Contents

KU-635-821

AQA introduction

Nelson Thornes has worked in partnership with AQA to ensure this book and the accompanying online resources offer you the best support for your A Level course.

All resources have been approved by senior AQA examiners so you can feel assured that they closely match the specification for this subject and provide you with everything you need to prepare successfully for your exams.

These print and online resources together **unlock blended learning**; this means that the links between the activities in the book and the activities online blend together to maximise your understanding of a topic and help you achieve your potential.

These online resources are available on **kerboodle!** which can be accessed via the internet at **www.kerboodle.com/live**, anytime, anywhere. If your school or college subscribes to this service you will be provided with your own personal login details. Once logged in, access your course and locate the required activity.

For more information and help visit **www.kerboodle.com**

Icons in this book indicate where there is material online related to that topic. The following icons are used:

🔆 Learning activity

These resources include a variety of interactive and non-interactive activities to support your learning.

☑ Progress tracking

These resources include a variety of tests that you can use to check your knowledge on particular topics (Test yourself) and a range of resources that enable you to analyse and understand examination questions (On your marks…).

🔧 Research support

These resources include WebQuests, in which you are assigned a task and provided with a range of web links to use as source material for research.

How to use this book

This book covers the specification for your course and is arranged in a sequence approved by AQA.

The book content is divided into chapters matched to the sections of the AQA Law specification for Units 1 and 2. Unit 1A (Law making) and 1B (The legal system) cover Unit 1 and Unit 2A (Criminal liability), 2B (Tort) and 2C (The law of contract) cover Unit 2. The chapters within each section provide full coverage of the AQA specification.

The features in this book include:

In this topic you will learn how to:

Each chapter is made up of two or more topics. At the beginning of each of these topics, you will find a list of learning objectives that contain targets linked to the requirements of the specification.

Key terms

Terms that you will need to be able to define and understand.

Links

These refer you back to other points in the book which consider similar points.

■ Key cases

Cases that demonstrate a key legal concept.

■ Activity

Things for you to do that will reinforce the information you have just learned.

AQA Examiner's tip

Hints from AQA examiners to help you with your study and to prepare for your exam.

AQA Examination-style questions

Questions in the style that you can expect in your exam. AQA examination questions are reproduced by permission of the Assessment and Qualifications Alliance.

You should now be able to:

A bulleted list of learning outcomes at the end of each chapter summarising core points of knowledge.

■ Web links in the book

As Nelson Thornes is not responsible for third party content online, there may be some changes to this material that are beyond our control. In order for us to ensure that the links referred to in the book are as up-to-date and stable as possible, the websites are usually homepages with supporting instructions on how to reach the relevant pages if necessary.

Please let us know at **kerboodle@nelsonthornes.com** if you find a link that doesn't work and we will do our best to redirect the link, or to find an alternative site.

Table of cases

Table of statutes

1A Law-making

Introduction

Chapters in this section:

Unit 1A together with Unit 1B constitutes Unit 1 of the AS specification. Unit 1A is about law-making and Unit 1B is about the legal system. Unit 1A and Unit 1B are examined together on one examination paper, which constitutes 50 per cent of the overall marks for the AS qualification and 25 per cent of the overall marks for the A2 qualification. The Unit 1 examination is of 1.5 hours' duration. Candidates must answer three questions: one question from Unit 1A; one question from Unit 1B; and another question, which may be from Unit 1A or 1B. There will be a choice of four questions in Unit 1A and four questions in Unit 1B. There will be one question on each topic area within the specification and no duplicate or omitted topic areas.

All questions are worth 30 marks each. Each question is divided into three parts, each part normally being worth 10 marks. Candidates must answer all parts of each question they choose to answer. All parts of each question relate to the same topic area of the AQA Law AS specification, that is, the same chapter of this book. Parts (a) and (b) will normally be a test of your knowledge and understanding, and part (c) will normally be evaluative.

Questions require essay-style answers. Attainment of high grades is dependent on correct identification of the issues raised by the question, sound explanation of each of the points and illustration. Illustration may be in many forms, for example, legislation, cases, research, statistics, material from the media. Further exam tips are provided throughout each topic and at the end of the chapter.

Unit 1A comprises four chapters:

1 **Parliamentary law-making**: concerned with the explanation and evaluation of how Parliament makes law.
2 **Delegated legislation**: explains and evaluates how law is also made by bodies to whom Parliament has delegated law-making powers.
3 **Statutory interpretation**: considers how the judges approach the task of interpreting Acts of Parliament.
4 **Judicial precedent**: concerned with the explanation and evaluation of law made by the judges in cases which come before them in the courts.

Parliamentary law-making

- describe a range of influences on Parliament

- give appropriate examples of each influence

- evaluate the effectiveness of each influence.

Key terms

Parliament: made up the House of Commons, consisting of elected MPs; the House of Lords, consisting of Lords who have either inherited their position or who have been appointed to the title; and the Queen. All three parts have to agree on a law in order for it to be made and come into force.

Government: responsible for the day-to-day running of the country. It is drawn from MPs from the largest party in the House of Commons and a smaller number of Lords. The head of the Government is the Prime Minister, who is assisted by senior Ministers in the Cabinet.

Law Commission: a full-time law reform body, independent of the Government. It was created by The Law Commission Act 1965. This Act gives it its powers and duties.

Influences on parliamentary law-making

Parliament is the supreme law-making body in the United Kingdom and can make laws for England and – in some areas – for Wales, Scotland and Northern Ireland. Pressure on Parliament to make or reform the law comes from a variety of sources. Many laws are introduced by the **Government** to implement its political agenda. Other ideas come from the Law Commission, pressure groups and the media. There are many other pressures operating on Parliament which candidates may wish to research even though they are outside the specification, for example Royal Commissions and the European Union.

The Government is responsible for the day-to-day running of the country. It is drawn from MPs from the largest party in the House of Commons and a smaller number of Lords. The head of the Government is the Prime Minister, who is assisted by senior Ministers in the Cabinet.

The Law Commission

The **Law Commission** is an independent, permanent and full-time law reform body set up by the Law Commission Act 1965. It has a full-time staff, headed by five Law Commissioners one of whom is the Chairman. The Chairman is responsible for promoting the work of the Law Commission and is its public face and voice. The Chairman also oversees the repeal and consolidation aspects of the Commission's work. The Chairman is a High Court Judge and the other four Law Commissioners are well qualified, experienced practising or academic lawyers. Each of the Law Commissioners is supported by a 'team' typically made up of barristers and solicitors, parliamentary draftsmen, researchers and administrative staff.

Under s3(1) of the 1965 Act the role of the Law Commission is to 'keep under review all the law.' This includes in particular the codification and consolidation of the law, the repeal of obsolete law and the simplification and modernisation of the law.

Codification

Codification is the bringing together of all the law on a particular topic into one Act of Parliament. Unlike other countries, which typically have all the law on a particular topic in one document, the law in Britain has been developed piecemeal over hundreds of years by Parliament and judges. As a result the law is quite difficult to access and understand because to decide what the law is, it is necessary to research all possible sources of law. Initially, when it was first created, the Law Commission embarked on a major programme aiming to codify contract law, landlord and tenant laws, family law and the law of evidence. In 1989 a draft Criminal Code was published although it has yet to be implemented. The Law Commission has gradually accepted that its initial plans for codification were over-ambitious, and that codification of smaller areas is preferable. For example, the Criminal Law and Evidence team published its report on the Law of Murder and Homicide in November 2006 and is currently working towards the codification of the General Principles of Criminal Law.

Consolidation

Consolidation brings all the statutory provisions relating to a particular area into one Act. As with codification, this makes the law more understandable and accessible. It does not necessarily require changes in the law. Examples of consolidation laws include the Education Act 1996 and the Powers of Criminal Courts (Sentencing) Act 2000.

While codifying and consolidation Acts make it easier to find out and understand what the law is, they require constant updating to truly fulfil their purpose. It is not usually very long before the Act is interpreted by the courts or is amended by further legislation thus requiring cross-referencing to another source of law.

Repeal

Repeal of obsolete law is the removal of laws that have no further use. Many laws become out of date or irrelevant due to passage of time. It is important to remove these Acts as they make research of the law more time-consuming and cause confusion. With limited exceptions, once an Act of Parliament has been passed it can only be repealed or altered by another Act.

Through these processes of codification, consolidation and repeal, the law is simplified and modernised. However, it is also necessary to suggest changes to existing laws and to create new areas of law in response to social change and technical developments. In the past the Law Commission has suggested changes such as the Occupiers' Liability Act 1984, which made occupiers of land responsible for injury caused to trespassers while on their land, and the Computer Misuse Act 1990, which was passed to deal with the problem of computer hacking.

The Law Commission investigates matters referred to it by Government departments and also decides for itself which areas to investigate. In addition, pressure may come from other sources, for example, the Criminal Attempts Act 1981 was a result of a Law Commission report prompted by academic pressure. Most areas of law considered by it are politically non-contentious.

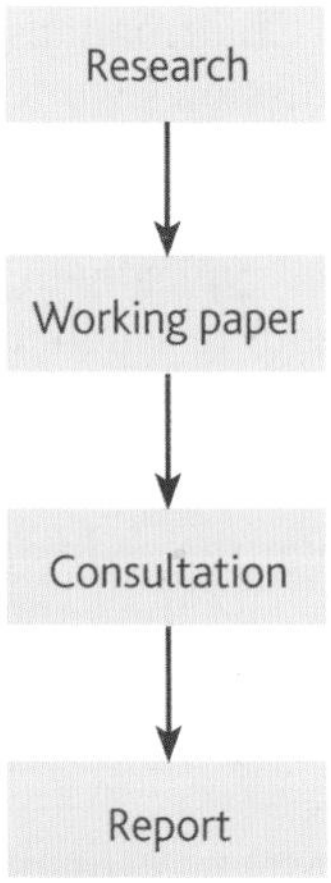

A Law Commission investigation will typically begin with research of the issue. A working paper is then produced, which sets out the current law, the problems within this, and the suggestions for reform. Consultation then follows of anyone interested in commenting on the issue. After the consultation, the Law Commission produces a Report including a draft Bill. The Government can then choose whether to implement the recommendations. Another example of a law passed to implement a Law Commission recommendation is the Law Reform (Year and a Day Rule) Act 1996, which abolished the previous requirement for a murder victim to die within a year and a day of the act which leads to the death.

Research

↓

Working paper

↓

Consultation

↓

Report

Fig. 1.1 *A flow chart summarising a typical Law Commission investigation*

Advantages of the Law Commission

The Law Commission possesses considerable legal non-political expertise. There is considerable research conducted into the issues it investigates. As a result its recommendations are well informed. This will help to avoid problems when the law is brought into force.

The Law Commission is an independent body. This ensures that all the law is kept under review and not just those areas the current Government wishes to focus on. The Law Commission may decide for itself to investigate a particular area, or a body other than the Government may ask it to do so.

AQA Examiner's tip

Note the use of examples – essential for attaining high marks when explaining the influence of the Law Commission on Parliament.

Disadvantages of the Law Commission

A major disadvantage of the Law Commission is that many of its recommendations, about one third, are not implemented. The Government of the day is not obliged to implement any of its proposals. Often the nature of recommendations do not always suit the political agenda of the Government.

The lack of power possessed by the Law Commission is further illustrated by the fact that the Government is not obliged to consult the Law Commission on any law it proposes to introduce.

The investigation of the current law is often lengthy and it can sometimes be years before a report is produced. An investigation may be interrupted by investigations into other areas.

The Law Commission investigates more than one matter at a time. Often 20 or 30 areas are under review. Consequently each investigation may not be as thorough as it could be.

Pressure groups

Pressure groups are groups of individuals. They range from a single person to several hundred thousand, who may influence Parliament to legislate on an issue. They may employ a variety of methods to support their campaign including lobbying Ministers and MPs, marches, petitions, demonstrations and publicity campaigns. This lobbying can often be made more effective through media coverage.

There are two main types of pressure group – sectional or interest groups, and promotional or 'cause' groups.

Key terms

Pressure group: a group of people who campaign for reform of the law.

Sectional pressure groups

Sectional or interest groups exist to further the interests of a section of society. Examples of sectional groups include the National Farmers Union, which exists to promote the interest of farmers, the British Medical Association, which promotes the interests of the medical profession and the Law Society, which promotes the interests of solicitors.

The degree of influence yielded by sectional groups varies according to whether the Government supports their particular interest. The major sectional groups are always influential because they represent large sections of society, and Government often needs their support. A Government which upsets a major sectional group will often suffer losses at election times. Because they are wealthy these groups can afford to employ research staff and mount publicity campaigns. Active members of the group are often influential and wealthy. The group may have direct access to Ministers and civil servants working in Government departments, as well as to backbench MPs.

Because of the wealth and influence of these groups it is rare for Government to introduce a law directly affecting the interests of a sectional group without consulting it. The content of the law may be influenced by this consultation process.

Cause pressure groups

Cause groups promote a particular ideal or belief. Examples of cause groups include:

- Greenpeace and Friends of the Earth, both of which believe in the preservation of the environment
- RSPCA, which believes in the elimination of unnecessary animal suffering
- Fathers 4 Justice, which believes in the right of fathers to have access to their children.

The influence wielded by these cause groups is usually less than that wielded by sectional groups. They are less likely to be consulted at the formative stage of laws as they do not generally enjoy close links with Government Ministers or departments. However, well organised cause groups are often able to publicise their point and succeed in some kind of reform. The RSPCA is a long-established charity which has considerable support of the British public. They have campaigned for many years using many methods, including leafleting and advertisements through the media, for animal welfare legislation. They were active in promoting the Animal Welfare Bill, which was passed as an Act in 2006 and requires animal owners to provide their pets with food, water, shelter, veterinary care and freedom to move about.

Sometimes one person may campaign for a certain cause. In the 1970s Mary Whitehouse campaigned to prevent child pornography and successfully pressured Parliament into enacting the Protection of Children Act 1978. More recently Jamie Oliver has campaigned for healthier meals to be served in schools. He has successfully used the media to publicise his campaign. There was a television series devoted to it, and he gained the support of many sectional groups including the National Union of Teachers and the British Medical Association. In 2006 the Department for Education and Skills issued The Education (Nutritional Standards for School Food) (England) Regulations, to come into force on 1 September 2007, which contained many provisions similar to those suggested by Jamie Oliver.

Table 1.1 *Characteristics of sectional and cause pressure groups*

Type of pressure group	Explanation	Illustration
Sectional	They exist to further the interests of a particular body of people.	British Medical Association, Trade Union Congress, National Union of Teachers, Law Society.
Cause	They exist to further a particular ideal.	Jamie Oliver – school dinners campaign – The Education (Nutritional Standards for School Food) (England) Regulations 2006. The RSPCA Animal Welfare Act 2006.

Advantages of pressure groups

Through a broad range of tactics, pressure groups are able to raise public awareness of matters affecting their interest or cause. Fathers 4 Justice has been particularly successful in raising public awareness of the plight of many fathers denied access to their children after a divorce. They have done this through stunts, including dressing up as Batman and scaling the walls of Buckingham Palace.

Fig. 1.2 *A Fathers 4 Justice demonstration*

Pressure groups raise awareness of, and remind Parliament of, the importance of an issue. Parliament is sometimes consumed with debating issues on the Government's political agenda. Pressure groups perform a valuable role, often using the media, in keeping Parliament in touch with issues that members of the public believe to be important. Environmental pressure groups are an example. They are having a greater influence on all political parties, as the public are becoming increasingly concerned about global warming. For example, car tax rates have been changed in favour of smaller, more fuel-efficient vehicles.

Some pressure groups have huge memberships which exceed those of the main political parties. These large pressure groups, for example the TUC representing over 6 million members, are able to raise awareness of issues of importance to large numbers of people.

Pressure groups possess considerable expertise. They have to have sound knowledge of their interest or cause in order to put their point across convincingly. Law enacted as a result of the influence of pressure groups should therefore benefit from extensive background knowledge. Jamie Oliver is clearly an expert on nutrition and will be able to advise on the key foods which should and should not be available to children at school.

Disadvantages of pressure groups

The main disadvantage of pressure groups is that they are inevitably biased in favour of their interest group or their cause. They are only concerned with promoting their side of the argument. Campaigns by pressure groups frequently do not involve presentation of an objective, balanced argument. For example, Fathers 4 Justice rarely recognise that the courts and mothers are genuinely (even if sometimes mistakenly) attempting to achieve the best outcome for the children of the family.

Views are often held passionately. This sometimes results in pressure groups resorting to undesirable tactics, involving criminal behaviour, to promote their cause. Examples include occasions when animal activists damaged scientific laboratories experimenting on animals, and when members of the Countryside Alliance demonstrated in the House of Commons.

An outsider group such as Fathers 4 Justice will have no contact with or access to Ministers or those with power to change laws, so they will have limited say in bringing about changes in the law.

Opinions held by a pressure group may only be those of a small minority of the population. However, if the pressure group is well organised and influential it may still be successful.

🖳 The media and public opinion

The term '**the media**' covers the channels by which information is transmitted. It includes newspapers, magazines, radio and television. There is a clear connection between the media and public opinion. Members of the public can make their views known to Parliament by joining a pressure group, by writing to their MP or to a Government Minister, or by contacting the media. In reverse, matters of concern can be highlighted to the public using the media. As with the school dinners campaign the media may be used by pressure groups to highlight their interest or cause and bring about change. The media may both represent public opinion and influence public opinion. As MPs in the House of Commons are democratically elected by the voters it is inevitable that the media are able to exert considerable influence on reform of laws.

As well as day-to-day reporting of news, the media also campaign to reform a law. An example was the 'name and shame' campaign run by the *News of the World* newspaper in 2000 following the murder of a child by a paedophile. The paper gathered public support by regularly raising the issue. Perhaps the most influential tactic was naming convicted paedophiles, publishing their pictures, and detailing where they lived. The Government was forced to act because the population was becoming increasingly alarmed by the revelations. There was also the worry of individuals being harmed by the public. Indeed on one occasion someone who was innocent was targeted. A law was passed requiring a register of convicted paedophiles to be maintained by the police.

It can be seen that law reform is sometimes prompted by pressure from more than one of the influences operating on Parliament. An example is the Criminal Justice Act 2003. This reformed the 'double jeopardy' rule, by allowing a suspect to be re-tried for a crime for which he had been formally acquitted, if there was compelling new evidence. This law came into effect in April 2007. This change in the law was brought about through a media campaign following the acquittal of the suspects in the Stephen Lawrence case despite the overwhelming evidence against them. Eventually media pressure led to a Government inquiry led by Sir William Macpherson, which in turn led to the Law Commission investigating and then recommending that the double jeopardy law be changed.

Advantages of the media

The media raise Government awareness of certain matters and help to inform Government of concerns held by the public. These views of the public are often publicised by pressure groups and these pressure groups in turn are sometimes supported by the media. Following the shooting of several young pupils at a school in Dunblane a pressure group called the Snowdrop Campaign was set up. Many newspapers, for example the *Daily Mail*, and television channels helped the Snowdrop Campaign to publicise its concerns to both the Government and the public, and this eventually led to legislation being introduced to ban handguns.

The media also raise public awareness. It is essential to raise public awareness in order for the Government to feel pressured into making legislative reforms. The Government are ultimately answerable to the electorate and will fear losing favour with the public because this could lead to a defeat at an election.

Disadvantages of the media

While radio and television channels are required to remain politically neutral, this is not the case with newspapers. Some newspapers, both tabloids and broadsheets, promote their own views. Sometimes the owners of newspapers hold particular political or moral views and their papers will report favourably on those views. Some newspapers lend their support to a political party. *The Sun* traditionally supported the Conservative Party and reported favourably on the policies of the Thatcher Government. However, *The Sun* now supports the current Labour Government and generally reports favourably on its proposals for reform when they are in conflict with the other parties.

Newspapers are in business to make a profit. They publish material which will sell copies and expand their readership, rather than merely keep the general public informed.

They can easily whip up a moral panic by reporting on matters that are rare in occurrence yet worry people when they are reminded of them. This was clearly what happened with the *News of the World* 'Name and Shame' campaign. Another example of law introduced in a hurry is the Dangerous Dogs Act 1991. This Act was introduced partly as a response to dangerous dogs attacking children and partly as a result of the media whipping up this issue.

Handguns to be banned in the UK

The British Government has announced plans to outlaw almost all handguns following the shocking massacre at Dunblane in Scotland.

On 13 March Thomas Hamilton walked into the gym at Dunblane Primary School and killed 16 young children and their teacher. He also injured 13 other children and three teachers. Hamilton, a former scout master, then shot himself.

Today's announcement follows publication of Lord Cullen's inquiry into the massacre which concluded Hamilton's horrific attack could not have been predicted.

But it made 23 recommendations to tighten rules on gun ownership and monitor those who work with children.

The proposal to ban all handguns – except .22-calibre target pistols – would leave Britain with some of the toughest laws on private possession of guns.

Home Secretary Michael Howard told a packed House of Commons he would make sure the measures were passed as quickly as possible through Parliament.

But the move has angered both those for and against private gun ownership.

The Snowdrop Campaign, set up by victims' families after Dunblane, wants to see a total ban on handguns and called the plan an 'unacceptable compromise'.

The opposition Labour Party welcomed the report and the Government's swift reaction to it but urged Ministers to bring about a complete ban.

Shadow Home Secretary Jack Straw said politicians should have acted in a similar vein nine years ago after the Hungerford massacre.

Former Tory Cabinet Minister David Mellor also felt the proposals did not go far enough.

He asked, 'Isn't it time to conclude that, literally and metaphorically, the game is up for handguns now?'

But gun club owners warned thousands of jobs would be in jeopardy if the proposal became law.

Speaking to the Daily Mirror newspaper, Ross Armstrong, owner of Medway Shooting Club in Kent said, 'People are killed by drunk drivers but no-one demands a ban on cars. Further restrictions suit no-one.'

www.wwc-coe.org

Activities

Read the above extract and answer the following questions:

1. Why was the Snowdrop Campaign formed?

2. Is the Snowdrop Campaign a cause group or a sectional group?

3. Does the Snowdrop Campaign represent the views of everyone?

4. How did the legislation introduced by the then Conservative Government fall short of that wanted by the Snowdrop Campaign?

5. When and by what Government were handguns eventually completely banned?

You should now be able to:

- understand a range of influences upon Parliament
- give examples of each influence
- evaluate each influence
- answer past paper questions on the topic of influences on Parliament.

In this topic you will learn how to:

- describe and give examples of different types of Bill and the stages in the passage of a Bill through Parliament
- explain the role of the House of Commons, House of Lords and the Crown in the creation of an Act
- evaluate the law-making process in Parliament.

Key terms

House of Commons: one of the two Houses of Parliament. The more powerful House, as its members are democratically elected.

Democracy: actions are carried out by the elected Government in the name of and on behalf of the electorate.

2 The legislative process

Parliamentary law-making

Laws made by Parliament are called Acts of Parliament. They are also referred to as 'statutes' and 'legislation'. In order to make an Act, a Bill must be introduced to Parliament. The Bill must then be debated and proceed through, and be approved by, both Houses of Parliament – the House of Commons and the House of Lords – and receive Royal Assent from the Queen.

Composition of the House of Commons

The **House of Commons** contains approximately 650 members: MPs. Each MP represents a constituency. MPs are elected at general elections, which usually take place every five years. The Government is drawn from the party with the greatest number of elected MPs. The leader of the party with the greatest number of MPs is the Prime Minister. The Prime Minister and his chosen Ministers make up the central Government, also referred to as the Cabinet. Elected MPs from the other political parties are called the opposition.

The role of the House of Commons

The role of Government is to make policy and to decide how to run the country. New policies require new laws. It is the role of the House of Commons to debate, scrutinise and vote on whether to approve the laws proposed by Government. During debates MPs are able to put forward the views of their constituents – the people they represent. MPs also directly challenge Government Ministers through rigorous questioning. In this way the Government is 'held to account'. The role played by the House of Commons ensures the legislative process is democratic, that is, carried out in accordance with the tenets of **democracy**.

Fig. 1.3 *The House of Commons*

The House of Lords

There are approximately 700 members of the **House of Lords.** They are unelected and unpaid and attendance is voluntary. Sitting in the House of Lords are:

- Hereditary peers, who inherit their title
- Life peers, who have been awarded a peerage because of their contribution to society or politics, an example being Lady Thatcher; the life peerage ends on death and is not passed on to descendants
- 26 Bishops
- Law Lords: the most senior judges; it is proposed to remove the Law Lords from the House of Lords when the Supreme Court begins operation in 2009.

The role of the House of Lords

The role of the House of Lords is to complement the work of the Commons and also to scrutinise and amend proposed legislation. Laws can be introduced in this House. In addition, the Lords pose questions to the Government, and debate policy issues and matters of current concern. Many peers also sit on specialist committees, for example the European Union Committee, which has approximately 70 members and scrutinises proposed European legislation.

The role of the Crown

The Crown is the title given to the monarch, who is the Head of State. Little real power remains with the monarchy. However in relation to parliamentary law-making the Crown has three key functions, these being to:

- open each parliamentary session – a traditional ceremonial event during which the monarch reads a speech prepared by the Government which outlines the legislative proposals to be considered in the coming session
- give Royal Assent to all legislation
- appoint and dismiss the Prime Minister, who is generally the leader of the party with the most MPs in the House of Commons.

Key terms

House of Lords: one of the two Houses of Parliament. Membership is by appointment or hereditary.

The Crown: the King or Queen, who is also the Head of State. The Crown's approval is necessary to all laws passed by Parliament before they come into force.

Table 1.2 *A summary of the role of the Commons, the Lords and the Crown in the legislative process*

Role of the House of Commons	Role of the House of Lords	Role of the Crown
Where most new laws are introduced.	Where some new laws are introduced.	To open each parliamentary session and announce the Government's legislative proposals.
To debate Government policy and hold Government to account.	To scrutinise and amend proposed legislation including Government proposals.	To give Royal Assent to all legislation.
To scrutinise and amend proposed legislation.	To scrutinise proposed EU legislation.	
To debate matters of current concern.	To question Government and debate legislative proposals.	
To represent the views of the electorate.	To debate policy issues and matters of current concern.	
	To delay legislation so as to allow further time to research and consult.	

Types of Bills

There are three main types of **Bill**: public Bills, private Bills and hybrid Bills.

Public Bills

Public Bills affect the general public. Some public Bills apply to the whole of the UK, while others apply only to England and Wales. Since the establishment of the Scottish Parliament and the Welsh Assembly, power to make legislation on certain matters has been devolved to these bodies. Parliament has retained power to make law applicable to the whole of the UK in what are called 'reserved' matters, including defence and foreign affairs.

There are two types of public Bills: Government Bills and private members' Bills.

Government Bills

The majority of Bills introduced into Parliament each year are **Government Bills.** Most proceed to become Acts of Parliament as they are supported by the Government. Government Bills are introduced into Parliament by a Minister.

Approximately a quarter of Government Bills are routine and are introduced irrespective of which party is in power; for example money Bills, dealing with collecting taxes. Government Bills are introduced for a variety of reasons. They may be introduced:

- to honour manifesto promises, that is, promises made during election campaigns on issues such as health or education
- in response to a specific incident or matter of concern; for example the Football (Disorder) Act 2000, which allows magistrates to ban potential trouble-making fans from travelling abroad for five days before an international match and until the match has been played
- in order to comply with international treaties, for example, the Treaty of Rome, which has prompted a vast amount of legislation on matters such as consumer and worker's rights
- following recommendation by a law reform body such as the Law Commission.

Before the Government introduces a Bill, it may issue a consultation document, called a Green Paper. This will set out the Government's outline policy proposals and invite comments from interested parties. Having considered any responses the Government may then publish a White Paper. This contains more detailed proposals for future legislation. Sometimes the White Paper will invite comments. Following the White Paper the Government will introduce their definite proposals in the form of a Bill which will be introduced into Parliament.

There is no formal requirement for the issue of a Green Paper or for a White Paper to follow a Green Paper. However, consultation with interested parties is important, as it ensures that any potential problems are fully considered before the legislation is enacted. It was because of a lack of consultation concerning the Dangerous Dogs Act 1991 that amendments were later necessary to make it workable. The Every Child Matters Green Paper 2003 was the precursor to The Children Act 2004 which provides for greater protection of children.

Since being elected in 1997 the Government has promoted the introduction of draft Bills. A number of these have been published in each parliamentary session enabling consultation and pre-legislative scrutiny before they are introduced into Parliament. An example of a draft Bill is the Draft Climate Change Bill published in March 2007 by the Department for Environment, Food and Rural Affairs, which provides a framework for reducing greenhouse gas emissions.

Private members' Bills

Private members' Bills are introduced into Parliament by individual backbench MPs who are not part of the Government. Comparatively few private members' Bills ever become law because of the shortage of parliamentary debate time allocated to them. The Government decides how this time is allocated so give their own Bills priority. Nevertheless some notable examples of Acts introduced as private members' Bills include the Murder (Abolition of Death Penalty) Act 1965, introduced by Sidney Silverman MP, and the Abortion Act 1967, introduced by David Steel MP.

Despite the fact that private members' Bills rarely become law, they play an important role in raising public and Government awareness of an issue and often lead to future Government legislation. An example of this is Ken Livingstone's Wild Animals (Hunting with Dogs) Bill, which failed in 2000 and which was then introduced as a Government Bill, eventually becoming the Hunting Act 2004.

Private members' Bills can also be introduced by peers in the Lords. An example of a Bill introduced this way is Lord Joffe's Assisted Dying for the Terminally Ill Bill in 2006. Although this failed to progress beyond a second reading in the Lords it did lead to much public debate on the issue.

Private Bills

Private Bills affect individuals, organisations or specific areas. These Bills are introduced into Parliament through a petition by the individuals, organisations or local authorities concerned. They are rare compared with public Bills. An example is the Edward Berry and Doris Eileen Ward (Marriage Enabling) Act 1980, the result of a Personal Bill, which was passed to allow a stepfather and stepdaughter, who first met as adults, to marry.

> AQA **Examiner's tip**
>
> It is a good idea to find a recent example of a Green Paper and a White Paper to include in your answers.

Example of why consultation = important! (handwritten note)

> **Key terms**
>
> **Private members' Bill:** a public Bill introduced into Parliament by a backbench MP in the Commons or by a peer in the House of Lords.
>
> **Private Bill:** a Bill affecting a particular individual or organisation, or a specific locality.

Hybrid Bills

Hybrid Bills are so called because they are a cross between a public Bill and a private Bill. They are introduced by a Government Minister and, if enacted, will affect particular individuals, organisations or localities. An example of an Act that began life as a hybrid Bill is the Channel Tunnel (Rail Link) Act 1996, which had a particular impact on landowners and residents in Kent.

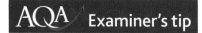

Examiner's tip

Note that an explanation of the formal legislative process should include an explanation of each reading and stage.

The process through which a Bill passes to become an Act of Parliament

To become an Act of Parliament the Bill must pass through both the House of Commons and House of Lords, and must receive Royal Assent. A Bill can start in either House unless it is a money Bill, which must start in the Commons.

Table 1.3 *A summary of the types of Bill*

Type of Bill	Explanation	Illustration
Public Bills	Affect the general public. Two types: Government Bills and private members' Bills. Government Bills are introduced into Parliament by Government Ministers. Private members' Bills are introduced by backbench MPs or peers.	Legislation which started as a Government Bill: the Football (Disorder) Act 2000, the Children Act 2004, the Dangerous Dogs Act 1991. Legislation which started as a private members' Bill: The Abortion Act 1967, The Murder (Abolition of the Death Penalty) Act 1965, the Bail (Amendment) Act 1993.
Private Bills	Affect a particular person or organisation or locality.	The Edward Berry and Doris Eileen Ward (Marriage Enabling) Act 1980.
Hybrid Bills	A cross between a Public Bill and a Private Bill. Introduced by a Government Minister but only affect a particular person, locality or organisation.	The Channel Tunnel (Rail Link) Act 1996.

First reading

The title and main aims of the Bill are announced and copies of it are distributed. There is no debate at this stage but a verbal vote is taken to decide whether the Bill should progress to the second reading. Many private members' Bills fail to progress beyond this stage. If the vote is in favour of the Bill a date is then set for the Bill's second reading.

Second reading

The House debates the whole Bill and is focused on the general principles behind the Bill. The Minister or other promoter of the Bill starts the debate. At the end of the debate there is a vote for or against the Bill progressing further. Should the Bill progress beyond this stage it is quite likely it will eventually become an Act of Parliament.

Committee stage

The Bill is passed to the Standing Committee which is made up of between 16 and 50 MPs selected per party strength. The MPs selected will generally have a particular interest in the Bill or specialist knowledge of its content. The Standing Committee scrutinises the Bill clause by clause and makes amendments as required to ensure it conforms to the general approval given by the House at the second reading. All amendments made to the Bill are voted on. Some Bills, for example money Bills, are subjected to examination by the whole House at this stage. In the House of Lords there are generally no specialist Standing Committees. The whole House scrutinises the Bill.

Report stage

The Standing Committee report the amendments made to the Bill during the Committee Stage back to the whole House. Each amendment is debated and a vote is taken to decide whether it should be accepted or rejected. The House may make additional amendments at this stage provided these are approved by a vote. Should no amendments be made at the Committee Stage there is no need for the Report Stage and the Bill progresses directly to the third reading.

Third reading

This is a review of the whole Bill and a vote is taken to decide whether the Bill should proceed to the other House. This stage is often a formality. As the Bill has successfully completed its earlier stages it is unlikely to now fail. In the House of Lords further amendments can be made at this stage.

After the third reading, the Bill is passed to the other House where it goes through the same stages.

The limited power of the House of Lords

If the Lords propose amendments to a Bill which has completed the process in the Commons, the Bill is returned to the Commons for a stage called Lords Amendments Considered. At this stage the Commons may approve or reject the Lords' amendments. Approximately 90 per cent of Lords' amendments are accepted by the Commons at this stage. In the event that the Lords do not approve a Bill that has been approved by the Commons, then under the **Parliament Acts 1911 and 1949** the Lords can delay the passage of a money Bill for one month and all other Bills for one year. Once the time has elapsed the Commons can send the Bill for Royal Assent without the Lords' agreement. In order to exercise this power the Bill must be re-introduced into Parliament in the next session and pass successfully through all the stages again. Only four Acts have been passed using the Parliament Acts, these being the War Crimes Act 1991, the European Parliamentary Elections Act 1999, the Sexual Offences (Amendment) Act 2000 and the Hunting Act 2004.

The supremacy of the House of Commons stems from the fact that it is a democratically elected body, answerable to the electorate. The Lords have retained the power to reject a Bill that attempts to extend the duration of Parliament beyond five years.

Royal Assent

Once a Bill has passed through both Houses, it requires Royal Assent to become law. It is not customary for the Monarch to assent in person; the last time was in 1854. Assent is now given by the Speaker in the House of Commons and the Lord Speaker of the House of Lords. The granting of Royal Assent is a formality. It has not been refused since Queen Anne refused to give assent to the Scottish Militia Bill in 1707. There is now a constitutional convention that assent will never be withheld as this would jeopardise the future position of the monarchy.

On the day Royal Assent is granted, the Bill becomes an Act of Parliament. Most Acts come into force at midnight following Royal Assent; however, implementation of some Acts has to be delayed so

AQA Examiner's tip

When explaining the legislative process, candidates frequently omit information about the delaying power of the House of Lords. Remember to include it in your answers.

Key terms

The Parliament Acts 1911 and 1949: they limit the power of the House of Lords to delay or defeat proposed legislation.

AQA Examiner's tip

An explanation of Royal Assent must be included in an explanation of the legislative process.

as to allow necessary resources to be prepared and put into place: for example, the Police and Criminal Evidence Act 1984, which was brought into effect in stages so as to give sufficient time to the police to train personnel and acquire equipment necessary for compliance with the Act. Acts of Parliament such as this are usually brought into force by delegated legislation, which is discussed in Chapter 2.

■ Activity

Identify and discuss the errors in the following account of the legislative process:

■ A Bill must start the legislative process in the House of Commons. The Bill has to go through, generally, the same process in each House. The first stage of the process is called the first reading. The title of the Bill is announced, there is a debate and a vote. A date is set for the second reading. At the second reading there is no debate. A vote is taken to see whether the Bill should progress further. At the third reading amendments can be made by the Lords but further discussion of the Bill can only take place in the Commons if at least six MPs request it. There is a vote to see if the Bill should progress further.

■ At the Committee Stage the Committee scrutinises the Bill and makes amendments. This stage is the same in the House of Commons and the House of Lords. At the Report Stage the whole House considers the amendments made by the Committee and vote on whether to approve them. There is generally no requirement for this stage in the Lords. A final vote is taken to decide whether the Bill should proceed to the other House.

■ Generally speaking there is no disagreement between both Houses. However, under the Parliament Acts 1911 and 1949, the House of Lords can only delay a Bill approved by the Commons for one month, one year if it is a money Bill. If the House of Lords make amendments to a Bill approved by the Commons then the Bill goes back to the Commons who can choose whether to adopt the amendments. Royal Assent is the final stage of the process. The Queen reads through the Bill and decides whether it should become law or not.

You should now be able to:

- ■ describe the role of the House of Commons and House of Lords
- ■ describe the different types of Bill
- ■ explain the legislative process
- ■ answer past paper questions on the topic of the legislative process.

In this topic you will learn how to:

- ■ discuss the advantages of parliamentary law-making
- ■ discuss the disadvantages of parliamentary law-making.

3 Advantages and disadvantages of parliamentary law-making

Advantages of parliamentary law-making

Scrutiny

The legislative process (passing through both Houses and receiving Royal Assent) is very thorough. There are three readings and two stages, which take place in both Houses of Parliament. This provides several opportunities for debate, scrutiny and amendment, ensuring that any mistakes or poor drafting can be corrected.

Democratic

Parliamentary law-making is democratic. MPs in the House of Commons are democratically elected to make laws. During the debates on the proposed law each MP should have the opportunity to put forward the view of his or her constituents. Members of the House of Lords are not democratically elected, so they cannot veto a Bill that has the approval of the Commons. Under the Parliament Acts 1911 and 1949 the delaying power of the Lords is limited to one month in respect of money Bills and one year for other Bills. The role of the Monarch, also unelected, has been reduced to a formality.

Government control

Government has considerable control over parliamentary law-making. For example, it controls the parliamentary timetable for debates and is likely to win at each voting stage of the process unless a number of its own MPs vote against it. This is democratic because the Government is the preferred choice of a significant proportion of the population.

A Government Minister introducing a Bill to Parliament has knowledge in his field of responsibility and the support of a civil service department with considerable expertise.

The House of Lords

The House of Lords acts as a checking mechanism. It can guard against laws being passed solely to fit the Government's political agenda. If the House of Lords exercises its power of delay there will be further opportunity for debate and amendment of the Bill's provisions.

The House of Lords contains many peers with considerable expertise spanning numerous issues. Because of this, the quality of scrutiny and debate in the Lords is very high.

Members of the Lords are able to act independently when debating and voting. However MPs often have to follow instructions from the party leadership.

Special rules exist in respect of money Bills. For example, the whole House will sit at the Committee stage in the House of Commons when a finance Bill is being considered. This helps guard against unlawful taxation.

Flexibility

There are several types of Bill which can be introduced in either House. This means that not only the Government but all MPs and Lords have the opportunity to propose new laws. This may be useful when the Government has not given thought to a particular matter or does not want to be seen to introduce controversial legislation. Examples of potentially controversial legislation were the Abortion Act 1967, and the Marriage Act 1994, which allowed marriages to be made in places other than Churches and Registry Offices.

Disadvantages of parliamentary law-making

Undemocratic

It is undemocratic. Neither the House of Lords nor the Queen is elected. Arguably, the unelected House of Lords should not have the power to delay Bills that have been approved by the democratically elected House of Commons. However, while the House of Commons is democratically elected, MPs are persuaded to vote with their party rather than in accordance with the wishes of their constituents. A Government with a large majority may be able to introduce any legislation it pleases and is only answerable to the electorate every five years.

AQA Examiner's tip

It is important with advantages and disadvantages questions not to produce a mere list. Each point should be explained fully and, where possible, provide examples.

Note the use of legislation as illustrative material and an alternative point.

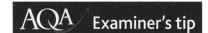

Government control

As the Government has a majority of MPs in the House of Commons, it can vote out any private members' Bill that does not fit its political agenda. Very little parliamentary time is allocated to private members' Bills. In comparison to Government Bills, very few private members' Bills are enacted each year. In the 2005–2006 parliamentary session only three private members' Bills made it into the statute book out of a total 130 that were introduced.

The Government is arguably too powerful as it is able to by-pass the House of Lords by invoking the Parliament Acts. The most recent example of this is the Hunting Act 2004. Any law desired by the Government may be passed despite the House of Lords' objections.

Slow

The process is slow. A Bill has to go through many readings and stages in both Houses. This takes many months and is not appropriate when important laws need to be made quickly.

The Royal Assent has become a formality. This is arguably a rather pointless stage and makes the whole legislative process more time-consuming.

Dated processes, language and statistics

When drafting a Bill, parliamentary draftsmen use words and phrases that are ambiguous, unclear, obscure and over elaborate. This sometimes means it is up to the judiciary to determine what the Act is meant to say. Approximately 75 per cent of cases heard by the House of Lords in its capacity as the final appeal court are about how words in an Act should be understood. Further, the language used is often incomprehensible to the average layman (and even to some lawyers!) Problems with the language and structure of Acts were originally identified in the Renton Committee's Report on Preparation of Legislation in 1975. Also the structure of Acts was reported to be illogical with sections of individual Acts having no obvious sequence and there being no clear connection between Acts dealing with the same topic. Similar problems were identified by the Hansard Society Commission lead by Lord Rippon in 1992.

These language and structural problems make law inaccessible to the ordinary person. It is also difficult to discover what the law on a particular issue is. Also there is a problem with finding out which sections of an Act have come into force. Not all Acts become law at the point of Royal Assent. They may be brought into force by a Government Minister. In such situations it will be necessary to research regulations issued by the Minister.

An example of an Act that had to be implemented in many stages was the Police and Criminal Evidence Act 1984. This Act required Custody Officers – a new role – to be introduced in every police station monitoring the detention of suspects. It also required interviews with suspects to be recorded. Sufficient time had to be allowed for police to be trained and for the acquisition of new equipment so that compliance with the Act was possible.

You should now be able to:

- explain the advantages and disadvantages of parliamentary law-making

- answer past paper question on the topic of parliamentary law-making.

4 Parliamentary supremacy

Parliamentary sovereignty

The supremacy of Parliament was established in the 17th century. In 1689 the Bill of Rights was enacted, which deemed Parliament to be the supreme law-maker. Article IX states, 'the freedom of speech and debates or proceedings in Parliament ought not to be impeached or questioned in any court or place out of Parliament.' The Bill of Rights provided further that Parliament was to be freely elected every three years, that the levying of tax was subject to parliamentary consent and that it was illegal for the Monarchy to interfere with the law as enacted by Parliament save for to grant Royal Assent.

The meaning of **parliamentary sovereignty** was expressed clearly by A.V. Dicey, a 19th century constitutional lawyer. In his work *Introduction to the Study of the Law of the Constitution*, first published in 1885, he wrote, 'The principle of parliamentary sovereignty means ... that Parliament ... has the right to make or unmake any law whatever; and, further, that no person or body is recognised by the law of England as having a right to override or set aside the legislation of Parliament.'

Parliamentary sovereignty means that:

- Parliament's power is unlimited and it can make law on any topic.
- The validity of parliamentary law cannot be questioned by anybody including the courts, the church and the monarchy.
- No one Parliament can limit the law-making power of any future Parliament. It is impossible, therefore, for any Parliament to pass a permanent law, or in other words to entrench an Act of Parliament.

The effect of the European Union on parliamentary sovereignty

The United Kingdom (UK) joined the EEC (now the **European Union – EU**) on 1 January 1973. The **Treaty of Rome 1957** and subsequent amendment treaties, together with secondary legislation – that is, law made under the authority of the treaties – was given effect in the UK by the **European Communities Act (ECA) 1972**. The effect of s2(1) of the ECA is that all the provisions of EU law are given the force of law in the UK. Section 2(4) has the effect of making UK Acts of Parliament subject to directly applicable EU law. Since the enactment of the ECA, Parliament is no longer the supreme law-maker in the UK. In the event of a conflict between an Act of Parliament and EU law, EU law prevails. As a result of this, membership of the EU challenges Dicey's theory.

The supremacy of European law over UK legislation was clarified by the European Court of Justice (ECJ) in *Costa* v *ENEL* (1964). The ECJ stated, 'The transfer by the states from their domestic legal system to the Community legal system of the rights and obligations arising under the Treaty carries with it a permanent limitation of their sovereign rights, against which a subsequent unilateral act incompatible with the concept of the Community cannot prevail.' This case clarified the requirement for both pre-existing domestic Acts and those made in the future to comply with EU law.

Arguably the greatest challenge to parliamentary sovereignty was that in **Ex parte Factortame No 2 (1991)**. The case was about the rights of Spanish fishermen to fish in British waters. The Spanish fishermen claimed that the Merchant Shipping Act 1988 was contrary to Community law and sought interim relief from the provisions of the

In this topic you will learn how to:

- explain the doctrine of parliamentary supremacy
- consider limitations on the doctrine of parliamentary supremacy.

Key terms

Parliamentary sovereignty: Parliament is the supreme law-maker in the UK.

European Union (EU): a group of countries that have signed international treaties with the common purpose of creating an economic union.

The Treaty of Rome 1957: the founding Treaty of the European Economic Community now known as the European Union.

The European Communities Act (ECA) 1972: the Act of Parliament that incorporates EU law into UK domestic law. The effect of this Act is that Acts of Parliament are now subordinate to European Law.

AQA Examiner's tip

A question that asks for consideration of the limitations on parliamentary sovereignty also requires an initial explanation of parliamentary sovereignty.

Key cases

Ex parte Factortame No 2 (1991): the ECJ held that domestic courts must suspend domestic legislation while waiting for a ruling from the ECJ as to whether the domestic legislation contravenes European Community law.

Act pending a trial of the issue. Both the Court of Appeal and House of Lords held that the 1988 Act should be enforced throughout the period in question, because no national court had the power to suspend an Act of Parliament. However, the European Court of Justice decided that national courts were obliged to suspend the Act of Parliament in these circumstances. This decision thus gave the right to the national courts to set aside an Act of Parliament, although in limited circumstances, and is clearly contrary to the principle of parliamentary sovereignty.

Following the ECJ decision in Factortame, when a piece of UK legislation is directly in conflict with EU law, the UK court must follow the EU law. By virtue of the ECA, parliamentary sovereignty is now limited by all sources of European Union law. Until the UK Parliament decides to withdraw the UK from the EU, an increasing amount of legislation will continue to be passed in order to comply with our membership obligations. This challenges UK parliamentary sovereignty, because Parliament is making law because the EU requires it to and not of its own free will. The Department of Trade in 1993 estimated that one-third of existing legislation had been enacted to implement EU law.

It is legally possible that the UK Parliament has surrendered sovereignty to the European institutions until it decides otherwise. By virtue of the doctrine of parliamentary sovereignty, the ECA can be repealed, as no Act of Parliament can be entrenched. In reality this is unlikely to happen due to economic ties that the UK now has with the European Union.

The effect of the Human Rights Act 1998 on parliamentary sovereignty

The European Convention on Human Rights

Before the enactment of the **Human Rights Act (HRA) 1998**, rights of the citizens of the UK were safeguarded by the **European Convention on Human Rights (ECHR) 1950**, which is an international treaty created by the Council of Europe. The purpose of the ECHR was to prevent the atrocities committed against European citizens during the war from happening again. The ECHR is concerned with the protection of human rights and fundamental freedoms. The UK signed the ECHR in 1950.

The Human Rights Act 1998

The Human Rights Act 1998 (HRA), which came into force in October 2000, incorporated the ECHR into UK domestic law. The main provision of the HRA, as far as parliamentary sovereignty is concerned, is that the HRA requires all legislation passed by Parliament to be interpreted and given effect so far as is possible to comply with Convention rights. Section 19 of the Act requires a Government Minister to declare before a Bill is given its second reading whether it is compatible with the HRA. In the event of incompatibility of existing legislation, the courts can quash or refuse to apply subordinate legislation (law made by bodies to whom Parliament has delegated law-making powers), and may make a declaration of incompatibility in respect of an Act of Parliament. This prompts a Government Minister to make a remedial order amending the legislation so that it is compatible with Convention rights.

Since the coming into force of the HRA there have been approximately 20 declarations of incompatibility made by the courts and around half-a-dozen of these have been overturned on appeal by either the Court of Appeal or House of Lords. An example of a declaration of incompatibility that has led to a change in the law is *A and others* v *Secretary of State for the Home Department* (2004). In this case, the provisions of the

Key terms

The European Convention on Human Rights (ECHR) 1950: an international treaty signed by 45 countries of Europe with the common purpose of protecting fundamental rights and freedoms of citizens.

The Human Rights Act (HRA) 1998: an Act of Parliament that incorporates the European Convention on Human Rights into UK domestic law.

Anti-Terrorism, Crime and Security Act 2001 were challenged. The Act provided that foreign nationals who were suspected international terrorists, and who could not be deported from the UK, could be held indefinitely without charge or trial. The House of Lords declared the 2001 Act to be incompatible with Arts 5 and 14 of the ECHR. The incompatibility was later remedied by the passing of the Prevention of Terrorism Act 2005.

It can be concluded that the effect of the HRA on parliamentary sovereignty is limited. The courts have the power to declare that domestic legislation is incompatible with the HRA, but do not have the power to declare the domestic legislation invalid. Any amendment or repeal of legislation must be done by Parliament. Similarly, while a Government Minister must declare whether domestic legislation being introduced is compatible with the HRA, there is no specific requirement that it must be. This would appear to provide that parliamentary sovereignty remains.

Devolution

Following referendums in Scotland and Wales and by the Scotland Act 1998 and the Government of Wales Act 1998, the Westminster Parliament has devolved certain powers to the Scottish Parliament and to the Welsh Assembly. This means that they can make laws for their own countries without referring back to Westminster. As a result the sovereignty of the Westminster Parliament has been removed in these areas. As with EU law, in theory the Westminster Parliament could repeal the Acts devolving power and regain their sovereignty. The Westminster Parliament has, however, retained powers to make laws in areas such as defence, which affect the whole of the UK.

> **Key terms**
>
> **Devolution:** the statutory granting of certain powers from the Westminster Parliament to Parliaments of Scotland and Wales.

Fig. 1.4 *The Scottish Parliament at Holyrood in Edinburgh*

The limitations on parliamentary sovereignty:

- Parliament can make law on any topic it wishes.
- The validity of law passed by Parliament cannot be questioned by anyone, including judges.
- Parliament cannot bind itself or future Parliaments.

■ Existing and future UK legislation must comply with EU law. The effect of the European Communities Act is that UK legislation is subordinate to EU law.

■ Parliamentary sovereignty is not ultimately affected by the Human Rights Act. Government Ministers must declare whether new legislation derogates from the HRA but no justification for derogation is needed.

■ The Westminster Parliament has granted devolved powers to the Scottish Parliament and to the Welsh Assembly.

Activity

Copy and complete the table below:

Table 1.4

European body	Founding international treaty	Principal aims	Court in which treaty is upheld	UK legislation incorporating the treaty into UK law
European Union				
European Commission of Human Rights				

You should now be able to:

■ describe the doctrine of parliamentary supremacy

■ discuss the effect of EU law on the doctrine of parliamentary supremacy

■ discuss the effect of the Human Rights Act 1998 on the doctrine of parliamentary supremacy

■ discuss the effect of devolution on the doctrine of parliamentary supremacy

■ answer exam questions on parliamentary sovereignty.

2 Delegated legislation

Link

Primary legislation is law passed by Parliament. For more detail, see Chapter 1 (Parliamentary law-making), p3.

Key terms

Delegated legislation: a law made by a person or body to whom Parliament has delegated (or given) law-making power.

Enabling Act: an original Act passed by Parliament which enables another person or body to make law.

Parent Act: this term can equally be used because the delegated legislation can be viewed as the offspring or product of the original Act.

1 Types of delegated legislation

The verb 'delegate' means to pass power, responsibility or authority to another person or body. **Delegated legislation** is law made by a person or body to whom Parliament has delegated law-making power; hence the term 'delegated legislation'.

Most laws passed by Parliament each year provide a framework for new law. There is often a need to complete more detailed rules. Parliament does not have enough time or expertise to make all these more detailed laws. There is often only time in a parliamentary session for debate of a limited number of new laws and policy issues, especially as Parliament also has to hold the Government to account. The reason for detailed new laws may be because:

- A new law may be required for a specific area of the country, for which case specialist local knowledge may be required.
- Alternatively, a new law on a technical matter such as health or agriculture will require specialist technical knowledge.
- Sometimes, an emergency or a new situation may require new law to be made very quickly. Parliament often does not possess the necessary specialist local or technical knowledge to make law quickly. Also the formal legislative process (outlined in Chapter 1), requiring readings in both Houses of Parliament, is not suitable when there is an emergency.

For these reasons it is necessary for Parliament to delegate law-making power to people and bodies who are better equipped to make the necessary, detailed legal reforms.

The parent (or enabling) Act

In order to delegate its power to another there is a need for a **parent Act**, otherwise known as an **enabling Act**. By this piece of primary legislation, Parliament gives authority to others to make law. The parent Act will enable further law to be made under this authority.

The parent or enabling Act contains the outline framework of the new law. Within the Act there will be authority for a specified person (such as a Government Minister) or body (such as a local authority) to make further more detailed law. It is these provisions of the enabling Act that delegate the power to make law.

It is likely that the Act will specify the area within which law can be made and any procedures that the delegated person or body must follow when making the delegated laws.

Law-making power is given to the person or body best equipped with the knowledge and resources to make the type of law required.

As with the law banning smoking, power to make law on such a technical matter is given to a Government Minister who has the support of a specialist civil service department.

If power is given to a local authority to make delegated legislation, they will have the required local knowledge. If it is given to another body, such as a train or bus company, it will be given to make laws in respect of their property (for example to enforce the payment of fares).

Types of delegated legislation

Orders in Council

Historically, the Monarch used to rule the country through the Privy Council. As the powers of the Monarchy were eventually reduced and Parliament emerged as the sovereign power, the powers of the Privy Council diminished. One of the remaining functions of the Privy Council is to make **Orders in Council**. Orders in Council are drafted by the Government and given formal approval by the Queen and the Privy Council.

There are currently some 420 members of the Privy Council; however only three or four current Government Ministers attend meetings at which Orders in Council are made.

The **Privy Council**, in full, consists of all current and former Government Ministers, senior politicians (for example, leading members of the opposition parties), members of the Royal Family, two Archbishops, senior judges, the British Ambassador and leading individuals of the Commonwealth. Appointment is made by the Queen on the advice of the Government and is for life.

Orders in Council are used in many situations, including:

- transferring responsibilities between Government departments, or from Westminster departments to the Scottish Parliament and the Welsh Assembly; this was done by the Scotland Act 1998 (Transfer of Functions to the Scottish Ministers etc.) Order 1999 and the National Assembly of Wales (Transfer of Functions) Order 1999
- dissolving Parliament before an election
- bringing an Act of Parliament into force
- compliance with EU Directives, for example, the Consumer Protection Act 1987 (Product Liability) (Modification) Order 2000, which was passed to comply with a Product Liability Directive
- dealing with foreign affairs, for example, the Afghanistan (United Nations Sanctions) Order 2001, which makes it an offence to make funds available to Osama Bin Laden or the Taliban or any person or body connected with Osama Bin Laden or the Taliban
- in times of national emergency, when Parliament is not sitting. An example of an emergency situation in which an Order in Council was made, is as a result of the terrorist attacks on 11 September 2001. The Terrorism (United Nations Measures) Order 2001, made on 10 October 2001 under the provisions of the United Nations Act 1946, made it an offence to provide funds to anyone involved in terrorism and allowed for the freezing of any such funds. A further example is The Extradition (Terrorist Bombings) Order 2002, which was made under the provisions of the Extradition Act 1989. It came into force on 27 August 2002 and allowed for persons suspected of terrorist activities to be extradited, that is, transferred from one country to another country for questioning and trial. Another emergency situation that required an Order in Council to be made was the fuel crisis in 2000. Truck drivers protesting about the price of fuel had blockaded some refineries preventing fuel tankers from leaving, with the result that many petrol stations ran out of fuel. The Energy Act 1976 (Reserve Powers) Order 2000 was made under the provisions of the Energy Act 1976. It came into force on 11 September 2000

Key terms

Orders in Council: laws made by the Queen and Privy Council which are enforceable in courts.

Privy Council: a body made up of senior current and former politicians, senior judges and members of the Royal Family.

and enabled movement of fuel throughout the country. In the case of emergencies, powers are given by parent Acts which authorise the Queen and Privy Council to make law. Other examples of such parent Acts include the Emergency Powers Act 1920 and the Civil Contingencies Act 2004.

Statutory instruments

As seen by the example of implementing the smoking ban in Activity 1 (p29), **statutory instruments** are laws made by a Government Minister under the authority of a parent/enabling Act within the area of their Ministerial responsibility. They are drafted by the legal department of the relevant Government department.

Statutory instruments are often used to update a law; for example, a statutory instrument might be used to change the amount of a fine for a criminal offence. Another example is the regular increase in the amount of the national minimum wage under the National Minimum Wage Act 1998.

Sometimes wider powers are given to the Government Minister to fill in the necessary detail which is too complex to be incorporated into the Act.

Statutory instruments are often referred to as 'Regulations' or 'Orders'.

Statutory instruments are often made in the form of Commencement Orders. These are orders made by a Government Minister specifying when an Act or part of an Act must come into force. Look at the following example.

2007 No. 62 (C. 2)
TRANSPORT
RAILWAYS
The Railways Act 2005 (Commencement No. 8) Order 2007
Made 16th January 2007
The Secretary of State makes the following Order in exercise of the powers conferred by section 60(2) of the Railways Act 2005:
Citation
1. This Order may be cited as the Railways Act 2005 (Commencement No. 8) Order 2007.
Commencement
2. (1) The provisions of the Railways Act 2005 specified in paragraph (2) shall come into force on 29th January 2007.
   (2) Those provisions are—
     (a) section 3 to the extent that it is not already in force;
     (b) section 4;
     (c) section 59(6) in so far as it relates to the provisions of Schedule 13 brought into force by this Order;
     (d) Schedule 4; and
     (e) in Part 1 of Schedule 13—
       (i) the entry relating to Schedule 4A of the Railways Act 1993 to the extent that it is not already in force; and
       (ii) the entry relating to paragraph 11 of Schedule 28 to the Transport Act 2000.
Signed by authority of the Secretary of State for Transport
Tom Harris
Parliamentary Under Secretary of State
16th January 2007

Sometimes there may be several Commencement Orders made in respect of the same Act. For example, the Town and Country Planning Act 1971 was brought into force by 75 Commencement Orders! There is generally no time limit within which a Commencement Order must be made after an Act has been passed. This means that some Acts are never actually brought into force, an example being The Easter Act 1928 which specifies a fixed date for Easter, but the Act has never been brought into force.

Law that is made to comply with directives from the European Union is usually made in the form of a statutory instrument. For example:

■ the Unfair Terms in Consumer Contracts Regulations 1999 were made in order to comply with the Unfair Terms in Consumer Contracts Directive 1993, and

■ the Sale and Supply of Goods to Consumers Regulations 2002 were made in order to comply with the Sale of Consumer Goods Directive 1999.

Both of these regulations provide extra protection to consumers.

A large volume of law is made in the form of statutory instruments each year.

Statutory instruments can be enforced in the courts and are just as much part of the law of the country as are Acts of Parliament. Some apply to the whole of the UK and others apply only to certain countries within the UK, for example, to England and Wales.

By-laws

By-laws are made by local authorities and public corporations or companies. They must be 'confirmed' (approved) by the relevant Government Minister and are enforceable in the courts.

Local authorities can make laws which apply just within their geographical area. A County Council can pass laws affecting a whole county, while a City-, Town- or District Council may pass laws affecting that city, town or district. These laws may deal with many issues, for example, drinking alcohol in public places or the fouling of public areas by dogs.

A parent Act in respect of dog fouling is the Dogs (Fouling of Land) Act 1996. Under this Act a local authority can designate areas of land as poop scoop areas. Those who are responsible for dogs which foul this designated land and who do not clear up the faeces are subject to a fixed penalty of £50. Failure to pay the fixed penalty is an offence. A local authority can designate a specific area of land to which this applies. For example, look at this public notice issued by Eastbourne Borough Council specifying the land they propose to designate.

> ### Dog Control Orders
>
> #### Failing to remove dog faeces
>
> This notice is to inform anyone with an interest that Eastbourne Borough Council is considering making a Fouling of Land by Dogs Order to make it an offence for anyone to fail to remove dog faeces deposited by a dog for which he or she is responsible. The land to be designated is all land within the Borough of Eastbourne of the following descriptions, being open to the air and to which the public are entitled or permitted to have access with or without payment:
>
> Roads, footpaths, road verges, walkways, alleyways and passageways
>
> Beaches, Promenades, Seafront Gardens and walkways

Key terms

By-laws: laws made by local authorities and public bodies. They are enforceable in the courts and apply to a local authority area or to the public body only.

Parks and Gardens, Recreation and Sports Grounds

Open amenity areas

Surface car parks

Open Downland (including Farmland)

Woodland Areas within Parks and in all other locations

www.eastbourne.gov.uk

Authority to make by-laws is given in many Acts of Parliament. Many by-laws are made under the authority of the Local Government Act 1972. For example, many local authorities make it an offence to drink alcohol or to skateboard or roller-skate in designated public places in their area, punishable with a fine. These designated areas have to have small signs supporting the prohibition; they are generally found on lampposts. See if you can find one in your area.

Public bodies and some companies are authorised to make laws regulating the behaviour of the public while on their property. For example, under the Railways Act 1993 railway companies can issue by-laws about behaviour of the public on their stations and trains. By-laws made by public bodies and companies are enforceable in the courts. In *Boddington* v *British Transport Police* (1998) the defendant was caught smoking on the train in breach of a by-law made in 1965 by British Rail under the Transport Act 1962. The Magistrates' Court fined him £10 and the decision was upheld on appeal. Similar by-laws apply for the payment of fares and are enforceable by a penalty fare and/or fine.

Fig. 2.1 *This is a common local authority by-law*

Table 2.1 *A table summarising the types of delegated legislation*

Type of delegated legislation Who makes it?	In what circumstances is it used?	Examples
Orders in Council. Made by the Queen and Privy Council.	To transfer responsibilitites between Government departments. To dissolve Parliament.	National Assembly of Wales (Transfer of Functions) Order 1999.
	To bring Acts of Parliament into force. To comply with European Directives.	Consumer Protection Act 1987 (Product Liability) (Modification) Order 2000.
	To deal with foreign affairs.	Afghanistan (United Nations Sanctions) Order 2001.
	To deal with national emergencies.	Terrorism (United Nations Measures) Order 2001.
Statutory instruments. Made by Government Ministers.	To update an Act of Parliament.	To increase the amount of a fine or the amount of the national minimum wage.
	To bring an Act or part of an Act into force – a commencement order.	Railways Act 2005 Commencement Orders.
	To comply with directives from the European Union.	Sale and Supply of Goods to Consumers Regulations 2002.
By-laws. Made by local authorities and public corporations or companies.	To make laws for the good government of local areas.	By-laws made under the Dogs (Fouling of Land) Act 1996.
	To make laws regulating the behaviour of the public on property belonging to a public body or company.	By-laws restricting smoking on trains and stations.

STATUTORY INSTRUMENTS

2006 No. 3368

PUBLIC HEALTH, ENGLAND

The Smoke-free (Premises and Enforcement) Regulations 2006

Made   13th December 2006

Laid before Parliament   18th December 2006

Coming into force   1st July 2007

The Secretary of State for Health, in exercise of the powers in sections 2(5), 10(1) and (2) and 79(3) of the Health Act 2006, makes the following Regulations:—

Citation, commencement, application and interpretation

1. (1) These Regulations may be cited as the Smoke-free (Premises and Enforcement) Regulations 2006 and shall come into force on 1 July 2007.

   (2) These Regulations apply in relation to England only.

   (3) In these Regulations 'the Act' means the Health Act 2006.

Enclosed and substantially enclosed premises

2. (1) For the purposes of section 2 of the Act, premises are enclosed if they—

   (a) have a ceiling or roof; and

   (b) except for doors, windows and passageways, are wholly enclosed either permanently or temporarily.

   (2) For the purposes of section 2 of the Act, premises are substantially enclosed if they have a ceiling or roof but there is—

   (a) an opening in the walls; or

   (b) an aggregate area of openings in the walls, which is less than half of the area of the walls, including other structures that serve the purpose of walls and constitute the perimeter of the premises.

   (3) In determining the area of an opening or an aggregate area of openings for the purposes of paragraph (2), no account is to be taken of openings in which there are doors, windows or other fittings that can be opened or shut.

   (4) In this regulation 'roof' includes any fixed or moveable structure or device which is capable of covering all or part of the premises as a roof, including, for example, a canvas awning.

Enforcement

3. (1) Each of the following authorities is designated as an enforcement authority for the purposes of Chapter 1 of Part 1 of the Act—

   (a) a unitary authority;

   (b) a district council in so far as it is not a unitary authority;

   (c) a London borough council;

   (d) a port health authority;

   (e) the Common Council of the City of London;

   (f) the Sub-Treasurer of the Inner Temple and the Under Treasurer of the Middle Temple; and

   (g) the Council of the Isles of Scilly.

Signed by authority of the Secretary of State for Health

Caroline Flint

Minister of State for Public Health Department of Health

13th December 2006

Activities

1 On page 28 is an extract of a recent piece of delegated legislation called a 'statutory instrument'. Answer the following questions about the extract:

   a Who was this piece of delegated legislation made by?

   b Under what piece of primary legislation (enabling Act) is it made?

   c To which part of the UK does the law apply?

   d Section 2 of the Health Act 2006 allows for the appropriate national authority to define, in delegated legislation, what 'enclosed premises' mean. How have they been defined?

   e How have 'substantially enclosed premises' been defined?

   f Who is responsible for enforcing the 'no smoking' ban?

   g Why was there a gap of six months between the making of the law and it coming into force?

2 Suggest which type of delegated legislation would be used in the following circumstances:

   a to transfer the responsibilities for university education from the Education Department to the newly created Department of Higher Education;

   b designating a new road;

   c a law introducing updated health and safety requirements;

   d increasing the amount of a fine for failing to travel with a valid train ticket;

   e declaring a 'state of emergency' to cope with widespread floods.

You should now be able to:

- describe how delegated legislation is made
- describe how each of the main types of delegated legislation are made
- answer exam questions on the topic of creation of delegated legislation.

2 Control of delegated legislation

We have seen that the power to make law is delegated to many different people/bodies. It is clear that some control must be exercised. Broadly speaking, there are two methods of control over delegated legislation, these being parliamentary control and judicial control.

Parliamentary control

The initial control Parliament exercises over delegated legislation is through the limits it sets in the parent/enabling Act. Only the people or body specified in the parent Act have power to make law, and the extent of that power is also specified. In addition, the parent Act will set out how the delegated legislation must be made and may set out certain procedures, such as consultation, to be followed. Parliamentary supremacy is not compromised because Parliament ultimately remains in control of what law is made and how it is made. Although law-making is

In this topic you will learn how to:

- describe parliamentary controls on delegated legislation
- describe judicial controls on delegated legislation
- evaluate the effectiveness of these controls.

removed from the elected House of Commons through the parent Act, it
specifies the limits of that power.

Parliament may repeal or amend the piece of delegated legislation.
This control also upholds parliamentary supremacy, as Parliament can
make or unmake any law. However, the effectiveness of this control is
limited because, due to the volume of delegated legislation made each
year, Parliament will not be able to check it all.

All by-laws are confirmed or approved by the relevant Government
Minister. For example, by-laws made by Hampshire County Council under
the Children and Young Persons Act 1933 regulating the local employment
of children were approved by the Secretary for Health. This should
ensure that all locally made law is overseen by those with expertise of the
technical issues involved. While the local authorities are perhaps more
aware than Parliament of local issues, the civil service department working
for the Minister possesses considerable technical expertise.

The Joint Select Committee on Statutory Instruments, more commonly
known as the Scrutiny Committee, is made up of MPs and peers. Its role
is to review statutory instruments and to refer provisions requiring further
consideration to both Houses of Parliament. The main grounds for referring
a statutory instrument back to the Houses of Parliament are because:

- It appears to have gone beyond or outside the powers given under the
  parent/enabling Act.
- It has not been made according to the method stipulated in the
  parent Act.
- Unexpected use has been made of the delegated power.
- It is unclear or defective.
- It imposes a tax or charge – only Parliament has the right to do this.
- It is retrospective in its effect, and the parent/enabling Act did not
  allow for this.

This is arguably one of the more effective controls, as many statutory
instruments are subject to some scrutiny. It is however impossible for
the Scrutiny Committee to review all statutory instruments because over
3,000 are created each year. Furthermore, the powers of the Scrutiny
Committee are limited in that it has no powers to amend the statutory
instrument, merely to report its findings back to either the House of
Commons or to the House of Lords. Research by the Hansard Society,
reported in 1992, revealed many findings of the Scrutiny Committee
were ignored.

The House of Lords Delegated Powers Scrutiny Committee checks all
Bills for any inappropriate enabling provisions. Any such provisions are
brought to the attention of the House of Lords before the Bill goes to the
Committee stage. This is an effective control because, if the enabling
provisions are made appropriately, it is more likely the law made under
the authority of them will also be.

Most statutory instruments must be laid before Parliament. This
requires the statutory instruments to be laid on the table of the House.
The parent Act will state whether the statutory instrument must be
laid before Parliament and which method must be used. There are two
methods of laying delegated legislation before Parliament:

First, there is **the positive (or affirmative) resolution procedure**. This
means that the statutory instrument must be approved by one or both
Houses of Parliament within a specified time, usually between 28 and 40
days, before it can become law. An example is the Human Rights Act 1998.

Section 1(4) authorises the Secretary of State to make amendments to the Act as he thinks fit, to reflect the rights in protocols that have been ratified or have been signed with a view to ratification by the UK. By virtue of s20 any such amendments are subject to the affirmative resolution procedure.

The disadvantage of this form of control is that it is time-consuming, defeating one of the main objects of delegated legislation, which is to save Parliament time. Furthermore, the statutory instrument cannot be amended by Parliament, only approved, annulled or withdrawn. The control is also limited in that, while it exists to control Ministerial power, the Government, by virtue of its majority in the House of Commons, will usually win a vote. As a result of these disadvantages the affirmative resolution is not used very often. However, statutory instruments subject to the affirmative resolution must always be debated by Parliament, and it is therefore more effective than some of the other controls. For this reason it is used for very important and potentially controversial issues.

Secondly, most statutory instruments are subject to the **negative resolution procedure**. The statutory instrument is laid before Parliament, usually for 40 days, during which time either House of Parliament can annul the instrument. All members of both Houses can put down a motion known as a 'prayer' calling for annulment. There is then a debate and a vote. If either House vote to pass the annulment motion, the statutory instrument does not become law. More often however, the statutory instrument is not annulled during the 40-day period, and so automatically becomes law.

It is arguable that this control is of limited effect, as there is no requirement for MPs to look at the statutory instrument. Most delegated legislation subject to this method is not challenged and automatically becomes law after 40 days. However, this method of control does give an opportunity for any member of either House to raise objections. This in turn may provide for more debate and consideration to be given to the provisions of the statutory instrument.

Publication

The Statutory Instruments Act 1946 provides a defence to someone in breach of a statutory instrument if it has not been issued – published – by Her Majesty's Stationery Office. The effect of this is that all statutory instruments must be published.

Although publication does not mean that everyone will be aware of the statutory instrument, this requirement does at least mean that the public have access to it.

Questions

Another form of parliamentary control is that the responsible Minister can be questioned by Parliament at Question Time or during debates. This method of control gives publicity to the delegated legislation due to the presence of the media in Parliament. It also makes the responsible Minister explain and justify the legal provisions. However, questioning politicians is often only as helpful as the particular politician wants to be. Politicians are notoriously skilled in not answering questions directly, and instead putting forward their own view.

Removing power

The final control is that Parliament may remove the power to legislate from the delegated person or body. This can be done by amending or repealing the parent or enabling Act.

▪ **Key terms**

Negative resolution procedure: the statutory instrument is laid before Parliament, usually for 40 days, and becomes law unless either House votes to annul it.

This control upholds parliamentary supremacy. It should also mean the delegated person or body takes care in the preparation of delegated legislation knowing that their legislative power could be taken away. However the volume of delegated legislation again limits the effectiveness of this control because many provisions will inevitably remain unnoticed by Parliament.

Control by the judiciary

The validity of a piece of delegated legislation can be challenged in the High Court through the judicial review procedure. **Judicial review** was defined by Mr Justice Simon Brown – now Lord Brown – in *Ex parte Vijayatunga* (1988) as the 'exercise of the court's inherent power at common law to determine whether action is lawful or not'. Judicial review is not concerned with the merits of the delegated legislation or the reasons behind it, only whether it is lawful.

When the delegated legislation is made beyond the powers conferred by the parent/enabling Act, the delegated legislation can be declared *ultra vires* by the court and void. **Ultra vires** means 'beyond the powers' or 'exceeding the authority of'. Any individual may challenge the validity of delegated legislation provided he is affected by it.

There are two types of *ultra vires*: procedural *ultra vires* and substantive *ultra vires*.

Procedural ultra vires

Procedural *ultra vires* is concerned with how the delegated legislation is made. Some parent Acts specify procedures which must be followed. Any delegated legislation which is made without following these procedures can be declared *ultra vires* and void. An example is *Agricultural, Horticultural and Forestry Training Board* v *Aylesbury Mushrooms Ltd* (1972), commonly known as the *Aylesbury Mushroom* case. An order was declared void against mushroom growers because a letter informing the Mushroom Growers' Association of the new law did not comply with the requirement in the parent Act to consult interested parties.

Substantive ultra vires

Substantive *ultra vires* is concerned with whether the content of the delegated legislation is within the limits set out in the parent Act. Any delegated legislation beyond these limits can be declared *ultra vires* and therefore void. In *A-G* v *Fulham Corporation* (1921), the parent Act gave the Corporation power to provide clothes washing facilities for the public. In 1920 the Corporation set up a commercial laundry where council employees washed the residents' clothes. This was held to be *ultra vires* because the parent/enabling Act did not give authority to the Corporation to wash clothes for others. Another example is *Customs and Excise Commissioners* v *Cure and Deeley Ltd* (1962). The parent/enabling Act gave the Commissioners power to make laws concerning the collection of taxes. The Commissioners made a law deciding the amount of tax due when a tax return was submitted late. This was substantive *ultra vires*. The Commissioners had power to make rules concerning the collection of tax due by law, not to make laws concerning the amount of tax due.

Unreasonableness

The courts may also declare the delegated legislation to be *ultra vires* and therefore void on the basis that it is unreasonable. This judicial control was established in *Associated Provincial Picture Houses* v *Wednesbury Corporation* (1948) and is commonly known as 'Wednesbury unreasonableness'. It is commonly argued in judicial cases such as in *R (Rogers)* v *Swindon NHS Trust* (2006), when a woman with early-stage breast cancer was prescribed Herceptin by her doctor. The NHS Trust refused to provide this non-approved drug because (it said) her case was not exceptional. The Court of Appeal said this policy was irrational and unreasonable and therefore unlawful. The Trust was unable to put forward any clear reasons for providing the drug for some patients and not for others.

Other circumstances where the delegated legislation may be declared void

Courts may also declare a piece of delegated legislation *ultra vires* and therefore void:

- where it levies taxes
- where it allows sub-delegation – no body to which law-making powers have been delegated has power to delegate to another body
- where all interested parties have not been consulted as required by the parent/enabling Act
- where the delegated legislation conflicts with European legislation.

Effectiveness of judicial control

Although there are quite a broad range of controls, the effectiveness of judicial control is limited. This is because the courts are dependent on cases being brought before them. It is quite rare that a person will question the validity of a law which it is claimed they have contravened. To do so requires considerable legal knowledge, financial resources and time. Even when a judge is presented with the opportunity to review a

Table 2.2 *A table summarising the controls on delegated legislation*

Parliamentary controls	Judicial controls
The parent Act sets out the limits within which delegated law must be made or the procedures to be followed.	Procedural *ultra vires*. The delegated legislation is void, because the procedures set out in the parent Act for creating it have not been followed, as in the *Aylesbury Mushroom Case* (1972).
Parliament can repeal or amend the delegated legislation.	
All delegated legislation, including by-laws, are made under the authority of Government Ministers.	Substantive *ultra vires*. The delegated legislation is void, because the content exceeds the limits set out in the parent Act: for example, *Customs and Excise Commissioners* v *Cure and Deeley Ltd* (1962).
It is the role of the Scrutiny Committee to review statutory instruments and refer any requiring further consideration back to the Houses of Parliament.	
The House of Lords Delegated Powers Scrutiny Committee checks the enabling provisions of the parent Acts.	Unreasonableness. The delegated legislation is void, because it is so unreasonable: for example, *R (Rogers)* v *Swindon NHS Trust* (2006).
The affirmative resolution procedure. The SI is laid before Parliament and becomes law if approved by both Houses.	
The negative resolution procedure. The SI is laid before Parliament and automatically becomes law unless annulled.	
The Statutory Instruments Act 1946 requires all SIs to be published.	
Ministers can be held to account at Question Time or during debates.	
Parliament can remove the power to make delegated legislation.	

piece of delegated legislation, he cannot amend it, only declare it void. However, when delegated legislation is challenged in the courts, a judge is able to ensure that it has been made in accordance with the instructions set out by the democratically elected House of Commons within the parent Act. This upholds parliamentary supremacy because while a judge can declare a piece of delegated legislation to be void, he can only do so if it does not conform to the instructions given by Parliament.

■ Activities

The Roads Act gives the Highways Minister power to make changes to the Highway Code by statutory instrument. A new Code is introduced which requires cyclists to wear helmets at all times while cycling and to cycle only in designated cycle lanes. The Order becomes law on the date stated on it, but will be annulled if either House passes a motion calling for its annulment within a certain time. This time period is 40 days including the day on which it was laid.

1. Is the Order subject to the affirmative or negative resolution procedure?

2. The Keep Cycling Campaign consider that these changes are the biggest threat to cycling for decades. Advise them how the these changes can be removed from the new Code.

Nuclear consultation was flawed

Queen's Bench Division
Published 20 February 2007
Regina (Greenpeace Ltd) v Secretary of State for Trade and Industry
Before Mr Justice Sullivan
Judgement February 16, 2007

Where it had been stated in a Government White Paper that there would be the fullest public consultation before making a decision on a matter of substantial public policy but information as to major relevant issues had emerged only after consultation had closed, then the decision-making process was fatally flawed.

Mr Justice Sullivan so held in the Queen's Bench Division in allowing the application of Greenpeace Ltd for judicial review by way of an order to quash the decision of the Secretary of State for Trade and Industry to announce Government support for the building of new civil nuclear power generation facilities.

Mr Nigel Pleming, QC and Ms Kassie Smith for Greenpeace; **Mr Richard Drabble, QC** and **Mr David Forsdick** for the secretary of state.

MR JUSTICE SULLIVAN said that a 2003 White Paper had said that a new nuclear build was not proposed and that there would be the fullest public consultation before a decision was made.

The consultation process was very seriously flawed. As an issues paper the Government's consultation paper was perfectly adequate. As the consultation paper on an issue of such importance and complexity it was manifestly inadequate.

It contained no proposals as such; even if it had, the information given to those consulted was wholly insufficient to enable them to make an intelligent response.

On both the economics and the waste issues all, or virtually all the information of any substance emerged only after the consultation period had concluded.

Elementary fairness required that those consulted should be given a proper opportunity to respond to the substantial amount of new evidence. There could be no proper consultation, let alone the fullest public consultation if the substance of these two issues was not consulted upon before the decision was made.

There was therefore procedural unfairness and a breach of legitimate expectation that there be the fullest public consultation before a decision was taken to support a new nuclear build. The application succeeded.

Solicitors: **Harrison Grant**, Kentish Town; **Treasury Solicitor**.

The Times, 20 February 2007

Activity

Read through the report from *The Times* on p34 and answer the following questions on this law report:

1 Which organisation is challenging the Government?

2 In which court was the case heard?

3 Is this a case of procedural or substantive *ultra vires*?

4 What kind of order was requested?

5 What is the effect of the order granted by the judge?

6 Why could this order be seen, by some, as an attack on the Government by the judge?

You should now be able to:

- understand how delegated legislation is controlled by Parliament and the courts

- discuss the effectiveness of these controls

- attempt previous questions on controls of delegated legislation.

3 Advantages and disadvantages of delegated legislation

Advantages of delegated legislation

Time-saving

Delegated legislation saves Parliament time. Parliament does not have enough time to pass all the new detailed and local laws required each year. There is often only enough time in the parliamentary session to pass all Government Bills introduced. There is very little time left for other types of Bills, and making over 3,000 statutory instruments as well as local by-laws and emergency provisions each year would be impossible.

Delegated legislation can be passed quickly to deal with situations when they arise, and in emergencies. If it was necessary to follow the parliamentary procedure, it would take too long before the law was introduced. This would be wholly inappropriate and ineffective in emergency situations.

Produced with specialist knowledge

People with specialist knowledge are involved in the preparation of delegated legislation. Parliament does not necessarily possess this specialist knowledge. For example, local councils have greater knowledge of the local area. Bristol City Council has several by-laws relating to the Clifton and Durdham Downs. These by-laws regulate behaviour on the Downs and amongst other things prohibit vehicles and grazing. Government Ministers and their civil service departments have considerable technical knowledge within their particular area of responsibility. For example, the Cableway Installation Regulations 2004, made by the Transport Minister in order to comply with a European Directive, required detailed technical knowledge of cablecars, drag lifts and ski lifts, etc.

In this topic you will learn how to:

- discuss advantages of delegated legislation

- discuss disadvantages of delegated legislation.

AQA Examiner's tip

Try to use details in the discussion, in the form of names of delegated legislation, case names or statistics.

Parliamentary control

There is some control over delegated legislation. In Parliament, statutory instruments are subject to affirmative or negative resolutions or are scrutinised by the Scrutiny Committee. By-laws must be approved by the relevant Minister, and a judge can declare any delegated legislation which has gone beyond its powers void. This range of control should ensure that all delegated legislation conforms to the requirements of the parent Act and therefore the will of Parliament.

Democratic

Delegated legislation is, to an extent, democratic because Government Ministers, who are responsible for issuing statutory instruments and who also approve by-laws, are elected. Local councillors, responsible for making by-laws, are also elected. Orders in Council are drafted by the Government, though they are approved by the Queen and Privy Council, neither of which is an elected body.

Disadvantages of delegated legislation

Partly undemocratic

The process of making delegated legislation is to an extent undemocratic. Delegated legislation is not debated by Parliament, the exception being those statutory instruments subject to the affirmative resolution procedure. Statutory instruments are drafted by unelected, permanently employed civil servants and often only rubber-stamped by the appropriate Minister. As discussed above, the Queen and Privy Council are not elected yet approve Orders in Council.

Lack of publicity

Delegated legislation is insufficiently publicised. Because delegated legislation is not debated by Parliament there is not the same opportunity for the press to raise public awareness of it as there is with an Act of Parliament. This, added to the fact that there is no general effective way to publicise delegated legislation, means that an enormous volume of law is passed without the public being aware of it. Much remains unpublicised after coming into force.

No effective control

There is lack of proper control. Many of the parliamentary and judicial controls are limited in effect. For example, not all statutory instruments are subject to an affirmative or negative resolution and those subject to the latter may be overlooked. Judicial controls are dependent on a person challenging the validity of the law, which due to limited knowledge, finance and time, rarely occurs. Consequently some delegated legislation that is *ultra vires* is never challenged, and so remains in force.

Contradicts the separation of powers

Some delegated legislation offends the doctrine of separation of powers. Under this doctrine there are three branches of power: the executive, the legislature and the judiciary. Noone should be a member of more than one of the three branches of power, and the three branches should operate separately from each other. They should not perform each other's duties.

The executive is the Government and is responsible for formulating policy. In theory Government Ministers should not also be making law.

The legislature is the Houses of Parliament and is responsible for making law.

AQA Examiner's tip

A point can be argued both as an advantage and as a disadvantage. It is an advantage that delegated legislation is to an extent democratic yet a disadvantage that it is to an extent undemocratic.

AQA Examiner's tip

This is another disadvantage with a contradictory advantage. It is an advantage that there is control, yet a disadvantage that there is a lack of control.

The judiciary should ensure the law passed by Parliament is applied. According to this theory they should not be declaring whether the law is valid or not.

Risk of sub-delegation

There is a risk of sub-delegation where the body or person who has been given the power to make law may pass this power down to another. For example, statutory instruments are supposed to be made by Government Ministers. In reality they often merely rubber-stamp laws actually made by their civil servants.

Table 2.3 *A table identifying the advantages and disadvantages of delegated legislation*

Advantages of delegated legislation	Disadvantages of delegated legislation
It saves Parliament time.	It is, to an extent, undemocratic.
It is flexible.	There is a lack of effective control.
It is made by people with local and technical expertise.	There is a lack of publicity.
There is control over delegated legislation.	Some delegated legislation offends the separation of powers.
It is, to an extent, democratic.	There is a risk of sub-delegation.

You should now be able to:

- discuss advantages of delegated legislation
- discuss disadvantages of delegated legislation
- answer past paper questions on advantages and disadvantages of delegated legislation.

Statutory interpretation

Key terms

Statutory interpretation: the interpretation of Acts of Parliament by the judges.

The literal rule: words or phrases in an Act are given their ordinary, natural or dictionary meaning. The literal rule does not allow a judge to create law. It requires application of the law as stated by Parliament.

AQA Examiner's tip

- Candidates should ensure that descriptions of each rule are complete and supported with authority to attain the highest marks.

- Notice how these explanations of the cases include reference to the words or phrase in the Act that the judge was interpreting.

Key cases

Whiteley v Chappell (1868); Fisher v Bell (1961): the literal rule of interpretation was used by the court in these cases and produced an unexpected outcome.

1 Approaches to statutory interpretation

Acts of Parliament, sometimes referred to as 'legislation' or 'statutes', are usually drafted by parliamentary counsel (draftsmen). However, while it is the role of Parliament to create legislation, it is the role of the judges to apply it. Despite the best efforts of parliamentary counsel to make the Act as clear and as understandable as possible, some words or provisions may be ambiguous – that is, have more than one meaning – or may be unclear. Sometimes an Act may be deliberately drafted in broad terms to allow the Act to be flexible enough to cover unforeseen circumstances or matters which may arise in the future, for example improved technology. These are some of the reasons that the judge may be required to interpret the Act/legislation/statute so as to provide for an appropriate outcome in the case before him/her – hence the term **statutory interpretation**.

While it is only the minority of Acts that pose such interpretation problems, 75 per cent of cases heard by the House of Lords are concerned with statutory interpretation.

In addition to materials both inside and outside the Act, judges are assisted by certain 'rules' and presumptions. These 'rules' have been developed by the judges themselves and are not rules in the strict legal sense, but are alternative ways a judge can approach interpreting an Act. A judge will make certain presumptions when interpreting Acts of Parliament. The main presumptions are that Acts of Parliament are not retrospective (that is, they only apply to situations arising after the Act is passed), that the Crown is not bound, that there is no change in the common law unless the Act expressly states that there is, and that *mens rea* (a guilty mind) is required in criminal cases. Presumptions are beyond the scope of the AQA specification and will therefore not be considered further in this chapter.

The rules of interpretation

The literal rule

Note the use of a judicial quote here to clarify the explanation of the rule.

The literal rule requires the judge(s) to give the word or phrase its natural, ordinary or dictionary meaning, even if this appears to be contrary to the intentions of Parliament. As Lord Reid said in *Pinner v Everett* (1969), 'In determining the meaning of any words or phrase in a statute, the first question to ask is always *what is the natural and ordinary meaning of that word or phrase* in its context in the statute.'

Application of the literal rule may lead to unexpected results that were not intended by Parliament. In **Whiteley v Chappell (1868)** an Act made it an offence to impersonate 'any person entitled to vote at an election.' The defendant attempted to vote in the name of a deceased person, but the court held no offence had been committed because when 'any person entitled to vote' is interpreted literally, it does not include dead people.

Application of the literal rule also produced an unexpected result in **Fisher v Bell (1961)**. The defendant displayed flick knives in his shop window. He was charged under The Restriction of Offensive Weapons

Act 1959. The Act made it an offence to 'sell or offer for sale' an offensive weapon. In contract law the display of goods in a shop window is not an offer for sale but an invitation to treat; the display of goods thus invites the customer to make an offer to buy the goods. The court found the defendant not guilty despite the obvious aim of the Act being to prevent such behaviour.

The golden rule

This rule is an extension of the literal rule. It allows the court to look at the literal meaning of a word or phrase, but then avoid using a literal interpretation which would lead to an absurd result. There are two approaches taken while applying the golden rule, these being the narrow approach and the broad approach.

Where a word or phrase is capable of more than one literal meaning, the narrow application of the golden rule allows the judge(s) to select the meaning which avoids an absurdity. For example, in **Allen (1872)** the defendant married for a second time. He was charged under the Offences Against the Person Act 1861, which states it is an offence to marry again without the previous marriage being ended by a divorce. Allen argued that it was not possible to be legally married twice, so he could not have committed an offence. This interpretation of the word 'marry' would mean that the offence is impossible to commit. The court had to decide whether 'marry' means to become legally married to another person, or whether it means to go through a ceremony of marriage. To avoid an absurd result the court adopted the second meaning and held Allen was guilty under the Act.

Where there is only one literal meaning of a word or phrase, but to apply it would cause an absurdity, then under the broad approach the court will modify this meaning to avoid the absurdity. In **Adler v George (1964)** the defendant was charged under the Official Secrets Act 1920 with obstructing a member of the armed forces 'in the vicinity of a prohibited place.' The defendant argued that he was actually in the prohibited place, not in the vicinity of it, that is, near to it. Had the court applied this literal interpretation of the phrase the defendant would not have been guilty. The court therefore interpreted the phrase 'in the vicinity of' to include 'in' a prohibited place to avoid the absurd result.

The golden rule provides an opportunity for judicial law-making. The narrow approach allows the judges to choose between two or more meanings of the words as stated by Parliament. The broad approach provides further scope for judicial law-making because it allows the judges to modify the meaning of the words as stated by Parliament.

The mischief rule

Under this rule the court looks at the gap in the law which Parliament had felt it necessary to fill when passing the Act. It then interprets the Act to fill that gap and to remedy the mischief Parliament had been aiming to remedy.

In **Heydon's Case (1584)** the judges said that the court should consider four things when attempting to interpret a statutory provision:

1 What was the common law before the Act was passed?
2 What was the defect or mischief for which the common law did not provide a remedy?
3 What remedy does the Act attempt to provide so as to cure the defect?
4 What is the true reason for the remedy?

Broadly speaking, therefore, the rule requires that where an Act has been passed to remedy a weakness or defect in the law, the interpretation which will correct that weakness or defect is the one to be adopted.

The mischief rule was applied in **Smith v Hughes (1960)**. Under the Street Offences Act 1959 it is an offence to solicit 'in the street or public place'. Prostitutes solicited men from a balcony and through a window while in their home. The accused was found guilty of the offence even though she had not been in the street when the soliciting took place. Parker LCJ said that regard should be had to the mischief at which the Act was aimed. He said 'everybody knows this was an Act designed to clean up the streets.' The court held therefore that, as the Act aimed to prevent people from being solicited whilst they were in the street or public place, it did not matter where the soliciting originated from.

The mischief rule provides scope for judicial law-making because it allows the judges to decide what they think Parliament was trying to put right in the previous law. The judges do not focus on the words as stated by Parliament.

The purposive approach

The mischief rule involves the court looking back to the common law position before the Act was passed to find the gap in the law that Parliament was trying to fill. The purposive approach focuses on what Parliament intended when passing the new law. The purposive approach is a modern version of the mischief approach. It is generally recognised by academics and the judiciary that the distinction between these two approaches is a minor technicality. In *Pepper (Inspector of Taxes) v Hart* (1993) Lord Browne-Wilkinson said 'the fine distinctions between looking for the mischief and looking for the intention in using words to provide the remedy are technical and inappropriate.'

In recent years, in particular since joining the European Union, the English courts have increasingly used the purposive approach when interpreting legislation. Unlike English legislation, European law is drafted in broad terms. In *Bulmer Ltd v J Bollinger SA* (1974) Lord Denning MR compared the two. 'The draftsmen of our statutes have striven to express themselves with the utmost exactness … In consequence the judges have followed suit. They interpret a statute as applying only to the circumstances covered by the very words. They give them a literal interpretation … How different is this treaty! It lays down general principles. It expresses its aims and purposes … All the way through the treaty there are gaps and lacunae. These have to be filled in by the judges, or by regulations or directives. It is the European way.'

In order to ensure the consistent application of European law throughout all the member states the United Kingdom judges recognised that, when interpreting European legislation or domestic legislation enacted to comply with European law, the purposive approach to interpretation should be adopted. In *Bulmer Ltd v J Bollinger SA* (1974) Lord Denning said of the judge's role: 'No longer must they examine the words in meticulous detail. No longer must they argue about the precise grammatical sense. They must look to the purpose or intent. To quote the words of the European Court in the *Da Costa* case they must deduce from the wording and the spirit of the Treaty the meaning of the Community rules.' This preference for the purposive approach was extended to United Kingdom legislation by the House of Lords in *Pepper (Inspector of Taxes) v Hart* (1993). Lord Griffiths said 'the days have long passed when the courts adopted a strict constructionist view of interpretation which required them to adopt the literal meaning of the language. The courts now adopt a purposive approach which seeks to give effect to the true purpose of legislation and are prepared to look at much extraneous material that bears on the background against which the legislation was enacted.'

Another influence operating on the United Kingdom judges which encourages the use of the purposive approach is the Human Rights Act 1998. This Act provides that all United Kingdom legislation must be interpreted so as to be compatible with the European Convention on Human Rights (ECHR). The ECHR is drafted in broad terms as is the law of the European Union. The European Court of Human Rights thus adopts a purposive approach when interpreting the ECHR and this approach is now followed by United Kingdom judges when interpreting legislation in Human Rights Act cases.

While the judges continue to use the literal, golden and mischief rules, there has clearly been a considerable shift from a preference for the literal rule to a preference for the purposive approach. This is in accordance with the recommendations of the Law Commission Report on The Interpretation of Statutes (1969), which has not to date been implemented. In this report it is stated, 'The principles of interpretation would include: the preference of a construction which would promote the general legislative purpose over one which would not.'

Examples of cases in which the judges have used the purposive approach include **Pepper (Inspector of Taxes) v Hart (1993)** and **Jones v Tower Boot Co. (1997)**.

In *Pepper (Inspector of Taxes)* v *Hart* (1993) the issue was how to interpret s63 of the Finance Act 1976. Teachers at an independent school for boys were having their children educated at the school for a fifth of the price charged to the public. This was a taxable benefit based on the 'cash equivalent' of the concession. Under s63 of the 1976 Act, the words 'cash equivalent' could be interpreted to mean either the additional cost of providing the concession to the teachers or the average cost of providing the tuition to the public and the teachers. The House of Lords referred to statements made by the Financial Secretary to the Treasury during the committee stage which revealed that the intention of Parliament was to tax employees on the basis of the additional cost to the employer of providing the concession.

> ■ **Key cases**
>
> **Pepper (Inspector of Taxes) v Hart (1993); Jones v Tower Boot Co. (1997):** the purposive approach was applied by the court.

In *Jones* v *Tower Boot Co.* (1997) the Court of Appeal had to decide whether the physical and verbal abuse of a young black worker by his workmates fell within 'the course of employment' under s32 of the Race Relations Act 1976. The employer had argued that these actions fell outside the course of the workmates' employment, because such behaviour was not part of their job. The Employment Appeal Tribunal agreed with the employer's argument and found that the employer could not therefore be held responsible to the young black worker for his workmates' behaviour. This decision was reversed by the Court of Appeal using the purposive approach to interpret s32. Parliament's intention when enacting the Race Relations Act was to eliminate discrimination in the workplace and this would not be achieved by applying a narrow construction to the wording.

The purposive approach provides scope for judicial law-making because the judge is allowed to decide what he/she thinks Parliament intended the Act to say rather than what the Act actually says.

1 Answer the following questions concerning cases considered in this topic.

   a What rule of interpretation do you think influenced the Court of Appeal in *Jones* v *Tower Boot Co.*?

   b What would the outcome have been in *Smith* v *Hughes* had the court applied the literal rule?

   c What would the outcome have been in *Whiteley* v *Chappell* had the court applied the golden rule?

2 Explain, using examples, the rules judges may use when interpreting Acts of Parliament.

3 Taking into account the exam tips throughout this topic make a bullet point essay plan in respect of the above question.

You should now be able to:

- explain the four approaches to statutory interpretation

- use cases to illustrate the rules of statutory interpretation

- attempt past paper questions on the topic of statutory interpretation.

In this topic you will learn how to:

- state the different intrinsic aids to interpretation

- state the different extrinsic aids to interpretation

- give relevant examples of intrinsic and extrinsic aids to interpretation

- state the different rules of language

- give relevant examples for each rule of language.

■ Key terms

Intrinsic aids: aids found within the Act.

💡② Aids to interpretation

There are certain materials both inside and outside the Act that the judge can refer to which help him/her interpret the words or provisions of the Act. These are known as 'aids to interpretation'. There are two types of aids: intrinsic aids and extrinsic aids.

Intrinsic aids

Intrinsic aids to interpretation are found within the Act itself. The judge may use other parts of the Act to understand the meaning of the word or phrase in question.

The long and/or short title of the Act may be referred to as guidance. The long title of the Abortion Act 1967 is 'An Act to amend and clarify the law relating to termination of pregnancy by registered medical practitioners.' This was referred to by four of the five Law Lords who heard the appeal in *Royal College of Nursing of the United Kingdom* v *DHSS* (1981).

Older statutes may contain a preamble which is a statement preceding the main body of the Act, setting out the purpose of the Act in detail. Newer Acts may contain an objectives or purposes section at the beginning of the Act. For example, the purposes section of the Climate Change and Sustainable Energy Act 2006 states:

> **1 Purposes**
>
> 1 The principal purpose of this Act is to enhance the United Kingdom's contribution to combating climate change.
>
> 2 In performing functions under this Act, the relevant persons and bodies shall have regard to—
>   a the principal purpose set out in subsection (1),
>   b the desirability of alleviating fuel poverty, and
>   c the desirability of securing a diverse and viable long-term energy supply.

> 3   In this section 'the relevant persons and bodies' means—
>   a   the Secretary of State;
>   b   any public authority.

www.opsi.gov.uk

Schedules appear as additions to the main body of the Act. These can be referred to in order to make some sense of the main text. In some cases it will be necessary to refer to the Schedules to understand the Act. For example s2(1) of the Hunting Act 2004 provides 'Hunting is exempt if it is within a class specified in Schedule 1.' The exempt classes of hunting are then specified in Schedule 1.

Most modern Acts contain a special interpretation definition section, which explains the meaning of key words used in the Act. For example, the Law Reform (Year and a Day Rule) Act 1996 provides that the defendant can be guilty of a fatal offence where the death follows more than a year and a day after the defendant's act or omission. Section 2(3) defines fatal offence as:

a   murder, manslaughter, infanticide or any other offence of which one of the elements is causing a person's death, or

b   the offence of aiding, abetting, counselling or procuring a person's suicide.

Punctuation is now recognised to have an effect on the meaning of words and can be taken into account in determining the meaning of statutory provisions. In *Hanlon* v *The Law Society* (1981) Lord Lowry said:

> I consider that not to take account of punctuation disregards the reality that literate people, such as parliamentary draftsmen, punctuate what they write, if not identically, at least in accordance with grammatical principles. Why should not literate people, such as judges, look at the punctuation in order to interpret the meaning of the legislation as accepted by Parliament.

Extrinsic aids

Extrinsic aids are materials found outside the Act that may be referred to by the judge.

Dictionaries can be used to find the literal meaning of words. In *Vaughan* v *Vaughan* (1973) the Court of Appeal had to interpret the word 'molest'. The defendant had been the subject of injunctions in respect of previous violence towards his ex-wife, who was afraid of him. The defendant argued that pestering his ex-wife to resume their relationship by going to her home early in the morning and late at night, and also calling on her at work did not amount to molesting her. The judges consulted the dictionary which defined 'molest' as to 'cause trouble, vex, annoy, or put to inconvenience' and held that the defendant's behaviour did amount to molestation.

Previous Acts may be referred to. In *Wheatley* (1979) the Court of Appeal had to interpret the provisions of the Explosive Substances Act 1883. The long title of the Act was 'An Act to amend the law relating to explosive substances, amending the Explosives Act 1875.' The Court of Appeal therefore looked at the earlier Act to made sense of the 1883 Act.

The Interpretation Act 1978 provides definition of certain words which are often used in Acts. For example it provides that masculine shall include the feminine and singular words include the plural unless a contrary intention appears within an Act. Section 6 provides:

Key terms

Extrinsic aids: aids to interpretation found outside the Act.

Fig. 3.1 *Someone loitering outside a house at night*

In any Act, unless the contrary intention appears,

a words importing the masculine gender include the feminine;

b words importing the feminine gender include the masculine;

c words in the singular include the plural and words in the plural include the singular.

The court may look at Reports of the Law Commission, Royal Commissions and other official law reform bodies. A Law Commission Report can highlight what is wrong with the old law and suggest options. A report usually includes a draft Bill.

International Treaties may be referred to in order to ascertain the overriding objective of the Treaty which the Act is intended to comply with. This will often arise when judges are interpreting EU law.

Since *Pepper (Inspector of Taxes)* v *Hart* (1993) the courts have been able to refer to the Parliamentary debates recorded in Hansard. However the House of Lords in this case held that Hansard can only be referred to in certain circumstances:

■ The Act must be ambiguous or obscure, or a literal interpretation would lead to an absurdity.

■ Judges may look only at statements made by a Minister or other promoter of the Bill.

■ The statements must be clear in order for them to be relied upon.

Since 1999 Acts have been issued with explanatory notes. These are not part of the Act, hence they are an external rather than an internal aid. Explanatory notes are written by the Government department responsible for the Act once the Act has been given Royal Assent.

Text books may be referred to for guidance as to the meaning of a word or phrase. For example, in *Re Castioni* (1891) J. F. Stephen referred to his own text, *History of the Criminal Law of England*, when interpreting the words 'political crime'.

Table 3.1 *Examples of intrinsic and extrinsic aids*

Intrinsic aids: aids within the Act	Extrinsic aids: aids outside the Act
Long/short title	Dictionaries
Preamble/objectives/purposes section	Previous Acts
Schedules	Interpretation Act (1978)
Definition section	Reports of Law Reform bodies
Punctuation	Hansard
	International Treaties
	Explanatory notes
	Textbooks

The rules of language

In addition to the four main rules explained earlier, there are other rules of language, sometimes referred to as subsidiary rules.

The ejusdem generis rule

Under this rule, where general words follow particular words, the general words are interpreted to be of the same kind as the particular words. For example, in the phrase 'dogs, cats and other animals', the particular

AQA Examiner's tip

As with the four rules of interpretation considered in Topic 1, you should use case illustration to explain these rules.

words are 'dogs' and 'cats'. The general words are 'other animals'. Under the ejusdem generis rule the general words would be interpreted in line with the particular words. Therefore, since dogs and cats are domestic animals, then the general words of 'other animals' would be interpreted to mean other domestic animals.

In **Powell v Kempton Park Race Course** (1899), the defendant company kept an open-air enclosure reserved for bookmakers. Under a Regulation it was prohibited to keep a 'house, office or other place' for betting purposes. The court applied the *ejusdem generis* rule and held the defendant was not liable because his open-air enclosure was not a covered place. The general words of 'other place' referred to covered places, since the places specifically mentioned, that is 'house' and 'office' are covered places.

Expressio unius est exclusio alterius

Translated, this means the expression of one thing implies the exclusion of another. Where particular words are used and these are not followed by general words, the Act applies only to the instances specified (the particular words). For example, in **Inhabitants of Sedgley (1837)** rates were charged on 'land, titles and coal mines.' Therefore rates could not be charged on any mine other than coal mines.

Noscitur a sociis

Under this 'rule' the meaning of a word is to be gathered from the context in which it is written. For example, the Refreshment Houses Act 1860 stated that all houses, rooms, shops or buildings kept open for 'entertainment' during certain hours of the night must be licensed. In **Muir v Keay (1975)** the defendant kept his café open to the public during the night without a licence. The court applied the *noscitur a sociis* rule and held that 'entertainment' in the context of the Act did not mean only musical or theatrical entertainment, but meant other forms of enjoyment, such as drinking coffee late at night. Therefore the defendant had committed an offence under the Act.

Key cases

Powell v Kempton Park Race Course (1899): the *ejusdem generis* rule was applied by the court.

Inhabitants of Sedgley (1837): the *expressio unius est exclusio alterius* rule was applied by the court.

Muir v Keay (1975): the *noscitur a sociis* rule was applied by the court.

Activities

1 The following are real cases. Decide the outcome of these cases by reference to the rules of language.

Wood v Commissioner of Police of the Metropolis (1986)
The court had to interpret the meaning of s4 of the Vagrancy Act 1824, which includes the phrase, 'any gun, pistol, hanger, cutlass, bludgeon, or other offensive weapon'. The defendant was in possession of a piece of glass which had fallen out of a door and was charged under this provision. Was he guilty?

Allen v Emmerson (1944)
Section 33 of the Barrow-in-Furness Corporation Act 1872 required 'theatres and other places of entertainment' to have a licence. The court had to decide whether a 'funfair' required a licence.

Pengelley v Bell Punch Co. Ltd (1964)
The court had to decide whether part of a factory floor used for storage fell within 'floors, steps, stairs, passages and gangways', as stated in s28 of the Factories Act 1961.

2 Look up the Times Law Report, 31 October 1990: *Cheeseman* v *Director of Public Prosecutions*. Answer the following questions.

a What extrinsic aid was referred to in order to determine the meaning of the word 'street'?

b According to that extrinsic aid what did the court decide was the meaning of the word 'street'?

c Did the court decide that the public lavatory fell within the meaning of the word 'street'?

d What extrinsic aid was referred to in order to determine the meaning of the word 'passenger'?

e According to that extrinsic aid what did the court decide was the meaning of the word 'passenger'?

f Did the court decide that the policemen were 'passengers'?

You should now be able to:

■ explain the different aids to interpretation

■ explain the different rules of language

■ explain how cases illustrate the aids to interpretation and rules of language

■ attempt past paper questions on the topic of aids to statutory interpretation.

In this topic you will learn how to:

■ state the advantages and disadvantages of each approach to statutory interpretation using cases to illustrate each

■ state the advantages and disadvantages of each rule of language using cases to illustrate each

■ state the advantages and disadvantages of the aids to interpretation using cases/ Acts of Parliament.

3 Advantages and disadvantages of the rules of interpretation

Advantages of the literal rule

Under this rule parliamentary sovereignty is respected, that is, the principle that Parliament is the supreme law-maker. Judges are given a restricted role. They must keep to the constitutional position of applying the law as set by Parliament.

Law-making is left to those elected for the law-making role, that is, MPs in Parliament. Judges are not elected and it is therefore not democratic for them to be involved in the creation or even modification of the law. If the law needs to be changed then this is the responsibility of Parliament. Application of the literal rule can highlight to Parliament the problems with an Act and then Parliament can amend the legislation. Literal interpretation in *Fisher* v *Bell* (1961) and *Partridge* v *Crittenden* (1968) prompted Parliament to amend the law so that invitations to treat are treated the same way as offers for sale. In *Partridge* v *Crittenden* (1968) the defendant had advertised some species of protected birds for sale. He was found not guilty because advertisements are invitations to treat and not offers for sale.

Disadvantages of the literal rule

As we have seen above the application of the literal rule can produce absurd results. Examples of absurd results include *Whiteley* v *Chappell* (1868) and *Fisher* v *Bell* (1961).

Application of the literal rule also produces unjust results. For example, in *LNER* v *Berriman* (1946) an Act placed railway companies under a duty to provide a look-out man whenever a railwayman was 'repairing or relaying' the track. Mr Berriman's job was to top up the oil which lubricated the points on the line. His employer, a railway company, did not provide him with a look-out man or any other warning system and Mr Berriman was killed by a train. Mr Berriman's widow claimed compensation, but was unsuccessful. The courts applied the literal rule and the words 'repairing and relaying' did not cover oiling points since this was merely maintaining the line.

The literal rule cannot be said to always give effect to the intention of Parliament, as Parliament would not intend the Act to produce absurd or unjust results.

Where there is more than one possible dictionary definition of a word the literal rule alone cannot provide the solution. Another interpretation rule or aid is required.

Application of the literal rule requires the assumption that the parliamentary draftsmen will always do their job perfectly. This is virtually impossible as not only will they sometimes be careless as is human nature, but language has its limitations. In its Report on The Interpretation of Statutes (1969), the Law Commission said:

> To place undue emphasis on the literal meaning of the words of a provision is to assume an unattainable perfection in draftsmanship … ignores the limitations of language, which is not infrequently demonstrated even at the level of the House of Lords when Law Lords differ as to the so-called 'plain meaning' of words.

AQA Examiner's tip

It is important with advantages and disadvantages questions not to produce a mere list. Each point should be explained fully. Questions could require consideration of a specific number of advantages and/or disadvantages. To ensure the highest marks candidates should select the points they are able to most fully explain and illustrate.

Advantages of the golden rule

Application of the golden rule prevents the absurd and unjust results that may be produced by application of the literal rule. Examples of cases where absurd or unjust results have been avoided by the use of the golden rule include *Re Sigsworth* (1935) and *Allen* (1872). In *Re Sigsworth* (1935) the judge had to apply the Administration of Estates Act 1925, which states that when a person dies without making a will the estate should be divided among the 'issue', that is, children of the deceased. The dead woman had only one son but he had murdered her. The court applied the broad application of the golden rule to avoid the absurd result whereby a murderer could inherit his/her victim's estate.

The application of the golden rule is more likely than the literal rule to produce a result that would have been intended by Parliament. Parliament would want to avoid absurd and unjust outcomes such as those in *Fisher* v *Bell* (1961) and *LNER* v *Berriman* (1946).

Disadvantages of the golden rule

There is no clear definition of what amounts to an absurd result. Use of the golden rule is therefore unpredictable which in turn makes the outcomes of cases unpredictable. This makes it more difficult for lawyers to advise their clients on whether to pursue a case. For example, in *LNER* v *Berriman* (1946) and *Whiteley* v *Chappell* (1868) a different court might have chosen to avoid the absurd outcomes of these cases.

Too much power is given to judges as they have to decide when and how to use this rule. They are not elected so should not be empowered in this way. It is undemocratic.

Michael Zander has described this rule as a 'feeble parachute'. It allows the court to escape from problems caused by the literal rule but the courts are still limited in what they can do.

Advantages of the mischief rule

Application of the mischief rule avoids absurd and unjust outcomes which might result from application of the literal rule. In *McMonagle* v *Westminster City Council* (1990) the court had to interpret the Local Government (Miscellaneous Provisions) Act 1982, which provided that it was an offence to use premises as a live sex encounter establishment without a licence from the local authority. The definition of 'sex encounter establishment' in the 1982 Act referred to performances, services and entertainments 'which are not unlawful'. The defendant claimed that his use of the premises for peep shows was unlawful and that therefore he could not be convicted. The House of Lords said that, in order to avoid the absurd result whereby a person could be convicted if the use of the premises was lawful but not if the use was unlawful, the words 'which are not unlawful' should be ignored. The guilty verdict was upheld.

The mischief rule promotes flexibility, enabling the law to be applied as intended by Parliament as opposed to merely applying the law as stated by Parliament in the Act. It was the flexibility promoted by this rule, through the focus on what Parliament meant rather than what is stated in the Act, that allowed the judges to make the decision in *Smith* v *Hughes* (1960) (considered on p40). In his judgment, Parker LCJ specifically referred to what the Act was intended to do.

In 1969 the Law Commission described this rule as a 'rather more satisfactory approach' than the literal and golden rules and suggested it should be the only rule used.

Disadvantages of the mischief rule

The main criticism of the mischief rule is that it gives far too much power to the unelected judiciary to determine not what the law actually says but what they think Parliament meant to say.

In some cases it can be argued that the judiciary have updated the legislation. It is the role of Parliament to update legislation through an amending Act. In *Royal College of Nursing of the United Kingdom* v *DHSS* (1981) the House of Lords had to interpret the Abortion Act 1967. Section 1(1) states that no criminal offence is committed 'when a pregnancy is terminated by a registered medical practitioner.' In 1967 abortions had been surgical and carried out by doctors. In 1972 medically induced abortions were introduced, which involve a doctor inserting a catheter into the womb and then nurses administering fluid into the womb via a pump or drip to induce labour. The nurses act upon instructions from the doctor, but the doctor is not always present. As it is the fluid that induces the labour, the abortions are effectively carried out by nurses. The question for the Lords was whether this method of abortion was within the provisions of the 1967 Act, that is, is the pregnancy terminated by a 'registered medical practitioner'? The Court of Appeal held that such abortions were unlawful, but the House of Lords reversed the decision, reinstating the decision of the first instance judge. Out of the nine judges overall who heard the case, five thought the induced abortions were unlawful. The majority of the House of Lords justified the decision on the basis that the mischief at which the Act was aimed was the unsatisfactory and unclear state of the old law, under which many abortions were carried out in unhygienic conditions. Therefore, the Act could apply to the situation whereby a registered medical practitioner retained overall responsibility. The dissenting Law Lords felt that the majority were rewriting the Act. Lord Edmund-Davies referred to the decision as 'redrafting with a vengeance'.

It is not always easy for the mischief the Act was intended to remedy to be discovered. Discovering the mischief requires research of the old law and the reports concerning how the law should be reformed. The old law may be contained partly in legislation and partly in cases. Reports may contain many different viewpoints on how the new law should remedy the mischief. For these reasons it may be difficult to identify the precise intention of Parliament.

The mischief rule is considered to be out of date for the following reasons:

- It was laid down in the 16th century, when common law was the main source of law.
- In the 16th century, parliamentary supremacy was not so established.
- In the 16th century, Acts contained lengthy preambles which spelt out the mischief the Act was intended to remedy.
- Judges in the 16th century usually drafted Acts on behalf of the King so were well qualified to determine the mischief the Act was meant to remedy.
- In the 16th century, drafting was not the exact science that it is today.

Advantages of the purposive approach

Advantages of the purposive approach are much the same as those given for the mischief rule. However, there is another important advantage of this rule. The purposive approach is the approach to interpretation used in courts in other EU countries. Since the UK joined the EU in 1972, our courts have increasingly used the purposive approach. This is bringing us more into line with our European counterparts. It is now recognised by the judiciary that when interpreting Acts which have been passed to comply with European Union law the correct approach to use is the purposive approach.

In some situations the purposive approach is more likely to give effect to the intention of Parliament than the more restrictive literal approach. In *Coltman* v *Bibby Tankers* (1987) the court had to interpret the meaning of the word 'equipment' in the Employers' Liability (Defective Equipment) Act 1969. An employee had been killed when a ship provided by the employer sank. The question was whether a ship was 'equipment'. The Act defined 'equipment' as 'any plant and machinery, vehicle, aircraft and clothing'. The House of Lords applied a purposive approach and held the employer liable on the basis that a ship was equipment. Had a more restrictive literal approach have been taken the employer would not have been liable.

In general Lord Denning preferred the purposive approach to the literal approach. In *Magor and St Mellons* v *Newport Corporation* (1950) he said:

> We do not sit here to pull the language of Parliament and of Ministers to pieces and make nonsense of it. That is an easy thing to do and it is a thing to which lawyers are too often prone. We sit here to find the intention of Parliament and of Ministers and carry it out, and we do this better by filling in the gaps and making sense of the enactment than by opening it up to destructive analysis.

Disadvantages of the purposive approach

As with the mischief rule, the purposive approach gives too much power to the unelected judiciary. It leaves it up to the judiciary to determine the intention of the democratically elected Parliament rather than merely applying the law as stated by Parliament.

In some situations judges can further overstep their role by making decisions based on public policy, a matter which should be left to Parliament. In *Fitzpatrick* v *Sterling Housing Association Ltd* (1999) the House of Lords, using the purposive approach, interpreted the word 'family' in the Rent Act 1977 to include a homosexual relationship. This was a majority decision. The dissenting judges stated that recognition of homosexual relationships was a matter of public policy and therefore for Parliament to decide.

Table 3.2 *Advantages and disadvantages of the rules of interpretation*

Rule	Advantages	Disadvantages
Literal rule	Respects parliamentary sovereignty. Leaves law-making to democratically elected Parliament.	Produces absurd/unjust outcomes. Does not always give effect to Parliament's intentions. Sometimes there is more than one dictionary definition. Assumes perfection from draftsmen.
Golden rule	Prevents absurd/unjust outcomes. More likely to give effect to Parliament's intentions.	Uncertainty as to what is an absurd outcome. Too much power to the judiciary. Michael Zander – 'feeble parachute'.
Mischief rule	Avoids absurd/unjust results. Promotes flexibility. Preferred approach of the Law Commission.	Too much power to unelected judiciary. Used by judges to update legislation. Not always easy to identify the mischief. Out of date.
Purposive approach	Consistent with European approach. Gives effect to Parliament's intentions. Denning: preferable to destructive analysis.	Too much power to unelected judiciary. Judicial decisions based on policy.

Advantages and disadvantages of the rules of language

Advantages and disadvantages of the ejusdem generis rule

An advantage of this rule is that there is no requirement for the draftsmen to write an exhaustive list of everything that is included. This means that the Act can cover circumstances which may not have been considered by the draftsmen but which they would have included had they thought about it. It also allows the Act to adapt to changes in society.

A disadvantage of this rule is that it is not always predictable what the judges will consider to be of the same category as the specific words. For example, in *Kensington and Chelsea LBC ex p Kihara* (1996) four homeless asylum-seekers claimed that they were in priority need for housing due to their extreme financial hardship, caused by a withdrawal of benefits. The Housing Act 1985 gave priority to those who were 'vulnerable as a result of old age, mental illness or handicap or physical disability or other special reason.' The question for the court was whether extreme financial hardship amounted to 'other special reason'. The Court of Appeal held that it could, despite the particular words referring to mental and physical needs.

The rule also allows for judicial law-making, which is not desirable, as the constitutional role of the judiciary, according to the separation of powers, is to apply the law as enacted by the democratically elected Parliament.

Advantages and disadvantages of the noscitur sociis rule

As with the *ejusdem generis* rule, an advantage of this rule is that there is no need for the draftsmen to foresee every particular circumstance. There is scope for the Act to be adapted to suit unforeseen circumstances.

However, because of the scope for judicial development it can also be said that this rule offends the separation of powers by allowing for judicial law-making.

There is also the disadvantage that the outcome of cases is unpredictable because of the scope for judicial discretion. This is a particular problem in criminal law because the liberty of the individual is at stake, not only in terms of the punishment that may be imposed, but also because criminal liability results in the defendant having a criminal record which may limit life opportunities in the future, for example, access to certain jobs.

Advantages and disadvantages of the exclusio alterius rule

An advantage of this rule is that a finite list is provided, which makes the outcome of cases more predictable. This means lawyers can advise their clients on whether to pursue a legal action and the likelihood of success.

Another advantage of this rule is that it respects the separation of powers. The judges apply the law as stated by the elected Parliament.

However a disadvantage of this rule is rigidity. There is no scope for development of the Act to suit a new or novel situation which the draftsmen may have intended the Act to cover had they foreseen it. This in turn may result in unfair and unjust outcomes.

Advantages and disadvantages of the intrinsic aids

The long and short titles are of limited use, but the long title in particular may remind the court of what the Act is trying to achieve. It may therefore be useful when using the mischief or purposive approach. In *Black-Clawson International Ltd* v *Papierwerke etc.* (1975) Lord Simon of Glaisdale said the only reason for referring to the long title was when it provided the 'plainest of all guides to the general objectives of a statute.' For example, the long title of the Chrismas Day Trading Act 2004 is 'An Act to prohibit the opening of large shops on Chrismas Day and to restrict the loading or unloading of goods at such shops on Christmas Day.' This long title makes it clear that the aim of the Act is to stop large shops trading on Christmas Day.

The preamble, objectives or purposes sections are also useful aids when the judge is adopting the mischief or purposive approach.

The schedules are useful as a guide to understanding the provisions of the Act they refer to, and in some instances it is essential to refer to them. For example, if a defendant were to argue that his/her activity was exempt from the Hunting Act 2004 it would be crucial to refer to Schedule 1 as the exempt activities are contained in Schedule 1 and not in the main body of the Act.

Most Acts contain a definition section. This is useful for interpreting the words included in that section. It is more likely that this is of assistance when using the mischief or purposive approach unless the interpretation section defines the word(s) in the same way as a dictionary.

The doubt as to whether punctuation should be taken into account arose because, prior to 1850, punctuation was not used in Acts of Parliament. It was sometimes inserted after Royal Assent. However, normal use of punctuation is used in modern Acts. Therefore, when interpreting the provisions of an Act, punctuation can guide the judge as to the meaning of those provisions as intended by Parliament.

Advantages and disadvantages of the extrinsic aids

Dictionaries are clearly a very useful aid when using the literal approach to interpretation, but are not always very helpful when using another approach that is more concerned with giving effect to Parliament's intention. This can be seen in the cases where the literal approach has produced unexpected or absurd outcomes.

Referring to other Acts, particularly to older Acts can be useful when determining the precise mischief at which the new Act is aimed and may also be necessary when interpreting an Act passed to amend a previous Act.

The Interpretation Act is useful for interpreting words or phrases commonly used in Acts of Parliament. However, it is limited in scope and does not generally provide a useful aid to the judge who is interpreting more technical or specialised provisions.

The reports of the Law Commission, Royal Commissions and other law reform bodies are clearly useful when applying the mischief or purposive approach. In *Anderton* v *Ryan* (1985), the House of Lords did not take account of the Report of the Law Commission that preceded the Criminal Attempts Act 1981. The appellant thought that a video recorder she had bought was stolen, when in fact it was not. She was found not guilty of attempting to handle stolen goods. This was despite the wording of the Act and the report of the Law Commission being quite clear that a person could be guilty of attempting to commit an offence even when the facts are such that commission of the offence is impossible. Had the Law Lords taken account of the Law Commission Report, the defendant would have been guilty. This decision was clearly an error and the House of Lords had to use the Practice Statement to overrule it at the earliest opportunity which arose in *Shivpuri* (1986).

Referring to an International Treaty is particularly useful when the judge is interpreting law made to give effect to the provisions of that International Treaty and seeking to apply the purposive approach.

Hansard is useful when the judge is applying the mischief or purposive approach. In *Pepper (Inspector of Taxes)* v *Hart* (1993), the case in which the House of Lords held that Hansard could be consulted, the purposive approach was adopted. Lord Denning had admitted in earlier cases to consulting Hansard when he was seeking to discover the intentions of Parliament. In *Davis* v *Johnson* (1979) Lord Denning consulted Hansard to help him interpret the Domestic Violence and Matrimonial Proceedings Act 1976. He was aware that such consultation was not permitted. He said:

> Some may say – and indeed have said – that judges should not pay any attention to what is said in Parliament. They should grope about in the dark for the meaning of an Act without switching on the light. I do not accede to this view … Although it may shock

the purists, I may as well confess that I have sometimes done it. I have done it in this very case. It has thrown a flood of light on the position.

The explanatory notes that accompany most modern Acts are a very useful aid. The language used is generally more accessible than that used in Acts of Parliament and this may help to clarify the meaning of technical and specialist terms used within the Act.

Activity

Including reference to case illustration, make three tables identifying:

a the advantages and disadvantages of the rules of interpretation;

b the advantages and disadvantages of the rules of language; and

c the advantages and disadvantages of the intrinsic/extrinsic aids.

You should now be able to:

- understand the advantages and disadvantages of each of the rules of interpretation and use cases to illustrate

- understand the advantages and disadvantages of the rules of language and use cases to illustrate

- understand the advantages and disadvantages of the internal and external aids to interpretation and use cases to illustrate

- answer past paper questions on the topic of the evaluation of rules of interpretation, aids to interpretation and the rules of language.

Judicial precedent

Key terms

Stare decisis: 'to stand by what has been decided'.

1 The doctrine of judicial precedent

The doctrine of judicial precedent is based upon the principle of *stare decisis*, meaning 'to stand by what has been decided'.

Under this doctrine, legal principles made by judges in the higher courts set a precedent to be followed by that court and all courts below it in future cases of similar fact.

For the system to operate successfully, three things are required:

1   a settled court structure;
2   a *ratio decidendi*;
3   accurate records of the decisions made by the superior courts.

The court structure

It is necessary for there to be a settled court structure as the judges need to know which decisions they are bound to follow. The English court structure/hierarchy as it stands today was largely established by the Judicature Acts 1873–75. The House of Lords was made the final appeal court in 1876 under the Appellate Jurisdiction Act.

In addition to the court structure established by these Acts it is important to consider the European Court of Justice and the Judicial Committee of the Privy Council.

The European Court of Justice

The European Court of Justice (ECJ) is not part of the English court structure. It does not hear national cases. However, under Art 234 of the Treaty of Rome 1957, an English court may refer a point of European law to the ECJ for interpretation. The interpretation made by the ECJ is binding on all courts throughout the European Union. Once the ECJ has decided how a piece of European law must be interpreted, all English courts and other courts throughout the European Union must interpret that piece of law in that same way.

The ECJ is not, however, bound by the doctrine of precedent. It does not have to follow its own previous decisions but does, nevertheless, try to be consistent.

The Judicial Committee of the Privy Council

The JCPC is considered in more detail later in this chapter. The Judicial Committee of the Privy Council (JCPC) like the ECJ is not part of the English court structure. The decisions of the JCPC are not binding on English courts, but are persuasive. This means that judges in the English courts do not have to follow the decisions of the JCPC but may do so if they choose. The importance of the JCPC in the doctrine of precedent lies in the fact that it is the final appeal court for many Commonwealth countries. It also has jurisdiction to hear and decide 'devolution issues'. Certain powers were devolved to legislative and executive authorities in Scotland and Northern Ireland by the Scotland Act 1998 and the Northern Ireland Act 1998 respectively, and also to the Welsh Assembly under the Government of Wales Act 1998. When questions arise concerning the exercising of these powers they are referred to and resolved by the Judicial Committee of the Privy Council. Another reason that decisions of this court are so highly regarded is that it is staffed by the Lords of Appeal in Ordinary – Law Lords – the same judges that decide cases in the House of Lords.

The House of Lords

The House of Lords (HL) stands at the top of the English court structure and its decisions are binding on all lower courts. It is the final appeal court in the United Kingdom for both criminal and civil cases.

From October 2009, appeal cases currently heard by the House of Lords, and the devolution issues currently heard by the Judicial Committee of the Privy Council, will be heard by a newly created Supreme Court. The creation of the Supreme Court was provided for by the Constitutional Reform Act 2005.

Until 1966, the HL regarded itself as bound by its own previous decisions, unless the previous decision was made *per incuriam* – that is, through lack of care – a mistake for example, where the previous decision was made without reference to a relevant Act of Parliament or precedent. This was the approach as stated by the House of Lords in *London Street Tramways* v *London County Council* (1898).

In the **1966 Practice Statement** issued by the House of Lords, Lord Gardiner stated that the HL would in future be free to depart from its own previous decision 'where it appears right to do so'. However, the Practice Statement emphasised that this freedom should be used 'sparingly' so as to maintain certainty and consistency in decisions.

An example of the House of Lords departing from its previous decision is **British Railways Board v Herrington (1972)** when the HL departed from its own previous decision made in *Addie* v *Dumbreck* (1929). In *Addie*, the HL held that an occupier of premises did not have a duty to prevent injury/death to children who trespassed on his/her land. Although this decision was repeatedly criticised, it was not until after the Practice Statement of 1966 that the HL could depart from it and, even then, it was another six years after the Practice Statement before a case of similar fact reached the HL. In *BRB* v *Herrington* (1972) the HL held that an occupier of land owes child trespassers a duty to protect them from injury. Another example of the use of the Practice Statement is **Hall v Simons (2000)**. The HL held that advocates – lawyers representing a client in court – should no longer be immune from being sued for negligent performance in court. This decision overruled the earlier decision of the HL in *Rondel* v *Worsley* (1967).

The Court of Appeal

The Court of Appeal (CA) is directly below the HL in the English court structure. It is bound by the decisions of the HL. It is divided into two divisions, these being the Civil Division and the Criminal Division. Decisions of the Civil Division are binding on all the courts below it in civil cases, and decisions of the Criminal Division are binding on all the courts below it in criminal cases. Each division is usually bound by its own decisions, with some exceptions (set out below), but the two divisions do not bind each other.

As a general rule, the Court of Appeal is bound by its own previous decisions. However, in *Young* v *Bristol Aeroplane Co.* (1944), the CA

Key terms

Per incuriam: the decision is found to be based on a mistake and is therefore not a binding precedent.

The Practice Statement 1966: a statement made by Lord Gardiner in 1966 which permits the House of Lords to depart from its own decisions.

Key cases

British Railways Board v Herrington (1972): the House of Lords used the Practice Statement to overrule its decision in *Addie* v *Dumbreck* (1929).

Hall v Simons (2000): the House of Lords used the Practice Statement to overrule its decision in *Rondel* v *Worsley* (1967).

listed the circumstances where it can refuse to follow one of its own previous decisions:

- If its previous decision conflicts with a later HL decision, then the CA must follow the decision of the HL.
- If there are two conflicting previous CA decisions (which in theory should not happen but in reality sometimes does) then the CA must choose between them. The rejected decision then loses its binding force.
- If its previous decision was made *per incuriam*, that is, through lack of care, in ignorance of relevant legislation or case law. In this situation, the *per incuriam* decision will again lose its binding force.

Fig. 4.1 *The Royal Courts of Justice*

Key cases

Parmenter (1991): The Court of Appeal departed from a previous decision using the Young v Bristol Aeroplane Co. exception, which allows the CA to reject one of its own decisions which conflicts with another.

A case in which the CA had to decide which of two conflicting previous decisions to follow is **Parmenter (1991)**. The defendant had caused serious injuries to his baby son while handling him very roughly. It could not be proved that the defendant had foreseen the risk of injury, so his conviction for inflicting grievous bodily harm under s20 of the Offences Against the Person Act 1861 was quashed. The CA then had to decide whether he could be convicted of assault occasioning actual bodily harm under s47. In *Spratt* (1990) the CA had decided that foresight of harm was required for a conviction under s47. However, on the same day in *Savage* (1991) another court of the CA had decided that foresight of harm was not required. In *Parmenter* (1991) the CA chose to follow the decision in *Spratt* (1990). The defendant could not be found guilty under s47 because foresight of harm was required. However, the case was then appealed to the HL, which reversed the decision and held that the decision in *Savage* (1991) was correct. The defendant could be found guilty under s47 because foresight of harm was not required.

The CA Criminal Division has one more exception, this being where it considers the previous decision was wrong and will do injustice to the defendant. In such circumstances the CA Criminal Division may not follow it. There is more of a need for flexibility with criminal appeals compared to civil appeals, because the liberty of the individual is at stake. It is important to remember in this respect that criminal convictions result not only in a sanction but also a criminal record.

The High Court

The High Court has two roles. It is a court of first instance and an appeal court. The High Court is divided into three divisions, these being the Family Division, the Chancery Division and the Queen's Bench Division. Each of these three divisions has its own Divisional Court.

Lower courts and the High Court itself are bound by decisions made in *appeal* cases in the Divisional Courts of the High Court. However, the exceptions set out in *Young v Bristol Aeroplane Co.* (1944) also apply to the Divisional Courts of the High Court. In criminal appeals heard in the Divisional Court of the Queen's Bench Division, the additional exception concerned with avoiding injustice and the liberty of the individual also applies.

First instance decisions of the High Court must be followed by the lower courts, but need not be followed by other High Court Judges, although they are highly persuasive and are usually followed.

The lower courts

The Crown Court, County Courts and Magistrates' Courts do not set binding precedents, although the decisions of the Crown Court are persuasive. Because of this, decisions of these courts are not usually recorded in law reports.

Table 4.1 *The civil and criminal court structure*

The civil courts	The criminal courts
European Court of Justice Binds lower courts on matter of European law.	House of Lords Binds all lower courts. Generally follows its own decisions except when using the Practice Statement.
House of Lords Bound by the European Court of Justice. Binds all lower courts. Generally follows its own decisions except when using the Practice Statement.	Court of Appeal (Criminal Division) Bound by the House of Lords. Generally follows its own decisions but takes a more flexible approach than the Civil Division in order to protect the liberty of the individual.
Court of Appeal (Civil Division) Bound by the European Court of Justice and the House of Lords. Binds all lower courts. Bound by its own decisions except in the circumstances outlined in *Young v Bristol Aeroplane Co.*	
Divisional Courts of the High Court Bound by the European Court of Justice, the House of Lords and the Court of Appeal. Binds all lower courts. Bound by their own decisions except in the circumstances outlined in *Young v Bristol Aeroplane Co.*	Queen's Bench Divisional Court Bound by the House of Lords and Court of Appeal. Generally bound by its own decisions but takes a flexible approach in order to protect the liberty of the individual.
High Court Bound by the European Court of Justice, the House of Lords, the Court of Appeal and the Divisional Courts. Binds all lower courts.	Crown Court Bound by the House of Lords, Court of Appeal and the Queen's Bench Divisional Court. Not bound by its own decisions and does not bind another court.
County Court Bound by the European Court of Justice, the House of Lords, the Court of Appeal, the Divisional Courts and the High Court. Not bound by its own decisions and does not bind any lower court.	
Magistrates' Court Bound by the European Court of Justice, the House of Lords, the Court of Appeal, the Divisional Courts and the High Court. Not bound by its own decisions and does not bind any other court.	Magistrates' Court Bound by the House of Lords, Court of Appeal and the Queen's Bench Divisional Court. Not bound by its own decisions and does not bind another court.

Ratio decidendi

The legal principle upon which the decision of the court is based is known as the **ratio decidendi**, meaning 'the reason for deciding'. In each case, the judge will listen to the legal arguments put forward by the parties and come to his/her decision. In his/her judgment (the speech made by the judge at the end of the case) the judge will explain the legal reason for the decision. It is this legal reason which forms the *ratio decidendi*. It is the *ratio decidendi* which *must* be followed in future cases of similar fact by the same court and all courts below it.

An example of a *ratio decidendi* is provided by the case of **Howe (1987)**. The House of Lords held the defendant was guilty of murder because the defence of duress, which he had pleaded was not available to a defendant charged with murder. A further example is provided by **Brown (1993)**. The defendants were found guilty of offences under ss47 and s20 of the Offences Against the Person Act 1861, because the defence of consent, which they had pleaded in respect of their sado-masochistic practices at a private party, was not available to defendants charged with such offences.

Another example of a *ratio decidendi* is provided by **Donoghue v Stevenson (1932)**, often referred to as 'the snail in the ginger beer' case. The facts were that the claimant went to a café with her friend. Her friend bought her a drink of ginger beer. The drink was delivered to the table in an opaque (dark glass) bottle. Some of the drink from the bottle was poured into a glass and the claimant drank it. She then poured the remaining contents into the glass and a decomposed snail emerged from the bottle. The claimant suffered shock and gastroenteritis (a stomach bug). She could not bring a legal action against the shop in contract law because she had no contract with it, as her friend had bought the drink. Instead, she sued the manufacturer for negligence. The House of Lords decided that her claim should succeed. The *ratio decidendi* was that manufacturers owe a duty of care to the ultimate consumers of their products. This was an **original precedent**, which judges can create when a new situation arises and/or where there is no existing precedent or legislation.

Unfortunately, the judges rarely make it clear what the *ratio decidendi* of their decision is. Judgments are not set out with clear headings. Therefore, it is up to the lawyers and judges reading the judgment to find what the *ratio decidendi* is. Furthermore, in the appeal courts, decisions are given by more than one judge. Even if all the judges reach the same decision in the case, they may each give a different reason for their decision. In such cases, it is difficult to determine which reason forms the *ratio*.

Obiter dicta

Obiter dicta (a plural noun; singular '*obiter dictum*') are things said 'by the way', or 'other things said'. These statements are not crucial to the outcome of the case. In the judgment the judge may discuss not only the *ratio decidendi* but other matters. He/she may speculate on what the outcome of the case would have been had the facts been slightly different. For example, in **Howe (1987)** the *ratio decidendi* of the case was that duress is no defence to murder. The House of Lords also expressed the opinion that duress is also no defence to attempted murder. This opinion was clearly made *obiter*, because it did not relate directly to the facts of the case as Mr Howe was charged with murder, not attempted murder. Similarly, in **Brown (1993)** the *ratio decidendi* of the case was that consent is no defence to sado-masochistic practices. The House of Lords also expressed the opinion that consent was a defence in other circumstances such as ritual circumcision, tattooing, ear and body piercing and violent sports.

Obiter dicta are important because they are persuasive (see under 'Binding and persuasive precedent' below). Should a judge choose to follow the *obiter dicta* of an earlier case, that *obiter dictum* then becomes the *ratio decidendi* of the later case. For example, in *Gotts* (1992) the defendant was charged with attempted murder and pleaded the defence of duress. Following the *obiter dicta* of *Howe* (1987), the House of Lords held the defendant was guilty on the basis that duress is no defence to attempted murder. Similarly, in *Wilson* (1996) the defendant was charged under s47 and pleaded the defence of consent. He had branded his initials on his wife's body with a hot knife with her approval. Following the *obiter dicta* of *Brown* (1993), the House of Lords held the defendant was not guilty, on the basis that this was a form of body decoration similar to tattooing, and that consent was therefore a defence.

Binding and persuasive precedent

A **binding precedent** is a precedent which *must* be followed. The *ratio decidendi* of a case is a binding precedent. It is binding on courts of the same level and on all courts below.

A **persuasive precedent** is a precedent which *may* be followed by judges in future cases of similar fact, should they so choose. As we have seen, one form of persuasive precedent is *obiter dicta*. There are other types of persuasive precedent.

Decisions of lower courts may be persuasive. For example, decisions of the Court of Appeal may be followed by the House of Lords in later cases of similar fact.

Decisions of Scottish courts, courts of other countries such as the US, and especially decisions of courts in Commonwealth countries such as Australia, New Zealand and Canada are persuasive. This is because these countries have legal systems based on the English legal system, due to previous or continuing dependence. In **R v R (1991)**, the Court of Appeal, and then the House of Lords, followed a previous decision made by the Scottish courts holding that a man can be guilty of raping his wife. Another example is *Lister* v *Hesley Hall* (2001). The House of Lords held that a residential school was vicariously liable (that is, legally answerable) for the sexual abuse of several former pupils by the warden of the school. The barrister representing the former pupils drew the House of Lords' attention to two recent decisions of the Canadian Supreme Court in support of his clients' case. The House of Lords then chose to follow the approach of the Canadian Supreme Court in these two cases and in so doing overruled the previous decision of the Court of Appeal in *Trotman* v *North Yorkshire County Council* (1999).

Decisions of the Judicial Committee of the Privy Council, which is the final appeal court for commonwealth countries, are highly persuasive. The court is equivalent in rank to the House of Lords, and it is staffed by Lords of Appeal in Ordinary (Law Lords), the same judges who sit in the House of Lords. A case which illustrates the considerable influence of the Judicial Committee of the Privy Council is *Holley* (2005). The case was about the defence of provocation, which reduces a murder charge to voluntary manslaughter. This decision is in conflict with the decision of the House of Lords in *Smith (Morgan)* (2000). The decision in *Holley* (2005) has raised the question of whether the courts should still be following the decision in *Smith (Morgan)* (2000). However, the Privy

Key terms

Binding precedent: a precedent which must be followed.

Persuasive precedent: a precedent which may be followed should judges so choose.

Key cases

R v R (1991): the decision in this case was based on the persuasive authority of the Scottish courts.

Council in this case comprised nine Law Lords, six of whom were in the majority, and the Court of Appeal has now followed the Privy Council decision rather than the House of Lords decision in three cases, these being *James* (2006), *Karimi* (2006) and *Mohammed* (2005).

Dissenting judgments are also persuasive. In the appeal courts, that is, the Court of Appeal and the House of Lords, the case is heard by more than one judge. Sometimes the decision is reached by only a majority of the judges. In this situation the judges in the minority will also give reasons for reaching a different decision. This is called a dissenting judgment. An example of a dissenting judgment which was followed in a later case was that of Lord Denning in **Candler v Crane Christmas (1951)**, in which he expressed the opinion that a person who suffers financial loss as a result of a negligent mis-statement ought to be able to recover compensation. This judgment was followed in *Hedley Byrne* v *Heller and Partners* (1966) and now forms the basis of the law regarding negligent mis-statement.

Key cases

Candler v Crane Christmas (1951): Lord Denning's dissenting judgment in this case was followed by the House of Lords in Hedley Byrne v Heller and Partners (1966).

Table 4.2 *Types of persuasive precedent*

Type of persuasive precedent	Illustrative material
Obiter dicta – things said by the way	*Howe* (1987) – duress is not a defence to a charge of attempted murder.
	Brown (1993) – consent can be a defence to a charge of actual or grievous bodily harm in certain circumstances.
Decisions of lower courts	*Miliangos* v *George Frank (Textiles) Ltd* (1976) – the House of Lords was influenced by the decision of the Court of Appeal in *Schorsch Meier GmbH* v *Hennin* (1975) (further details of these cases are given on p68 of this chapter).
Decisions of leading foreign courts	*Lister* v *Helsey Hall* (2001) – the House of Lords followed the decision of the Canadian Supreme Court.
	R v *R* (1991) – the House of Lords followed the approach of the Scottish courts.
Decisions of the Judicial Committee of the Privy Council	*Holley* (2005) – this JCPC decision has now been followed by the Court of Appeal despite conflicting House of Lords authority in 2000.
Dissenting judgments – the decisions of the minority judges	*Hedley Byrne* v *Heller and Partners* (1966) – decision followed Lord Denning's dissenting judgement in *Candler* v *Crane Christmas* (1951).

Law reports

It is crucial to the operation of the doctrine of precedent that accurate records be kept of the decisions of the superior courts, because it must be made possible for the binding and persuasive precedents to be found. Records of the decisions of the superior courts are kept in law reports.

Until the mid-19th century, law reports were published privately. Standards varied and some reports consisted of little more than incomplete jottings of lawyers or students. However, law reporting became more comprehensive and systematic when the Incorporated Council of Law Reporting was established in 1865. It is responsible for a series of reports known as the Appeal Cases (AC), which covers cases from the House of Lords, Court of Appeal and all three divisional courts of the High Court. The ICLR also publishes the Weekly Law Reports which, as the name suggests, are published weekly and thus help legal practitioners keep up-to-date with legal developments.

There are also private law reports. These include the All England Law Reports, published by Butterworths since 1936. This series is also published weekly and covers the cases heard in the superior courts.

AQA Examiner's tip

Candidates frequently fail to address the issue of law reporting, despite it always being required by the mark scheme in questions about the operation of the doctrine of precedent; or if they do address the issue, they frequently give it a brief mention. Consequently, answers that are otherwise excellent fail to attain the highest marks.

Some series of law reports are more specialised, focusing on a particular area of law. Examples of such series include the Family Law Reports, the Industrial Relations Law Reports and the European Human Rights Reports.

Law Reports are also published by the media. Some newspapers have their own law reports. The most notable are *The Times* Law Reports; however, law reports are occasionally published in the *Guardian* and the *Independent*. Law Reports may also be found in journals such as the *New Law Journal* and the *Law Society Gazette*.

Purity ring is not intimately linked to religious belief

Queen's Bench Division
Published July 23, 2007
Regina (Playfoot) (a Child) v Millais School Governing Body
Before Mr Michael Supperstone, QC
Judgment July 16, 2007

A school's refusal to allow one of its pupils to wear a purity ring, demonstrating her commitment to sexual abstinence prior to marriage, did not infringe her right to freedom of thought, conscience and religion protected by the European Convention on Human Rights.

Mr Michael Supperstone, QC, sitting as a deputy Queen's Bench Division, so held when dismissing the claim of Lydia Playfoot, suing by her father as next friend, for judicial review of the refusal of Millais School, Horsham, West Sussex, to let her wear a purity ring. Mr Paul Diamond instructed directly, for the claimant; Mr Jonathan Auburn for the school.

HIS LORDSHIP said that the claimant sought judicial review of the decision of the school which she attended not to permit her to wear a purity ring as a symbol of her commitment to celibacy before marriage.

She contended that that decision unlawfully interfered with her right to manifest her religion or beliefs contrary to Article 9.1 of the Human Rights Convention.

The issues between the parties were: whether the wearing of the ring was a manifestation of the claimant's religious belief, whether refusing to permit her to wear the ring interfered with her freedom to manifest her belief, and, if so, whether such interference was justified by Article 9.2.

Guidance as to what amounted to manifestation was to be found in decisions of the House of Lords in R (Shabina Begum) v Governors of Denbigh High School (The Times March 23, 2006; [2007] 1 AC 100) and R (Williamson) v Secretary of State for Education and Employment (The Times February 25, 2005; [2005] 2 AC 246).

In Williamson, it was held that in deciding whether a person's conduct constituted manifesting a belief and practice for the purposes of Article 9 it was necessary to identify the scope of the practice.

If the belief took the form of a perceived obligation to act in a specific way, then, in principle, doing that act pursuant to that belief was itself manifestation of that belief in practice. In such cases the act was intimately linked to the belief.

The claimant was under no obligation by reason of her belief to wear the ring and, in his Lordship's judgement, the act of wearing it was not intimately linked to the belief in chastity before marriage.

In any event, the claimant's Article 9 rights had not been interfered with because she voluntarily accepted the school's uniform policy and there were other means open to her to practise her belief without undue hardship or inconvenience.

Moreover, the rules on uniform and the school's decision to enforce them were proportionate.

Solicitors: Miss Diane Henshaw, Chichester.

The Times, 23 July 2007

Records of decisions are also kept online. Some reports are available on a subscription basis such as LEXIS – available in the United Kingdom since 1980 – and JUSTIS. However, many reports are freely available on the internet. The House of Lords, the European Court of Justice, the European Court of Human Rights and some leading foreign courts put their decisions on the World Wide Web within hours of being made.

Most law reports, such as the one on p61, follow a similar structure. A law report will usually include the name of the case, the court in which the case was heard, the names(s) of the judge(s) and the date of the hearing. There then follows a summary of the facts and legal issues and the decision of the court in which the case was first heard (court of first instance). There is a list of cases and statutes referred to and the names of the counsel appearing in the case. Finally there is the judgment in which the judge will consider the arguments and legal issues cited by the counsel for each side and give his/her conclusion.

The formal rule is that a law report must be vouched for by a barrister or solicitor with rights of audience who was present in court when the judgment was delivered. This is often demonstrated by the appearance of the person's name at the end of the report. This confirms accuracy and authenticity.

■ Activities

1 Find a law report either on the internet or in a recent copy of *The Times*. Make a note of:
   ■ the name of the case;
   ■ the court that heard the case;
   ■ the names of the judge(s) who heard the case;
   ■ the facts of the case, legislation and previous decisions referred to;
   ■ the *ratio decidendi* of the case.

2 Find another example of the House of Lords using the Practice Statement. Make a note of:
   ■ the name of the previous case which the House of Lords chose to depart from;
   ■ the facts of the previous case, the *ratio decidendi* which the House of Lords chose to depart from;
   ■ the name of the new case;
   ■ the facts of the new case;
   ■ the new *ratio decidendi*.

You should now be able to:

■ explain the elements of the doctrine of precedent

■ attempt past paper questions requiring a description of the doctrine of precedent.

🔲 2 Methods of avoiding judicial precedent

We have seen that the House of Lords, and the Court of Appeal and High Court, may in certain circumstances avoid following precedent. The House of Lords may use the Practice Statement and the Court of Appeal and the High Court can use the exceptions set out in *Young* v *Bristol Aeroplane Co.* (1944). In addition there are some mechanisms which the judges in both these courts and other courts may use to depart from a precedent.

Distinguishing

Distinguishing is the main device used by the judges in all courts for avoiding a binding precedent. No two cases are exactly the same. Therefore, the judges may regard the facts of the present case as sufficiently different from the facts of the case in which the binding precedent was set. In these circumstances, the judges are not bound to follow the previous precedent; they may distinguish the case on its facts. This creates a second binding precedent. The previous precedent remains binding in cases of similar fact.

In *Balfour* v *Balfour* (1919), the CA decided that an agreement made between a husband and wife that the husband should pay the wife £30 per month was not a legally binding agreement that could thus be enforced by the courts. This was because of the legal principle that, unless otherwise stated, agreements between a husband and wife are not intended by them to be legally binding. The wife failed in her claim to enforce the agreement.

In **Merritt v Merritt (1971)** there was an agreement made between a husband and wife after they had separated. The husband agreed that he would sign the matrimonial home over to the wife if she continued to pay the mortgage. The wife continued to pay the mortgage, but the husband refused to sign the home over to her. He relied on the principle of *Balfour* v *Balfour* (1919), claiming that as they were husband and wife the agreement was not legally binding. The court disagreed. It distinguished *Balfour* v *Balfour* (1919) on the basis that this couple had already separated, and held that they had thus intended to create a legally binding agreement. This was a new and distinct precedent, which now exists alongside the precedent set in *Balfour*.

Fig. 4.2 *Balfour v Balfour and Merritt v Merritt*

In this topic you will learn how to:

- define the terms 'overruling', 'reversing', 'distinguishing' and 'disapproving precedent'
- identify and explain cases illustrating those terms.

AQA Examiner's tip

- Questions asking for an explanation of the methods judges may use require you to consider distinguishing, overruling, reversing and also the positions of the *Young* v *Bristol Aeroplane Co.* exceptions and the Practice Statement. Answers should include illustration to attain the highest marks.
- It is important that you understand that the 1966 Practice Statement only applies to the House of Lords, and the exceptions in *Young* v *Bristol Aeroplane Co.* (1944) only apply to the Court of Appeal and High Court.

Link

Unit 4 of A2 Law: Judicial creativity. The material in this topic is particularly useful when answering a question about how and to what extent the rules of interpretation allow judges to create and/or develop the law. All of the methods of departure from binding precedent allow a judge to create law.

Key terms

Distinguishing: the judge does not follow the decision in an earlier case because the facts are materially different.

Key cases

Merritt v Merritt (1971): the CA distinguished the earlier case of *Balfour* v *Balfour* (1919).

Another example of distinguishing is provided by **Evans v Triplex Safety Glass Ltd** (1936). The facts of this case were that a car windscreen shattered, injuring the occupants of the car. The claimant sued the manufacturer of the windscreen. The court distinguished the facts of this case from those of *Donoghue* v *Stevenson* (1932) and did not hold the manufacturer liable in negligence. In *Donoghue* v *Stevenson* (1932) there had been no opportunity for tampering with the contents of the bottle between it leaving the manufacturer and reaching the consumer. The facts of *Evans* v *Triplex Safety Glass* (1936) were materially different in this respect. The car windscreen had been processed by a third party, that is, the manufacturer of the car.

Overruling

Overruling is where a higher court does not follow a precedent set in a *previous* case, either by a lower court or by itself. An example of a superior court overruling a previous precedent set by a lower court is *Hedley Byrne* v *Heller and Partners* (1964). The House of Lords overruled the decision of the majority in the Court of Appeal in *Candler* v *Crane Christmas* (1951) and held that there can be liability for making a negligent mis-statement.

Reversing

This is similar to overruling, but occurs where a higher court does not follow a precedent set by a lower court in the same case. In other words, reversing is where the same case has gone to appeal and the appeal court reaches the opposite decision to that of the lower court. For example, in *Fitzpatrick* v *Sterling Housing Association Ltd* (2000), the Court of Appeal refused to allow the homosexual partner of the deceased tenant to take over the tenancy as he could not be considered part of his family as required under the Rent Act 1977. He appealed to the House of Lords who reversed the decision of the Court of Appeal and held that he could take over the tenancy on the principle that a same-sex partner could prove the familial link as required by the legislation.

Disapproving

Disapproving is not a method of avoiding precedent, but rather a mechanism which facilitates a departure from precedent in a future case. When a judge disapproves of a precedent he/she makes clear that he/she believes the precedent is wrong. These disapproving comments are persuasive and thus may be followed by judges in future cases who wish to avoid the precedent. For example, the *ratio decidendi* of the House of Lords in *Anns* v *Merton London Borough Council* (1978) was that purchasers of defective buildings could recover compensation from local authorities when the defects were caused by the negligent failure of the local authority to inspect the foundations during construction. This decision was heavily disapproved before the House of Lords overruled it 12 years later in *Murphy* v *Brentwood District Council* (1990).

Table 4.3 *The methods of departure from precedent*

Method	Explanation	Illustration
The exceptions in *Young* v *Bristol Aeroplane Co.* (1944)	The Court of Appeal can depart from its own decisions in three circumstances: i when the decision conflicts with a House of Lords decision; ii when the decision was made *per incuriam*; iii when there are two conflicting decisions.	*Parmenter* (1991)
The Practice Statement 1966	The House of Lords can depart from its own decisions 'when it appears right to do so'.	*British Railways Board* v *Herrington* (1972) departed from *Addie* v *Dumbreck* (1929) *Hall* v *Simons* (2000) departed from *Rondel* v *Worsley* (1967)
Distinguishing	The binding decision is not followed because the facts of the cases are materially different.	*Merritt* v *Merritt* (1971) distinguished *Balfour* v *Balfour* (1919) *Evans* v *Triplex Safety Glass* (1936) distinguished *Donoghue* v *Stevenson* (1932)
Overruling	The court does not follow a precedent set in an earlier case by a lower court or by itself.	*Hedley Byrne* v *Heller and Partners* (1964): the House of Lords overruled the decision of the Court of Appeal in *Candler* v *Crane Christmas* (1951)
Reversing	A case is heard on appeal and the court makes the opposite decision to the earlier court.	*Fitzpatrick* v *Sterling Housing Association Ltd* (2000)
Disapproval	Comments of a persuasive nature are made indicating the judge's belief that the precedent is wrong.	*Anns* v *Merton London Borough Council* (1978)

Activities

1 Make a note of the key similarity and the key distinction between overruling and reversing.

2 Consider whether *Donoghue* v *Stevenson* should be distinguished in the following circumstances:

   a A person suffers sickness having found a baby mouse in the empty bottle of cola he had just drunk.

   b A person suffers food poisoning having eaten half a bar of chocolate containing raisins, some of which turn out to be dead flies.

   c A girl has half of her hair burnt off by a faulty hairdryer.

   d A woman suffers a broken ankle when the heel of her new shoe falls off.

   e A man suffers multiple injuries when his car engine blows up.

You should now be able to:

- understand the ways of avoiding precedent
- use cases to illustrate the ways of avoiding precedent
- attempt past paper questions requiring a description of the doctrine of precedent.

In this topic you will learn how to:

◼ state the advantages and disadvantages of the doctrine of precedent

◼ use examples relevant to those advantages and disadvantages

◼ state the advantages and disadvantages of the methods of avoiding precedent

◼ use examples relevant to those advantages and disadvantages.

AQA Examiner's tip

It is important with advantages and disadvantages questions not to produce a mere list. Each point should be explained fully and supported by examples. More recent exam papers have included questions which require consideration of a limited number of advantages and/or disadvantages. To attain the highest marks in questions where the numbers are specified candidates should select the points they are able to most fully explain and provide illustration.

◼ **Key cases**

R v R (1991): the House of Lords overruled previous decisions and held that marital rape is a crime.

Gillick v West Norfolk and Wisbech Area Health Authority (1985): the House of Lords made an original precedent holding that girls aged under 16 could be prescribed contraceptives without parental consent.

💡 3 Advantages and disadvantages of the doctrine of judicial precedent and the methods of avoiding precedent

Advantages of the operation of precedent

Consistency

The doctrine of precedent brings consistency to the English legal system, in that cases with similar facts will be treated in the same manner. It prevents judges making random decisions, and promotes justice and equal treatment. The law remains the same, which helps people plan their affairs.

Predictability

Lawyers are able to advise their clients with some degree of certainty. They can tell their client, for example, that their proposed course of action would be likely to be upheld by the court, or that they will probably lose their case and should therefore settle out of court or cease their legal action. Predictability is also important in determining who should qualify for Government help in funding their legal action. The Government do not fund cases which have little chance of success as this would be a waste of taxpayers' money.

Flexibility

The judges can sometimes develop the law by, for example overruling an out-dated precedent. The House of Lords can also use the Practice Statement. This means that the law can be developed in areas not considered important or not considered at all by Parliament. Modernising decisions may prompt Parliament to review the legislation and bring it into line with precedent. For example, after the decision in **R v R (1991)**, Parliament amended the Sexual Offences Act 1956, stating that marital rape is a crime.

Detailed practical rules

There is a wealth of detail contained in the reported cases. The principles set out in the cases are a response to real-life situations which have occurred and can be a guide to future litigants.

Original precedents

The doctrine of precedent allows for new or 'original' precedents to be created. This occurs when there is no previous decision on the matter before the court and there is sometimes no legislative provision. An original precedent therefore makes legal provision on a matter for which there was previously no law. In **Gillick v West Norfolk and Wisbech Area Health Authority (1985)** the House of Lords had to decide whether or not girls under the age of 16 could be prescribed contraceptives without parental consent. The matter had not arisen before the courts before, and Parliament had provided no guidance. The Lords decided that girls could be prescribed contraceptives in such circumstances, provided they were able to understand the issues involved.

Disadvantages of the operation of precedent

Complexity

The judgments are often complex and it is sometimes difficult to decide what the *ratio decidendi* of a case is. Furthermore in the Court of Appeal and House of Lords there is more than one judgment to consider and a common *ratio* has to be decided by the judges in future cases. Furthermore one judge may give more than one *ratio*. An example is **Rickards v Lothian (1913)**. The facts were that due to a blocked sink, water from an upper floor property had escaped to lower floor properties, causing flooding. The claimant brought an action under the rule in *Rylands* v *Fletcher* (1868), which requires: i) a non-natural use of land; ii) an escape of the non-natural thing from the land; and iii) damage caused by the escape. Lord Moulton gave two reasons for his decision, that is, two ratios, for not holding the defendant liable. His first reason was that bringing water onto land for normal use was not a non-natural use of land. His second reason was that the escape of the water had been caused by a stranger for whom the defendant was not responsible.

Volume

It is difficult for anyone to research the law. Hundreds of judgments are made every year, so to discover the precise law on a matter, a person may have to search through many volumes of law reports. The complete official law reports are estimated to run to almost half a million pages.

Fig. 4.3 *The law is difficult to research*

Uncertainty

By using the mechanism of distinguishing cases and other methods of departure, the judges can avoid following precedents. This causes uncertainty as to how cases will be decided.

Rigidity

An unjust precedent can lead to further injustices. For example, once the HL sets an unjust precedent, it cannot be overruled unless and until another case of similar fact goes to the HL on appeal. This may not happen for many years. Similarly, the law may become out-of-date and need modernising. For example, judges had felt since the 1960s that the old law whereby a builder did not owe a duty of care to the person to whom he/she sold a property was unfair. Lord Denning made *obiter* comments to the effect that a duty should be owed; however, the law was not changed until 1978, in *Batty* v *Metropolitan Property Realisations Ltd*. Also, judges are sometimes reluctant to act as law-makers and would rather leave it to Parliament to change the law. In the *President of India* case (1984), Lord Brandon said that to overrule the 19th century decision that no interest was payable on a contract debt 'would be an unjustifiable usurpation of the function which properly belongs to Parliament.'

Lord Denning recognised the rigidity of the system of precedent and for many years campaigned for the Court of Appeal to be allowed greater flexibility. He argued that the Court of Appeal should not consider itself bound by decisions of the House of Lords. During the years that he sat in the Court of Appeal he sometimes put these views into practice. In *Broome* v *Cassell and Co. Ltd* (1971) Lord Denning and the other judges in the Court of Appeal refused to follow the decision of the House of Lords in *Rookes* v *Barnard* (1964). Similarly, in *Schorsch Meier GmbH* v *Hennin* (1975) the Court of Appeal did not follow the decision of the House of Lords in *Re United Railways of the Havana and Regla Warehouses Ltd* (1961). In *United Railways* the House of Lords had held that damages could only be awarded in sterling – English currency. In *Schorsch Meier* the Court of Appeal, presided over by Lord Denning, held that damages could be awarded in a foreign currency. The *Schorsch Meier* case did not continue to the House of Lords; however, a year later another case concerning the same point did. In *Miliangos* v *George Frank Textiles Ltd* (1976) the House of Lords overruled its decision in *United Railways*, thus indicating that they agreed with the approach to awarding damages adopted by the Court of Appeal. The House of Lords, however, reminded Lord Denning of the rules of precedent. Lord Cross stated

> In the Schorsch Meier case, Lord Denning MR ... took it on himself to say that the decision in the Havana case that our courts cannot give judgment for payment of a sum of foreign currency – though right in 1961 – ought not to be followed in 1974 because the 'reasons for the rule have now ceased to exist'... The Master of the Rolls was not entitled to take such a course. It is not for any inferior court – be it a county court or a division of the Court of Appeal presided over by Lord Denning – to review the decisions of this House. Such a review can only be undertaken by this House itself under the declaration of 1966.

Lord Denning also argued that the Court of Appeal was no longer bound by its own decisions. He said the same rules applied to the Court of Appeal as applied to the House of Lords, and that it was not only in the circumstances outlined in *Young* v *Bristol Aeroplane Co.* (1944) that the Court of Appeal could depart from its earlier decisions. In *Gallie* v *Lee* (1969) he said:

> I do not think we are bound by prior decisions of our own, or at any rate, not absolutely bound. We are not fettered as it was once thought. It was a self-imposed limitation: and we who imposed it can also remove it. The House of Lords have done it. So why should not we do likewise?

In *Gallie* v *Lee* (1969) Lord Denning did not convince the other judges sitting on the case of his argument. However, an example of a case in which the Court of Appeal did depart from its earlier decision is *Davis* v *Johnson* (1979). In this case, the Court of Appeal had to decide whether the Domestic Violence and Matrimonial Proceedings Act 1976 could be applied so as to protect a mistress (as distinct from a wife) from domestic violence. In the earlier cases of *B* v *B* (1978) and *Cantliff* v *Jenkins* (1978) the Court of Appeal had held that the Act only protected wives, and did not protect mistresses, unless the mistress was the sole owner or the sole tenant of the property. Lord Denning did manage to persuade two of the other four judges hearing the case to depart from the earlier decisions and provide protection to the mistress. He said:

> On principle, it seems to me that, while this court should regard itself as normally bound by a previous decision of the court, nevertheless it should be at liberty to depart from it if it is convinced that the previous decision was wrong. What is the argument to the contrary? It is said that if an error has been made, this court has no option but to continue the error and leave it to be corrected by the House of Lords. The answer is this, the House of Lords may never have an opportunity to correct the error, and thus it may be perpetuated indefinitely, perhaps for ever.

The essence of Lord Denning's argument is that the Court of Appeal should be able to depart from its own decisions because in the majority of cases the Court of Appeal is the last court to hear the case. Comparatively few cases are appealed to the House of Lords, largely due to financial and time constraints. It is not therefore an adequate safeguard against wrong, unjust or out-of-date decisions to only allow them to be corrected by the House of Lords. While Lord Denning's argument has been convincing in some cases, it is the requirement for certainty that has prevailed. Even in cases such as *Schorsch Meier GmbH* v *Hennin* (1975) and *Davis* v *Johnson* (1979) where the House of Lords has subsequently upheld the decisions of the Court of Appeal the Law Lords have stressed that the only time the Court of Appeal should depart from its earlier decisions is when the case falls within the *Young* v *Bristol Aeroplane Co.* exceptions.

Unconstitutional

It is often argued that judges are overstepping their constitutional role by actually making the law rather than simply applying it. It is the role of Parliament to create the law and the role of the judiciary to enforce/apply the law as set by Parliament.

Undemocratic

Only persons who are elected, that is, the Government and MPs should be able to create law. The judges are not elected and should therefore not engage in law-making.

Retrospective effect

Unlike legislation made by Parliament, the law created by judges is backward-looking. It applies to events that occurred before the case came to court. This is unfair, because the parties involved would rightly have considered themselves to be acting within the law (legally) at the time. For example, in *R* v *R* (1991) the husband had not been acting illegally when he subjected his estranged wife to sexual intercourse without her consent. The retrospective effect of case law can be compared to the prospective effect of legislation (law made by Parliament). Legislation usually only applies to events occurring after the legislation has come into effect.

Lack of research

Unlike legislation which is made with the benefit of research by interested and knowledgeable bodies, there is no opportunity for the judge to commission research or consult experts on the likely outcomes of their decisions. Judges are confined to making their decisions on the basis of the arguments presented in the course of the case.

Table 4.4 *Advantages and disadvantages of precedent*

Advantages of precedent	Disadvantages of precedent
Consistency	Complexity: *Rickards* v *Lothian* (1913)
Predictability	Volume
Flexibility: *R* v *R* (1991)	Uncertainty – due to methods of departure. Use illustrative material from Topic 2
Detailed practical rules	Rigidity: Lord Denning campaigned for more freedom to depart in Court of Appeal: *Broome* v *Cassell and Co. Ltd* (1971), *Schorsch Meier GmbH* v *Hennin* (1975), *Davis* v *Johnson* (1979)
Original precedent – to deal with new situations or where there is no existing law: *Gillick* v *West Norfolk and Wisbech AHA* (1985)	Unconstitutional
	Undemocratic
	Retrospective: *R* v *R* (1991)
	Lack of research

Advantages of the methods of avoiding precedent

Potential for growth

It is because there are methods the judges can use to avoid precedent that case law is not totally rigid. The avoidance mechanisms give the judges the opportunity to modernise and develop the law when necessary. Examples of cases already considered which illustrate this advantage include **Hall v Simons** (2000) and *British Railways Board* v *Herrington* (1972). In *Hall* v *Simons* (2000) the House of Lords overruled the decision in *Rondel* v *Worseley* (1967) and held that barristers were no longer immune from being sued for the work they do in court. Lord Steyn said:

> 'The appearance is that the law singles out its own for protection no matter how flagrant the breach of the barrister. The world has changed since 1967. The practice of law has become more commercialised: barristers may now advertise; they may now enter into contracts for legal services with their professional clients; they are now obliged to carry insurance. On the other hand, today we live in a consumerist society in which people have a much greater awareness of their rights. If they have suffered a wrong as a result of the provision of negligent professional services, they expect to have the right to claim redress. It tends to erode confidence in the legal system if advocates, alone among professional men, are immune from liability for negligence.'

Unfair laws can be replaced

In some circumstances precedents are developed which are then seen to be unfair. The methods of avoiding precedent allow these unfair laws to be abandoned and replaced with more appropriate decisions. In **R v G and R (2003)** the House of Lords had to decide whether the two young defendants, aged 11 and 12, should remain convicted of arson. For the convictions to stand it had to be proved that the boys had been reckless, that is, taken an unjustified risk. The meaning of recklessness was central to the decision. Was it based on a subjective test or an objective test? Should the defendant be judged by what he/she foresaw as a risk or be judged by what the reasonable person in the defendant's position would have foreseen as a risk? In a previous case, *Caldwell* (1981), the House of Lords had held that a defendant should be judged on what the

■ Key cases

Hall v Simons (2000): the House of Lords modernised the law and held that barristers could be sued by their clients for negligently presenting a case in court.

R v G and R (2003): in this case, the House of Lords abolished objective recklessness, whereby defendants were judged by what the reasonable person would have foreseen as a risk.

reasonable person would have foreseen. This decision had received a lot of criticism from academics and the legal profession. It was clearly unfair to judge the young defendants in *G and R* (2003) by the standard of the reasonable person, and so the Lords used the Practice Statement to overrule their previous decision. Recklessness is now based on a subjective test, which requires the defendant to have foreseen the risk.

Disadvantages of the methods of avoiding precedent

Retrospective law-making

When judges avoid following a precedent they change the law. This is unjust, because the precedent that is set applies to events that have already happened. In *R v R* (1991) the defendant was found guilty of raping his estranged wife after he forcefully entered her parents' house and had sexual intercourse with her without her consent. Up until this case, the law applied by the judges for over 250 years had been as stated by Sir Mathew Hale in his work *History of the Pleas of the Crown*, published in 1736, that is, that a man cannot be guilty of raping his wife because, upon marriage, she irrevocably gives consent to sexual intercourse. While this decision in itself seemed to make the law more appropriate to modern thinking, it was unfair to the defendant who was then imprisoned for an act which at the time of commission had been within the law.

Uncertainty

The possibility of judges avoiding precedent makes the outcomes of cases uncertain. This is not desirable, because justice requires that people are treated in the same way and know how to conduct their lives within the law. It is also problematic for lawyers, who are less able to advise their clients on the likelihood of pursuing a successful case. Certainty is particularly desirable in criminal law, where the defendant's liberty is at stake. In *Howe* (1987), the House of Lords held that duress is not a defence to a charge of murder, whether the defendant is the principal (that is, the actual killer) or an accessory to murder (that is, someone who participates in the murder but is not the actual killer). This overruled the earlier House of Lords decision in *DPP v Lynch* (1975), in which the it had been held that duress was available as a defence when charged with being an accessory to murder.

Non-conformity with the separation of powers

According to Montesquieu's theory of the separation of powers, it is Parliament that should create new law, while the role of the judiciary is to apply the law. However, when judges avoid following precedent, then unless they do so to conform to the requirement of an Act of Parliament, they inevitably create new law.

You should now be able to:

- explain the advantages and disadvantages of the doctrine of precedent
- use examples to support your explanation of the advantages and disadvantages of the doctrine of precedent
- explain the advantages and disadvantages of the methods of avoiding precedent
- use examples to support your explanation of the advantages and disadvantages of the methods of avoiding precedent.

Activities

1 Make a table of the advantages and disadvantages of the methods of avoiding precedent. Include reference to illustration.

2 Summarise the arguments put forward by Lord Denning as to why the Court of Appeal should not be bound by its own decisions.

AQA Examination-style questions

Chapter 1: Parliamentary law-making

1   (a) Briefly explain the roles of the House of Commons, House of Lords and the monarch
         in the formal process of statute law creation.   *(10 marks)*
    (b) Describe **two** influences on Parliament as a law maker.   *(10 marks)*
    (c) Discuss the advantages and disadvantages of **one** of the influences you have described
         in your answer to (b) above.   *(10 marks)*

2   (a) Explain what is meant by the doctrine of parliamentary supremacy and briefly explain
         one limitation on this doctrine.   *(10 marks)*
    (b) Describe the role and powers of the House of Lords in the law making process.   *(10 marks)*
    (c) Discuss the advantages of the process of law making in Parliament.   *(10 marks)*

Chapter 2: Delegated legislation

1   (a) Using examples, describe **two** forms of delegated legislation.   *(10 marks)*
    (b) Briefly explain the controls on delegated legislation.   *(10 marks)*
    (c) Discuss the disadvantages of delegated legislation.   *(10 marks)*

2   (a) Briefly describe the different forms of delegated legislation.   *(10 marks)*
    (b) Explain the controls put on delegated legislation by parliament.   *(10 marks)*
    (c) Discuss the effectiveness of parliamentary control of delegated legislation.   *(10 marks)*

Chapter 3: Statutory interpretation

1   (a) Describe any **two** aids that can be used by judges when interpreting an Act
         of Parliament.   *(10 marks)*
    (b) Describe any **two** rules of (approaches to) statutory interpretation which help
         judges to interpret an Act of Parliament.   *(10 marks)*
    (c) Consider the **disadvantages** of the **two** rules (approaches) described in your answer
         to (b) above.   *(10 marks)*

2   (a) Explain, using examples, the purposive approach to statutory interpretation.   *(10 marks)*
    (b) Explain the difference between internal and external aids to statutory interpretation. *(10 marks)*
    (c) Explain the advantages to the rule of approach.   *(10 marks)*

Chapter 4: Judicial precedent

1   (a) Briefly explain what is meant by the doctrine of precedent.   *(10 marks)*
    (b) Describe **two** ways in which judges can avoid following precedent.   *(10 marks)*
    (c) Identify and discuss the disadvantages of the doctrine of precedent.   *(10 marks)*

2   (a) In the context of the doctrine of precedent, explain what is meant by, and outline
         the importance of the terms *ratio decidendi* and *obiter dicta*.   *(10 marks)*
    (b) Describe the hierarchy of the courts and the role of law reporting in precedent.   *(10 marks)*
    (c) Identify and discuss the advantages of the doctrine of precedent.   *(10 marks)*

1A   Review and examination techniques

Answering questions on law-making in AQA Law 1

There are a number of different aspects of learning that need to take place to answer the questions fully:

- being able to understand and explain the basic principles
- being able to illustrate the principles by reference to decided cases
- being able to select appropriate material for a given question
- being able to evaluate the legal principles and come to an appropriate conclusion.

The aspects listed above will enable examination questions to be tackled. The examination questions come in two formats:

- Theory or knowledge questions, on the lines of 'Describe **two** influences on Parliament as a law-maker.'
- Evaluation questions, such as 'Discuss the advantages and disadvantages of **one** of the influences you have described in your answer to (b) above.'

It can be expected that the examination paper will contain law-making questions in Section A of the Unit 1 examination paper. There will be four questions on Section A of the paper, one question from each of the four topic areas in the AQA specification. These specification areas match Chapters 1–4 of this book. Each question will be divided into three parts, each worth 10 marks. You will therefore have, on average, a maximum of 10 minutes to answer each part question. The first two parts of each question will be theory or knowledge questions and the final part, Part (c), will be evaluative.

In the first type of question, theory or knowledge only, no reference needs to be made to evaluation. All you are expected to do is describe or explain the topic in the question asked for, using relevant examples. These examples might be decided cases, Acts of Parliament or general examples, depending on the topic. The second type, evaluation, requires advantages and/or disadvantages to be stated, giving examples to demonstrate the point. You will need to read the question carefully, as you can be required to look at advantages only, disadvantages only, or both.

Answering a theory or knowledge only question

A theory only question might be:

Briefly describe the aids to interpretation used by judges. *(10 marks)*

The potential content in the mark scheme would be:

(A) Brief **description** of the aids.

A good answer would include a description of each of the aids with an example of each.

Answering an evaluation question

An evaluative question is set out below:

Discuss the advantages and disadvantages of one of the rules of (approaches to) statutory interpretation that you have described in Part [X] of this question. *(10 marks)*

Note that the question does not ask you to describe your chosen rule, as the examiner has asked you to do that earlier in the question. You can refer back to that material, and should not waste time repeating the information.

A good answer would include:

■ Advantages, which can include, for example: literal rule, respect for parliamentary supremacy and certainty; and golden rule, avoidance of absurd outcome. Each point exemplified.

■ Disadvantages, which can include, for example: literal rule, rigidity, following bad decisions; and golden rule, judicial law-making, too much flexibility. Each point exemplified.

> ### Key terms
>
> **Descriptions:** these can relate to, eg., long title, short title, preamble, headings marginal notes, Hansard, dictionaries, etc.

> ### Activities
>
> **1** Write up, using continuous prose, your answer to the two parts of the question set out above.
>
> **2** Now attempt two questions from Section A of the sample paper in 60 minutes. Your teacher will be able to provide you with a copy of this.

You should now be able to:

■ apply the principles in AS examination questions involving law-making.

Introduction

Unit 1A, together with Unit 1B, constitutes Unit 1 of the AS specification. Unit 1A is about law-making and Unit 1B is about the legal system. Unit 1A and Unit 1B are examined together on one examination paper, which constitutes 50 per cent of the overall marks for the AS qualification and 25 per cent of the overall marks for the A2 qualification. The Unit 1 examination is of 1.5 hours' duration. Candidates must answer three questions: one question from Unit 1A; one question from Unit 1B; and another question, which may be from Section 1A or 1B. There will be a choice of four questions in Unit 1A and four questions in Unit 1B. There will be one question on each topic area within the specification and no duplicate or omitted topic areas.

All questions are worth 30 marks each. Each question is divided into three parts, each part normally being worth 10 marks. Candidates must answer all parts of each question they choose to answer. All parts of each question relate to the same topic area of the AQA Law AS specification, that is, the same chapter of this book. Parts (a) and (b) will normally be a test of your knowledge and understanding, and part (c) will normally be evaluative.

Questions require essay-style answers. Attainment of high grades is dependent on correct identification of the issues raised by the question, sound explanation of each of the points and illustration. Illustration may be in many forms, for example, legislation, cases, research, statistics, material from the media. Further exam tips are provided throughout each Topic and at the end of the chapter.

Unit 1B comprises four chapters:

5 **The civil courts and other forms of dispute resolution:** concerned with an outline of the civil court structure and a description and evaluation of ways in which civil disputes are resolved without going to court.

6 **The criminal courts and lay people:** concerned with an outline of the criminal court structure and a description and evaluation of the role and work of lay magistrates and of jurors.

7 **The legal profession and other forms of advice and funding:** investigates the legal profession, including solicitors, barristers and legal executives. It goes on to describe and evaluate the funding of legal services today.

8 **The judiciary:** looks at the different types of judge that exist and considers the concept of their independence from different aspects of the State.

The civil courts and other forms of dispute resolution

Key terms

Judicial review: the procedure by which the High Court may review a decision of a body (for example, a tribunal) to ensure that the rules of natural justice have been followed. Natural justice means, for example, that all parties be given the opportunity to put their case forward.

Claimant: the party who brings a claim in the civil courts and is usually claiming some form of redress for a loss or harm suffered. The commencement of a civil claim is known as the issue of proceedings.

Defendant: the party who is alleged to have caused the loss or harm and who may have to compensate the claimant for the loss or harm.

Jurisdiction of a court: the extent of that court's power over certain legal disputes.

🔆 1 Outline of civil courts and appeal system

Fig. 5.1 *The civil court structure in diagrammatic form*

Courts of first instance

Civil disputes are, generally, between individuals, partnerships, companies and/or local or national Government departments. Any or all of the above may disagree about, for example, a contract, a negligence claim or a landlord and tenant relationship. Further, local or national Government departments may be the subject of a claim for **judicial review**.

The dispute will be between the **claimant** and the **defendant**. The claimant will issue proceedings in a civil court by giving to the court a description of the claim on a set form, together with the court fee. This claim is then sent to the defendant for a response, usually in the form of a defence to the claim.

There are two main civil courts in which civil claims may be issued: the County Court and the High Court. The Magistrates' Court is primarily a criminal court, but does have some civil **jurisdiction**.

These courts are known as courts of first instance, as claims may be commenced and decided there. If the decision of the court is disputed, then a party may be able to ask a higher court to reconsider the case – known as an appeal (see 'Appeal hearings', below).

There are about 250 County Courts in England and Wales, of which approximately 170 have the jurisdiction to hear family cases as well as civil disputes. Trials in the High Court (which has jurisdiction to hear all types of civil disputes) may be in London or may be heard in one of the 26 High Court District Registries in England and Wales.

Magistrates' Court

The Magistrates' Court has jurisdiction over most family matters (except divorce). It can deal with the recovery of unpaid council tax and charges for water, gas and electricity. It can also hear appeals from the local authority about whether to grant licences for gambling or the sale of alcohol.

County Court

The County Court deals with many types of civil disputes, including cases on contract, tort (for example, negligence), bankruptcy, property and divorce. Civil cases are divided into three types: cases involving less than £5,000 are transferred to the small claims track and are dealt with and heard by District Judges; cases involving between £5,000 and £15,000 are transferred to the fast track and are generally heard by a Circuit Judge; cases over £15,000 are usually transferred to the multi-track and may be heard by a Circuit Judge or may be transferred to the High Court if, for example, the case concerns professional negligence and/or there is a complicated point of law in issue.

High Court

The High Court has three divisions: the Queen's Bench Division, the Family Division and the Chancery Division. These Divisions are then sub-divided into the court where civil claims may be issued and the court where appeals from lower civil courts will be heard (see 'Appeal hearings', below). There are approximately 120 High Court Judges. Cases allocated to the multi-track may be heard in this court rather than the county court, due to the legal complexity of the case, the large amount of money involved, or if the case is of a certain type, for example, professional negligence or claims against the police.

- Queen's Bench Division: This is the main court and deals primarily with contract and tort cases. There are approximately 70 High Court Judges sitting in this court. The cases are often heard in the **Royal Courts of Justice** in The Strand, London, but may be heard in one of the High Court's District Registries around the country, of which there are approximately 26.

- Family Division: This court deals with all aspects of family matters, including divorce, related children and financial claims, adoption and care proceedings.

- Chancery Division: Historically, this court dealt with cases in which the rules of **equity** could be used. The modern version of this court deals with cases such as partnership disputes, company law, disputes about wills or trusts, bankruptcy, the sale of land and the creation of mortgages. There are approximately 20 judges who sit in the Chancery Division. The Chancery Division includes specialist courts, for example the Companies Court. Cases will be heard at the Royal Courts of Justice, or in one of the eight specified Chancery centres in the country.

Appeal hearings

An appeal is when a party to a civil case is dissatisfied with the court's decision and requests a higher court to review the earlier decision. Following the **Access to Justice Act 1999**, the majority of appeals will only be allowed to proceed if either the original court or the appeal court has given such authorisation. Permission is only granted if it involves a matter of great importance or the appeal has a good chance of success.

The 1999 Act will, generally, only allow one level of appeal. For example, if the Family Divisional Court (see below) has already considered an appeal from a Magistrates' Court's decision then no further appeal will be allowed. The only exception to this rule is if the appeal raises a point of great legal or procedural importance.

The High Court as appeal court

As mentioned above, the High Court is both a court of first instance and an appeal court.

Queen's Bench Divisional Court: This court has **appellate jurisdiction** in respect of judicial review (see Topic 2, p79). This court may review the decisions made by local and national Government departments and by tribunals. Technically, judicial review is not an appeal but a consideration by this court as to whether the rules of fairness have been broken in the decision-making process by the body under review. This court may also hear appeals on a point of law by way of **case stated** from a

Key terms

Royal Courts of Justice: based in The Strand in London, this is where High Court Judges mainly sit.

Equity: a branch of law which developed from the end of the 13th century. It is based on the court's application of 'fairness' to a decision in a case, in response to the occasional unfairness of the inflexible rules of common law.

Access to Justice Act 1999: amended the law on appeals in order to restrict the number and type of appeals allowed to proceed.

Appellate jurisdiction: the authority of a higher court to review the decision of a lower court.

Case stated: a means by which a case may be reviewed by a higher court at the request of an inferior court in order for a point of law to be confirmed or clarified.

Magistrates' Court, Crown Court or tribunal. Finally, a party who claims to be unlawfully detained may apply for a 'writ of habeas corpus' for the decision to detain to be overturned.

Family Divisional Court: This court hears appeals from the decisions of Magistrates' and County Courts in respect of family-related matters.

Chancery Divisional Court: This court hears appeals on decisions made in bankruptcy and insolvency cases originally decided in the County Court.

The Court of Appeal

There are approximately 35 judges (known as Lords Justices of Appeal) who sit in the Court of Appeal, the most senior being the Master of the Rolls. The Court of Appeal has a Civil Division, which specialises in civil cases.

In general terms the Court of Appeal hears appeals from:

- the County Court (District Judge or Circuit Judge)
- the High Court in its capacity as a first instance court (all three Divisions)
- the High Court in its capacity as an appellate court (all three Divisions)
- the Employment Appeal Tribunal.

These appeals are generally heard by three to five judges, although appeals may be heard by two judges if, for example, the parties agree. In the majority of cases **leave to appeal** to the Court of Appeal is required.

The appeal is not a rehearing of the original trial with the calling of witnesses, etc., but a review of the case. The Court of Appeal will reconsider the application of the law and, for example, the admissibility of evidence at the original hearing. The barristers in the Court of Appeal must provide, in advance, written and concise statements of their arguments to the court and the opposing barrister. This saves time and cost to all parties. These statements are called 'skeleton arguments'.

The Court of Appeal may reverse the original decision, vary it or confirm it. An example of an appeal case to the Court of Appeal is *Goodwill v British Pregnancy Advisory Service* (1996). In *Goodwill*, the court had to decide the difficult question of whether the BPAS was liable for the negligent advice given to a married male patient (who underwent a vasectomy), which he passed on to his girlfriend, who relied on this advice and fell pregnant. The court held that, as the BPAS was unaware of the girlfriend, there was no liability.

The House of Lords

The House of Lords is the final court of appeal in civil law for England, Wales and Northern Ireland. This court is part of the civil court system, but is also a part of the legislative body of Parliament. This link has resulted in the creation of a replacement court (see below).

There are at present 12 judges of this court, called **Lords of Appeal in Ordinary** (or 'Law Lords'). The House of Lords hears about 200 cases each year, the majority of which are civil. These cases are on matters of general public importance. Two such cases are **Donoghue v Stevenson** (1932) and **British Railways Board v Herrington** (1972).

Most appeals are heard by three or five Law Lords. Leave to appeal must be obtained from the original court or from the House of Lords itself.

Key terms

Leave to appeal: when a party wishes to appeal and authority for the appeal must be obtained, either from the original court or from the appeal court.

Lords of Appeal in Ordinary: judges who sit in the House of Lords.

Key cases

Donoghue v Stevenson (1932): Lord Atkin created the 'neighbour' principle, on which the modern law of negligence is based. As a result, the manufacturer of ginger beer was liable to the end consumer who suffered harm due to the presence of a decomposed snail in the beer.

British Railways Board v Herrington (1972): The House of Lords decided an occupier of land should owe a (limited) duty of care to a trespasser on the land.

The majority of the appeals are from the Civil Division of the Court of Appeal. However, there is a 'leap-frog' procedure provided by the Administration of Justice Act 1969. If a High Court Judge certifies the case as suitable for the House of Lords and the House of Lords agrees to grant leave to appeal, the case will go straight from the High Court to the House of Lords. The case must be on a point of law, and one:

- of public importance in relation to the statutory interpretation of an Act of Parliament or a piece of **delegated legislation** or

- when the trial judge is bound by a **precedent** of the Court of Appeal or House of Lords.

It should be noted that the Constitutional Reform Act 2005 created a Supreme Court to replace the House of Lords (this is expected to be fully functional from October 2009). This court will no longer have any connection with Parliament. It will have its own building, staff and budget, and the appointment process will be reformed. The number of judges will remain at 12 and the jurisdiction of the court will increase to include cases on devolution.

The Court of Appeal is, in effect, the highest court in England and Wales. It has a civil and criminal division and hears many more cases per year than the House of Lords: the Court of Appeal hears about 2,000 cases a year, whereas the House of Lords hears about 200, only a minority of which involve criminal issues. The decisions of the Court of Appeal are more likely, therefore, to have an impact on the man in the street. Generally, the House of Lords is restricted in the cases it decides to those that involve important legal issues.

You should now be able to:

- outline the civil court structure

- describe the jurisdiction of each court

- attempt past paper questions on the civil court structure.

Key terms

Delegated legislation: a law made by a person or body other than Parliament but with the authority of Parliament.

Precedent: the principle that an inferior court must follow the earlier decision of a higher court.

Activities

1 Alan wishes to sue Ben for £12,500 for a breach of contract. Advise Alan of the court to be used to commence the claim and the track to which the claim will be allocated. How would your advice be different if the claim were for £72,500?

2 Carol wishes to divorce David and claim residence (formerly known as 'custody') in respect of the child of the family. David is a wealthy businessman and Carol has just inherited a large amount of money from a long-lost relative. Advise Carol of the two courts in which she may start the proceedings.

3 Alan was unsuccessful in his claim against Ben for £72,500. Advise Alan on the different civil courts in which his appeal may be heard.

5.2 Other forms of civil dispute resolution

Reasons for alternatives to the court system

When **parties** are involved in a dispute that cannot be resolved, the parties will often apply to the civil courts for a decision. Topic 1 of this chapter outlined the types of civil courts available and the jurisdiction of each court.

However, for many reasons, these courts are not always the most suitable or appropriate method to resolve such disputes. As will be explained and discussed in Topic 3 of this chapter, the civil courts are, for example, expensive and slow. Alternative methods for resolving such disputes have developed, or been created, which are often less costly and speedier than the courts.

In this topic you will learn how to:

- state reasons why there is a need for other forms of dispute resolution

- describe the people involved in each of the other forms of dispute resolution

- outline the procedures in each of the other forms of dispute resolution

- allocate types of dispute to each form.

Tribunals

Since the late 1940s there has been a growth in parliamentary legislation affecting individuals in their private lives. Examples are laws affecting employment rights, social security benefits, housing, education, immigration and mental health.

These laws inevitably result in disputes, for example whether an individual is entitled to a particular State benefit. A system had to be constructed to allow these disputes to be resolved. The court system could not cope with the number of disputes so **tribunals** were created for each area, for example, the Social Security Appeal Tribunal.

In 1957, the Franks Committee on Tribunals reviewed how tribunals were working and recommended that tribunals should be based on, for example:

■ independence (from Government)

■ openness (all hearings should, if possible, be in public)

■ accessibility (so that all parties could understand the procedure involved, and legal representation was not essential).

As a result of this Committee's report, the Tribunal and Enquiries Act 1958 created the Council of Tribunals to review the running and workings of tribunals. The Council has 15 members, who observe cases and deal with complaints. The Council cannot insist on reforms, but may make recommendations. After a recommendation, the Government set up the Leggatt Committee in 2001, which advised that all tribunals should be dealt with under the Tribunals Service from April 2006.

Types of dispute dealt with by tribunals

There are many tribunals but they may be classed as two main types: **administrative** and **domestic**.

Administrative tribunals deal with disputes between the individual and the State. The tribunal will apply the relevant law to the dispute between the parties. Examples include:

■ the Social Security Appeal Tribunal, which deals with disputes arising out of claims for State benefits such as unemployment benefit, income support, etc.

■ the Immigration Tribunal, which deals with disputes over rights to enter and remain in the UK

■ the Mental Health Review Tribunal, which deals with applications by patients for release from secure hospitals.

However, some administrative tribunals deal with disputes between individuals. Examples include:

■ Rent tribunals, which deal with disputes between landlords and tenants over levels of rent

■ Employment (formerly Industrial) tribunals, which deal with disputes between employers and employees on unfair dismissal, equal pay, sex discrimination and redundancy.

Domestic tribunals are 'in-house' tribunals often set up by professional bodies. The tribunal will apply the rules of the particular organisation to the dispute between the parties. Examples include:

■ the Solicitors Disciplinary Tribunal, which deals with solicitors who have behaved badly, whether professionally or personally

- the Bar Council, which covers the same areas, but in relation to barristers
- the General Medical Council, which covers the medical profession
- the Football Association, which deals with disputes between members of the Association.

People involved

Most tribunals consist of three members, namely a legally trained chairperson (for example, a qualified lawyer) and two lay members, who are selected from a panel of persons who have expertise in the matter under dispute. For example, an Employment tribunal will consist of a legally qualified chairperson, plus two lay members who have experience of industry and commerce and who represent the views of the employee and of the employer.

Some tribunals will have a chairperson who has expertise in the area of the parties' dispute.

Generally, parties are encouraged to represent themselves and not use lawyers. The parties will attend, as will their witnesses.

Procedure

The parties and their witnesses give evidence. All will be available for questioning by the other party and by the chairperson and lay members.

Tribunals are not bound by the strict rules of evidence and procedure that apply in the civil courts. Furthermore, tribunals are not bound by the strict rules of precedent, so each case may be decided on its individual facts.

A party does not need to employ a lawyer for representation at the tribunal. The party may choose to represent himself, be represented by a friend or by someone with an understanding of his complaint, such as a trade union member.

Tribunals are free: no fees are charged, so as to keep the system available to all.

If a party chooses to be represented by a lawyer it is most unlikely that public funding will be available. A few exceptions include the Lands Tribunal, the Mental Health Review Tribunal and the Employment Appeals Tribunal. Unlike in the civil courts, each party must meet their own legal costs, regardless of who wins the case. This helps to discourage people from using lawyers and maintains the lower cost compared to a civil court.

Most tribunals are obliged to give reasons for their decisions, which has allowed for more tribunal decisions to be challenged on appeal. Where the appeal is heard depends upon which type of tribunal made the original decision. The appeal may be to another tribunal, for example, appeals against decisions of an Employment tribunal pass to the Employment Appeals Tribunal and finally to the Court of Appeal. However, most appeals are to the Queen's Bench Division of the High Court.

Tribunals must follow the rules of natural justice, which means, for example, that both parties must be given time to prepare the case and be given a fair hearing. The Queen's Bench Division of the High Court can reverse a tribunal's decision where the rules of natural justice have not been followed by the tribunal.

Tribunals were created to allow the public access to fast and inexpensive ways of resolving disputes which may otherwise have clogged up the civil justice system.

Lord Woolf conducted a two-year investigation into means of reforming the civil justice system. His reports in 1997 proposed streamlining the civil court procedure and the growth of **Alternative Dispute Resolution** (ADR). The Civil Procedure Rules 1998, passed as a result of Lord Woolf's proposals, place a duty on the courts to encourage the use of ADR. The Court of Appeal has held that the courts do not have the power to force parties to try ADR as this would be a breach of a person's right to a fair trial under Art 6 of the European Convention on Human Rights, as can be seen in *Halsey* v *Milton Keynes General NHS Trust* (2004). However, if a party unreasonably refuses to try ADR and then wins the case at court, that successful party may not be awarded their costs to be paid by the losing party: see *Dunnett* v *Railtrack plc* (2002).

Arbitration

Arbitration is where the parties refer the dispute to a third party, who will act like a judge and give a decision on the dispute, which is called an award.

The arbitrator will usually be a person with both legal and specialist knowledge of the subject matter of the dispute, for example, a surveyor may arbitrate in a building dispute between a builder and developer. Arbitration is governed by the Arbitration Acts 1979 and 1996, which set out rules for arbitration and the various grounds for appeal from an arbitrator's award.

Types of dispute dealt with by arbitration

Most large commercial contracts will contain an arbitration clause allowing for arbitration to occur if a dispute arises under the contract. A number of trade and professional organisations offer an arbitration facility. For example, the Association of British Travel Agents (ABTA) can arbitrate on a disagreement about a package holiday. Most disputes may use the arbitration process and the **Chartered Institute of Arbitrators (CIA)** can suggest and supply an independent arbitrator, if requested.

If a claim is started at the Employment tribunal (see above), a copy of the employee's claim and employer's response is sent automatically to the **Advisory, Conciliation and Arbitration Service (ACAS)**. The ACAS representative is an expert in employment law and can, if the parties agree, act as an arbitrator.

People involved

The arbitrator is independent of the parties and is usually an expert in the area of the dispute. The parties may name a specific arbitrator in their contract or name a professional body that can appoint the arbitrator should a dispute arise. An example would be the CIA above or, if the dispute involved building, the professional body for surveyors, namely the Royal Institute of Chartered Surveyors.

The parties will present their case to the arbitrator (see Procedure, below) which may involve witnesses.

Procedure

Arbitration is covered by the Arbitration Act 1996. The arbitration agreement must usually be in writing, but how the arbitration proceeds is open to the parties to agree. The parties may include an arbitration clause in their original contract, committing them to arbitration in the event of a dispute. This is known as a *Scott* v *Avery* clause. The clause will specify who will act as arbitrator (where the parties choose one themselves) or the process for appointing one (for example nomination by the CIA).

Where this type of clause has been included within a contract, the court will refuse to deal with any dispute unless and until it has gone to arbitration. An example of an arbitration clause in a contract is a package holiday contract, which may include a clause providing for arbitration through ABTA.

An agreement to go to arbitration can also be reached after a dispute has arisen.

The Act sets out the powers of the parties to shape the process according to their needs, together with the powers of the arbitrator. Both the parties and the arbitrator agree the arbitration hearing procedure together. The hearing can be set at a time and place of mutual convenience to the parties and the arbitrator. The hearing is carried out in private. The process usually involves each party putting forward its own arguments and evidence, either in writing or orally. Witnesses may be called to give evidence and be cross-examined.

The arbitrator makes the final decision (the award), which is binding on the parties. An arbitrator has the power, for example, to order one party to pay money to the other.

The process of arbitration is free, but the arbitrator will charge a fee. The parties are allowed to be represented by a lawyer if they wish, but this is discouraged.

There is no automatic right of appeal. However, under s68 of the Arbitration Act 1996, a party may appeal to the High Court if there is a 'serious irregularity', for example, the arbitrator did not carry out the arbitration in the manner as agreed by the parties. Under s69 of the 1996 Act, a party may appeal on a point of law that arises in the arbitration decision.

Mediation

Mediation is a process by which a third party acts as a messenger between the parties to assist in resolving the dispute. The parties do not have to meet and the **mediator** will pass on the offers, counter-offers and general comments between the parties.

The mediator is to help the parties define the issues in dispute and the emphasis is on the parties themselves creating a solution to the dispute. The mediator is not to act as adviser to either party, who must make their own judgements on the offers made.

Mediators may be selected from mediation bodies such as the Centre for Dispute Resolution (which has approximately 300 trained mediators).

Types of dispute dealt with by mediation

The Family Law Act 1996 has encouraged separating couples to use mediation instead of court action. If a party wishes to obtain public funding for legal advice and representation then it will be a condition that mediation must first be attempted. The mediation may cover disputes over children, property and finance.

There are now a growing number of mediation services aimed at resolving small disputes. For example the West Kent Independent Mediation Service offers a free service from trained voluntary mediators to try to resolve neighbour disputes over noise and boundaries.

AQA **Examiner's tip**

Remember that the parties agree to arbitration and it is not forced on them. The parties may choose the arbitrator or the manner in which the arbitrator is chosen.

Key terms

Mediator: an independent third party who will assist the parties in their attempt to resolve the dispute.

People involved

The mediator will organise the mediation at a time and place convenient to all parties. The parties attend with legal advisers (if any). The mediator will pass on information from one party to another. The parties may be in separate rooms from each other if they prefer.

Procedure

Mediation takes place in private and in a neutral setting. Procedures vary, but typically each party puts forward its position, followed by private meetings between the mediator and each party in turn. The mediator acts as a 'go-between', whereby the two parties in dispute communicate and negotiate through the mediator. The mediator remains neutral and does not suggest any solutions to the problem and cannot force settlement on the parties. The mediator encourages the two parties to reach an agreement.

Each party may be legally represented, but this is discouraged. Each party must meet their own legal costs but public funding is available for family mediation. Witnesses are rarely involved in mediation.

If the parties reach an agreement then this may be written down and, if the parties agree, the agreement becomes legally binding. The agreement is enforceable by the civil courts should either party fail to follow the terms of the agreement. If no agreement is reached, the matter may be taken to court or a tribunal.

Conciliation

This is a similar process of ADR to mediation. However, the conciliator is able to intervene in the negotiations, actively suggest terms of settlement and comment on terms put by one party to another. It is important for the parties to realise that the **conciliator** is neutral and is not acting as their representative (such as a lawyer).

Types of dispute dealt with by conciliation

ACAS (see above) operates a conciliation scheme in industrial disputes, for example in Employment tribunal cases. In a tribunal case ACAS will be sent a copy of the employee's claim and employer's response. The ACAS representative is an expert in employment law and, with the parties' agreement, can act as a conciliator in the dispute.

People involved

The conciliator will organise the conciliation at a time and place convenient to all parties. The parties attend with legal advisers (if any). The conciliation will proceed as mediation except for the conciliator's added powers of intervention.

Procedure

The procedure is very similar to mediation. The conciliator and the parties will meet and the conciliator will listen to the grievances and will make suggestions how the problem can be resolved. If the parties agree then the agreement may be made legally enforceable as for mediation. If no agreement is reached, the matter may be taken to court or a tribunal.

Mediation and conciliation are very similar. Remember the subtle differences between the two and that ACAS is a good choice as an example of arbitration and conciliation.

Key terms

Conciliator: an independent third party who will actively assist the parties in their attempt to resolve the dispute. The conciliator will suggest terms of settlement to the parties and advise on offers put forward by the parties during negotiations.

Negotiation

Negotiation is usually the first method in trying to resolve a dispute. The parties will communicate directly with each other to try and agree matters without going to court. This communication may be face-to-face, by letter, telephone, email, text, etc.

If either or both of the parties are legally represented, the lawyer(s) will continue to negotiate throughout their involvement. Many cases are settled on the morning of a court hearing.

Types of dispute dealt with by negotiation

Any dispute may be resolved by negotiation. Mediation and conciliation are forms of negotiation, but using third parties to assist in the process.

Low-key disputes are best resolved by negotiation without expensive court action. A neighbour disagreement or a dispute between an electrician and the homeowner are examples of when a negotiated settlement would be appropriate.

People involved

The only people involved are the parties themselves or their representatives, if they have one.

Procedure

There is no fixed procedure, but often a meeting will commence with each party stating their position. For a successful negotiation the parties must focus on the issues rather than personalities. A successful negotiation will always require each party to compromise their position to a certain extent.

There are no costs involved with negotiation unless representatives are involved. Should an agreement not be reached, the parties may then instruct lawyers.

However, lawyers will encourage their clients to reach an agreement without resorting to the court and/or try to negotiate on behalf of the clients. Obviously, it is cheaper and quicker to reach the agreement without involving lawyers.

Key terms

Negotiation: an informal method of dispute resolution. It may take place between the parties or between their representatives.

AQA Examiner's tip

Remember that tribunals and the four types of ADR are outside the civil court justice system. They are alternative ways of resolving civil disputes. Each type of ADR is separate from the other and the parties will not move from one type to another automatically but only through choice. For example, negotiation may lead to mediation, but conciliation and arbitration will not necessarily follow.

Activities

1. List the two main types of tribunals with examples and descriptions of each. Describe the people who sit on tribunals and the procedure at a tribunal hearing.

2. List the types of disputes dealt with by each of the four types of ADR.

3. Imagine you run a successful company and have contracted with another professional for you to supply specified goods and materials. Choose the area of business, and negotiate with the professional about whether an arbitration clause should be contained in your contract. Prepare that clause between you so that it covers all the potential disputes that may arise under the contract.

You should now be able to:

- understand the other forms of civil dispute resolution

- explain the operation of each form

- attempt past paper questions on other forms of dispute resolution.

■ Key terms

Public funding: the State paying for, or contributing to, the costs and expenses incurred by a party to a case (formerly known as Legal Aid).

Remedies: what the successful claimant is awarded by the court at the trial.

Civil Procedure Rules (CPR): introduced into all civil courts in April 1999, they were the result of a review of the civil justice system by Lord Woolf. Their purpose is the 'overriding objective', namely to simplify the system, reduce costs and delay.

■ Links

■ For more information on Judicial precedent, see Chapter 4 (Judicial precedent), p54.

■ For more on the procedure of the courts, see Chapter 12 (The courts: procedure and damages for negligence cases), p227.

3 Advantages and disadvantages of forms of civil dispute resolution

The civil courts: advantages

Legal expertise/experience

The judges sitting in the county or High Court have acquired experience of the law and the legal system over many years, both as lawyers acting for parties and as judges. They will be able to guide the parties through the court process. The final decision will be supported by an explanation of the result of the case with a detailed description of the law used to reach the decision.

Availability of public funding

The Community Legal Service oversees the granting of public funding for civil cases. **Public funding** is available for some civil cases, for example, a financial claim related to divorce.

Remedies

The civil court has the power to award the successful party a variety of **remedies**. Compensation (known as 'damages') may be ordered to be paid from the defendant to claimant. The court also has the power to order a party to cease an act or activity (an 'injunction') or to complete a contract ('specific performance'). These remedies are enforceable by the court.

New procedure under the **Civil Procedure Rules (CPR)**:

■ Pre-action protocols: Since 1999, parties must now complete certain procedures before issuing a court case. These procedures cover a full exchange of relevant information, for example, the disclosure of an accident book in a place of work. This enables the parties to consider the merits of their respective claims before issuing a claim.

■ Emphasis on encouraging settlement: The civil courts must now actively encourage the parties to try and achieve a settlement without continuing with the case, for example, by the use of ADR (see Topic 2, p79).

■ Case management by judges: Judges order the parties, and lawyers, to complete certain formalities by set dates, for example, the exchange of witness statements. This means the case will proceed at a reasonable speed.

■ Part 24 strike-out provisions: The CPR allows the court to strike out (dismiss) a claim at any time after the claim is issued. This stops the defendant from incurring unnecessary legal costs in a claim that has no merit.

■ Part 36 offers to settle: The CPR allows the parties to make offers to settle the claim to the court and to the other party in a simple and effective manner. Cases may be compromised (settled) without the need for a trial.

The civil courts: disadvantages

Lack of technical knowledge

Judges may have limited knowledge of the subject-matter of the dispute, as it may be of a technical or obscure nature. The judge will have to rely on the view of an expert appointed by the court rather than on his/her own expertise, for example, a surveyor in a building dispute.

Slow process

Despite the CPR, the civil justice system is still slow and delays do occur. For example, in cases allocated to the 'fast track' (see Unit 2, Chapter 12) the final hearing must be within 30 weeks, but this track only covers cases where the claim is less than £15,000. Larger claims will take longer to come to trial.

Lack of flexibility in court process

The parties have little control over the court process and procedure. Evidence at a trial is restricted by technical rules, and hearings are set by the court, which may be inconvenient to either or both parties. The court is limited in the remedies it may award, for example, a letter of apology may be part of a suitable remedy, but the court is unable to order this.

Need for lawyers

Due to the complexity of the law and the continuing complications in the civil court process, lawyers are required by parties. A party may represent themselves but will inevitably be at a disadvantage.

General cost

Parties must pay fees, which can run into hundreds of pounds, to the court when commencing a claim. Lawyers' costs are high, as are expert witnesses, who may be required to give evidence.

Adversarial process

The English civil court system is still based on winning a case, whether on a legal, factual or procedural point. The CPR attempted to banish tactical manoeuvring by lawyers, but such tactics still exist.

Publicity

Most cases heard in the civil courts are open to the public and the press. This may prove to make the experience of resolving a dispute in the courts an even more stressful and embarrassing experience.

New procedure under CPR:

 Under pre-action protocols, parties must now incur costs at an early stage in the case, which may finally prove unnecessary. For example, a claimant in a personal injury case has to incur the cost of a full medical report before beginning a case, and may then discover the defendant is not liable.

 Case management is not effective as it should be as there is under-funding, for example limited IT access for judges on cases currently running in court.

Tribunals: advantages

Expertise

A tribunal **chairperson** and members usually have expertise in the matter under dispute. For example, in an Employment Tribunal the chairperson is usually an experienced lawyer in employment disputes and the lay members have practical experience of business due to their respective connections with employers and employees.

Reasons for decisions

Under s10 of the Tribunals and Enquiries Act 1992, most tribunals must give reasons for their decisions. This allows the parties and the public to understand why a particular decision has been reached.

> ### Activity
> At this stage, make a mind-map or spidergram of the advantages and disadvantages of the civil court justice system.

> ### Key terms
> **Chairperson:** usually, a legally qualified individual who leads a tribunal, with the assistance of two legally unqualified persons (lay members).

Cost

Legal representation is not essential. Tribunals do not charge a fee. In a tribunal, each party usually pays their own legal costs, rather than the losing party paying all the costs of both parties. Public funding is available in a few tribunal cases, for example, before a Mental Health Review Tribunal.

Informality

Two of the tribunal members are lay persons, and neither they nor the chairperson wears an official outfit. This lack of formality allows the parties to relax and present their case with confidence.

Flexibility

Because tribunals do not operate strict rules of **judicial precedent**, they are more flexible in their decision-making. This allows the tribunal to judge each case on its own merits. Strict **rules of evidence** do not apply in tribunal hearings.

Speed

Tribunal cases are usually heard quickly. The hearing date is fixed within a short period of the start of the claim, giving details of place, date and time. The final hearing is usually completed within one day.

Privacy

Proceedings taken before a tribunal are often not as highly publicised as court hearings.

Congestion

Tribunals relieve congestion in the civil court system. If the volume of cases heard by tribunals were heard in the civil courts, the court system would be overloaded and this would cause further delays.

Tribunals: disadvantages

Influence of chairperson on lay members

The chairperson is usually a legally qualified person. The chairperson may influence the lay members of the tribunal panel because of this expertise and professional experience.

Lack of availability of public funding

Generally, public funding is not available for legal representation before a tribunal. This affects the more disadvantaged members of society, as the other party may be able to afford legal representation. For example, in an Employment Tribunal an employer will probably be able to afford a lawyer while the (former) employee may not. The tribunal system was created to assist the weaker members of society and this defect devalues the system.

Appeals procedure

There are different rights and routes of appeal from different tribunals which may make the process complicated. For example, an appeal from an Employment Tribunal is to the Employment Appeal Tribunal (but only on a point of law). However, all tribunal decisions may be reviewed by the High Court under the principle of judicial review if, for example, there has been a breach of natural justice.

> ### ■ Key terms
>
> **Judicial precedent:** the rule by which courts must follow the decisions of earlier cases made by more senior courts.
>
> **Rules of evidence:** restrict the evidence that may be given to a court.

Inconsistencies in decisions

Tribunals are not bound by the rules of judicial precedent, nor by the strict rules of evidence. As a result, tribunal decisions will sometimes be inconsistent, which creates uncertainty for future cases.

Publicity

Because of the lack of publicity for tribunals, cases of public importance are not given the attention and consideration they deserve.

Formality

Following the recommendations of the Franks Committee, the chairperson must be legally qualified. This has led to greater formality of proceedings, which are sometimes conducted in the same way as a court hearing. The attendance of lawyers, representing their clients, also makes the procedure and atmosphere more formal.

Arbitration: advantages

Expertise

The arbitrators have specialist knowledge of the relevant area under dispute, which allows fair and speedy decisions. For example, the arbitrator in a building dispute is likely to be a surveyor.

Privacy

The proceedings are conducted in private and the decision is not publicised in the media. The parties may not wish their domestic or business affairs to be made public.

Convenience

The parties agree the time, date and venue to meet with the arbitrator.

Enforceability of the award

Arbitration will result in a conclusion to the dispute between the parties. The award made by the arbitrator is binding on the parties. This means the parties must comply with the terms of the award and, if they do not, the court will enforce it.

Informality

The process may be less formal than the courts. There are no complicated rules of evidence and the use of lawyers is discouraged. For example, in a dispute about a holiday dealt with through ABTA, the parties may represent themselves and need not have a detailed knowledge of the relevant law to achieve a successful conclusion.

Speed

Arbitration is quicker than the civil courts. The hearing will take place earlier than a typical court date and the hearing will usually take only one day or part of a day.

Cost

There are no court fees, and the use of lawyers is discouraged.

Cost-saving to the State

The use of arbitration frees the court from dealing with many disputes. Many small disputes (for example, holiday cases or employment disputes) may be dealt with by arbitration, as may many large disputes of a technical nature (for example, the building dispute that arose over the creation of the new Wembley Stadium).

Arbitration: disadvantages

Lack of legal expertise

The arbitrator will often lack the legal expertise possessed by a judge. Where a dispute hinges on a difficult point of law, the arbitrator may not be able to judge the matter, due to this lack of legal knowledge. In courts, the parties have to depend on witnesses giving expert evidence.

Inconsistencies in decisions

The arbitrator is not bound by the rules of judicial precedent. Each case is judged on its own merits, providing no real guidelines for future disputes. This leads to inconsistent decisions and conclusions.

Cost

The costs may be high. This is due to the length of time that some disputes may take to be resolved, and to the possibility that arbitrators may charge high fees for their professional services. For example, a surveyor will charge an hourly or daily rate to act as an arbitrator in a building dispute.

Appeals

Under ss68 and 69 of the 1996 Act, appeals may be made on limited grounds to the High Court (see Topic 2). This prolongs the arbitration process and increases cost, which are factors arbitration is supposed to resolve.

Lack of awareness/popularity

There is a low take-up rate for arbitration. Some cases are not appropriate for alternative dispute resolution, and some parties may not want to try it, because they do not understand it or have faith in it. Cases dealt with by arbitration have not increased since the CPR reforms introduced by Lord Woolf in April 1999, which aimed to promote more use of all forms of alternative dispute resolution.

Mediation: advantages

Speed and convenience

The process is quicker than the ordinary courts. The meeting will be arranged at the earliest date which is agreeable to the parties. The parties can arrange the date, time and venue for the meeting rather than wait for the court to fix a hearing date. The process allows the parties to continue their business or personal relationship after the mediation is completed.

Lack of formality

The process is less formal than the courts. There are no complicated rules of evidence and the use of lawyers is discouraged. For example, in a family dispute, the parties can use the mediator, but may always negotiate directly if both agree.

Empowerment

The system empowers the parties because it does not force a decision upon them, but encourages them to reach a mutual agreement. The process generally leads to both parties being satisfied with the outcome. This is indicated by research conducted by Professor Hazel Genn (2002).

Cost

The process is not expensive. There are no court fees and the use of lawyers is discouraged. For those who qualify, public funding is available for mediation in family cases.

Expertise

Mediators are usually specialists in the area of dispute. Mediators are usually trained in the art of mediation (for example, by the Centre for Dispute Resolution). It is difficult to facilitate the resolution of a dispute between parties who may have strong emotions, for example, in a family case.

Privacy

The proceedings are conducted in private and the decision is not publicised in the media. This enables the parties to keep their business and domestic disputes between themselves.

Mediation: disadvantages

Imbalance of power

One party is usually weaker than the other, whether financially or emotionally. That party is susceptible to intimidation by the stronger party, whereas this would not be allowed in a courtroom setting. An example of this would be one party in a personal relationship still having the power to inhibit the other in a mediation situation.

Lack of legal expertise

Mediators may not be legal experts. When the resolution of a dispute involves a difficult or complicated point of law, the mediator may not have the ability to deal with the mediation in an appropriate manner.

Lack of certainty

There is no certainty as to the outcome of the mediation. This is due to the mediation not having to conform to the rules of precedent and the possibility that one or both parties may choose not to accept offers made to compromise the dispute. The recent Paul McCartney and Heather Mills divorce is an example of an unsuccessful mediation resulting in increased costs and a court hearing.

Enforceability

Unless the parties agree otherwise, the mediation settlement is not binding and the parties cannot enforce the agreement in the courts. Therefore, the mediation may not lead to a satisfactory conclusion. This means time and costs will have been wasted and the dispute will have to proceed to court in any event.

Conciliation: advantages

Pro-active element of conciliator

The conciliator is independent of the parties and has the power and ability to suggest and advise on offers made by parties during conciliation. This allows the parties the security of knowing the advice, etc., came from a neutral source. This may mean the dispute is settled on agreed terms.

Expertise

The conciliator has expert knowledge and experience of the types of disputes under conciliation. For example, ACAS conciliators are experts in the area of employment law. They can comment on, and suggest compromises for, settlement of employment disputes with confidence.

Conciliation: disadvantages

Imbalance of power

One, or both, of the parties may feel the conciliator is not neutral in their comments and/or suggestions. This may lead to a non-resolution to the dispute.

The other disadvantages are similar to mediation.

Negotiation: advantages

Speed

The process is often quicker than that in the ordinary courts. The parties meet at a mutually convenient time, which is probably shortly after the dispute arises. Time has not passed, which sometimes may exaggerate and enlarge the subject matter of the dispute in the minds of the parties.

Formality

The process is less formal than the courts. Simple negotiation is a process by which the parties discuss the issues between themselves, probably face to face. The terms of settlement may be in any form acceptable to the parties, and may be in a form not allowed or sanctioned by the court process. For example, an employer might agree to supply a letter of apology to a (former) employee, a neighbour might agree to allow a third party to prune an overhanging tree or a business might allow a customer a choice of products from his stock.

Cost

The process is the least expensive of all forms of ADR. There are no court or legal fees, unless solicitors are instructed at a later date. The only expense may be the parties' time, postage or the cost of a telephone call.

Privacy

The proceedings are conducted in private. The agreement is not publicised in the media. The parties are secure in the knowledge that the settlement is confidential and that no one outside the agreement need know about the dispute or its compromise.

Negotiation: disadvantages

Imbalance of power

There is an imbalance of power. As with the other forms of alternative dispute resolution, one party is often weaker than the other and is acting less voluntarily. Not all parties wish to resolve their disputes by negotiation. Some disputes are not appropriate for this method of alternative dispute resolution and some parties may not want to use it, for example, due to serious personality clashes.

Lack of legal expertise

There is a lack of legal expertise. Lawyers are not used, although they could be consulted on a point of law or might be instructed where no agreement is reached. The parties may agree a settlement of the dispute which is not practical or enforceable. The dispute may then resurface and the parties may have little choice but to instruct solicitors for advice.

Lack of certainty

There is lack of certainty as the negotiation process does not follow the rules of precedent. The parties have no security that there will be a successful negotiation, and the process may itself re-ignite the dispute between the parties.

Enforceability

The agreement negotiated between the parties may become enforceable by the civil courts. However, the parties involved may have no appreciation of this point. One party may believe the agreement is a binding agreement, but the other may feel it is not enforceable by the civil court unless agreed otherwise. This causes confusion and upset.

Overall evaluation

The examiner will expect you to be able to explain the types of tribunal and ADR clearly, with relevant examples. You must be able to expand this explanation with a discussion of the relevant merits or otherwise of tribunals and the types of ADR. Ensure you reach a reasoned but brief conclusion of this discussion.

Activities

1. Pick a type of ADR and a dispute to be resolved. List the advantages and disadvantages of the process to be undertaken compared to a civil action in the courts.

2. Divide into two groups. Group 1 will argue that the civil court justice system is the preferable forum to resolve a civil dispute. Group 2 will argue that ADR generally, and/or a particular type of ADR, is a better option.

3. Divide into four groups. Group 1 is the neighbour to Group 2, and there is a falling-out concerning late, loud parties held by Group 1, which annoy Group 2. Group 3 is the mediator or conciliator, who must assist the parties to reach a compromise. Group 4 is neutral, and takes notes on the reasons for the success or failure of the mediation/conciliation process.

You should now be able to:

- understand the ways of resolving civil disputes
- answer examination questions on civil dispute resolution.

Link

For more information on the Criminal Appeal Structure, see Chapter 10 (The criminal courts: procedure and sentencing), p189.

1 Outline of criminal courts and appeal system

The outline in this section will provide the background to the work that is done by lay people in the criminal court system. The court structure has been explained in Chapter 5, and now should be reviewed.

This topic concentrates on the jurisdiction (the powers and types of case dealt with) of the Magistrates' Court and the Crown Court in criminal matters.

The overall criminal court structure can be seen in the diagrams set out below:

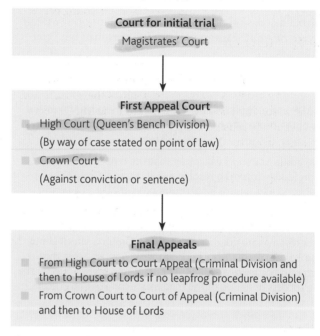

Court for initial trial
Magistrates' Court

First Appeal Court
High Court (Queen's Bench Division)
(By way of case stated on point of law)
Crown Court
(Against conviction or sentence)

Final Appeals
From High Court to Court Appeal (Criminal Division and then to House of Lords if no leapfrog procedure available)
From Crown Court to Court of Appeal (Criminal Division) and then to House of Lords

Fig. 6.1 *Criminal appeal structure: Magistrates' Court trial*

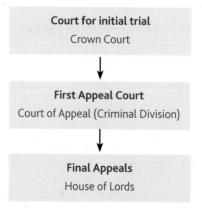

Court for initial trial
Crown Court

First Appeal Court
Court of Appeal (Criminal Division)

Final Appeals
House of Lords

Fig. 6.2 *Criminal appeal structure: Crown Court trial*

This chapter looks at the lay people who perform a central role in the criminal courts, either as magistrates or as jurors.

The Magistrates' Court jurisdiction

Whilst the Magistrates' Court has some limited civil jurisdiction, most of its work is dealing with criminal offences involving adult defendants. This includes issuing arrest and search warrants, deciding on **bail**, conducting sending for trial hearings where **indictable offence** cases, such as murder, are transferred to the Crown Court, trying **summary offences** such as assault, and trying **either-way offences** that are to be tried summarily, such as theft.

The magistrates also deal with young offenders in the Youth Court. This is a specialised form of Magistrates' Court. Unlike the Magistrates' Court, the Youth Court is not open to the general public, and only those directly involved in the case will normally be in court. It deals with almost all cases involving young people under the age of 18. A hearing in the Youth Court is similar to one in the Magistrates' Court, although the procedure is adapted to take account of age of the defendant. The magistrates who sit in the Youth Court receive specialist training on dealing with young people.

The Crown Court jurisdiction

The Crown Court deals exclusively with serious criminal cases. The work includes trying indictable offences such as murder, trying either-way offences that are to be tried on indictment, such as theft, sentencing where the case has been sent by the Magistrates' Court to the Crown Court for sentence (usually because the magistrates' sentencing powers are limited), and appeals from the Magistrates' Court against conviction or sentence.

Appeals from the Crown Court go to the Court of Appeal (Criminal Division). Possible grounds for appeal include misdirection of law or facts, failure to refer to a defence, inappropriate comments by the judge, or jury irregularity. The Court of Appeal will allow an appeal (and possibly order a new trial) if it considers the conviction unsafe. Where the Court of Appeal quashes a conviction on a point of law and the verdict of the jury shows that it was satisfied that some other offence had been committed, the Court of Appeal may substitute a conviction for that other offence.

You should now be able to:

- outline the criminal court structure
- describe the jurisdiction of each court
- attempt past paper questions on the criminal court structure.

Key terms

Bail: release of a defendant from custody, until his next appearance in Court.

Indictable offence: a criminal offence that can only be tried by the Crown Court (see below).

Summary offence: a criminal offence which can only be tried by a Magistrates' Court.

Either-way offence: an offence, such as theft, for which the accused will be tried by the Magistrates' Court or in the Crown Court where the defendant will be tried by jury.

AQA Examiner's tip

Make sure you answer any question on the jurisdiction of criminal courts accurately. In particular, the different appeal structures from the Magistrates' Court and Crown Court can be confused.

Activity

Draw a chart comparing the appeal structure for a summary offence, an either-way offence and an indictable offence.

Magistrates

Magistrates are also known as Justices of the Peace. They can be traced back to 1195, when Richard I required some of his knights to preserve the peace in unruly areas. They were responsible to the King for ensuring that the law was upheld; they preserved the 'King's Peace' and were known as Keepers of the Peace. In 1327 an Act of Parliament set out the appointment of men in every county to 'guard the peace'. In 1361 the term 'Justice of the Peace' was first used and the role has developed since then.

There are just under 29,000 lay magistrates in England and Wales. They are unpaid, except for expenses, although the annual training budget is

In this topic you will learn how to:

- describe the qualification, selection and appointment of a magistrate
- describe the training, role and powers of magistrates.

approximately £500 per head. The magistracy is comprised of roughly equal numbers of men and women. It is supposed to reflect society as a whole, so it is expected to have a race and gender balance that reflects the make-up of the country and, more importantly, of the local area in which magistrates sit. They are all part-time, but give a commitment to be able to sit as a magistrate at least 26 half-days a year. There are constant appointments of people to be magistrates. During 2005/2006, 1,132 men and 1,080 women were appointed Justices of the Peace. This level of appointments does not just include growth in the number of magistrates, but also turnover, as magistrates retire or otherwise stop being able to continue being a magistrate.

The growth can be seen in Table 6.1 below.

Table 6.1 *Numbers of Justices of the Peace in England and Wales*

Year	Total	Men	Women
1978	23,483	14,633	8,850
1988	27,926	15,992	11,934
1990	28,667	16,090	12,577
1991	29,062	16,098	12,964
1992	29,441	16,105	1,336
1993	29,686	16,087	13,599
1994	30,054	16,151	13,903
1995	30,088	16,045	14,043
1996	30,326	15,951	14,375
1997	30,374	15,858	14,516
1998	30,361	15,713	14,648
1999	30,260	15,561	14,699
2000	30,308	15,544	14,764
2001	28,735	14,639	14,096
2002	24,526	12,439	12,087
2003	28,344	14,392	13,952
2004	28,705	14,555	14,150
2005	28,253	14,256	13,997
2006	28,865	14,519	14,346

www.official-documents.gov.uk

Link

For more information on District Judges (Magistrates' Courts), see Chapter 8 (The judiciary), p133.

Lay magistrates sit as a bench of three magistrates and have a role in all criminal cases in some way, dealing with the entire criminal process for 95 per cent of all cases. There are approximately 1 million cases heard in the Magistrates' Court in each year, with nearly 850,000 convictions in 2006–7. Many of these cases will have involved more than one hearing, so the workload is enormous. There are some full-time, paid, legally qualified magistrates, called District Judges (Magistrates' Courts). They are described in Chapter 8. This chapter will now focus on the lay magistrate.

How magistrates are qualified, selected and appointed

Qualifications and eligibility to be a magistrate

Lay magistrates require no special qualifications. The first requirement is to have the correct personal qualities and be able to commit the time and effort to being a magistrate. There are six general personal qualities that applicants to become a magistrate should possess. These are:

1 To be of good character, including having personal integrity, keeping confidences and the respect and trust of others.

2 To have understanding and communication. This is needed, as a magistrate will have to understand documents, identify facts, follow evidence and concentrate for long periods of time. A magistrate also needs to be able to communicate effectively, both in court and out of court.

3 To have social awareness, including an appreciation and acceptance of the rule of law, respect for people from different ethnic, cultural or social backgrounds, and an understanding of their local community.

4 To be mature and of sound temperament. This will include an awareness and understanding of people, and a sense of fairness, as well as humanity and courteousness.

5 Being of sound judgement. This requires the ability to think logically, to weigh arguments and come to a sound decision, as well as having an open mind, being objective and recognising and controlling prejudices.

6 Having commitment and reliability. This includes being committed to serving the community and making the necessary time commitment. The applicant must be willing to undergo training, and be in sufficiently good health to undertake magistrate duties on a regular basis. Support of family and employer is essential.

The second requirement is the willingness to take the Oath of Allegiance. However, British nationality is not a requirement, although those who are in the process of seeking asylum cannot be appointed to be a magistrate. Even then, certain professions or occupations are ineligible, because they could cause concern about the magistrates' duty to be impartial. These professions and occupations include the police and the armed forces; and it is also relevant if the magistrate has been selected as a prospective candidate for election to the House of Lords, or any other parliament or assembly. There is discretion in this area, but the key is whether there is likely to be a conflict of interest, so the list of excluded occupations could be extended in individual cases. These guidelines apply also to the occupation of the potential magistrate's spouse, partner and even close relatives. The guidance notes for applicants give more details, as it would be unacceptable if previous occupations or professions prevented a person from becoming a magistrate. Applicants also have to disclose whether they are a freemason.

The third requirement relates to criminal convictions and civil claims. In a way, this is an extension of the quality of good character and integrity. Applicants must disclose any convictions, however minor, including motoring offences for which a fixed penalty was payable and even police cautions. Disclosure is also required of other criminal or civil orders, including details of divorce and maintenance orders. The Rehabilitation of Offenders Act 1974 does not apply to the application, so even minor motoring offences that are 20 years old have to be disclosed. The effect of this is that anyone who, or whose spouse or partner, has been convicted of a serious offence or even a number of minor offences will not be appointed if it is thought by the Advisory Committee (which advises on the appointment of magistrates) that the public would not have confidence in them as a magistrate. For these purposes, a serious offence is regarded as anything other than a minor motoring conviction for which one received points on one's licence and/or a fine, although very old convictions of this nature are not regarded as serious.

There is no formal age requirement, except that applicants must be a minimum of 18 years old in order to apply. Magistrates retire from the bench at the age of 70, and five years' service is normally expected before retirement. This means that anyone aged over 65 is unlikely to be appointed.

Selection of a new magistrate

The selection process has a number of stages. When new magistrates are needed, there is usually an advertisement placed in the area where the need has arisen. This is often part of a local campaign to recruit more magistrates. There are public awareness days in some courts, so that potential magistrates can learn more about what is involved. A person can apply to be a magistrate in either their home or work locality. There is a standard application form available from the Ministry of Justice, which can also be downloaded or printed from its website. A DVD is also included in the application pack. A person who has decided to apply to be a magistrate must complete an application form. This is straightforward, and reflects the eligibility criteria. It can be completed online, or as a hard copy.

Once the form is submitted, it is checked to make sure that, in general, the applicant is eligible to apply. If the applicant is eligible, an invitation to a first interview is sent by the Advisory Committee. The local Advisory Committees consist of local people, including some magistrates.

If successful at the first interview, there is a second interview, at which practical examples of the sort of cases magistrates deal with are discussed. At this stage, background checks are made for conflicts of interest. In making their recommendations, Advisory Committees consider the suitability of candidates and the number of vacancies. The view of the Advisory Committee is then sent to the Lord Chancellor, who will make the appointments.

Appointment of a new magistrate

Magistrates are then appointed by the Secretary of State and Lord Chancellor on behalf of, and in the name of, The Queen. New magistrates will then meet their colleagues and begin their training.

How magistrates are trained

The Judicial Studies Board has overall responsibility for overseeing magistrates' training. The training operates through regional Courts Board areas. Each area has responsibility for delivering the training to magistrates. The Justices' Clerk (who is the magistrates' legal adviser) for the area is responsible for delivery, and a local Magistrates' Area Training Committee sets the training priorities and agrees a training plan each year. The Magistrates' Association is consulted on training, and works with the Judicial Studies Board to develop materials.

Each year the Court Service and the Judicial Studies Board produce a document setting out the minimum training provision for magistrates.

This sets out the essential minimum training provision and desirable additional training. Not all training is for all magistrates.

The compulsory training programme for newly appointed magistrates is designed to prepare them for sitting in court. The training is usually delivered locally by the justices' clerk. The training includes a basic introduction to the role and responsibilities of a magistrate, which includes preliminary reading and three days of training, at least three court observations, a visit to a prison, a young offenders institution and a probation service facility. After this has been successfully completed, the new magistrate can start to sit in court. The new magistrate will then develop in their role as they deal with real cases as one of the three magistrates sitting on the bench.

After about a year, a new magistrate will receive consolidation training. This will normally be for the equivalent of two days, and includes training on law and procedure as well as skills development.

The most effective way to develop as a magistrate is to learn from the experience of sitting in court. All new magistrates are therefore given a mentor. Mentors are experienced magistrates who have been specially trained to take on the role. During the first year, a new magistrate will have six sessions with a mentor. These sessions are used to discuss the day's events in court with the mentor (who has been present through the day) and to reflect on how knowledge and skills have been applied during the day. One possible outcome is to identify further training and development needs. After the first year, the new magistrate will have their first appraisal.

After at least two years there may be opportunities to do specialised training, to sit in either the Youth Court or the Family Proceedings Court, or to undertake training to become chairman of the bench. Training is also undertaken to cover things such as new legislation or sentencing policy as well as refresher training.

The Judicial Studies Board training for magistrates for 2007–2008 is extensive, and supplements the large volume of electronic material that is available for day-to-day guidance. The material includes the adult bench book, the family bench book, the youth bench book and a workbook that is provided to all new magistrates. The adult bench book includes help on sentencing, as can be seen in Fig. 6.3 (overleaf).

The role and powers of magistrates

The Lord Chancellor's Directions for Advisory Committees on Justices of the Peace state that 'each bench should broadly reflect the community it serves in terms of gender, ethnic origin, geographical spread, occupation and political affiliation.' This enables the magistrates to act in an appropriate manner to ensure that the community in which they serve can deal with local issues.

A magistrate is required to sit for at least 26 half-days each year. Magistrates normally work as part of a bench of three magistrates. There is a chairman and two wingmen, who are often less experienced than the chairman. As magistrates are not legally trained, they always have available to them the advice of a qualified legal adviser. This is a justices' clerk or assistant clerk, who is also responsible for effective case management and the avoidance of delay in court.

The legal adviser explains the relevant points of law and legal procedures to the magistrates and gives advice on possible sentencing options. The

Assault – actual bodily harm	Offences Against the Person Act 1861 s.47 Triable either way – see Mode of Trial Guidelines Penalty: Level 5 and/or 6 months

CONSIDER THE SERIOUSNESS OF THE OFFENCE
(INCLUDING THE IMPACT ON THE VICTIM)

IS DISCHARGE OR FINE APPROPRIATE?

IS IT SERIOUS ENOUGH FOR A COMMUNITY PENALTY?

GUIDELINE: ➜ *IS IT SO SERIOUS THAT ONLY CUSTODY IS APPROPRIATE?*

ARE YOUR SENTENCING POWERS SUFFICIENT?

THIS IS A GUIDELINE FOR A FIRST-TIME OFFENDER PLEADING NOT GUILTY

 ## CONSIDER AGGRAVATING AND MITIGATING FACTORS, CULPABILITY AND HARM

for example	for example
Abuse of trust (domestic setting) Deliberate kicking or biting Extensive injuries (may be psychological) Headbutting Group action Offender in position of authority On hospital/medical or school premises Premeditated Victim particularly vulnerable Victim serving the public Weapon *This list is not exhaustive*	Minor injury Provocation Single blow *This list is not exhaustive*

If offender is on bail, this offence is more serious
If offender has previous convictions, their relevance and any failure to respond to previous sentences should be considered – they may increase the seriousness. The court should make it clear, when passing sentence, that this was the approach adopted.

TAKE A PRELIMINARY VIEW OF SERIOUSNESS, THEN CONSIDER OFFENDER MITIGATION

for example
Age, health (physical or mental)
Co-operation with police
Evidence of genuine remorse
Voluntary compensation

CONSIDER YOUR SENTENCE

Compare it with the suggested guideline level of sentence and reconsider your reasons carefully if you have chosen a sentence at a different level. Consider a reduction for a timely guilty plea.

DECIDE YOUR SENTENCE
NB. COMPENSATION – Give reasons if not awarding compensation

© The Magistrates' Association   **14**   Published October 2003 and revised December 2006

Fig. 6.3 *Extract from sentencing guidelines in adult bench book*

actual decisions are made by the magistrates alone, as they decide on guilt or innocence based on the findings of fact that they make. Similarly, the magistrates decide on sentence, but must act within their powers. The adviser will make sure that the magistrates are aware of the latest guidelines and policies on sentencing, but the magistrates make the decision and the chairman of the bench announces it to the court.

The adviser carries out many administrative roles, such as preparing for court sessions and making sure that all relevant papers and exhibits are ready, reading charges to the court, dealing with the paperwork for legal aid and completing bail forms, managing court schedules and training magistrates. This means that the magistrates can concentrate on the evidence in the case and the appropriate sentence, rather than being burdened with tasks that require specialist knowledge and expertise.

Magistrates hear less serious criminal cases and commit serious cases to the higher courts, where the case will be heard by a judge or recorder. Magistrates cannot impose sentences of imprisonment of more than six months (or 12 months for consecutive sentences) or fines exceeding £5,000. Magistrates can also sit in the Crown Court with a judge to hear appeals from Magistrates' Courts against conviction or sentence; and proceedings on committal to the Crown Court for sentence.

Removal of magistrates

Magistrates must retire at the age of 70. Complaints about the conduct of magistrates are dealt with under the Judicial Discipline (Prescribed Procedures) Regulations 2006. There are likely to be a number of complaints, given the number of magistrates. Criticism of a magistrate's behaviour, in or out of court, may come from sources including other magistrates, people in their court, members of the public, the press, the police or the Crown Prosecution Service. Complaints are investigated on behalf of the Lord Chancellor and the Lord Chief Justice by Advisory Committees and their support staff, and staff in the Office for Judicial Complaints.

Failure to meet the standards of behaviour required, or to attend sufficient sittings, can result in removal. In the Office for Judicial Complaints' first year from 2006, there were 28 complaints that resulted in disciplinary action against magistrates. The action was removal of 15 magistrates. One complaint was of Alan Mitchell, a 68-year-old magistrate who was reprimanded after complaining about 'bloody foreigners' in a Manchester courtroom. He made the remark after dealing with his list of cases. He was overheard by a colleague, who complained, saying she was married to an Iranian and that she was unhappy with his comments.

You should now be able to:

- understand the workings of lay magistrates
- attempt past paper questions on lay magistrates.

Activities

1 Explain how lay magistrates are chosen and appointed.

2 Describe, in outline, the work of lay magistrates.

3 Identify and discuss the advantages and disadvantages of using lay magistrates in the criminal justice process.

4 In small groups, discuss whether you would like to be appointed a magistrate. List the positive and negative points to your view of becoming a magistrate.

In this topic you will learn how to:

- describe the qualification and selection of jurors
- describe the role of jurors.

💡 3 Jurors

Trial by jury has been a feature of English law for hundreds of year. The way in which the jury operates has developed over the years, and is now seen as central to the administration of justice for serious criminal offences. Whilst there are other, more limited, roles for the jury, this section deals exclusively with the jury in criminal trials. The main legislation with respect to juries is the Juries Act 1974, as amended.

Nearly 500,000 people are summoned for jury service each year. It is normally for a period of two weeks, but there is no guarantee that there will be a trial to hear on any particular date. Some trials are lengthy, and service continues until the trial ends. Each juror attends at court each day. On occasions when the trial has a high media profile, there is a danger, once the jury has retired to consider its verdict, that the jurors may be exposed to reports which might influence the verdict. In such cases, the jury stays together until the verdict is reached; and, if this is overnight, the jury is accommodated in a hotel and kept away from media reports.

If a person does not reply to the summons, fails to attend without good reason, or is not available or unfit through drink or drugs when called, that person may be prosecuted and fined.

Jury service is one of the most important civic duties. All members of the public are expected to perform this duty if called upon to do so. However, some people are not eligible, or are disqualified from jury service, while others may be asked to have their service deferred, as their personal circumstances make it difficult to carry out their duty at the time. Whilst a person might be summoned for jury service more than once, a few people are excused further jury service after completing a trial. Since electronic records were created in 1999–2000, the Jury Central Summoning Bureau's database shows that by 2006, the most that any one person has served on a jury is four times, and that was only one person.

The juror's role in the criminal justice system is to decide, based on the evidence presented, whether a defendant is guilty or not guilty of the crime with which he has been charged. A jury trial takes place only in the Crown Court. A jury is made up of 12 jurors, who should come to a unanimous decision, although this can be reduced to 11:1 or 10:2 in some situations. As with magistrates, jurors are unpaid, except for expenses and some compensation for loss of earnings, and are not expected to have any legal knowledge.

Qualification and selection of jurors

Eligibility

Jurors are chosen at random from the electoral roll to serve on a jury at a Crown Court reasonably close to where the juror lives. Any person is eligible for jury service, provided they fulfil certain conditions. This means that a person may be summoned if all the conditions set out below are satisfied:

- He or she is aged at least 18 and under 70 on the day on which the jury service is due to start.
- He or she is registered on the electoral roll.
- He or she has lived in the UK, Channel Islands or Isle of Man for at least five years after the age of 13.
- The jury summons is prepared on a random basis by a computer. This is dealt with by the Jury Central Summoning Bureau.

Disqualification

A person is not qualified for jury service whilst on bail, or following certain convictions for criminal offences, or suffering from a mental disorder or other mental health problem. The following situations each disqualify a person from jury service, and are set out in the Criminal Justice Act 2003:

▓ Bail: if a person summoned is on bail for a criminal offence.

▓ Conviction: if a person summoned has ever been sentenced to:

   a   imprisonment, detention or custody for life; or

   b   imprisonment for public protection or detention for public protection; or

   c   five or more years' imprisonment or youth custody; or

   d   certain extended sentences in Scotland.

▓ Conviction: if a person summoned has in the past ten years:

   e   served any part of a sentence of imprisonment, or a sentence of detention; or

   f   had a suspended sentence passed on them; or

   g   had various community orders imposed, such as a community rehabilitation order, a community punishment order, a community punishment and rehabilitation order, a drug treatment and testing order.

▓ Mental disorders or mental health problems: if the person summoned:

   h   suffers from, or has suffered from, a mental disorder or mental health problem, and as a result is a resident in a hospital or other similar institution; or

   i   regularly visits the doctor for treatment for the mental disorder or mental health problem; or

   j   has a guardian under the Mental Health Act 1983; or

   k   as a result of mental health problems, the court has decided that they are not capable of managing their own affairs or property.

It should also be noted that a juror can be discharged from his duties if the judge considers that, because of physical disability (such as deafness) or insufficient understanding of English, the juror would not be able to perform his duties properly.

Deferral

Anyone can apply for deferral of their jury service. If the application is successful, the effect is that the jury service is carried out later within the following 12 months. The new dates may be given as soon as an application for deferral is accepted. The application for deferral needs to be a good reason, such as examinations, a date for an operation in a hospital, or a holiday that has already been booked. Most applications for deferral are granted, but anyone refused deferral can appeal to the head of the Bureau. Jury service can only be deferred once up to a maximum of 12 months from the original date. Home Office research into deferral of jury service found that almost three-quarters of all deferrals were for either work commitments or holidays. Guidelines are being produced to ensure consistency in deferral and excusal of jury service.

Excusal

A person can be excused from serving as a juror at any time during the following 12 months, as opposed to just deferring jury service. As excusal effectively takes a person off the list for jury service for 12 months

AQA Examiner's tip

Do not confuse disqualification, deferral and excusal – many candidates do confuse the terms!

and therefore requires a further random selection before the person is summoned again. It is only available in exceptional circumstances.

A person may be excused if he or she has been on jury service in the criminal courts (not a coroner's jury) in the previous two years. This also applies where the court has excused someone for further jury service for a period that has not yet ended. This can occur after a particularly long or distressing trial, such as the Soham murders. This ensures that no individual should feel overburdened by the duty.

A full-time member of the armed forces may also be excused, if the commanding officer certifies to the Jury Summoning Officer that absence would prejudice the efficiency of the service. The list of those who have a right to be excused jury service or to apply for discretionary refusal is:

- those who are over 65 years of age
- those who have served within the last two years
- those whose religious beliefs are incompatible with jury service
- full-time members of the armed forces
- certain members of the medical profession
- representatives of the Assembly of the European Communities (Euro MPs)
- Members of Parliament.

This can create difficulties for some potential jurors, particularly solicitors, barristers and judges, who are familiar with the process and may be seen by other jurors as 'knowing what the result should be'. Equally, they may be acquainted with some or all of the solicitors, barristers and judge involved in the case, which could lead to a suggestion of bias.

To assist barristers who are summoned for jury service, guidance is given by the Bar Council; similarly, the Lord Chancellor has given guidance for judges.

Jury vetting — Check of Jurors = suitable

The European Convention on Human Rights requires trial by an independent and impartial tribunal. Jury vetting, where the members of a jury are checked out before they are allowed to be selected to serve as a juror on a particular trial, would appear to go against the principle. However, there are three concerns that need to be balanced against this principle.

The first concern is that jurors may be corrupt or biased. The second concern is national security. These concerns suggest that jury vetting would be beneficial. However, a further concern is that the Government might use jury vetting to ensure a politically attractive verdict in the trial. This might outweigh the advantages of jury vetting relating to the first two concerns. The defence will not have access to the information available to the prosecution, but may also wish to check for disqualified persons or seek assistance in obtaining information regarding a totally unsuitable juror on the ground of bias. This right to challenge a juror can only be done 'for cause', that is, ineligibility, disqualification or assumed bias. The defence will only have this option where a juror is known to a member of the legal team. For example, this challenge could be used where a person of known racist views was selected for a trial involving racial hatred.

Beneficial
① May be corrupt / biased
② National security

The role and process of the jury

The jury offers to the defendant the opportunity of being tried by his equals. The role of the jury can be seen as simply to return verdicts of guilty or not guilty. This is done by determining the facts. The jury then must apply the law, as explained by the judge in his summing up, to those facts, and give their verdict. The verdict should be unanimous, that is, all 12 jurors should reach the same verdict, but a majority verdict can be accepted by the judge when all the jurors cannot agree. In this situation, the judge decides that the jury's decision is acceptable if at least ten of the jurors agree. A majority decision can only occur when the judge considers that enough time has elapsed; this is usually at least two hours. This will depend on the case, and might not be until the next day.

The jury is independent and should be free from bias. The random nature of the selection of jurors by the computer starts the process. When the juror reaches court there is another random element in the selection of the individual trial for which that juror may be involved. When the individual juror arrives at court, he goes to the assembly area. This is a room in the courthouse where jurors have to check-in at the start of their service and have their identity confirmed. The assembled potential jurors are shown a DVD explaining their role as a juror and what happens in a courtroom.

When a court is ready to select a jury, a court official chooses a group of people at random from those in the jury assembly area. More people are called into the courtroom than the 12 required to make up the jury: usually 15 people are called forward. This is to allow for the random selection process to continue, to make sure that no one is a juror on a case with which they have a connection and, if a case is expected to go on for more than two weeks, to allow for the fact that there will be some people who will be unable to serve on the jury for that long.

The average trial lasts about a day and a half. People may be called to sit on more than one trial, which may mean more than one per day, but that depends on the number of trials going ahead, the size of the the juror pool at the court, and the random selection of jurors from that pool. At all times other than in the courtroom, the jury will be kept apart from the other people involved in the trial, except for the ushers, who help and guide the jurors to the correct place.

Jurors will listen to the evidence and see the exhibits, such as items involved in the crime, photographs, CCTV images and diagrams. A juror can take notes, but these can only be used in the courtroom and the jury room. They cannot be taken home. At the end of the trial, the notes will be destroyed, because the whole process of the jury's deliberation is secret.

When the evidence has been completed and the lawyers have finished their speeches, the judge sums up the case to the jury and explains the law. The jury then retire to the jury room to consider their verdict. Each juror can only take into the jury room any notes made during the trial, a copy of the indictment (the list of the offences with which the defendant is charged) and any exhibits submitted during the trial that are allowed to be taken (typically photographs and diagrams). Jurors may not have access to mobile phones, to ensure secrecy.

Activity

Read the extract from the guidance given to barristers who are called for jury service. Discuss the issues raised in the extract and consider whether barristers, solicitors and judges should be ineligible to serve on a jury.

3 A common problem is likely to be where a member of the Bar is summoned to attend as a juror where he/she practises and/or sits as a Recorder [judge]. It would be inappropriate for a juror to have any special knowledge of any person involved in a trial: that applies not just to defendants or witnesses, but also to members of the judiciary, and to the legal representatives involved in a trial. Personal knowledge of the jury bailiff or other court staff will not be considered a reason to be excused from service.

4 If a member of the Bar receives a summons to attend the court at which he/she regularly practises or sits as a Recorder, he/she should apply to the summoning officer not to serve at that particular court. If deferral would not solve the problem, the summoning officer should consider whether jury service could be undertaken at a different court. It is to be borne in mind that no juror is expected to travel more than one and a half hours from home in order to serve on a jury.

5 As with any other potential juror, valid professional or business reasons may justify deferral or excusal. However as the Guidance makes clear, such applications will be 'looked at closely and granted only if there would be unusual hardship.' If a member of the Bar has a fixture which was arranged prior to receipt of a jury summons, and where it would be contrary to the interests of the client to return the brief, then application for deferral should be made. Such an application should contain sufficient information to enable the summoning officer to make an informed decision.

www.barcouncil.org.uk

You should now be able to:

- understand the operation of the jury
- attempt past paper questions on juries.

In this topic you will learn how to:

- state the advantages and disadvantages of the use of magistrates

- give examples relevant to those advantages and disadvantages

- state the advantages and disadvantages of the jury

- give examples relevant to those advantages and disadvantages.

4 The advantages and disadvantages of using lay people in the criminal courts

There are many advantages and disadvantages of using lay people in the criminal justice system. The key advantages and disadvantages are set out below, but there are many other arguments that can be made. For most of the advantages or disadvantages stated, it is possible to argue the opposite view: for example, the cost of replacing magistrates with judges is shown as an advantage of having magistrates; it could be argued that the cost is relatively small if the result of the spending were a better criminal justice system. It is a useful exercise to think what the counter-arguments are for each advantage or disadvantage as you read this topic.

The advantages of the use of magistrates

Cost

Magistrates are unpaid, apart from their expenses. This means that the large majority of criminal cases are tried without the need for a Judge, Recorder or District Judge (Magistrates' Court), whose salary would be over £90,000 each. It is estimated that the annual saving is in the region of £100m. This figure takes into account the cost of the legal adviser in the court which would not be necessary for full-time salaried judges; an administrator for each court would still be needed.

Local knowledge

Magistrates' local knowledge is invaluable when it comes to understanding exactly where an offence took place. In Crown Court much time can be taken explaining exactly where the location of a crime was and where, in relation to the event, a witness was standing. Most importantly, sentencing can take into account local problems that can be helped by sensitive sentencing.

An example of this arises from that fact that, under the Drugs Act 2005, police can drugs test people arrested for a variety of 'trigger' offences such as theft, robbery or taking a motor vehicle. This was put into effect as a pilot scheme in three police areas where high levels of drug-related crime existed. Those who tested positive for drugs were obliged to attend a compulsory drug assessment and help them into treatment and other support. The scheme could be backed up by appropriate sentencing for those charged and convicted.

The approach of using local knowledge was seen in the case of *Paul v DPP* (1989), where the court had to decide whether a kerb-crawler was 'likely to cause nuisance to other persons in the neighbourhood.' The magistrates knew the area as a residential area in which kerb-crawling had become a problem. The defendant was convicted, and on appeal, Lord Justice Woolf said this was the sort of case that was particularly appropriate for trial by magistrates with local knowledge.

Availability of judges

If all magistrates were replaced by judges, approximately 1,000 judges would have to be appointed. This would require an entirely new approach to the appointment of judges as the pool of candidates at present would be nowhere near big enough.

Can deal with the issues that arise

Over 90 per cent of defendants plead guilty, and most trials deal with issues of conflicting evidence rather than questions of law. Magistrates are perfectly able to decide who is telling the truth and can also decide whether behaviour is reasonable in all the circumstances, such as when self-defence is pleaded. In many ways they are better able to do this as they reflect a cross-section of society better than the judiciary. This can be seen by comparing the respective statistics on race and gender.

Public confidence

The public have great confidence in the magistrates system, even though there is perhaps less confidence in magistrates than in the judiciary. Studies in 2000 and 2001 suggest that the public would neither understand nor support any moves to lessen the role of lay magistrates, who are seen as an example of active citizenship within the criminal justice system.

The disadvantages of the use of magistrates

Unrepresentative of society

Surveys reveal that the magistracy fundamentally remains socially unrepresentative, as it is disproportionately white, middle class, professional and wealthy. This situation varies from town to town, and

AQA Examiner's tip

A question evaluating lay people in the criminal courts is likely to appear quite often. You should:

- Make sure you read the question carefully to see whether it refers to magistrates, juries or both of them.
- If the question refers to lay people and does not state either magistrates or juries, answer the question using examples from both magistrates and juries and concentrate on points relevant to both.
- Check whether it is advantages, disadvantages or both that the question requires.

in general the local magistracy reflects at least to some extent the local racial mix. Efforts continue to attract appropriate magistrates, so the old adage that magistrates are 'middle class, middle aged and middle minded' is no longer completely true.

The magistracy remains disproportionately middle-aged in comparison to the population. Despite the reduction in the minimum age for a magistrate, only about five per cent are under 40 years old. Approximately two-thirds of magistrates have managerial or professional backgrounds, compared to one-third of the population. Two-fifths of magistrates are retired. The vast majority of defendants in the Magistrates' Court are under 25 years old.

However, there are an increasing number of young magistrates, but some people take the view that they lack experience. Some examples can be seen in the article set out below.

Controversy flares over magistrate aged 19

Kate O'Hara

A 19-YEAR-OLD law student has become one of Britain's youngest magistrates, the *Yorkshire Post* can reveal.

But the appointment of Lucy Tate to the Pontefract bench has caused resentment among some of her fellow justices, who believe a 19-year-old cannot possibly have enough life experience to carry out the role properly.

Miss Tate is studying for a law degree in Leeds, and has had only one sitting as a magistrate so far.

She was recruited after a £4m Government advertising campaign two years ago to recruit more young people and ethnic minority candidates to the bench.

Magistrates without legal qualifications deal mainly with minor criminal offences and some family cases. The minimum age was reduced from 27 to 18 in 2004.

Miss Tate is even younger than the 20-year-old man from north Sussex who became the country's youngest magistrate last year.

One magistrate told the Yorkshire Post: 'It is an absolute folly to have somebody so young making such important decisions.

'Some of the magistrates in Pontefract feel very disillusioned about what has happened and they just can't see where the Government is coming from by wanting to take people on so very young.

'It was all hushed up when she was sworn in because it was felt there might be bad publicity. There probably will be – what life experience does she have at 19?'

The chairman of the local advisory committee responsible for recruiting magistrates, Sue Vogan, said: 'Lucy was an exceptional candidate, and came through a rigorous recruitment process. The committee were very impressed with her personal maturity and judgment.

'Of course, the magistracy should reflect the community it serves and we can only emphasise that Lucy's appointment was based solely on merit having met all the selection criteria. The Lord Chancellor requires that advisory committees recruit people from a wide range of experiences and backgrounds.'

Miss Tate did not want to speak to the *Yorkshire Post* but issued a statement which said: 'I was very pleased to be appointed, and look forward to serving as a magistrate. I have had my first sitting, which was fascinating, and am grateful for the training and support which I have received, as all new magistrates do.

'I don't see myself as a role model, but rather as someone who wants to serve the local community in a useful and positive way.'

Inconsistent

Two of the major criticisms of magistrates have been inconsistency between neighbouring benches in the sentences they impose, and bail refusal rates. Research in the 1980s and 1990s pointed out such inconsistencies. Since then, there have been increased efforts to be more consistent without losing the ability to vary sentences to suit the needs of the individual offender and crime. The sentencing guidelines and revised principles on bail are major reasons for improvement. However, inconsistencies remain between sentencing in neighbouring benches; in 2005 research was undertaken in the Bath and Bristol area.

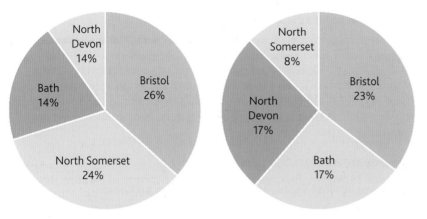

Fig. 6.4 *Percentage of those convicted given custodial sentences by magistrates for Actual Bodily Harm by region*

Fig. 6.5 *Percentage of those convicted given custodial sentences by magistrates for domestic burglary by region*

There may have been different circumstances justifying these differences, of course, but justice should be consistent across the country and not vary unduly according to views of local magistrates.

Case-hardened and biased

Magistrates often hear very similar cases, with similar evidence and with the same witnesses. For example, a magistrate may have 30 or more TV licence evaders to deal with in a morning's court. This can lead to a suspicion that the evidence is not really considered and that the convictions are rubber stamped, particularly if the defendant is not present. It is inevitable that the same police officer witnesses will appear to give evidence given the local nature of the courts. The magistrates could be suspected of knowing and always believing the police witnesses, particularly where a defendant is not properly represented. This leads to suspicions that magistrates may be too ready to believe the police and may be unlikely to accept the defendant's evidence. One quite old example of this is the case of **Bingham Justices ex p Jowitt (1974)**, where a motorist was charged with exceeding the speed limit. The only evidence was given by the motorist and a police officer. The evidence was contradictory. The magistrates found the defendant motorist guilty. The chairman of the magistrates said, 'My principle in such cases has always been to believe the evidence of the police officer.' The conviction was quashed on appeal, as any reasonable person would suspect that the chairman of magistrates was biased and there had not been a fair trial.

It should be noted that fewer than one in 100 Magistrate Court cases is appealed successfully on any ground whatsoever. This figure should be seen in the context of a very low acquittal rate, this resulting from

■ Key cases

Bingham Justices ex p Jowitt (1974): magistrates showed bias in favour of police evidence. This is an isolated example of magistrates being case-hardened and ignoring their neutral stance.

the Crown Prosecution Service not bringing cases to court that are unlikely to secure a conviction. For many categories of offence, the Crown Prosecution Service has achieved a conviction rate of over 90 per cent in parts of the country. In July 2007 there were just over 30,000 prosecutions across 42 Crown Prosecution Service areas for motoring offences. The conviction rate was 90.2 per cent. For burglary, there were over 2,300 prosecutions with a conviction rate of 85.7 per cent (including 100 per cent in Cumbria). For drugs offences, there were nearly 4,300 prosecutions with a conviction rate of 93.6 per cent (several CPS areas had 100 per cent conviction rates). With such statistics, it is not surprising that there is a cynical and unfounded view of bias.

Reliance on legal adviser

There is a suggestion that magistrates rely too much on their legal adviser. Whilst the adviser is not allowed to help the magistrates decide on a sentence, a defendant who sees the adviser constantly conferring with the magistrates and going in and out of the magistrates' retiring room may form the view that the magistrates are not in fact making the decisions. If you visit a Magistrates' Court, you can form your own judgement on this.

The advantages of the use of the jury

A balance against State interference in criminal trials

Lord Devlin, writing on jury trials, made the point that juries also provide a balance against the power of Government: 'The first object of any tyrant in Whitehall would be to make Parliament utterly subservient to his will; and the next to overthrow or diminish trial by jury, for no tyrant could afford to leave a subject's freedom in the hands of twelve of his countrymen.' This means that a jury can find defendants not guilty even if they are obviously guilty and the judge tells them to convict the defendant. This right was first seen in 1670, when the Quakers Penn and Meade were charged with riot, which allowed them to have a jury trial. The jury, led by a man called Bushel, refused to convict. The judge was so incensed that he committed the entire jury to Newgate prison until released under a writ of habeas corpus. The trial, which took place at the Old Bailey, established the independence of a jury to return a true verdict without fear of the consequences.

A modern example of this is the trial of Clive Ponting. He was an assistant secretary at the Ministry of Defence. He was the civil servant who had responsibility for 'the policy and political aspects of the operational activities of the Royal Navy' during the time of the Falkland Islands conflict. Ponting had to draft replies and answers on the sinking of an Argentinian warship, *The General Belgrano*, by the Royal Navy on 2 May 1982. Because he believed that the Government was deliberately misleading the Commons, a select committee and the public, and thought this was unethical, he acted out of professional conscience in sending two documents to an MP who would be horrified by the Government's action. Ponting was then prosecuted under the Official Secrets Act 1911. The prosecution lost the case, not because they were not correct in law, but because the jury refused to convict.

This is, however, a perverse verdict. A perverse verdict is one that could not reasonably be expected on the evidence given. For this reason, this can also be seen as a disadvantage of using a jury.

Handwritten margin notes:
- Public Confidence
- Cross Section of society
- Direct involvement of Lay people
- Not case hardened
- Jury Equity: Ponting Case.

A jury sometimes gives a **perverse verdict**

As we have seen in the Clive Ponting case, a jury sometimes comes to a perverse verdict, often as a view of public opinion and the justice of bringing a prosecution. Another example is the case of Kronlid. On the night of 29 January 1996, three women, Andrea Needham, Joanna Wilson and Lotta Kronlid, broke through the perimeter fence that surrounds the British Aerospace factory at Warton in Lancashire, where planes were being prepared for sale to the Indonesian government. At that time, Indonesia was in dispute over East Timor and many people were killed in the conflict. The women slipped past security guards to a hangar containing a Hawk jet and forced opened its door. Then, using household hammers, they smashed the £12m plane's sophisticated electronics.

The women made no attempt to escape and had draped the aircraft with banners bearing the slogans 'Swords into Ploughshares' and 'Peace and Justice in East Timor'. They had also left a video in the cockpit explaining the reasons for their actions. They then used a telephone in the hangar to call Angie Zelter (a conspirator with them), a press agency and security.

They were charged with causing nearly £2m of criminal damage to the plane. The defence prosecution stated that said that the attack 'was not a publicity stunt, but an act of last resort by women of principle who had so far unsuccessfully campaigned against the sale of the Hawks.' The prosecution told the court that the women's 'genuine and sincere' beliefs were irrelevant to the issues in the case. However, the jury of seven men and five women cleared them of the charges. This is clearly another example of a perverse verdict.

Juries are racially balanced

Research published in 2007 by the Ministry of Justice shows that there are no differences between white, black and minority ethnic people in responding positively to being summoned for jury service, and that black and minority ethnic groups are not significantly under-represented among those summoned for jury service or among those serving as jurors. The research also found that racially mixed juries' verdicts do not discriminate against defendants based on their ethnicity.

Public participation in the criminal justice system

The fact that juries are drawn from the general public reinforces the view that the criminal justice system serves society as a whole and is not totally removed from society as a Government agency might be. A report for the Home Office in 2004 found that over one-half of those included in the survey who received a jury summons claimed to be 'enthusiastic' or 'very enthusiastic', while just under one-third of respondents claimed to be 'reluctant' or 'very reluctant'. Reluctance was usually because of the inconvenience of serving on a jury, rather than the principle of it. Many jurors found the experience reinforced their confidence in the criminal justice system.

The disadvantages of the use of the jury

Juries do not have to give reasoned verdicts

Whilst it can be argued that not having to give reasons for the verdict speeds up the process and reinforces the secrecy of the jury room, it does mean that the individual jurors can give their verdict on a whim. This could be a result of 'going with the flow' to finish the trial and go home or to produce a genuinely perverse result. This means juries deliberate in private and no one can inquire into what happened in the jury room. The only time when the public finds out what happens in the jury room is when a juror complains and this leads to a retrial, as in the case in 1994 of insurance broker Stephen Young. He was granted a retrial after it emerged that a jury at Hove Crown Court had consulted an ouija board during their deliberations. Despite this, he was convicted at his retrial of the murder of Harry and Nicola Fuller.

The jury is not truly representative of the public

The jury represents the public, but many are excluded as being disqualified or ineligible. Once those excused have been added in, it is likely that the jury will have a higher proportion of older people (most people with relevant criminal convictions are under 25; mothers of young children are often excused jury service) and fewer people who are reluctant jurors as they will try harder to be excused or have their service deferred. Jury vetting may also affect the representative make-up of the jury.

Lack of ability to do the job

It is often suggested that jurors do not really understand the nature of the proceedings in a criminal trial. Lawyers make a point of ensuring the evidence is given in such a way that all jurors will understand the case being made. For many jurors this is seen as trying too hard, and some become suspicious that they are not really being told the truth. The real problem is claimed to be in long and complex fraud trials where there is now provision for a judge to sit without a jury, in order to avoid any problems of juror ability. All these arguments are based on conjecture, as the actual workings of real jurors cannot be studied because of jury secrecy. This is seen in the 1986 Report of the Fraud Trials Committee, which stated that the Committee was disadvantaged in determining whether or not jurors could understand the technical evidence and complex issues in fraud trials because they were prohibited from discussing this issue with jurors in such trials.

The effect of jury service on jurors

Most jurors find the experience interesting, and are reassured about the high standard of the criminal justice system. However, for some jurors, the experience can be very distressing, particularly where the case has similarities to a personal experience. There is some follow-up counselling, but only in 2007 had a system been set up. Members of Crown Court juries struggling to cope with horrific cases are now being put in direct touch with the Samaritans through court staff. Contact numbers and leaflets are now available in jury rooms after the launch of the partnership between the Samaritans and the Courts Service. Feelings of distress may not surface until some time after the trial. Although Samaritan volunteers are not allowed to talk to jurors about their deliberations, they can discuss their feelings and emotions without disclosing jury room secrets.

Activities

1 Identify and discuss the advantages and disadvantages of using lay people to decide cases in the Magistrates' Court.

2 Identify and discuss the advantages and disadvantages of using lay people to decide cases in the Crown Court.

You should now be able to:

■ understand the advantages and disadvantages of using lay people in the criminal justice system

■ answer examination questions on magistrates and jurors.

The legal profession and other sources of advice and funding

In this topic you will learn how to:

- describe the qualification, training and work of barristers
- describe the qualification, training and work of solicitors
- describe the qualification, training and work of legal executives.

AQA Examiner's tip

Look at examination questions carefully: some require a discussion of solicitors, some of barristers, some of legal executives, and some of all or two of them. You must answer the question that has been asked.

Key terms

Bar Council: the professional body for barristers in England and Wales.

Barrister: barristers are one branch of professional lawyers whose main work is to give specialist legal advice and represent people in court.

Queen's Counsel (QC): a barrister appointed to senior rank.

1 The legal profession

The legal profession consists of two main branches: barristers and solicitors. These branches of the profession are the traditional 'lawyer' and have rights of audience (that is, the right to appear and speak on behalf of their clients) in court. There are also legal executives, who are usually specialist employees of solicitors. Legal executives might work in areas such as conveyancing, debt recovery or wills. A legal executive does not have the same rights of audience in court as a solicitor or barrister.

Barristers

Barristers have been in existence since the 13th century. For many years they were the only profession that had the right to represent people in the higher courts, but this monopoly has gone. They cannot form partnerships, but use common facilities and support services in chambers (originally rooms, now effectively offices). England and Wales is divided into regions or 'circuits' for the purposes of the administration of justice, and barristers attach themselves to a circuit.

The **Bar Council** is the professional body for barristers in England and Wales. It provides representation and services for the Bar, and guidance on issues of professional practice. The Bar Standards Board was established in January 2006, the Bar Council separating its regulatory and representative functions. It is responsible for regulating barristers, for example, by setting entry qualifications and discipline.

Barristers of at least ten years' standing may apply to become **Queen's Counsel (QC)**. They undertake work of an important nature, and are referred to as 'silks', a term derived from the gown that QCs wear in court. Solicitors can now also apply to be a QC: the appointment as QC is often seen as a stepping stone to applying to be a judge. These senior lawyers are made Queen's Counsel as recognition of their outstanding ability. There are also a number of honorary QCs appointed each year from nominations made. These are appointments of people who do not intend to practise in the courts as a QC, but whose work in the law is deemed to deserve recognition.

Qualification

There are three stages to becoming a barrister. The stages are: the academic stage, the vocational stage and pupillage. The academic stage sets the minimum educational requirement for becoming a barrister. This is a qualifying degree in law at the minimum of a 2:ii. A qualifying law degree's requirements are set out by the Bar Council and the Law Society jointly, as required by the Courts and Legal Services Act 1990. This sets out a minimum law content for the degree course followed at a university. If a person's degree is in a subject other than law, or does not comply with the requirements for a law degree, a one-year conversion course must be completed. This conversion course is either the Common Professional Examination (CPE) or an approved Graduate Diploma in Law (GDL) course. This is so that all starting the next stage of training have a common basic foundation in legal principles. It is for this reason that some law degrees do not qualify for exemption from taking a conversion course.

Before starting the vocational stage, a person must join one of the four Inns of Court: Lincoln's Inn, Inner Temple, Middle Temple and Gray's Inn. The Inns are societies that provide various activities and support for barristers and student barristers. They also provide the use of a library, dining facilities, common rooms and gardens. Most importantly, the Inns alone have the power to call a student to the Bar, and admission to an Inn is required before registration on the Bar Vocational Course, the main part of the vocational stage of qualifying as a barrister. The purpose of the Bar Vocational Course is to ensure that students intending to become barristers acquire the skills and knowledge of procedure and evidence that will be required for the more specialised training in pupillage. The course runs for one academic year full-time or for two years part-time.

The final stage is **pupillage**. Here the pupil barrister undertakes practical training under the supervision of an experienced barrister. Pupillage is divided into two parts: the first is non-practising. In this six-month period pupils shadow, and work with, their supervisor barrister. During the second, practising, six-month period, pupils, with their supervisor's permission, can carry out legal services and have rights of audience in court. There is great competition for pupillage, and so a mini-pupillage is a useful starting point. It is a short period of work experience (usually one or two weeks) in a set of chambers. Some chambers require applicants to undertake an assessed mini-pupillage as part of the recruitment process, and others use it as one of their selection criteria. All applicants to the Bar are advised to undertake at least one mini-pupillage by the Bar Standards Board.

Training

Once a person has successfully completed the Bar Vocational Course, he can be called to the bar. This usually takes place towards the end of their first six months pupillage. As with most professions, there is a requirement for continuing training and updating. Barristers need to update and develop specialist areas of knowledge and improve their skills, particularly as there is increasing competition in the market for legal services.

The **Bar Standards Board** has set up an Education and Training Committee, which is responsible for setting the standards of education and training that people must pass before being able to practise as barristers, together with the further training requirements that barristers must comply with throughout their careers. At present, in the first three years of practice, a barrister must complete 45 hours of continuing professional development, including at least nine hours of advocacy training and three hours of ethics. After the first three years of practice, barristers are required to undertake 12 hours of continuing professional development each year under the established practitioners' programme. There is a wide range of courses available to cover most specialisms such as sentencing, aspects of tax law and patents and design law.

Pay

The Bar Council sets a minimum rate to be paid to pupils. In 2006–7 this was no less than £833.33 per month (£10,000 per annum) plus reasonable travel expenses. Once qualified, a barrister will have typical earnings as a self-employed barrister in a range from £25,000 to £150,000 gross within five years. There are huge disparities in annual earnings at the Bar, with some junior barristers working in criminal law earning as little as £50 per day. However, this is before deduction of tax and chambers' charges. It should also be noted that barristers rely on the

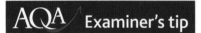

solicitors appointing them to pay the fee. This is because the contract is between solicitor and barrister, and not between the barrister and the person he represents. The fee is agreed by their clerk and is often paid at the end of a trial. This means much work is done several months before payment. Some solicitors used to be very poor at paying the barrister's fee; more recently, the Law Society has made it clear that solicitors should pay promptly. Despite this, many young barristers actually receive little or no income in the first year of practice.

Barristers' clerks were originally paid purely on commission. Today, the majority of chambers offer a pay package. This is a mixture of salary and bonus based on the income of the barristers. This has to be paid for on a proportional basis by all the barristers in the chambers. This could cost each barrister up to 15 per cent of all earnings, although each set of chambers has its own method of spreading the cost of running the chambers.

Work

Barristers are usually self-employed although there are an increasing number who are employed directly by large organisations and some who work in law centres. Barristers can now work for firms of solicitors. Until recently, it was not normally possible for members of the public to go to a barrister direct. Barristers were, and still are, normally accessed through a solicitor. However, the Bar Council has relaxed its rules relating to direct access and there are now three routes to accessing a barrister.

The first is professional client access, where a number of people can instruct barristers on behalf of clients or as a fellow professional. This usually means solicitors, but includes many overseas lawyers.

The second is public access, where members of the public and commercial and non-commercial organisations are now able to instruct barristers directly on most civil matters. This might be legal advice or involve drafting a document such as a will. Barristers do not have to accept any public access instructions. This is an exception to the 'cab-rank rule', which is that, subject to having the necessary expertise, a barrister must accept any brief or instructions and act for anyone. However, barristers who are willing in principle to accept public access instructions must observe a non-discrimination rule.

Finally, there are licensed access organisations that are suitable to instruct barristers, because they have expertise in particular areas of the law. They can apply to the Bar Council to be licensed to instruct barristers directly in those areas. Typical examples of those with licensed access are a firm of clinical negligence insurers and a financial services company.

Barristers are specialists, yet have a varied work load, including drafting documents and giving legal opinions. Barristers specialising in criminal law are likely to spend a great deal of time in court, whereas civil practitioners will probably attend court less often. Now that civil procedure encourages the use of alternative methods of dispute resolution, barristers may find that some time is spent in preparing and advising on this. Similarly, an increasing amount of time is spent in tribunals, but the vast majority of time is spent drafting documents and giving opinions as to the best way to progress a legal problem. For many barristers, much of their work is preparing for and then appearing in court. The key benefit of the barrister is that he is independent and objective and trained to advise clients on the strengths as well as the weaknesses of their case.

Key terms

Barristers' clerk: the person (who may be one of a team) responsible for running the business activities and administration of a barristers' chambers.

A typical day of a barrister

I work long hours, often up to 10–12 hours per day. There is a great deal of court work in property litigation and I usually attend court 3 or 4 times each week for interim hearings and trials. When not in court, I am usually preparing for hearings, drafting pleadings or advising on property disputes.

www.barcouncil.org.uk

Background of barristers

Barristers are the smaller branch of the legal profession. The breakdown of the profession shows that it is male dominated and largely white.

Table 7.1 *Bar statistics as at December 2006 (figures for 2005 in brackets)*

Called to the Bar

Total 1640 (1476)	Men 48.4% (51.1%)	Women 51.6% (48.9%)	UK 1,196 (1,091)

Pupillage (to July 2006)

Total 552 (527)	Men 48% (52.4%)	Women 52% (47.6%)	Ethnic Minority 15.3% (16.9%)

Practising Bar – Self-Employed and Employed

Total 14,890 (14,623)	Men 66.6% (67.1%)	Women 33.4% (32.9%)	Ethnic Minority 11.2% (11%)

Self-Employed Bar

Total 12,034 (11,818)	Men 69.6% (70%)	Women 30.4% (30%)	Ethnic Minority 10.4% (10.2%)

Employed Bar

Total 2856 (2805)	Men 53.9% (54.7%)	Women 46.1% (45.3%)	Ethnic Minority 15.1% (14.9%)

www.barcouncil.org.uk

Key terms

Solicitor: a legal professional who advises clients about the law, and acts on behalf of clients in legal matters.

Solicitors

The usual first port of call when someone recognises that he needs legal advice is to contact a solicitor. **Solicitors** are the general practitioners of the legal world, dealing with all kinds of legal problems. Solicitors are readily available within geographical reach of most people. Most solicitors are in private practice, working in firms ranging in size from those with hundreds of staff to a small office in the high street as sole practitioners (one person working on their own in their own business), and in firms of every size in between. Solicitors, unlike barristers, can form partnerships. The sole practitioner has chosen not to work in a partnership, but still may employ other solicitors or legal executives. Other solicitors have jobs in local government, law centres, the civil service, commerce and industry.

Qualification

There are three parts to becoming a solicitor: the academic training, which gives the fundamentals of legal knowledge; the vocational training, which provides the practitioner fundamentals; and the training contract. There are three starting points to becoming a solicitor, and each of these ways has a different form of academic training.

The first starting point is the law graduate route, which requires a person to complete successfully a qualifying law degree. The content of a qualifying law degree is set out in the Joint Statement on Qualifying Law Degrees prepared jointly by the **Law Society** and the Bar Council under the Courts and Legal Services Act 1990. However, to qualify as a solicitor, a person must achieve the required pass mark for each of the foundations of legal knowledge subjects. This is 40 per cent, regardless of the pass mark set by the educational institution itself. It should also be noted that the degree remains valid for seven years, after which it becomes stale. This is to ensure that solicitors have up-to-date basic legal knowledge.

The second is the non-law graduate route, in which a student graduates from a non-law degree course and then completes a Common Professional Examination (CPE) course or a Graduate Diploma in Law (GDL) course. This, like the first starting point, is exactly the same as for becoming a barrister.

The final route has different regulations for those who are non-graduates and those who are members of the **Institute of Legal Executives (ILEX)**. This route is not available for a person who wishes to become a barrister. A person who is a non-graduate may be able to undertake a Common Professional Examination (CPE) course or a Graduate Diploma in Law (GDL) course if that person is a mature student or holds certain other academic or vocational qualifications. A mature student must be over 25 years of age and have considerable experience in a suitable area of work and a good general education. Acceptance is at the discretion of the Law Society. This will also apply to people who hold a degree from outside the United Kingdom.

The second non-graduate route is the ILEX route. In this route, the person must pass equivalent examinations in the foundations of legal knowledge and a further legal subject. Provided that the person is an ILEX Member or Fellow, these examinations can be taken within the ILEX framework. This route may also exempt an ILEX member who wants to become a solicitor from needing to undertake a training contract.

The second part is the vocational training, which is common to all those seeking to qualify as a solicitor, whichever route they started from. This is the Legal Practice Course, which provides the professional training for a solicitor. The main purpose of the course is to learn how to apply the law to the needs of clients. At the end of the Legal Practice Course, a trainee solicitor will be able to enter a training contract with the necessary knowledge and skills to undertake appropriate tasks under proper supervision during the training contract. The course includes legal knowledge, skills and ethics.

The Legal Practice Course has some compulsory areas of study: Business Law and Practice; Property Law and Practice; and Civil and Criminal Litigation. There are also topics known as pervasives, which appear throughout the course at appropriate times. These focus on Probate and Administration, Professional Conduct and Client Care and Financial Services, Revenue Law and Solicitors' and Business Accounts, EU Law and Human Rights. There are also some optional, or elective, topics, which vary depending on the potential solicitor's interests and the specialisms of the institution offering the course. The skills needed to be a solicitor are also part of the course and include practical legal research, writing and drafting documents, advocacy and interviewing. The course can be taken on a full- or part-time basis with a number of providers across England and Wales.

Key terms

Law Society: the representative body for solicitors in England and Wales.

Institute of Legal Executives ILEX: the Institute of Legal Executives is the professional body representing legal executives.

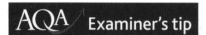

Examiner's tip

Make sure you are quite clear about the different routes to qualification: candidates often confuse the Common Professional Examination, the Graduate Diploma in Law and the Legal Practice Course.

■ Key terms

Training contract: a period of practice-based training for a trainee solicitor.

Solicitors Regulation Authority: the independent regulatory body for solicitors.

Examiner's tip

Make sure you can distinguish training from a training contract.

The final part is the **training contract**. The training contract is a period of practice-based training. The idea is that the trainee will gain practical training under supervision, and learn to apply a range of skills through working in a solicitor's office or the legal department of another organisation. As with a barrister's pupillage, trainees are paid with minimum amounts set. This is normally two years of full-time work, but can be part-time over a longer period.

On a training contract, the trainee solicitor will work in at least three areas of law, such as personal injury law, conveyancing, company law, environmental law or criminal litigation. The areas will depend on the nature of the firm or organisation and the interests of the trainee. Skills are developed through working on clients' cases, although with close supervision. The trainees' work will be regularly reviewed and as time goes on the trainee will deal with clients and learn to handle cases without supervision.

On completion of these three parts to the training, the trainee will be admitted as a solicitor and will get his/her practising certificate. This licence to work as a solicitor must be renewed annually.

Training

Solicitors, as with most professions, have a requirement for continuing professional development to be undertaken. This is designed to make sure that the solicitor is up to date with law and other matters essential for his/her work. The **Solicitors Regulation Authority** requires that all solicitors complete at least 16 hours of continuing professional development activities per year. These activities might be a tax law update, a study of the latest anti-money-laundering regulations or the solicitors' new code of conduct. In addition, new solicitors must complete the Law Society's Management Course Stage 1 by the end of their third year in practice. This is a one-day course that deals with basic aspects of management that are essential to a solicitor.

Work

Solicitors work in a range of roles and areas. The vast majority of solicitors (over 68,000) work in private practice, that is, a firm of solicitors such as you see on the high street. These range from sole practitioners to multinational firms with hundreds of partners and offices across the world. Most solicitors in private practice work with individual clients: the general public and local businesses.

A solicitor in a large firm will usually carry out work that is quite specialised. By contrast, a solicitor in a small firm may be involved in a great range of activities. Solicitors deal with a vast range of legal problems such as helping to buy and sell property, personal injury claims, advising on matrimonial problems such as divorce, or financial disputes between partners and immigration problems. They also represent people in court or instruct a barrister to represent them.

Solicitors do more work in court than is often imagined. In civil matters they represent their clients at most interlocutory hearings, that is, hearings before trial. They also usually appear in court in enforcement proceedings, such as repossession cases. In criminal cases, they often represent their client in the Magistrates' Court: indeed, this is a typical function of the duty solicitor, who will be the representative who usually makes a defendant's first bail application.

Businesses need help and advice in areas such as employment law, contracts and property leases. Bigger clients may be involved in company mergers and acquisitions. Some firms of solicitors have offices overseas which may involve advising local clients on English, EU or foreign law, or representing a UK person or business abroad.

This vast range of work is affected by the public perception of what amounts to a legal matter that a solicitor should be dealing with. For example, if a person has a problem with the Inland Revenue, a decision has to be made whether to go to a solicitor, an accountant or other adviser.

Other solicitors work directly for large businesses such as banks and multi-national companies. Others work for local authorities or central government. Others work for the Court Service, the Crown Prosecution Service, as a court clerk, for a charity, the armed forces or in a law centre.

Background of solicitors

There are approximately ten times as many solicitors as there are barristers, although approximately 20 per cent of them do not currently hold a practising certificate. Those who do not hold a practising certificate are still qualified solicitors, but are not at the time authorised to act as a solicitor. This could be as a result of a career change or a career break. There has been a rapid growth in the number of solicitors over recent years, with an even greater rise in the proportion of female solicitors and those from ethnic minorities. This is much the same as the changes in barristers.

Table 7.2 *Number and percentage of solicitors at 31 July 2006*

Male	74,098	56.4%
Female	57,249	43.6%
Total	131,347	100.0%

www.lawsociety.org.uk

Approximately 10 per cent of solicitors belong to minority ethnic groups, although many of them are resident outside the UK. However, there are a much higher proportion of solicitors from minority ethnic groups where the population as a whole has a high proportion of residents belonging to ethnic minorities. For example, in Central and South Middlesex areas, over a quarter of solicitors come from ethnic minorities.

The average age of solicitors has reduced with the rapid growth of the profession. At 31 July 2006 the average age of male solicitors was 43, and of females 37. The gender balance of solicitors has also been changing over recent years and the view that solicitors are all white and male should now be dispelled.

Legal executives

Legal executives are members of ILEX, which was set up in 1963 with the support of the Law Society. The aim was to provide a professional body recognising the work done by non-solicitors working in a solicitors' office. Legal executives are qualified lawyers specialising in a particular area of law and have at least five years experience of working under the supervision of a solicitor. There are currently around 22,000 legal executives who are members of ILEX. Their status as professionals is recognised throughout the legal profession and the courts. Whilst their

AQA Examiner's tip

Use extracts from articles and contacts with solicitors and barristers to get real examples of the work each does.

■ Key terms

Legal executive: a qualified lawyer who specialises in a particular area of law but is not a solicitor or barrister.

right to appear in court is limited, Fellows of ILEX with more than four years' post-qualification experience are equated with similarly experienced solicitors in terms of assessment of costs in court cases.

Qualification

Most trainee legal executives combine study for the ILEX qualification with practical experience of working in a law firm or legal department, usually being given day release from work to study. There are many starting points for qualifying as a legal executive, the routes varying depending on existing qualification. The usual minimum is four GCSEs at grade C or above, including English language.

There are three types of membership. The first is Student Membership, where academic training is started by taking a series of courses covering a range of the areas of law and legal practice encountered in the legal profession. The second type is Membership. Students apply for enrolment into this grade of ILEX on successful completion of both parts of the ILEX Professional Qualification in Law. This takes on average four years' part-time study to complete. Finally, there is Fellowship. To achieve the full qualification of Fellow, Members of ILEX must have five years' qualifying employment under the supervision of a solicitor, including a minimum of two years after passing all the examinations.

Training

For all ILEX Fellows, continuing professional development is compulsory. Systematic maintenance, improvement and extension of professional and legal skills and personal qualities are required on a continuing basis. Each year a Fellow is required to complete a minimum of 12 hours' continuing professional development, rising to 16 hours from 2008. Members will also be required to undertake continuing professional development: six hours from 2007 and eight hours from 2008. At least half of the requirement must be met through events relating to their specialist area of work. Failure to comply with these requirements is a breach of ILEX regulations and may result in disciplinary action.

Work

Legal executives specialise in a particular area of law such as conveyancing, wills, matrimonial matters or general litigation. Their day-to-day work is similar to that of a solicitor earning fees for the firm of solicitors for whom they work. Quite often all the work on a particular matter will be handled by a legal executive rather than a solicitor. Legal executives are usually expert in one field of work and concentrate exclusively on that type of work.

Activities

1 Outline how both a barrister and a solicitor are trained and become qualified.

2 Compare the work of a solicitor, a barrister and a legal executive.

Activity

Read the article from *The Times* set out here and discuss the points raised in the article about the life of a solicitor.

All take and no give? I'm afraid I'm off

Edward Fennell

The Law Society is worried about the high turnover of recently qualified staff, so why are so many people voting with their feet?

When people cease liking their jobs – and there is the prospect of another, better job elsewhere – they leave. And that is what has been happening at scores of large law firms. Young lawyers have been leaving in droves.

Getting hold of exact details is not easy. Understandably, individual firms are reluctant to talk about their figures. Nonetheless, just how serious the problem is was revealed by the most recent Pricewaterhouse Coopers (PWC) annual law firm survey. This announced that 'staff turnover levels are high, averaging 20 per cent for some top 25 firms. The turnover is highest in London and in the 3 to 5 years' postqualification experience [PQE] category. There are undoubtedly work-life balance issues here.'

Analyse the details of the survey and the findings are revealing – maybe even shocking. For example, at the three to five years' PQE stage almost half the top 25 firms had a turnover of between 16 and 20 per cent. More spectacularly, at almost one in five firms the turnover rate was more than 30 per cent. Even among the one to three-year PQE lawyers the turnover was between 26 and 30 per cent at a quarter of firms.

The indications are that turnover tends to be highest where younger lawyers have fewer flexible benefits and where maternity and childcare rights are stripped down to the minimum. As to sabbaticals? Forget it.

'The lack of flexibility in terms of both benefits and work arrangements has, perhaps, contributed towards firms suffering from high staff turnover,' PWC commented, adding archly that 'they may need to give further consideration to the value that employees put on flexibility in the workplace.'

It was anxieties about the scale of departures from firms that prompted in part the Law Society to undertake its Quality of Life investigation (lawsociety.org. uk/newsandevents/news/majorcampaigns/view). As it said when the programme was announced: 'The Law Society has launched a project on staff retention and job satisfaction aiming to drive forward the thinking on this subject through research and a sharing of experience. We'll cover issues such as the working practices that affect employees' decisions to stay or move on, the extent to which firms should adapt to fit with employees' life choices and the impact on the firms and employees that decide to adopt different working practices.' In defence of the employers, the society went on to claim that firms are starting to 'address urgently' issues of staff retention — not least because it is vital to their growth, innovation and competitiveness. 'Retaining staff and recruiting at mid-career level are becoming increasingly difficult. The pool of high-quality talent is not growing. In the services sector, businesses rely on the quality of their people. Turnover costs are around £150,000 for every £50,000 of salary.'

While some staff turnover is inevitable, there is clearly an emerging consensus that it has reached a worryingly high level. Firms are losing not merely the also-rans but, potentially, very able people in whom they have invested heavily.

Robert Sully, who works for Cripps Harries Hall in Tunbridge Wells, is typical of those who got away. He comes across as very bright, articulate, able and ambitious. Yet after six years of hard toil he left a well-known City name almost entirely because of work-life balance reasons. 'There was a macho atmosphere that came from the partners,' he says. 'I was doing well in the firm and that, maybe, was my downfall. I was staying very late night after night and the partners' attitude was, "So, what's the problem?" Personally I can't see how it's a good thing to have tired young lawyers working on a deal, but that was the general atmosphere. It's not so much the policies within the firms that matter but their culture.'

With a child on the way Sully decided that the time had come to leave the City but build on his experience in a positive way. He now works reasonable hours, lives five minutes from the office and does jobs that are comparable to his previous City life. 'The difference is,' he says, 'that if you are still working here at 9 o'clock at night people ask what's the matter with you.'

Source: The Law Society

The Times, *8 May 2007*

You should now be able to:

- discuss the qualification, training and work of different branches of the legal profession

- take an overview of the make-up of the different branches of the legal profession

- attempt past paper questions on the legal profession.

💡 2 Funding and other sources of legal advice

The law is open to everyone, but legal services can cost a great deal of money. Most people will need to use legal services at some time in their life, yet not everyone will be able to afford the legal services they need. The purpose of this topic is to investigate the sources that are available, and then, in the next topic, be able to evaluate the provision of legal services.

Litigation, the threat of and the process of taking legal action against another person or organisation in a dispute, can be extremely expensive. A person is primarily responsible for paying his lawyer's costs resulting from the litigation. It is often the case that the losing party will pay for the winning party's costs and expenses of pursuing the claim. However, that may not amount to all the legal fees and expenses, so the winner will still have a bill to pay. It is difficult to estimate the costs in advance, as there are many variables. For example, expert evidence might be required, the defendant may fight to have his day in court when the matter could have been settled early, or unexpected legal issues might arise.

These are questions that cannot be answered when a solicitor is first instructed. However, a good solicitor will know the probable or possible outcomes of the case and will explain the possible liability for paying the legal costs and will discuss the funding options.

What might appear to be a simple case can go on for a long time at great expense. In *Hall* v *Simons* (2000), one of the cases was a relatively straightforward divorce case, which had gone wrong and the client argued the solicitor had been negligent. The extract set out below shows the length of time, and therefore cost, likely to be involved in legal disputes.

Cockbone v Atkinson, Dacre and Slack

The marriage between Mr Clive Cockbone ('the Husband') and his wife, Mrs Patricia Cockbone ('the Wife'), was dissolved by a decree absolute pronounced on 25 September 1989, leaving outstanding the Wife's claim for ancillary relief. (He and the Wife were married in August 1958. They had five children. The Wife left the farm in February 1988.) In connection with that claim, on 20th June 1991, the Husband retained Atkinson, Dacre and Slack ('the Solicitors') to act for him.

The claim was settled at the Harrogate county court on 22nd August 1991 on terms that the Husband should pay £250,000 to the Wife by instalments, the unpaid part being secured on his farm in the meantime. An order to that effect was made, pursuant to s33A Matrimonial Causes Act 1973, by District Judge Grills on the same day. On 10th April 1992 the Husband, appearing in person, was refused leave to appeal from that order. In May and June 1995 the Husband started proceedings in the Leeds county court against, amongst others, the Solicitors claiming damages for negligent handling of his case, and for the use of undue pressure and blackmail inducing him to enter into the settlement and to consent to the order. On 30th October 1997 His Honour Judge McGonigal, sitting as a deputy judge of the Queen's Bench Division, struck out the Husband's claim against the Solicitors on the grounds that they were immune from suit in respect of their actions and advice leading to the settlement on 22nd August 1991. This is an appeal of the Husband from that order.

www.bailii.org

Note the length of time that a straightforward case took to be finally resolved and how that, even after the divorce was dealt with, there were still issues about the cost of the whole episode.

Private funding

There are three main ways of paying for your own legal services. The first is paying the bill out of your own resources, using your own money. The second way is when an insurance company will pay the bill. It is quite common to have legal expenses insurance with your house and contents insurance or car insurance. The final way is a conditional fee agreement. Most personal injuries claims are made using this agreement with your solicitor.

Own resources

This is what is done when you use a solicitor to make a will or undertake the conveyancing when buying or selling a house. Most individuals will not be able to afford to do this for more complex or lengthy legal work. Businesses have more need to pay directly for legal work, as most successful businesses have worked out that it makes better financial sense to seek advice first rather than have lawyers sort a problem out later. The solicitor's work is charged to the client at an hourly rate, plus expenses such as court fees. The hourly rate will vary with the location of the solicitors – central London is usually most expensive – and the level of seniority and expertise of the solicitor. Solicitors' costs in the Guide to Summary Assessment of Costs used by the courts reflect this and vary, as at January 2007, from up to £380 per hour for solicitors with over eight years' post-qualification experience, including at least eight years' litigation experience, working in Central London, to £95 per hour for trainee solicitors, paralegals and fee earners of equivalent experience working in areas where overheads are lower, such as Teesside or Devon. Some work, such as conveyancing or making a will, may be done for a fixed cost.

These sums soon make a solicitor's bill quite large. As has been seen in the extract above relating to *Cockbone* v *Atkinson, Dacre and Slack*, litigation can drag on at potentially great cost. In *Hall* v *Simons* (2000), the solicitors' bill that was unpaid had been sent in 1988 for about £10,500, and related to a building dispute where the sums involved totalled a little over £20,000.

Insurance

Insurance is the first part of risk-sharing using a legal expense insurer. There are two types of policy, a 'before the event policy' and an 'after the event policy'. A **'before the event policy'** is an insurance policy which can be taken out, usually with an annual premium, to provide cover for a possible future legal problem. This is often part of a home contents or car insurance policy. However, some of these policies are limited in what they cover and may include restrictions on choice of solicitor, the hourly rates that will be paid and other related expenses.

Conditional fees

This is effectively risk-sharing with lawyers. This is part of the change to the funding arrangements set up by the Courts and Legal Services Act 1990, to combat the huge cost of public legal funding. Before these changes, solicitors were not allowed to offer clients any risk-sharing arrangement. However, there are now a number of types available. Around 2.5 million people in the UK suffer accidental injuries every year.

Public funding through Legal Aid for these costs was withdrawn in 2000, leaving these people with the option of paying for legal action themselves or risk sharing in some way.

The first type of risk sharing with lawyers is a **conditional fee agreement**. This is often known, inaccurately, as a 'no win, no fee' arrangement. This is where the solicitor makes no charge if the case is lost. However, the disbursements (the costs incurred by the solicitor on behalf of the client such as court fees, or fees for medical reports) and the opponents' legal charges will still have to be paid. If the case succeeds, the solicitor charges a 'success fee' on top of the normal hourly rate. The loser may be ordered to pay at least part of these charges, including the success fee. Insurance is normally taken out at the client's expense to cover this risk with an 'after the event' policy.

An '**after the event policy**' is designed help to cover the cost of litigation once the dispute has arisen. If the premium is affordable, then it can provide some peace of mind against the possibility of the total litigation costs if you lose the case. There are also potential limitations to the amount payable under this type of policy. With some insurance policies, the client must pay the solicitor's bill and then reclaim the money from the insurance company, which can be difficult for some people.

The second is a contingency fee arrangement. Again, a person is not charged if he or she loses, but the fee, if he or she is successful, is a percentage of what is recovered. However, this arrangement cannot be used for cases which require court proceedings.

There are also other possible arrangements such as a discount conditional fee where an hourly rate is agreed as being payable if the case is won but the rate is reduced if the outcome is unsuccessful. Such an agreement could also provide for a success fee.

State funding

Community Legal Service

People often need legal advice, for example, in matters such as relationship breakdown, asylum and immigration, and community care issues. Sometimes it is enough to provide information leaflets or to direct people to other services, such as debt counselling or mediation. The first part is the information available in the leaflets and on the website. The **Community Legal Service** (www.clsdirect.org.uk) provides funds direct to solicitors and to other organisations such as the Citizens Advice Bureau. These organisations provide funds and promote civil legal services. This is provided in a number of categories from general information to advice and representation. These categories are known collectively as legal aid.

The most usual starting point is **Legal Help**. It allows people with a low income and few savings to get free legal advice and help from a solicitor or an experienced legal adviser. The solicitor or adviser must have a contract with the Legal Services Commission. It is designed to cover everything up to and including the preparation of a case to go to court. It can also cover the costs of mediation in non-family cases. If money is won as a result of the case, that money must, in most cases, first be used to pay the solicitors' costs. This is known as the statutory charge.

Help at Court then provides funding for a solicitor or adviser to represent a person in court. This might be used in representing someone who is being sued for a debt or who is defending eviction proceedings. Again, there are financial criteria to meet if a person is to get this assistance, just as there are criteria about the case itself: it must be a cost-effective method of dealing with the matter.

Family cases have always taken a large part of public legal funding. To ensure that family matters are dealt with as effectively and efficiently as possible, there are three types of funding available, all of which have financial criteria. The first is General Family Help, which covers preparation of a case to go to court and general advice on any legal problems related to a family matter. It also covers the costs of starting legal action and legal representation to get a court order and sort out arrangements following the order.

Whilst General Family Help can cover negotiations in family disputes where there is no mediation already happening, many family disputes are resolved by mediation. This might be about arrangements for contact with children. Legal aid for mediation in a family dispute is called Family Mediation and is used to help pay for the costs of the mediator.

The final part of legal aid for family matters is Help with Mediation. This would be used to help pay for drawing up the agreement reached between the parties or following up the agreement that has been made.

For other cases that a person might need to bring to court, there is Legal Representation. This is again subject to financial criteria, and the case must be one that the Legal Services Commission considers it reasonable to fund. It is also subject to the statutory charge. Funding can also be stopped if the solicitor involved does not think the case is strong enough. Types of cases that can be funded include consumer cases such as claiming against the seller of faulty goods, or an appeal to the Employment Appeal Tribunal (but not for representation at an Employment Tribunal). Legal Representation will not usually pay for the costs of taking a personal injury case to court, as this is covered by conditional fee agreements.

There is also Controlled Legal Representation, which is only representation before a Mental Health Review Tribunal or an Asylum and Immigration Tribunal. In many cases there are no qualifying criteria, financial or other.

The only other legal aid relates to criminal cases and is dealt with by the Criminal Defence Service.

Criminal Defence Service

Legal aid in criminal cases is organised by the **Criminal Defence Service**. There are three different types of help: free legal advice at the police station; advice and assistance before charge; and help with representation at court.

Free legal advice at the police station is the right to free independent legal advice from a duty solicitor. This has no financial or other criteria attached. However, this advice is not necessarily face-to-face, and may well be telephone advice. A person can also choose his own solicitor and the advice will be free if they have a contract with the Criminal Defence Service. On arrest, a person is given an information sheet explaining how to get legal help.

Even where a person has not been charged with an offence, he may need advice and assistance. This is however subject to financial criteria.

Help with representation in court comes in three forms. The first is a Representation Order. This applies in the Magistrates' Court and is subject to complex financial criteria, except for those under 16 or claiming most benefits, as well as a merits test: it must be in the interests

AQA Examiner's tip

When looking at State funding, be clear about the differences in funding for civil and criminal cases.

■ Key terms

Criminal Defence Service: provides legal advice and representation for people under police investigation or facing criminal charges.

of justice for the accused to be represented. The interests of justice test is is a requirement of Art 6 of the European Convention on Human Rights, which states that everyone charged with a criminal offence has the right, 'if he has not sufficient means to pay for legal assistance, to be given it free when the interests of justice so require.' The criteria used for this test are:

- whether it is likely that the court will impose either a custodial sentence or one which will lead to a loss of livelihood
- whether the case involves substantial questions of law or evidence of a complex or difficult nature
- whether the accused is unable to understand the proceedings or state their own case because of, for example, age, inadequate knowledge of English, or illness
- whether it is in the interests of someone other than the accused that the accused be legally represented
- whether the defence to be put forward is frivolous
- whether the accused has been remanded in custody pending the trial.

The recently introduced means test has not been well received by many, as it is seen to be in conflict with the right to a fair trial.

There are no financial conditions to getting a Representation Order in the Crown Court. However, the interests of justice test must be passed. This is unlikely for very minor offences.

The second type of legal aid is Advocacy Assistance. This covers the costs of a solicitor preparing a case and initial representation in certain cases such as anti-social behaviour orders or non-payment of council tax. Again there are no financial criteria to be met.

Finally there is free advice and representation at the Magistrates' Court from the duty solicitor, although this is not available for very minor cases. However, one can only use the services of the Duty Solicitor at one hearing – usually the first hearing – and not at a contested trial, so a Representation Order would then be needed.

Other sources of legal advice

Citizens Advice Bureau

The Citizens Advice Bureau provides legal advice as part of its service. Whilst the Citizens Advice Bureau is a charity, it gains a substantial amount of income from its contracts with the Legal Services Commission to provide legal advice to people with debt, welfare benefits, housing, employment and immigration issues. The advice it gives is free, and where the problem requires further action, appropriate agencies or solicitors are contacted. Many bureaux work with local solicitors firms, giving access to over 1,000 specialist solicitors, working on a pro bono basis, that is, without charge. Citizens Advice are also looking at new ways of delivering legal advice.

Law centres

Law centres have existed since the early 1970s. They are usually in less affluent areas, usually in large cities with poor public services. There are just over 60 law centres throughout the UK (excluding Scotland). They are designed to help people access the legal system, especially those who would find it hard to do so. A law centre may take up a case where legal aid is not available and are often open outside normal office hours.

Law centres specialise in social welfare law. This includes areas such as welfare rights, immigration and asylum, housing and employment rights. They are funded by a variety of sources. They hold contracts with the Legal Services Commission to provide casework services and receive grant aid from local councils. They employ solicitors, barristers, legal advisers and community workers. Many lawyers volunteer to help in their nearest law centre as part of pro bono work.

The concept behind law centres is being developed, with Gateshead Community Legal Advice Centre being the first in a series of new networks and centres being established for people with the greatest need of legal and advice services. This is a joint service between Gateshead Citizens Advice Bureau and Gateshead Law Centre, and provides integrated services from basic advice to representation at court to help people with social welfare and family legal problems. This particular project was set up because the Legal Services Research Centre's national civil law and social justice survey found that:

- civil justice problems lead to further problems
- those experiencing the most problems were likely to be socially excluded
- only about half of those who have problems seek advice
- one in seven people who try to get advice fails to do so, mainly because the adviser couldn't help
- the more times a person gets referred on, the less likely they are to continue seeking advice.

The topic of funding and access to justice will be useful for the 'concepts of law' section in Unit 4 of the A2 specification.

Other sources

Legal advice can sometimes be obtained from solicitors offering a fixed fee or free interview at a special session after hours, or on a Saturday morning. Advice is usually available from a person's trade union, not just on employment law matters. There is also legal expenses insurance either through a specialist policy, home insurance, car insurance or a motoring organisation. There is often free advice in the media; it often appears in newspapers printing articles on consumer affairs.

 Activities

1 Paveen has been injured in an accident. Explain from whom she could get advice about a possible claim for damages and how she might be able to pay for that advice.

2 Outline the legal aid available to Alan, who has been arrested for a serious criminal offence.

You should now be able to:

- understand the funding of legal services for an individual
- understand the sources of legal advice
- attempt past paper questions on funding and other sources of advice.

In this topic you will learn how to:

■ evaluate the legal profession

■ evaluate legal funding

■ evaluate sources of advice.

💡 3 Evaluation of the legal profession, funding and other sources of advice

The provision of legal services is an issue that most people do not consider until they find that they have an obvious need for help from a lawyer. The person needing help then has to find and choose someone to help them. This is often done without any guidance as to the quality of the help or the relative merits of different providers. However, the essential principles relating to the provision of legal services have not changed since they were stated in the 1979 Royal Commission on Legal Services as:

1 There should be equal access to the courts.

2 Equal access demands adequate legal services.

3 Financial assistance out of public funds should be available for every individual who, without it, would suffer an undue financial burden in properly pursuing or defending his rights.

4 The standard of legal services should be the same irrespective of whether or not provided at the public expense.

5 A free choice of lawyer should be available to each individual.

These principles need to take into account the fact that there is an unmet need for legal services, arising from a number of factors:

■ There has been the creation of new categories of legal rights without the funding to enforce them: this relates in particular to social welfare law.

■ People do not recognise their problem is a legal one that can be dealt with by a lawyer: an example of this is debt.

■ There is still poverty in the UK, and poorer people often have a fear of fees and bills.

■ There is general ignorance of funding methods available, despite the increase in advertising by the legal profession and other organisations such as accident helplines.

■ There may be fear of authority and unfamiliarity with the surroundings: lawyers are equated by many with the courts and the police and generally give a feeling of unease to many.

■ Unfamiliar language is used, that is, legal jargon and technical terms.

■ Lawyers may be inaccessible: this includes office hours usually matching times when people are at work.

■ Lawyers in the area may be unavailable: this does not just affect rural areas but inner cities too. There are, for example, perhaps 20 times more lawyers in Bournemouth than in the Huyton district of Liverpool.

■ Solicitors' training emphasises the business side of being a solicitor, so the emphasis is on the most lucrative business, not that which is unprofitable.

These general points need to be borne in mind when looking at specific points made below.

Evaluation of the legal profession

The evaluation of the legal profession is largely concerned with an analysis of how the profession could be improved from the point of view of the user. Much of the criticism that has been levelled at the legal profession has had to be put on hold as the effect of recent changes is considered.

AQA Examiner's tip

The general principles set out at the start of this topic can be used as a basis for evaluation of the legal profession and funding of legal services.

The work lawyers do

The large rise in the numbers of solicitors has led to a need for more work. All firms of solicitors face more competition from: each other; accountants for tax work; licensed conveyancers; independent will-makers; banks and building societies; and debt-collecting companies. Some types of work are more profitable than others, for example, business and commercial affairs, commercial property and probate, wills and trusts are most frequently considered to be profitable, whilst welfare benefits was regarded as the least profitable and indeed often loss-making. As solicitors, unlike barristers, do not follow the cab rank rule, they can cherry-pick the work they do, leaving some people without access to a lawyer. This situation is resolved where there is a law centre which specialises in welfare work and in other areas of low profitability.

Pay

The public perception of lawyers is that they are very well paid. The reports of million-pound earnings are true, but very rare. The average earnings of all solicitors in 2005 was £48,000 per annum. For example an assistant solicitor's average earnings in the North East of England was just under £22,000: less than many teachers. There are even more extreme variations for barristers. As a barrister is self-employed, he may earn nothing, yet have overheads for his place in chambers. The late George Carman QC was fond of saying that it took him five years at the Bar to earn as much as a Manchester bus driver without overtime.

Legal aid rates are arguably very low, yet in 2005–2006 barrister Balbir Singh was paid over £1.1m from legal aid. Another big earner is Jim Sturman QC, who said:

> When you aren't in court, you earn nothing and when you are you earn very little. In 1983 I was very grateful to go to the magistrates' court for £35. People sometimes go there now for £20. Take off travel, expenses and clerks' fees and it's very hard to make a living. I carried an overdraft for 20 years. Now, young barristers are paid uneconomic rates. I pay my plumber £90 an hour, yet a barrister can be paid £45 for hanging around all day.

http://business.timesonline.co.uk

A proposed fixed fee structure for legal aid cases was due to go ahead in October 2007, but the High Court decided that the method of implementing the reform breached EU rules. This leads to uncertainty as to implementation and uncertainty in the professions to the possible detriment of those needing to use legal aid.

From the consumer point of view, the high cost of lawyers is seen as a deterrent to using the law. The fact that some lawyers are very highly paid may also give the consumer a feeling that using the law is not for them, as they feel no connection with the lawyer and would rather avoid the situation.

Getting started

Combined with servicing the debt inevitably accumulated through university, the financial outlook for many potential lawyers is as poor as it was when the late George Carman QC started. In many cases the only way to progress is to take out more loans, even though there is no guarantee of success. For example, almost two-thirds of bar vocational course students never even get a pupillage. Whilst pay is made during pupillage or a training contract, there is no guarantee of work after qualification. For barristers, only one-third of pupils find a tenancy.

Control of the legal profession

Barristers had traditionally been immune from liability for poor work in court, but with limited protection for work done out of court. This immunity was effectively removed in the case of **Hall v Simons (2000)**, where the House of Lords decided that there was no good reason to treat solicitors or barristers any differently to other professionals with respect to liability in negligence.

However, in **Moy v Pettman Smith (2005)**, the House of Lords clearly gave a more lenient approach to barristers and other advocates working under pressure at the court door. In that case, solicitors Pettman Smith were instructed by Mr Moy to bring a clinical negligence action against a Health Authority following treatment of his broken leg. The solicitors failed to obtain and serve a key medical report within time, and a pre-trial application to admit it was refused. On the morning of the trial Moy rejected a court-door offer of £150,000 (half the value of the claim if the disallowed evidence were admitted). Jacqueline Perry, the barrister, gave advice that she expected that permission to call the extra evidence would be given. Unfortunately, it wasn't. Moy then had to take a reduced offer of £120,000 from the Authority. He then sued the solicitors, who joined the barrister in the claim, arguing that if she had advised Moy to take the £150,000, he would have been better off by £30,000 and would have avoided a lot of extra costs. The House of Lords acknowledged that stricter and more developed standards apply for the medical profession, giving the opinion that it would be too much of a burden for advocates to spell out their reasoning for advice to clients, and so found the barrister not liable in negligence. It seems that the standard of care required is not as high as that needed in many other areas of negligence. A claimant will need to prove that the decision was 'one which no reasonably competent member of the relevant profession would have made' if the claim is to be successful.

Barristers have always been subject to discipline for their actions by their governing body, the Bar Council. The Bar Council has now removed itself from direct involvement in complaints and discipline, except in giving general advice to its member barristers. It has set up the Bar Standards Board as the independent regulatory board of the Bar Council. It is responsible for regulating barristers independently and in the public interest. Professional negligence is outside the Bar Standards Board remit, although there are clearly some areas of overlap.

There are many bodies that can help with complaints about solicitors. The first approach about poor work or charges is the solicitor himself. If that does not provide a satisfactory solution, the Legal Complaints Service is the next step. It is an independent complaints handling body, part of the Law Society, but operating independently from the Law Society. Its services are confidential and free to use, aiming to try to find a solution that is acceptable to both sides. In most cases, the Legal Complaints Service hopes to resolve the matter through conciliation.

Solicitors, like barristers, have no immunity from claims for professional negligence although, again like barristers, they may have some protection for courtroom work, in that the standard of care may not be very high in this area of work. This can be seen from the case of *Moy v Pettman Smith* (2005), discussed earlier.

Where individual solicitors have not acted in the manner required, the Solicitors Regulation Authority may become involved. It is part of the

---

■ Key cases

Hall v Simons (2000): solicitors and barristers can be sued for professional negligence just like any other professional.

Moy v Pettman Smith (2005): in a claim for negligent advice given at the courtroom door, a barrister could be found negligent, but only in exceptional cases.

Law Society, but operates independently. Its purpose is to protect the public by ensuring that solicitors meet high standards and by acting when risks are identified. The standards are set out in the Solicitors' Code of Conduct 2007.

For legal executives, ILEX can take disciplinary action against members who breach the Code of Conduct or its rules, or whose behaviour is unbefitting membership of ILEX. This is very similar to the principles behind solicitors and barristers' disciplinary process. ILEX has the power to exclude a person from membership or take less severe action such as a reprimand or a fine. Usually, the first point of contact for poor work by a legal executive is the firm of solicitors or organisation he works for.

Despite all these safeguards, it is still a daunting task to take action against a member of the legal profession where the work seems to be unsatisfactory. Whilst there is no immunity from legal action, it is sometimes suggested that the standard required of the legal profession is, on occasions, lower than that of some other professions.

> **AQA Examiner's tip**
>
> When answering evaluation questions, make sure you use examples to prove the point you are making.

Evaluation of legal funding

Cost

Legal aid in England and Wales currently costs more than £2 billion per annum. This is nearly 50 per cent more than was spent on culture, media and sport. Successive Governments have been attempting to reduce the legal aid spending, but have only managed to contain it by reducing availability of it.

Availability

In the Select Committee on Constitutional Affairs Third Report in 2007, it was noted that legal aid suppliers had declined in numbers significantly. For example family legal aid contracts have reduced by over a third between 2000 and now, and cases starting had declined from 410,916 cases in 2000–2001 to 283,274 in 2005–2006. This represents a huge decline in access to justice for people with family problems, as firms gave up legal aid work because of the poor rates of pay, the bureaucracy and costs of administering legal aid contracts and difficulties in recruiting and retaining suitably qualified staff.

The Mental Health Lawyers Association stated to the Select Committee that 'the number of Law Society Panel Mental Health Panel Specialists has declined by close to 25 per cent since 2000, whilst those mentally unwell clients requiring representation at Mental Health Review Tribunals has risen by over 10 per cent in the same period.'

Sir Anthony Clarke, giving oral evidence to the Select Committee, expressed concern about unrepresented litigants in courts when he said:

> Actually, people with problems which give rise to civil dispute, especially in the mental health and housing fields, are extremely worthy of assistance and indeed may come from the very same families who find themselves before the criminal courts, so we are worried. In answer to your particular question, since that happened over the years there has been a big increase in litigants in person and it is very difficult for them.
>
> *www.publications.parliament.uk*

These examples of lack of availability demonstrate that there remains an unmet need for legal services and the principles relating to access to justice are not being achieved.

Conditional fee agreements

These agreements are a mix of financial and legal matters and are not always clearly understood by the non-lawyer. It is suggested that consumers are sometimes induced into signing conditional fee agreements inappropriately. Citizens Advice Bureau evidence is that the withdrawal of legal aid and the advent of conditional fee agreements has contributed to a system that involves relatively high legal costs and delays. In some cases, consumers are subjected to high-pressure sales tactics by unqualified people. Inappropriate marketing and sales practices are sometimes used, suggesting that solicitors are becoming 'ambulance chasers'.

The risks of conditional fee agreements are not always clearly explained at the outset. People are misled into thinking the system will be genuinely 'no win, no fee', but can often find that costs are hidden and unpredictable. Even the insurance against the costs of losing the case comes as a shock to some, who then finance the insurance with a high-cost loan that further erodes any compensation gained. The alternative of representing oneself in court is seen by many as impossible, so valid claims go unmade through fear and inertia.

The so-called compensation culture is focusing more people on the hope of money for nothing, rather than getting back to work after injury. Victims are not being helped to resume a normal life in both society and the workplace.

Conditional fee agreements create incentives for some solicitors to cherry-pick high value cases with high chances of success. A cab rank principle for such cases would be better, so that solicitors will not refuse to take on good small claims which may nevertheless be of great significance to the client, thus denying access to justice.

There is no effective regulation of conditional fee arrangements to provide protection on both quality of advice and costs. In particular, the activities of claims management companies seem to fall largely outside the system of regulation, yet they are increasingly the starting point of the claims process.

Other sources of advice and funding

The cost to the individual of funding legal advice varies. Much of the advice available is apparently free, for example through a trade union or a person's car insurance. In fact, this is not really free, as the cost is built into the subscription or insurance premium. However, that cost is often minimal. It is for this reason that many people have some form of legal expenses insurance attached to their car or house insurance. The disadvantage of this is that there is often a restricted choice of legal provider, and some policies limit the maximum amount payable.

You should now be able to:

- ▪ evaluate the legal profession
- ▪ evaluate legal funding
- ▪ evaluate sources of advice
- ▪ answer examination questions on the legal profession
- ▪ answer examination questions on funding of legal services and sources of advice.

Activities

1 Briefly discuss advantages and disadvantages of both private funding and of 'no win, no fee' arrangements in a civil claim.

2 Discuss in groups the extent to which the current funding of legal cases and structure of the legal profession helps achieve the principles of the provision of legal services stated in the 1979 Royal Commission on Legal Services.

8 The judiciary

Key terms

Superior judges: judges appointed to sit in the High Court and the appeal courts.

Inferior judges: all judges who are not superior judges.

Lord Chief Justice: head of the judiciary in England and Wales.

Judges

Judges perform a central function in the legal system. They have a number of different roles in both the delivery and the creation of the law. Judges can be seen as the pinnacle of the legal profession from which they are drawn. Unlike other countries, English judges are not elected and are not trained to be a judge as an alternative to starting a career as a solicitor or a barrister. This chapter will look at the selection, appointment and role of different types of judges, and provide material to help consider how well they perform. It should be noted that the AQA Law specification does not require reference to judges in Scotland or Northern Ireland, just those in England and Wales.

Types of judge

There are many types of judge and several different ways of categorising them. The most general distinction is between superior and inferior judges. **Superior judges** are those appointed to sit in the High Court and the appeal courts. Those sitting in the High Court are also known as puisne (pronounced 'puny') judges. Court of Appeal judges are also known as Senior Judges or, formally, Lords Justices of Appeal, and those sitting in the House of Lords are known as Law Lords or, formally, Lords of Appeal in Ordinary. All other judges are known as **inferior judges**. These include Circuit Judges, who are full-time judges sitting in the County Court or Crown Court, Recorders, who are part-time judges sitting in the County Court and Crown Court, and District Judges, who sit in the County Court and Magistrates' Court.

Judges can also be categorised by the court in which they sit, for example, a Crown Court Judge or a High Court Judge. They can also be categorised as either full- or part-time or even by their pay scale.

There are also specific titles that are assigned to a judge with a particular role in one of the courts, such as the Lord Chief Justice: you will have seen these titles in your study of the courts.

The Lord Chief Justice

The **Lord Chief Justice** is the head of the judiciary in England and Wales. The Constitutional Reform Act 2005 sets out his duties. It should be noted that he is not responsible for the House of Lords, as that court is a court for the whole of the United Kingdom and not just England and Wales. He has over 400 duties. Major ones include:

- representing the views of the judges to Parliament and the Government
- the provision and deployment of resources for the judiciary and the allocation of work of judges in the courts
- the welfare, training and guidance of judges
- responsibility (along with the Lord Chancellor) for the Office of Judicial Complaints, which deals with complaints about judges
- hearing important criminal, civil and family cases and many of the most important appeal cases, which helps him lead the judiciary, as he is closely involved with developments of the law

■ chairmanship of the Sentencing Guidelines Council, which aims to encourage consistency in sentencing

■ being President of the English and Welsh courts and, as such, being able to hear cases in any court in England and Wales: this means that he could hear a case in your local Magistrates' Court, if he so desired!

The Master of the Rolls

The Master of the Rolls is the title of the judge ranking immediately below the Lord Chief Justice. He is also the leading judge dealing with the civil work of the Court of Appeal and, as such, deals with the most difficult and sensitive cases. He has a number of other major responsibilities, including:

■ acting as the President of its Civil Division, which he also organises. This means he is responsible for the deployment and organisation of the work of the judges of the Division. He normally sits with two Lords Justices of Appeal, and there is occasionally a third member, such as a retired Lord Justice

■ being consulted by the Government on the civil justice system and rights of audience in the courts

■ officially authorising solicitors to practise. A solicitor is entered on the Roll of Solicitors when first qualifying to practise as a solicitor. He also deals with professional rules and regulations dealing with solicitors and appeals against rulings of the Solicitors' Disciplinary Tribunal

■ originally, being responsible for the safe-keeping of charters, patents and records of important court judgments written on parchment rolls. He still has responsibility for documents of national importance, being Chairman of the Advisory Council on Public Records and Chairman of the Royal Commission on Historical Manuscripts.

The Lords of Appeal in Ordinary

The Lords of Appeal in Ordinary are also known as the Law Lords. Each judge sitting in the House of Lords is a life peer and is therefore able to sit in the parliamentary House of Lords, although this opportunity is rarely taken except on legal matters. The 12 members of the House of Lords usually sit as a panel of five Law Lords when considering an appeal to their court. They do not have to be unanimous: indeed, there are often different views of the law and the way in which the law is to be developed. Where a different view to the majority is expressed, it is said to be a dissenting judgment. The Law Lords will automatically become judges in the new Supreme Court, which is due to come into existence in October 2009. Appointments after that date will no longer automatically confer a life peerage, which will go some way to addressing the possible conflict that exists under the doctrine of the separation of powers (see Topic 2).

Lords Justices of Appeal

The Lords Justices of Appeal sit in the Court of Appeal. They usually sit as a bench of three judges and can make a majority decision. The composition of the court for civil cases is any combination of the named Heads of Division and the Lords Justices. In criminal appeals, the three judges are Lord Chief Justice or the President of the Queen's Bench Division or one of the Lords Justices of Appeal, together with two High Court Judges or one High Court Judge and one specially nominated Senior Circuit Judge. This gives a greater depth of knowledge of current sentencing and criminal trends, but still allows a lead to be taken where there is a necessary development of the law to be made. This is the last stage of appeal in many cases and so these judges deal with most of the important cases and probably develop the law more than the House of Lords. The Lords Justices of Appeal's title is 'Lord/Lady Justice ...', or '... LJ' for short. There were 37 Lords Justices at 1 April 2007.

The Heads of Division, such as the Master of the Rolls, and Lords Justices of Appeal sometimes also sit with one or more High Court Judges in the Divisional Court, which hears appeals to the High Court from Magistrates' Courts and certain judicial review cases at first instance. This again helps develop the law and provides a consistency of approach to the application of the law.

High Court Judges

As at 1 April 2007 there were 108 High Court Judges appointed. They deal with the more complex and difficult cases. They usually sit in London, but they also travel to major court centres around the country in cities such as Cardiff, Bristol, Birmingham, Manchester, Liverpool, Leeds and Newcastle. They try serious criminal cases, important civil cases and assist the Lords Justices in hearing criminal appeals. High Court Judges are given the prefix 'the honourable', and are referred to as 'Mr/Mrs Justice ...'. Most High Court Judges are assigned to the Queen's Bench Division (72 of them), with 19 to the Family Division and 17 to the Chancery Division. They also sit in the specialist courts, such as the Commercial Court, within the three divisions of the High Court.

High Court Masters and Registrars

Masters and Registrars of the Supreme Court are the procedural judges for the majority of the civil business in the Chancery and Queen's Bench Divisions. They do not sit in open court, but in chambers (a private room within the court buildings) and do not dress in wig and robes. There is one Senior Master and nine Queen's Bench Masters. Outside London, their work is dealt with by District Judges or Deputy District Judges.

Circuit Judges

There were 637 Circuit Judges in post at 1 April 2007. Some of them are specialists either in criminal work, civil work or family work or in the specialised courts such as the Commercial Court. There are some senior Circuit Judges who take on additional responsibilities, and some who are semi-retired and sit part-time. These judges sit in the Crown Courts or County Courts in the region for which they are appointed, England and Wales being divided into six regions: South Eastern, Midland, North Eastern, Western, Northern, and Wales and Chester.

District Judges

District Judges deal with the majority of cases in the County Courts and the District Registries of the High Court. There were 431 of them as at 1 April 2007. They are appointed to work on a specific circuit and may sit at any of the county courts or District Registries of the High Court on that circuit. A District Registry is part of the High Court situated outside London and deals with High Court family and other civil business.

District Judges (Magistrates' Courts)

District Judges (Magistrates' Courts), as the name suggests, sit in the Magistrates' Court. They are full-time salaried judges, as are other District Judges, but do the same work as lay Magistrates. There were 139 of them as at 1 April 2007, and they are usually appointed to work in a large city such as Manchester or Hull. They sit alone, not as one of a panel of three as lay Magistrates do. They hear criminal cases (usually the more serious or complex cases), youth cases and also some civil proceedings in Magistrates' Courts. They can be authorised to hear cases in the Family Proceedings Courts or to deal with extradition proceedings and terrorist cases. District Judges (Magistrates' Courts) are also authorised to sit on an appeal from a Prison Adjudicator, who deals with disciplinary matters in prisons.

Non-salaried judges

There are a large number of part-time fee-paid (rather than salaried) judges who are used to deal with the changing workloads of individual courts. It is a requirement for appointment as a salaried judge that the candidate has a number of years experience as a part-time judge. The most numerous are Recorders (numbering about 1,200), then Deputy District Judges (numbering a little over 700) and then Deputy District Judges (Magistrates' Courts) (numbering a little under 200). Recorders may sit in both the Crown Court and County Courts, but most start by sitting in the Crown Court. Their work is similar to that of a Circuit Judge, but they will generally handle less complex or less serious matters coming before the court. Deputies work in a similar manner to their full-time equivalents. There are also a few Deputy High Court and Circuit Judges and Deputy Masters and Registrars. Non-salaried judges are usually appointed for a fixed period of time, so may not be reappointed if they are not seen to be satisfactory.

💡 The role and work of judges

The role of the judge in a civil case

The role of the judge in a civil case continues through many aspects of the case. At the start of the case is the role of case management. The main purpose of this is to ensure that the case proceeds as quickly and efficiently as possible. This will involve encouraging cooperation between the parties to the case, including arrival at a negotiated settlement or the use of an alternative method of dispute resolution. If this fails, then the role is one of controlling the different stages leading up to a trial by setting appropriate time limits and dealing with matters that are urgent before the trial. This might include granting an injunction or joining another party in the case.

Before trying a civil case, the judge reads the relevant case papers and becomes familiar with their details. The vast majority of civil cases do not have a jury, defamation trials being the main exception. The judge hears the case on his own, decides on the facts, applies the relevant law to the facts and then gives a reasoned judgment.

To decide on the facts, the evidence has to be obtained and understood by the judge. This will be a mixture of written evidence that the judge will have to read and oral evidence given to the court on oath. This oral evidence may well be subject to cross-examination, and the judge will have to decide what evidence is accurate and relevant to the case.

The judge must ensure that all parties involved are given the opportunity to have their case presented and considered as fully and fairly as possible. Even though the process is adversarial and not inquisitorial, the judge may ask questions on any point that he feels requires clarification, or that he feels is relevant and will help with his decision but has not been covered. He also decides on all matters of procedure that may arise during a hearing.

Once the judge has heard the evidence from all parties involved and any legal arguments, he delivers his judgment. This may be immediately

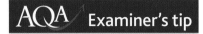

AQA Examiner's tip

Read the examination question carefully to make sure you know whether all judges are required to be dealt with in the answer or only some of them.

or, if the case is complicated, the judgment may be given at a later date. The task of the judge is to decide on what is the appropriate remedy, if any, and on the precise terms of it. Usually the judge will then have to decide on the amount of damages to compensate a successful claimant for the losses suffered as a result of the defendant's actions. There are other orders that he can make, such as an injunction to prevent certain activities continuing or a declaration as to where the boundary between two pieces of land actually runs.

Once the judgment in the case has been delivered, the judge must deal with the costs of the case and decide on the amount that the unsuccessful party to the case must pay the successful one. The general rule is that the unsuccessful party will have to pay the successful party's costs, but the judge can depart from this rule where he thinks that is the appropriate decision.

The role of the judge in a criminal case

The judge in a criminal trial is responsible for all matters of law, and for making sure that all the rules of procedure are properly applied. Before the criminal trial starts, the judge familiarises himself with the details of the case by reading the case papers. He may well have been involved in pre-trial matters such as whether or not to grant bail and the plea and directions hearing. He will need to read various documents such as the charges against the defendant, witness statements, details of exhibits and any previous documentation about the admissibility of evidence in the trial. At the start of the trial he supervises the selection and swearing-in of the jury and explains to the jury what their role is in the trial. He will make it clear that they are only concerned with deciding the facts and coming to a verdict. He warns them not to discuss the case with anyone else.

Once the trial has commenced, the judge makes sure that all parties involved are given the opportunity for their case to be presented and considered fully and fairly. The judge is active during the trial, controlling the way the case is conducted according to the rules of evidence and procedure. As the case progresses the judge makes notes of the evidence and makes any necessary decisions on legal issues, for example, whether evidence is admissible; if it is not, he or she will tell the jury to ignore that evidence.

Once all evidence in the case has been heard, the judge makes his summing-up to the jury. The judge sets out the law on each of the charges made and what the prosecution must prove if the jury are to find the defendant guilty on each charge. He will refer to notes made during the course of the trial and reminds the jury of the key points of the case. He will outline the strengths and weaknesses of the arguments for both prosecution and defence. He will then give directions to the jury about their individual and collective duties before they retire to the jury deliberation room to consider the verdict. He will answer any queries or matters that might arise during the deliberations of the jury and will advise the jury when a majority verdict is acceptable.

If the jury find the defendant guilty, then the judge will decide on an appropriate sentence once he has considered all of the factors relevant to the case. He will then discharge the jury, and if the case has been particularly lengthy or distressing, excuse the jurors from any further jury service. If the jury deliver a verdict of not guilty, the judge will free the defendant, discharge the jury and make any appropriate order about the cost of the trial.

If the defendant pleads guilty, then the judge's main function is to impose the appropriate sentence.

Examples of other judicial roles in courts

There are two main sorts of work that judges do with respect to family law. The first involves private cases such as disputes involving parents about their children and who they should live with, where they should go to school and so on, where the parents are separated or getting divorced.

The second sort of work is public work, when local councils take action to remove children from their parents' care because they are being mistreated, or because the parents cannot cope with the child. Other family matters include adoption and orders with respect to medical treatment for those adults who cannot make their own decisions. An example of this is *Re A* (2000). In that case there was a choice between allowing twins born joined together with shared organs being left without surgery, with the result that both were likely to die within a few months; and separating the twins surgically, which would give one of the twins a good chance of life but would inevitably kill the other. Here, the court made the decision to authorise the hospital to operate. The court was involved, as the parents refused their consent to an operation to separate the twins. The parents' refusal was primarily on the grounds that they could not consent to the killing of one of the twins. However, the doctors at the hospital were not prepared to accept the death of both children, if there were a real possibility of life for one of them.

There are also designated Immigration Judges who work with teams to maintain the quality of decisions and in the management of the hearing centres of the Asylum and Immigration Tribunal (AIT). This tribunal hears appeals against decisions made by the Home Secretary and his officials in asylum, immigration and nationality matters. Appeals are heard by one or more Immigration Judges.

The main types of appeal are made against decisions to:

- refuse a person political asylum in the UK or entry to the UK for a family visit
- refuse a person entry to, or leave to remain in, the UK for permanent settlement
- deport someone already in the UK.

The work of judges outside court

Judges perform a number of roles outside their normal court work. The main one is being the chairman of an inquiry. Under the Inquiries Act 2005, a Minister can set up an inquiry which often has a judge as its chairman. The judge will have to consult as to whether he should take up the role so that there is seen to be approval by their Head. The person who is to be consulted is set out in the table below:

Table 8.1 *Persons to be consulted*

Description of judge	Person to be consulted
Lord of Appeal in Ordinary	The senior Lord of Appeal in Ordinary
Judge of the Supreme Court of England and Wales, or Circuit Judge	The Lord Chief Justice of England and Wales

Because of the high cost and great length of public inquiries, there is often a reluctance to set one up. Notable recent inquiries have been the Hutton Inquiry which was set up to investigate the death of Dr David Kelly and his role in the Iraq weapons of mass destruction pronouncements, and the McPherson Inquiry on the murder of Stephen Lawrence.

AQA Examiner's tip

Make sure you are clear about the differing roles of a judge in a civil and a criminal trial.

Selection and appointment of judges

The Judicial Appointments Commission

The Judicial Appointments Commission was set up by the Constitutional Reform Act 2005 to select judicial office holders. The reform of the system of judicial appointments was part of a Government move to demonstrate judicial independence and to improve public confidence and the effectiveness of the appointment process. This was done by taking responsibility for selecting candidates for judicial office out of the hands of the Lord Chancellor and looking for a wide range of candidates. However, the new system has not been without its problems. This is exemplified by the article from *The Times* set out below:

Criminal trial chaos over lack of judges

An acute shortage of judges is causing long delays in bringing criminal trials to court, putting more pressure on overcrowded prisons and delaying justice for victims of crime.

The Times has learnt that Jack Straw, the Justice Secretary, received a list of approved candidates to fill the growing number of vacancies for Crown Court judges some weeks ago. But Mr Straw has not indicated how many appointments he will make nor when he will announce them.

Retired judges are being pressed into service, and part-time recorders are being repeatedly asked to serve for longer periods. Such ad hoc measures save money because the Government does not have to pay holiday allowance or pension contributions for retired or part-time judges.

As the criminal justice system struggles to cope, serious cases are being put back until 2008 and overcrowded remand prisons are holding record numbers of inmates.

Senior members of the judiciary have called for urgent talks with Mr Straw to resolve the crisis. Lord Phillips of Worth Matravers, the Lord Chief Justice, told judges at their recent annual dinner that 'judicial appointments can be made very much more swiftly and efficiently.'

He said that he had raised the issue with Mr Straw and called for urgent remedial action.

Mr Justice Calvert-Smith, another senior judge, has also spoken of 'severe problems' created by the judicial shortages, budget cuts and crumbling courthouses.

Relations between the new Justice Department and the judiciary are already poor and will not be helped by the widespread belief that much-needed judicial appointments are being delayed in order to save money.

There are at least 47 vacancies for Circuit Judges across England and Wales, with more than 30 of those in the South East Circuit where pressure on court space and time is most intense.

The courts in and around London already face difficulties finding courtrooms and judges to conduct the growing caseload of terrorist trials which routinely start later than scheduled and overrun by months.

The management of the fertiliser bomb plot trial, which was presided over by a judge brought out of retirement, has been particularly criticised after lasting a year.

A main cause of the delays in appointing judges has been the bungled handling of the process by the new Judicial Appointments Commission.

Established in April 2006 to make the selection of judges more meritocratic and representative, it has yet to complete the process of appointing a significant batch of Circuit Judges. It advertised for 32 Circuit Judges last year – 24 in the South East – with applications to be submitted by September. But in February this year the JAC had to write to candidates apologising for mishandling their applications by disregarding their references without consideration. The posts have still not been filled and the number of vacancies has continued to grow.

Writing in *The Circuiteer*, a magazine for lawyers on the South East Circuit, Mr Justice Calvert-Smith said that judges were facing mounting problems. 'We are at least 35 judges short on this circuit,' he wrote. 'The budget cuts and the fact that the vast majority of our expenditure is on salaries have meant that many staff are not replaced when they leave.

'Other results have been that in spite of all being agreed as to the need to modernise and/or extend courts around the circuit, the actual work has been delayed.'

Demands have also been made on judicial manpower by the current sentencing regime which requires increasing numbers of judges to review reports from the Parole Board.

The indeterminate sentence of 'imprisonment for public protection', which has to be imposed for 153 offences, is fuelling prison numbers with 3,000 prisoners now serving the sentence, a number the Home Office predicts to reach 25,000 by 2012. Sir Igor Judge, Deputy Lord Chief Justice, recently told the Constitutional Affairs Committee of MPs that judges had to review the Parole Board reports on such prisoners and to deal with that increase would need an extra 100 judges. 'Where will they come from?' he asked MPs.

Sally O'Neill, QC, vice-chairman of the Criminal Bar Association, said that the hiatus in appointing judges was having a damaging effect. 'It is necessary to keep the appointment system going to make sure younger people are coming through and promote the aim of having greater diversity in the judiciary,' she said.

The Ministry of Justice could not say what measures were being considered to speed up judicial appointments but said it expected vacancies to be filled 'very shortly'.

www.timesonline.co.uk

Qualities required to be a judge

The Judicial Appointments Commission has identified five main qualities required for judicial office. Different types of judge may require a different balance in the qualities. The first quality is intellectual capacity, which will be evidenced in a high level of expertise in a candidate's chosen area of work, the ability quickly to absorb and analyse information and an appropriate knowledge of the law and its underlying principles. This quality is required to ensure that all judges can deal with the intellectual demands of the job.

The second quality involves the personal qualities of the candidate. These include integrity and independence of mind, sound judgement, decisiveness, objectivity and an ability and willingness to learn and develop professionally. This is fairly obvious, given the nature of the role undertaken by a judge. The ability to learn is essential so that training and development of judges is speedy and effective.

The third quality is an ability to understand and deal fairly. A judge needs to be able to treat everyone with respect and sensitivity, whatever their background, and to have a willingness to listen with patience and courtesy to those involved in a court case. This is more than just being seen to be 'politically correct', but a genuine need to understand the disparate nature and needs of members of society so that justice can be obtained.

The fourth quality is stated to be authority and communication skills. A judge needs to be able to explain the procedure and any decisions reached clearly and succinctly to all those involved. He clearly needs to

Examiner's tip

When discussing the qualities required to be a judge, try to write a sentence or two on each quality and give a reason why that quality is important.

know and understand them himself, which is another example of the first and second qualities. He also needs the ability to inspire respect and confidence and to maintain authority when challenged, which he will surely do when faced with a determined litigant, solicitor or barrister. This quality can be illustrated by a judge in the County Court about 50 years ago, who gave a young solicitor appearing before him a very hard time. The judge had not seen the solicitor advocate before and the young advocate was a little nervous, given the judge's reputation for being demanding and fiery. When a senior barrister who had been in court on that day saw the judge socially later, he enquired whether it had been necessary to be so tough on the young man. The judge explained that if the young man could not stand up for himself, he could not see how he could stand up for his clients. Modern judges are much more likely to be patient, but can still be intimidating!

The final quality is efficiency. Given the cost of the legal process, this is one way of being cost-effective, and requires a judge to work at speed and under pressure. This means he needs an ability to organise time effectively and produce clear reasoned judgments quickly. This is key given the complaints made about judges in the past such as the High Court Judge Sir Jeremiah Harman, who resigned after a 20-month delay in delivering a judgment. Three appeal court judges said his conduct, in a 1998 case, 'weakens public confidence in the whole judicial process'. One of the lawyers involved in the case said he had written repeatedly to the judge, asking for the judgment, and even considered taking out life insurance on him to cover lost legal costs if he died before giving his ruling. An ability to work constructively with others (including leadership and managerial skills where appropriate) is also required, particularly with respect to case and court management.

The Judicial Appointments Commission is required to appoint as judges people who are of good character. This requires a decision as to whether there is anything in the candidate's past conduct or present circumstances (for example, business connections) that would affect the application for judicial appointment. Thus a criminal conviction will normally be fatal to a candidate's application – indeed the person description given to applicants makes this clear – unless it is well in the past, minor and did not lead to imprisonment. Thus, minor motoring offences will normally be disregarded, but not, say, a conviction for grievous bodily harm. The Rehabilitation of Offenders Act does not apply to judges.

Financial correctness is looked for – a person who has been bankrupt may, occasionally, be appointed a judge, but difficulties with the taxman or with respect to VAT may prove fatal to an application. This is to avoid a suspicion that the judge is dishonest or may be open to some form of blackmail or bribery.

When a judge has been appointed and later appears to fail to meet the criteria, then there is the likelihood of disciplinary action against the judge.

The stages in appointing a judge

The first stage is an advertisement. Most positions are advertised widely in the national press, the legal press and online. The Judicial Appointments Commission also runs roadshows and other outreach events. These are designed to explain the selection system to potential applicants and to encourage them to consider a judicial career, thus extending the likely range of candidates. Each appointment is started with the design of an application form and information pack. The application pack includes details of the eligibility criteria and guidance on the application process.

Here is an example from an advertisement for a District Judge (Magistrates' Courts) past:

> To be eligible for appointment as District Judge (Magistrates' Courts) you must meet the following requirements.
>
> Statutory requirement
>
> **The statutory requirement for applicants is as set out in Courts Act 2003, Part 2 (Justices of the Peace), s22.**
>
> Her Majesty may, on the recommendation of the Lord Chancellor, appoint a person who has a 7 year general qualification to be a District Judge (Magistrates' Courts).
>
> A general qualification is within the meaning of s71 of the Courts and Legal Services Act 1990.
>
> In order to meet the statutory qualifications for appointment, persons who wish to rely upon their qualification as solicitors, including those holding full-time judicial office, must appear on the Roll of Solicitors.
>
> **Previous service in a judicial office**
>
> To be considered for appointment the Lord Chancellor expects applicants to have served in judicial office in a fee paid or salaried capacity for at least two years or to have completed 30 sitting days by 22 June 2007. Such service is not the only criterion. You will also need to demonstrate the qualities and abilities required for this office.

Extract from judicial post information pack 00316

Once the candidate has completed the application form and it is received by the Judicial Appointments Commission it is checked to make sure of the candidate's eligibility for the post. At the same time an assessment is made of the good character of the candidate.

Candidates are asked on their application form to nominate up to three referees. The Judicial Appointments Commission may also seek references from a list of Commission-nominated referees, which is published for each selection exercise. In all cases, references will form part of the information that the Judicial Appointments Commission will use to make final selection recommendations. Shortlisting is then done.

The next stage of the assessment will vary depending on the nature of the post to be filled. Candidates might be asked to attend a selection day, which might entail a combination of role-plays and an interview. For some specialist and the most senior appointments, there might be only a panel interview, as the candidate's ability as a judge at one level is already known. Interview panel members assess all the information about each candidate, prepare reports on their findings and agree which candidates are best.

There is then a statutory consultation. This is required by the Constitutional Reform Act 2005 and means that the panel's reports on candidates are sent to the Lord Chief Justice and another person who has held the post or has relevant experience. The Commissioners consider all the information gathered on the candidates and select candidates to be recommended to the Lord Chancellor for appointment. There are then final checks. For existing judges seeking promotion, this is with the Office for Judicial Complaints, to see that there are no complaints outstanding against the candidates. For all other candidates recommended for appointment, a series of good character checks are done with the Police, Revenue and Customs and relevant professional bodies. The Lord Chancellor may also require candidates to undergo a medical assessment before the appointment is confirmed. This should then result in the best candidates being appointed and is a fair and open system.

For most appointments there are criteria for appointment although it is possible that some posts may be made attractive to academic lawyers who are not engaged in legal practice as a solicitor or barrister on a day-to-day basis. This is summarised in the chart below:

Table 8.2 *Judicial qualification requirements*

Type of judge	Qualifications
Law Lords	15-year Supreme Court qualification or be holding existing judicial office
Lords Justices of Appeal	10-year High Court qualification or be an existing High Court Judge
High Court Judge	10-year High Court qualification or be an existing Circuit Judge
Circuit Judges	10-year Crown Court or County Court qualification or be a Recorder or District Judge for three years
Recorders	10-year general qualification
District Judges	Seven-year general qualification

Reasons to become a judge

Judges are usually former top solicitors or barristers. They have often started working part-time judicially to see if the life of a judge is attractive. A number start from the point of view of putting something back into the system as well as the personal prestige that comes with the title. Many applicants are already financially secure and feel they can manage with the reduction in earnings that will come from the change and look forward to a pension that is perhaps the best in the UK. A judge's salary is in the public domain: it can be found on the Department of Constitutional Affairs' website.

The salary has to be sufficient to attract appropriate candidates and also sufficient that there is no danger of financial pressures tempting a judge to accept a bribe or otherwise act in any way other than impartially. A judge's salary for 2007–8 ranges from the Lord Chief Justice, whose salary with effect from 1 November 2007 is £230,400, to a District Judge, whose salary with effect from 1 November 2007 is £98,900.

The judge's pension scheme is particularly favourable. Unlike most pensions, it is calculated on the basis of 1/40th of final salary for each year worked as a judge, up to a maximum of 20/40ths (50 per cent) of final salary, together with a lump sum of 2.25 times the final pension, various enhancements for retirement due to ill health, and some tax concession on normal pension rules.

High Court Judges are expected to sit throughout the legal terms (189 days per year). The legal year traditionally begins in October, and courts sit for four terms during the year. In practice judges work long hours, as well as during court vacations, and are required to deal with a variety of judicial business, such as reading case papers and preparing reserved judgments

(judgments that are delivered in court some time after the end of the trial, so as to give time to reflect on the legal arguments and make a clearly reasoned decision) and to perform other public duties in addition to their actual sittings. However, this is often fewer days than many were working as a barrister or solicitor. Judges usually retire at age 70.

Training of judges

The Judicial Studies Board is directly responsible for training full- and part-time judges in England and Wales. It also oversees the training of lay magistrates and chairmen and members of tribunals. The Judicial Studies Board was set up in 1979, and its role is to carry out its objectives which are stated to be:

■ to provide high quality training to full- and part-time judges in the exercise of their jurisdiction in civil, criminal and family law

■ to advise the Lord Chancellor on the policy for, and content of, training for lay magistrates, and on the efficiency and effectiveness with which Magistrates' Courts' committees deliver such training

■ to advise the Lord Chancellor and government departments on the appropriate standards for, and content of, training for judicial officers in tribunals

■ to advise the Government on the training requirement of judges, magistrates and judicial officers in tribunals if proposed changes to the law, procedure and court organisation are to be effective, and to provide, and advise on the content of, such training

■ to promote closer international cooperation over judicial training.

Much of its training work is carried out through its publications, such as the 8th edition of the *Guidelines for the Assessment of General Damages in Personal Injury Cases*, or specimen directions for use by judges in criminal trials. These publications are generally written by members of the judiciary at the Judicial Studies Board's request.

The current activities of the Judicial Studies Board are: initial training for new judges and judges who take on new responsibilities; continuing professional education to strengthen and deepen the skills and knowledge of existing judicial office holders; and delivering change and modernisation by supporting major changes to legislation and to the administration of justice.

The initial training of a judge on appointment is an intensive residential induction course. This lasts between four and five days. The course concentrates on the practical aspects of sitting as a judge and running a court. Much of the training is done through group discussions, role-play and practical exercises.

Newly appointed judges also spend a period sitting in with an experienced judge for at least a week and, if they are to hear criminal cases, they must visit local prisons and the Probation Service.

Once new appointees have completed an induction course they must attend annual training days, which are held locally in their regions, and are called back for continuation training by the Judicial Studies Board every three years. In addition, judges must attend further induction courses before being able to sit in certain types of case, for example, family law. Experienced judges also attend 'refresher' seminars, generally on a three-year cycle, in all the areas of law in which they sit. The Judicial Studies Board also organises training programmes in response to legislative change.

A mentoring scheme is being developed to help judges perform their role initially and also to be able to progress up the judicial ladder. District Judges already mentor Deputy District Judges in the County Courts, and a range of other informal mentoring arrangements exists throughout the judiciary.

Dismissal and discipline

The Office for Judicial Complaints was set up by the Constitutional Reform Act 2005 to handle complaints about the personal conduct of all judges and to provide advice and assistance to the Lord Chancellor and Lord Chief Justice in the performance of their new joint role of considering and deciding about complaints. The objective is that all judicial disciplinary issues be dealt with consistently, fairly and efficiently. The complaints must be about the personal conduct of the judge and not the actual decision made by him.

In the Office for Judicial Complaints' first year of operation, from April 2006 to March 2007, there were 1,694 complaints against judicial office holders: this includes magistrates, coroners and tribunal members, as well as the judiciary. Some 800 of these complaints can be discounted as being outside the scope of the Office for Judicial Complaints, as they were about the judge's decision rather than his personal conduct. However, over half of the total (valid and invalid) complaints were against the judiciary, which is a surprisingly large number. When the complaints were processed, disciplinary action was taken against two judges, the action being a serious reprimand, as can be seen from the table below.

Table 8.3 *Disciplinary action taken*

	Judges	Coroners	Tribunals	Magistrates	Total
Formal warning/ advice	0	0	1	2	3
Reprimand	2	0	0	11	13
Removed from office	0	0	1	15	16
TOTAL	2	0	2	28	32

www.judicialcomplaints.gov.uk

None of the complaints is given in detail, as the anonymity of the judge or magistrate is preserved under the Constitutional Reform Act 2005. Anonymous case histories are not used either. However there has been a great deal of speculation about the judges involved. According to *The Times* on 7 August 2007:

How well behaved are Britain's judges?

Frances Gibb

Two current complaints … have, however, been very publicly aired: the referral by the Lord Chief Justice of Mr Justice Peter Smith, the judge who refused to step down from a case in which he had been acrimoniously linked with a law firm involved; and two immigration judges embroiled in the 'chilli hot stuff' black-mail case. On the first, a nominated Court of Appeal judge (one of three) will look at the case and advise whether disciplinary action should be taken or whether a further judicial investigation is needed.

The investigation into the other judge is now proceeding after the ending of the criminal proceedings.

The Times, 7 August 2007

The cases involved to date have resulted in no worse action than a reprimand. However, the ultimate sanction would be removal from judicial office, although for High Court Judges and above, judicial independence dictates that this would require a vote in both Houses of Parliament. Of course, the only way to complain about a judge's decision (rather than his personal conduct) is by way of an appeal.

It is highly unlikely to find a full-time serving judge needing to be removed. This has happened just once, in 1983, when a Circuit Judge, Judge Bruce Campbell, was removed from office after pleading guilty to several charges of smuggling whisky into England from Guernsey. In the last 200 years only one High Court Judge has been removed from office on a vote in both Houses of Parliament. This was Sir Jonah Barrington in 1830. He misappropriated money belonging to litigants. A number of judges have retired or resigned to avoid the possibility of such action, but judges still manage to behave in inappropriate ways, and that appears to hinder their career prospects.

Judge found guilty after drunken fracas

A COUNTY Court judge remained defiant last night after being found guilty of causing a drunken fracas in a kebab shop.

David Messenger said he planned to appeal against his conviction for being drunk and disorderly.

He was also convicted of obstructing two police officers and criminal damage of a police cell.

He was found guilty by magistrates following a three-day trial and fined a total of £800, ordered to pay £188 in compensation for damaging the bell button in his cell and pay more than £6,000 in court costs.

Messenger, 49, of Valley Bridge Parade, Scarborough, North Yorkshire, denied all the charges.

The judge was arrested at a takeaway in Scarborough, on May 2 and spent the night banging on his cell door, refusing to co-operate with officers and eventually damaging a cell bell button.

Messenger was arrested at the Best Kebab shop, in St Thomas's Street, after intervening in an incident that police were trying to sort out in the kitchen.

The court was told how Messenger called police officers 'ar******s' and said their behaviour would 'cost them £5,000' as they marched him out of the kebab shop.

Asked if he wanted to contact anyone after his arrest he asked to speak to the Chief Constable.

As the officers were taking him from the building and attempting to put him into a police van he shouted to passers-by: 'Tell them I'm a solicitor and a county court judge'.

He was eventually taken to the police station where his lack of co-operation continued.

The court was told the 'booking in' procedure took 40 minutes as the defendant refused to give his personal details.

Once Messenger was locked in a cell, he spent the night banging on the door to such an extent that other prisoners had to be moved so they could get some peace.

Later, an officer found a button in the cell, which operated the bell, was damaged, the court heard.

Messenger told magistrates that he had described two police officers as 'ar******s' because he was shocked and frightened about being frogmarched out of a kebab shop. He said he had been 'unlawfully arrested'.

He said he could not believe what was happening to him after he tried to help a client who was involved in an incident at the kebab shop.

However, the magistrates said the evidence of the two police officers had been compelling and they had good reason to be concerned there would be a breach of the peace.

Dr Jones said: 'Their actions were entirely justified and perfectly reasonable.

'The way in which Mr Messenger responded was to behave in a totally inappropriate way.'

The court was told Messenger's convictions would mean the end of his 'judicial aspirations'.

Outside court, he continued to maintain his innocence and said he would carry on working as a solicitor.

He is not sitting as a judge at present.

He said: 'It's been a very difficult five months. I maintained my innocence throughout and I still do.'

A Department for Constitutional Affairs spokesman said: 'This judge has not been sitting and a report on the issue will be prepared for the Lord Chancellor, who will make a decision about his sitting in future.'

Northern Echo, *30 September 2003*

Conclusion

There are many types of judge, but all have the primary role of managing and deciding cases. Whilst a judge is appointed until the age of 70, there are still examples of those appointed who retire or resign before that age.

Activities

1 Here is a typical examination question for you to attempt:

   a Outline the role of a judge in a Crown Court trial.

   b Briefly describe how superior judges are chosen, appointed and dismissed.

   c Consider why it is so difficult to dismiss a superior judge from office.

2 Read the article below and discuss within groups whether the new system of judicial complaints will work well.

Judges' misdeeds will remain secret

Clare Dyer

No naming and shaming in legal system shake-up

Judges who are disciplined for bad behaviour will not have the findings against them made public under a complaints regime to be launched next year.

The decision to treat judges differently to doctors, barristers, solicitors and police officers was announced by the Lord Chancellor and the Lord Chief Justice yesterday.

The exception, as at present, will be those judges whose misdeeds are trumpeted in the media – for example, those who make racist remarks in open court which are picked up by reporters.

In those cases, it is necessary for the sake of public confidence in the justice system to reveal the outcome of an investigation, the Lord Chancellor, Lord Falconer, said.

He disclosed that 250 complaints of misconduct against judges and tribunal chairmen had been investigated by the Department of Constitutional Affairs last year, 68 of which were upheld and resulted in disciplinary action. Eleven were serious enough to be referred to senior judges for investigation.

Judges have been admonished or reprimanded for such behaviour as racist language, sexual harassment, discourtesy in court, delays in delivering judgments and drink driving.

One referred in court to 'the nigger in the woodpile', while another said that fraud was an offence prevalent among Nigerians.

One who had previously been reprimanded for kissing a court usher had to apologise after saying, in reference to doctors writing sick notes: 'I know many people with duodenal ulcers who work like niggers'.

Yet another was reprimanded for falling asleep twice in a rape trial, causing the hearing to be abandoned.

Circuit Judges may be removed by the Lord Chancellor 'on the ground of incapacity or misbehaviour'.

This power has only once been exercised, in 1983 after a judge was convicted of smuggling whisky and cigarettes into Britain in his yacht.

From April 2006 a new Office for Judicial Complaints will deal with allegations about judges' personal conduct, though complaints over the way they conduct court proceedings will be outside its remit.

That will be part of a shake-up which will transfer the responsibility for choosing and promoting judges from the lord chancellor to a new Judicial Appointments Commission.

▶

A judicial appointments and conduct ombudsman will be appointed to oversee both the appointments commission and the complaints office.

Candidates for the bench who feel they have been treated unfairly will be able to take their cases to the ombudsman, as will a judge subject to a misconduct complaint or a complainant who feels the investigation has not been properly handled.

Unlike judges in the US and Canada, those in England and Wales will not normally be subjected to public disclosure of the fact that they have been disciplined.

An agreement between the Lord Chief Justice and the Lord Chancellor, under which they will share responsibility for disciplining judges as part of the new arrangements, says the two 'may agree in a particular case that public confidence in the justice system demands that the fact that a judicial office-holder has been subject to disciplinary action, or has been exonerated, be made public.'

The Lord Chief Justice, Lord Woolf, said he supported keeping judges' names under wraps: 'One has got to take into account the need still for the public to appear before the judge and for him or her to continue to perform his or her job as a judge.'

The Guardian, *30 June 2005*

You should now be able to:

■ understand the operation of the judiciary

■ attempt past paper questions on the judiciary.

💡 2 Independence of the judiciary

The independence of the judiciary

The Universal Declaration of Human Rights enshrines the principles of equality before the law, of the presumption of innocence, and of the right to a fair and public hearing by a competent, independent and impartial tribunal established by law.

In order to ensure the right to a fair and public hearing, three basic principles are needed:

■ Security of tenure: once appointed, a judge cannot be dismissed except for misconduct.

■ Immunity from suit: a judge cannot be sued or prosecuted for his performance in court.

■ An independent judiciary: that is, independent of the State and, therefore, independent of influence on its decisions.

In this topic you will learn how to:

■ define the term 'judicial independence'

■ explain the meaning of separation of powers

■ give examples of judicial independence and separation of powers.

Security of tenure

As we have seen in the previous topic, full-time judges have security of tenure. Once appointed, a full-time judge remains in office until retirement, unless he dies, resigns or is dismissed from office. Dismissal is very rare. However, there are an increasing number of complaints being made against judges. The fact that the systems in place result in few dismissals gives a judge confidence in his ability to act as he or she thinks is appropriate in every case. This is reinforced by the fact that the Office for Judicial Complaints cannot deal with any complaints about a judge's decision or about how he has handled a case.

Under the Judicial Discipline (Prescribed Procedures) Regulations 2006, there is provision for the Lord Chancellor or the Lord Chief Justice, upon receipt of information from any source which suggests that disciplinary proceedings might be justified, to refer that information to the Office for Judicial Complaints to be dealt with in accordance with their rules. This means that there does not have to be a formal complaint made by a member of the public, merely that information emerges that merits investigation. This can be from another judge, or as a result of a report in the press such as those referred to in the previous topic. This enables disciplinary proceedings to be started whenever there appears to be activity that suggests that a judge is not behaving entirely properly, and will help protect against abuses that might occur where litigants are unsure of what to expect and are not represented by a solicitor or barrister.

The same regulations suggest a large number of reasons why a complaint may be dismissed and not investigated at all, ranging from the fact that it relates to a judge who is no longer in office (hence some early resignations) to the complaint being vexatious (that is, it has been started maliciously and without good reason). This may explain why there have been so few disciplinary actions taken in comparison to the number of complaints. The result is that a judge will feel secure and therefore independent of outside pressures unless he knows that he has acted improperly.

Immunity from suit

Any **immunity from suit** is contrary to a person's fundamental right of access to the court. Therefore, any immunity from suit has to be justified. This principle is found both in the common law and in the decisions of the European Court of Human Rights. The fact that a judge cannot be sued for his court performance, and so has protection from negligence claims as a matter of policy, is central to the concept of an independent judiciary and therefore is the justification for the existence of this protection of a judge. It also gives a judge great peace of mind. As the number of cases that are brought before the courts in negligence increases, this is one of the last areas of the law of negligence where no duty of care is owed.

If a judge makes an error in the course of a hearing, the correct procedure is to use the appeal system. This is consistent with the Office for Judicial Complaints being unable to deal with a complaint based on complaints about a judge's decision or about how he has handled a case. It also preserves the independence of the judiciary, as senior judges do not count up how many appeals have been made from the decisions of particular judges.

Under the Court Settlement process (used in the Technology and Construction Court, which is part of the High Court Queen's Bench Division), it is made clear that the parties to the case agree that the Settlement Judge has the same immunity from suit in relation to a Court Settlement Process as the Settlement Judge would have if acting as a judge in the proceedings. This protects judges working towards alternative dispute resolution. Unfortunately, this is not clearly the case for mediators and conciliators.

The independent judiciary and the separation of powers

The idea of the independent judiciary stems from the doctrine of the **separation of powers**. For a political system to be stable, the holders of power need to be balanced against each other. In England, the holders of power are the Government, Parliament and the judiciary. The traditional theory, expounded by philosophers such as the Frenchman Montesquieu and the Englishman Locke, deals with three areas of power: legislative power

Key terms

Immunity from suit: protection from being sued (taken to court), for example, on the ground of a judge's conduct in court when acting in his or her capacity as judge.

Separation of powers: the idea that there are three powers in a State: legislative, executive and judicial.

(that is, the power to make law); executive power (that is, the power to carry the law into effect or oversee its enforcement); and judicial power (that is, the power to make judgements and to apply the law in particular cases).

There is obviously going to be some overlap between the three areas, and in England this overlap is demonstrated by the fact that it is the Cabinet of the Government that is the effective executive, while all the members of the Cabinet are also members of the legislature (Parliament); furthermore, the judiciary includes the Law Lords and the Judicial Committee of the Privy Council, who have a final say on legal issues but also sit in the legislature (the House of Lords). Removal of a judge from office requires approval by the legislature, which also makes the law relating to the appointment of judges.

Whilst this position is not entirely satisfactory, it is much improved since the Constitutional Reform Act 2005 limited the Lord Chancellor's role in the appointment of judges. Judges are effectively independent and have sufficient controls to ensure quality in their work. The controls also ensure that any hint of a lack of independence is dealt with effectively. This can be seen in the House of Lords case involving the extradition fight of Chile's former head of State, General Pinochet. The claim was made that one of the Law Lords, Lord Hoffmann, was biased against General Pinochet because of his links with the human rights group Amnesty International. Lord Hoffman's wife, Gillian, was also connected with Amnesty International. The original decision was reached by a panel of five Law Lords (by a 3:2 majority). In modern times House of Lords' rulings cannot be appealed, but in this case arrangements were made for the case to be reheard by an appeal committee of the Law Lords, so as to ensure there was no hint of possible bias. The original decision showed no trace of bias, but justice through a truly independent judiciary had to be seen to be done.

Judges take the doctrine of the separation of powers as meaning that they should not question the validity of an Act of Parliament; but the European Communities Act 1972 requires judges to give precedence to EU law over UK law where there is a conflict. Similarly, the Human Rights Act 1998 gives judges the power to declare that UK legislation does not comply with the requirements of the European Convention on Human Rights. The effect of this is to strengthen the independence of the judiciary, as judges can now, in certain circumstances, treat parliamentary-made law as ineffective. This has always been the case where the judges have been able to interpret an Act of Parliament in such a way as to make the statute ineffective, as has been seen in cases such as *Fisher* v *Bell* (1961).

Conclusion

The principle of judicial independence is interlinked with the doctrine of separation of powers. Most constitutional theories require that the judiciary is separate from and independent of the Government, in order to ensure that the law is enforced impartially and consistently, no matter who is in power, and without undue influence from any other source. Judicial independence can be seen in the decisions the judges make, their security of tenure and their immunity from suit.

You should now be able to:

- understand the principle of judicial independence

- understand the doctrine of separation of powers

- attempt past paper questions on judicial independence and the separation of powers.

Activities

Attempt these sample questions on this and the previous topic:

1. Explain what is meant by the principle of judicial independence.

2. Discuss the importance of this principle of judicial independence.

3 Evaluation of the judiciary

In this topic you will learn how to:

■ evaluate the judiciary.

Evaluation of the composition of the bench

Where magistrates have been said to be middle class, middle aged and middle minded, it could be argued that judges are upper class, old aged and conservative in outlook. The judicial statistics for 2005 (revised August 2006) show that they fail to reflect society to a far greater extent than magistrates do whilst carrying out a very heavy workload.

Table 8.4 *Type of work dealt with by different types of judges*

Days sat[1] by judges showing type of work dealt with, 2005

| | Court of Appeal | | High Court | | | | Crown Court | County Court | | | |
	Criminal	Civil	Chancery Division	Queen's Bench Division[2]	Family Division	T&C court[3]		General List	Public	Family Law Private	Total
Type of judge											
Lords Justices	720	2,666	42	135	58	15	–	55	24	51	3,766
High Court Judges	1,230	91	2,081	3,378	2,244	380	3,886	41	161	73	13,563
Deputy High Court Judges	108	109	1,098	929	399	267	185	90	1112	15	3,311
Circuit Judges	196	–	940	717	1,224	790	69,630	11,859	13,707	7,127	106,190
Deputy circuit Judges	–	–	1	13	1	–	1,098	459	321	202	2,094
Recorders	–	–	29	3	84	11	18,727	3,124	408	1,102	23,487
District Judges	–	–	301	176	2	–	–	51,615	2,473	22,797	77,362
Deputy district Judges	–	–	6	2	1	–	–	18,768	77	2,945	21,798
Total[4]	2,254	2,866	4,497	5,351	4,012	1,463	93,526	86,010	17,282	34,311	251,570

[1] Days sat in court and chambers
[2] Admiralty Court and Administrative Court sittings are included in the Queen's Bench Division figures
[3] T&C court – Technology and Construction Court, formally the Official Referee's court
[4] These figures represent only the days sat in court or in chambers in the jurisdictions shown. Judges sit in other areas, and also undertake a range of other functions outside the courtroom that are not shown here

www.official-documents.gov.uk

From these statistics it can be seen that fewer days are spent on criminal appeals than on civil appeals and that most work is done in courts below the High Court. This is reflected by the increased jurisdiction of the County Court and the relatively few trials in Crown Court. It is also interesting to see the workload of each type of judge and how this reflects the limited opportunities for promotion.

There is still a great imbalance between the number of judges who were formerly barristers and those who were solicitors. In the statistics published as at 1 April 2007, the split was roughly 90 per cent former barristers and 10 per cent former solicitors. When looked at from a gender point of view, the statistics show more women in judicial posts at the lower end of the judicial hierarchy which suggests that the gender imbalance will improve as promoted posts become available. This still is unlikely to match the magistrates who are almost 50:50 men and women.

Table 8.5 *Workload of different types of judges*

Days sat[1] by judges, by type of judge and circuit, 2005

Type of judge	London	Midlands	North East	North West	South East	South West	Supreme Court	Wales & Cheshire	Grand Total
Lords Justices	36	43	3	11	31	16	3,627	–	3,776
High Court Judges	574	1,174	724	1,404	535	364	8,262	527	13,563
Deputy High Court Judges	164	933	178	426	21	74	1,250	266	3,311
Circuit Judges	26,509	15,252	11,147	15,015	19,810	8,715	2,434	7,309	106,190
Deputy circuit Judges	395	42	128	265	819	281	1	164	2,094
Recorders	5,960	3,931	2,591	2,627	4,119	2,526	88	1,646	23,487
District Judges	12,604	11,463	11,024	11,879	15,633	8,894	–	5,866	77,362
Deputy district Judges	2,591	3,665	3,257	4,032	3,924	2,719	–	1,611	21,798
Total[2]	48,833	36,503	29,053	35,657	44,889	23,587	15,662	17,388	251,570

[1] Days sat in court and chambers
[2] These figures represent only the days sat in court or in chambers in the jurisdictions shown. Judges sit in other areas, and also undertake a range of other functions outside the courtroom that are not shown here

www.official-documents.gov.uk

The fact remains that the ethnic background of judges does not reflect the ethnic balance of people in England and Wales. There was only one non-white judge of High Court rank or above as at 1 April 2007, although these figures have significantly improved over recent years as there are many more members of the lower ranks of the judiciary who have a non-white ethnic background. This can be seen from the statistics which show that there were just over five per cent non-white District Judges (Magistrates' Courts) and four-and-a-half per cent non-white recorders.

In a report in 2002, the Labour research department found that the average age of judges was over 60, that two-thirds of them had been to public school and that 60 per cent had been to Oxford or Cambridge universities. In general, the higher the rank of judge, the more likely it was that the judge had been public school and Oxbridge educated.

Table 8.6 *Women judges in post (as at 1 April 2007)*

Post		Former Barristers	Former Solicitors	Total
Lord of Appeal in Ordinary	Women	1	0	1
	Men	10	0	11
	Total	11	0	12
	% Women	9.09	0	8.33
Heads of Division • Lord Chief Justice • Master of the Rolls • President of the Queen's Bench Division • President of Family Division • The Chancellor of the High Court	Women	0	0	0
	Men	5	0	5
	Total	5	0	5
	% Women	0	0	0

Post		Former Barristers	Former Solicitors	Total
Lord Justice of Appeal	Women	3	0	3
	Men	33	1	34
	Total	36	1	37
	% Women	8.33	0	8.11
High Court Judge	Women	10	0	10
	Men	97	1	98
	Total	107	1	108
	% Women	9.35	0	9.26
Circuit Judge	Women	59	13	73
(including judges of the Court of Technology and Construction)	Men	485	79	566
	Total	544	92	639
	% Women	10.85	14.13	11.42
Recorder	Women	152	27	179
	Men	945	77	1022
	Total	1097	104	1201
	% Women	13.86	25.96	14.9
Recorder In Training	Women	3	0	3
	Men	2	0	2
	Total	5	0	5
	% Women	60	0	60
District Judge	Women	15	86	101
(including Family Division)	Men	21	325	349
	Total	36	411	450
	% Women	41.67	20.92	22.44
Deputy District Judge	Women	59	159	219
(including Family Division)	Men	74	486	561
	Total	133	645	780
	% Women	44.36	24.65	28.08
District Judge (Magistrates' Courts)	Women	13	20	33
As at 31 August 2000 all Stipendiary Magistrates became District Judges (Magistrates' Courts)	Men	34	71	106
	Total	47	91	139
	% Women	27.66	21.98	23.74
Deputy District Judge (Magistrates' Court)	Women	18	24	42
As at 31 August 200 all Stipendiary Magistrates became District Judges (Magistrates' Courts)	Men	53	74	127
	Total	71	98	169
	% Women	25.35	24.49	24.85

www.judiciary.gov.uk

Judges themselves talk of their isolation and the great feeling of responsibility in the post of judge. Even where judges sit as a panel, this still holds true, as each appeal court judge and Law Lord writes an individual judgment or speech in making their decision. Admittedly, there is often a lead judgment to which some or all of the others agree in whole or in part.

The fact that judges are almost exclusively drawn from practising lawyers is positive, as it ensures that the judges start off being in touch with current practice and procedure. The fact that judges have a legal qualification (unlike most magistrates) means that they have a sound basic knowledge of the law and some procedures. However, not all judges come from the area of law in which they become a judge, and their training needs to be comprehensive and continuing.

Evaluation of the adequacy of training

The creation of the Judicial Studies Board has led to much improved training for judges, but the changes in the appointment system have meant that it now has an increasing workload on top of its larger role in training magistrates and tribunal members. The changes in the system of judicial appointments, particularly the increased emphasis on recruiting judges from more diverse backgrounds, means that a greater range of skills needs to be developed in some new judges. Some judges being trained have less courtroom experience than has been the case under the old system of appointments. The new Judicial Training Strategy has taken a great deal of effort to prepare, and it will be interesting to see if the strategy works in improving both the initial and continuing training of judges.

The Judicial Studies Board research in 2006 included a training needs analysis, which concluded that Circuit and District Judges needed training in judicial skills rather than substantive law. This would include training in those judicial skills that apply across the jurisdictions. The training would be annual rather than on a three-year-cycle, and would meet individual judge's needs as well as being assisted by technology.

The Judicial Studies Board research in 2006 also looked at the needs of senior judges. Its main recommendations included the following: there should be training of at least five days in the first year after appointment and at least two days per year after that; the training should include training in judicial skills for those who seek it; the induction package should be flexible and backed up by a formal programme of continuation training; there should also be an annual two-day residential seminar for Queen's Bench Division judges, covering all aspects of serious crime.

The fact that there has been so much training initiated by the Judicial Studies Board demonstrates that the previous lack of training is starting to be addressed. It is positive that the training is aimed at all levels of the judiciary and includes existing judges. The concern is that some judges who most need training may not get it for some time, and that it is not always clear how the training fits into the appraisal, mentoring and disciplinary systems.

Evaluation of performance

The performance of a judge is very difficult to monitor objectively. The fact that, when the 2006 complaints were processed, disciplinary action was only taken against two judges, suggests that the performance of the judges was excellent given the number of hearings that took place. However, the fact that there were over 800 complaints to the Office for Judicial Complaints in its first year of operation suggests that there were many unhappy litigants. Equally, the number of appeals and cases that have come to an agreed settlement rather than going to appeal is not known, but the number of days sat by appeal court judges is indicative of some dissatisfaction. The only well-documented evidence of dissatisfaction comes from the newspapers. This usually relates to unduly lenient or harsh sentencing decisions or excessive damages being awarded. Examples are difficult to find as most excessive damages cases are libel cases where the damages have been awarded by a jury such as the case of Sonia Sutcliffe's claim against *Private Eye* magazine. However in the so-called 'McLibel' case, which ended in 1997, there was no jury.

In that case, McDonald's won a partial victory in its libel trial against two environmental campaigners, Helen Steel and Dave Morris. They had published a leaflet entitled *What's wrong with McDonald's? Everything they don't want you to know*, accusing McDonald's of a series of unethical and environmentally destructive activities. At the end of the longest trial in English legal history, the judge, Mr Justice Bell, agreed that some of the claims made in the leaflet were unjustified. However, the judge's award of £60,000 damages to McDonald's conveyed to some that McDonald's had won the case on all bar a few minor points. In fact, most of the judge's findings of fact back up the criticisms made in the leaflet. In March 1999 the Court of Appeal reduced the amount of damages awarded to McDonald's from £60,000 to £40,000. This shows that judges have a sound view about the amount of compensation to award, whereas a jury often makes excessive awards.

There was a later appeal in 2005 to the European Court of Human Rights. That court decided that the denial of legal aid constituted a violation of Steel and Morris's right to a fair trial. More importantly, the court decided that, while the damages were relatively modest by British standards, because Steel and Morris were on a low income, the amount was disproportionate and violated their right to freedom of expression. In that sense, the judges at the original hearing and on appeal had not really grasped the impact of the European Convention on Human Rights and its effect on the workings of the English legal system.

There are also examples of unduly lenient sentences being given. One such was highlighted in a House of Commons debate in 1999 when the MP Teresa Gorman pointed out '… in the Ealing vicarage rape case. Three males were involved, two of whom abused her (the victim) in what even the judge referred to as a foul and disgusting way. They were given five-year sentences. A little bit was added on because they were there to commit a burglary. Nevertheless, one of those men was out after three years and the other served less than his five-year sentence. That is not uncommon. Many soft sentences are handed down by geriatric judges in our courts, often in cases that involve women and their sexual lives. Our courts are besmirched as a result of that and they need to do something about it. The Bill must deal with sentencing and the length of sentences.'

After the vicarage rape case, Lord Lane, who was then the Lord Chief Justice, said that the sentences had been too lenient. That is not surprising, because the third man in that case, who did not take part in the rapes but was involved only in the burglary, was sentenced to 14 years' imprisonment. That contrast shows that the courts make dreadful mistakes and inconsistencies, however senior the judge might be.

Judges are sometimes seen as out of touch with questions such as, 'Who are the Beatles?' 'Who is Gazza?' asked Sir Jeremiah Harman in 1990, 'Is it an opera?' A judge sitting at Highbury, near Arsenal's home ground, did not know that Arsenal was an FA Premiership football club. In 1999, Judge Francis Aglionby stopped a 'Teletubby' theft case and asked, 'What

AQA Examiner's tip

Do not make up examples of judicial errors. Examples should be sufficiently explained to demonstrate their source.

is a Teletubby?' Finally, some judges realised that being in touch with society is important: the late Judge Michael Argyle QC, when asked if judges were out of touch, stoutly defended his peers. 'A lot of judges play golf. And if you play golf you couldn't possibly be out of touch.'

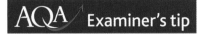

Behind the changes to the judicial system is a growing awareness that, to maintain confidence in the justice system, the judiciary needs to engage with the public. Society has moved on from the 1930s, when the Lord Chief Justice could say, 'His Majesty's judges are satisfied with the almost universal admiration in which they are held.' In 1999 the largest ever study of attitudes about judges and the justice system, funded by the Nuffield Foundation, revealed a lack of confidence across social class in the fairness of courts. Only 53 per cent of people believed they would get a fair hearing at court and 65 per cent agreed that 'judges are out of touch with ordinary people's lives.'

Evaluation of judicial independence

The current system of appointing judges is satisfactory, in that the judges are largely independent and are prepared to make decisions that are not popular with the Government of the day. The fact that the members of the judiciary remain in office when there is a change of Government supports this view, as do the changes to the process of appointing judges brought about by the Constitutional Reform Act 2005.

Conclusion

Whilst there are always criticisms of the judiciary, the systems in place ensure that, for the most part, the judiciary are effective and efficient and that the lapses that occur are usually ones that can be corrected within the system.

Activities

1 Discuss the effectiveness of the judiciary.

2 Read the following extract from *The Times* about the former High Court Judge, Sir Hugh Laddie.

Definitely no regrets: there is life beyond the High Court

[One difficulty that arises is that once a person becomes a High Court judge, there appears to be no going back as some judges may then refuse to have him appear as an advocate in their courts. However, in 2005, Sir Hugh Laddie announced that he was leaving the High Court Bench because he found it 'boring'. Since then he has gone to work part-time in a leading firm of intellectual property solicitors as a consultant and mediator. It means that he sees clients and can lecture and has taken up a part time post at University College London developing intellectual property law courses across the college.]

Laddie was a top patents silk when the 'tap on the shoulder' came in April 1995. 'I was at the Bar for 25 years. I had a truly stupendous time. I still think, if you're lucky and get a good practice, it's a great job.' But with the heavy and tiring workload – 'it was the only thing my wife and I would argue about' – he had no doubt about becoming a High Court judge. 'There was only one direction — down. You can't stay at the top for ever.'

For the first five years, he enjoyed it. But aspects jarred. 'One thing is that you are really isolated. You can go all day without speaking to another judge.'

So he set up a common room where judges could meet weekly for teas. Laddie, who was senior judge of the Patents Court, also believed strongly that the courts should serve litigants, not the profession. 'That meant I was determined to try to cut costs to a point where I used to irritate people.

'Everyone has egos – it's a matter of how difficult you find it to control.' Laddie did not endear himself to counsel when, at the start of a case, having read the papers, he would make clear his preliminary views. ' Obviously I had provisional thoughts – it would be amazing if I didn't. Some would say: he's made up his mind. I hadn't, of course.'

Laddie also objected to sitting on Chancery cases beyond his expertise. Had he taken a case outside his field at the Bar, he'd have left himself open to a negligence action, he says. But the moment he was a judge he was expected to do just that. 'It was challenging – like high-wire walking – but I didn't think it fair for clients to be learning at their expense.' Most worrying were the cases involving unrepresented litigants, with applications 'in an area of law that I knew nothing about.'

He remains outspoken in his criticisms. Litigation is reserved for the 'rich, mad or destitute', he says. 'The slowness of it; the expense of it.' The Woolf reforms had not had an impact on costs: he believes one answer is less oral advocacy with time limits on counsel's speeches. He also favours keeping the courts running in the long vacation.

There were unfounded fears that his departure would prompt an exodus or that people would simply go for the job for the knighthood. 'If that's what they thought, there must be an awful lot of unhappy judges. The other answer is: scrap the knighthood. They don't have them in Australia and have perfectly good judges. Or give it to all judges. Many do just as good a job as a High Court judge. One or two others may leave before their time is up "because they now see there's a door". But most like the job and will stay.'

Laddie acknowledges the 'great privilege' he had working with 'some spectacular people', although the company, he adds, 'was not exactly a cross-section of the population' and conversation inevitably limited to cases. It also has 'immense status'. But if people want to leave, they should be able to. 'We abolished slavery a long time ago. If you don't like it, get out. Keep the job for people who really want to do it.'

http://business.timesonline.co.uk

AQA Examiner's tip

Consider how this article helps you evaluate aspects of being a judge.

You should now be able to:

- evaluate the judiciary

- answer examination questions on the judiciary.

AQA Examination-style questions

☑

Chapter 5: The civil courts and other forms of dispute resolution

1 (a) Describe how tribunals work. *(10 marks)*

   (b) There are forms of dispute resolution apart than using the courts or tribunals. Describe any **two** of these forms, making reference to the types of dispute dealt with. *(10 marks)*

   (c) Discuss the disadvantages of the forms of dispute resolution you have described in (b) above. *(10 marks)*

2 (a) Arbitration is one form of Alternative Dispute Resolution. Explain how this form of Alternative Dispute Resolution works, and describe the types of cases dealt with by arbitration. *(10 marks)*

   (b) Describe the system of appeals through the courts of a civil case. *(10 marks)*

   (c) Discuss the advantages and disadvantages of arbitration. *(10 marks)*

Chapter 6: The criminal courts and lay people

1 (a) Describe the qualification, selection and appointment of lay magistrates. *(10 marks)*

   (b) Briefly describe the role of lay magistrates **and** a jury in the criminal process. *(10 marks)*

   (c) Identify and discuss the advantages of using **lay magistrates** in the criminal justice process. *(10 marks)*

2 (a) Explain how jurors may or may not qualify for jury service, and describe how jurors are chosen to serve on a jury. *(10 marks)*

   (b) Explain how a magistrate is selected and appointed. *(10 marks)*

   (c) Identify and discuss the advantages of using **a jury** in the criminal justice process. *(10 marks)*

Chapter 7: The legal profession and other forms of advice and funding

1 (a) Describe the work of solicitors both in **and** out of court. *(10 marks)*

   (b) Chris has been charged with robbery, an offence which is triable only on indictment. Briefly describe the different forms of legal advice and representation available to him. *(10 marks)*

   (c) Identify and consider the problems associated with these different forms of advice. *(10 marks)*

2 (a) Outline the stages in training and qualifying as a barrister. *(10 marks)*

   (b) Paveen has been injured in an accident. Explain from whom she could get advice about a possible claim for damages. *(10 marks)*

   (c) Briefly compare the roles played by solicitors, barristers and legal executives when acting for a defendant in a court case. *(10 marks)*

Chapter 8: The judiciary

1   (a) Naseem has been injured in a road accident. Briefly explain the role of the judge
         in Naseem's civil court claim for damages.   *(10 marks)*
     (b) Briefly describe how inferior judges are selected and appointed.   *(10 marks)*
     (c) Identify and comment on the problems associated with the methods of selection
         and appointment of judges.   *(10 marks)*

2   (a) Describe the role of a judge in **criminal** cases.   *(10 marks)*
     (b) Explain what is meant by the principle of judicial independence.   *(10 marks)*
     (c) Discuss the importance of this principle of judicial independence.   *(10 marks)*

AQA Examiner's tip

The examination paper has 10 marks out of a 30 mark question for evaluation. Do not waste time repeating in great detail facts stated in an earlier answer.

Answering questions on the legal system in AQA Law 1

There are a number of different aspects of learning that need to take place to answer the questions fully:

- being able to understand and explain the basic principles

- being able to illustrate the principles by reference to decided cases

- being able to select appropriate material for a given question

- being able to evaluate the legal principles and come to an appropriate conclusion.

The aspects listed above will enable examination questions to be tackled. The examination questions come in two formats:

- Theory or knowledge questions, on the lines of 'Outline the role of a judge in a Crown Court trial'

- Evaluation questions, such as 'Discuss the advantages and disadvantages of either tribunals or arbitration'.

It can be expected that the examination paper will contain legal system questions in Section B of the Unit 1 examination paper. There will be four questions on Section B of the paper: one question from each of the four topic areas in the AQA specification. These specification areas match Chapters 5–8 of this book. Each question will be divided into three parts, each worth 10 marks. You will therefore have, on average, a maximum of 10 minutes to answer each part question. The first two parts of each question will be theory or knowledge questions, and the final part, part (c), will be evaluative.

In the first type of question, theory or knowledge only, no reference needs to be made to evaluation. All you are expected to do is describe or explain the topic in the question asked for, using relevant examples. These examples might be decided cases, Acts of Parliament or general examples depending on the topic. The second type, evaluation, requires advantages and/or disadvantages to be stated, giving examples to demonstrate the point. You will need to read the question carefully, as you can be required to look at advantages only, disadvantages only, or both.

Answering a theory or knowledge only question

A theory only question might be:

> Briefly explain the work of a barrister.   *(10 marks)*

The potential content in the mark scheme would be: brief explanation of barristers' work, for example, specialist areas of work, giving pre-trial advice and drafting of documents, advocacy in court, advice and conduct on possible appeal, working from chambers, independent status, now direct access but also instructed through solicitors.

A good answer would include a description of each of these areas.

Answering an evaluation question

An evaluative question is set out below:

Consider the disadvantages of using juries in the English legal system.

(10 marks)

Note that the question does not ask you to repeat the description of your chosen rule, as the examiner may well have asked you to do that earlier in the question. You can refer back to that material and should not waste time repeating the information. You should note that in this case, the question looks for disadvantages only. A good answer would include:

Consideration of disadvantages of use of juries, for example, perverse verdicts, feelings of bias, unrepresentative nature, selection procedures, influence, media pressure, 'jury nobbling', complexity of issues.

Activities

1 Write up, using continuous prose, your answer to the two questions set out above.

2 Now attempt two questions from Section B of the sample paper in 60 minutes. Your teacher will be able to provide you with a copy of this.

You should now be able to:

- apply the principles in AS examination questions involving the legal system.

Introduction

Unit 2A, together with Unit 2B or Unit 2C, constitutes Unit 2 of the AS specification. Unit 2A is about criminal liability and is compulsory. Unit 2B is about tort and Unit 2C is about the law of contract. Candidates must answer the questions on either Unit B or C, but not both, as well as the questions on Unit A. Candidates choose to study either Unit 2B or Unit 2C in addition to Unit 2A from Unit 2.

All three are examined together on one examination paper, which constitutes 50 per cent of the overall marks for the AS qualification and 25 per cent of the overall marks for the A2 qualification. The Unit 2 examination is of 1.5 hours' duration. Candidates must answer all the questions from Section A and all the questions from Section B or Section C. There is no choice of question in any of the Sections.

The questions in each ection are worth 45 marks each. Each question is divided into several parts, each part normally being worth 5, 7 or 10 marks. Candidates must answer all parts of the question. All parts of the criminal liability question relate to criminal liability, and there can be no overlap between sections of the AQA Law AS specification.

The criminal liability section is covered by Chapters 9 and 10 of this book. Some parts of the question test the candidate's knowledge and understanding and some test application of the liability to the scenario that introduces the question. Question 1 is the criminal law question and is broken into three main parts with sub-parts. Part (a) usually tests knowledge and understanding only, whilst parts (b) and (c) test a mixture of knowledge, understanding and application.

Questions require answers to be written in continuous prose rather than note form. There are no short answer or multiple choice questions. Attainment of high grades is dependent on correct identification of the issues raised by the question, and sound explanation of each of the points, using authority. Authority is usually reference to a decided case or to an Act of Parliament, but may be examples taken from other sources. Further exam tips are provided throughout each topic and at the end of the chapter.

Unit 2A comprises two chapters:

9 **Underlying principles of criminal liability:** concerned with the basic terms used in criminal law, and goes on to look at five different non-fatal offences against the person. This provides the foundation for considering the criminal liability of the character or characters in the scenario in the question.

10 **The criminal courts: procedure and sentencing:** looks at the procedure that takes place in the criminal courts once a defendant has been charged with a crime, up to, but not including, his trial. The chapter continues to examine the way in which a guilty defendant is sentenced.

Underlying principles of criminal liability

In this topic you will learn how to:

- distinguish between the criminal process and the criminal law

- explain what is meant by criminal evidence and criminal procedure

- identify how cases and statutes are used to justify your answer to questions.

Key terms

Criminal law: the law that sets out the definitions of individual crimes.

Criminal process: the system used in a criminal case to manage the stages between the offence and conviction of the offender.

1 Introduction to criminal liability

Criminal law

Criminal law is concerned with the liability of an individual for wrongdoing against another individual, society, and/or the State. Not all wrongdoing is a crime, and some people consider that some crimes do not involve wrongdoing.

Society, through its lawmakers, has to decide what forms and types of conduct are to be criminal. Some forms of conduct, such as murder, have always been considered criminal. Other forms of conduct were criminal in the past but are no longer criminal, such as homosexual acts between consenting adults. Some activities have been made criminal, such as possessing certain types of drug. Some crimes have come into being to cover new situations, such as computer misuse.

The starting point for any criminal conviction is the criminal law. Crimes are defined either in an Act of Parliament or by reference to decided cases. This requires the use of the rules of statutory interpretation and the doctrine of precedent that are studied in Unit 1 of the AQA Law specification. The defendant's behaviour must match the definition of the crime for him to be guilty. The definition of the crime usually has two parts to it: the *actus reus* and the *mens rea*. The *actus reus* is the guilty act and the *mens rea* is the guilty mind.

These terms are examined in more detail in later topics in this chapter.

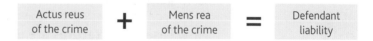

Fig. 9.1 *Link Between the definition of a crime and the defendant's liability*

The criminal process

The **criminal process** has the function of deciding whether the crime has been committed by the accused and, if so, what sentence should be imposed. Reporting a crime is just the beginning. Police investigations, prosecution decision-making, court processes and sentencing can be a long and complicated business for both the victim and the defendant. Once a person has been arrested and charged with a crime, they have to go to court to be tried and, if found guilty, to receive their sentence. The length and complexity of the process depends on the seriousness of the crime, whether the evidence is clear and how the defendant pleads. There are rules of procedure that set out the court in which the case will be heard and the framework for deciding the case.

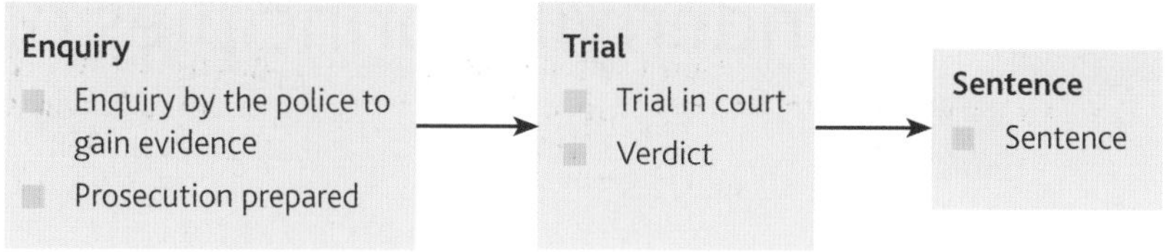

Enquiry	Trial	Sentence
■ Enquiry by the police to gain evidence ■ Prosecution prepared	■ Trial in court ■ Verdict	■ Sentence

Fig. 9.2 *The criminal process*

When information about a case is received from the police, a Crown Prosecutor will read the papers and decide whether or not there is enough **criminal evidence** against the defendant and whether it is in the public interest to bring that person to court. There are rules of evidence that set out how the facts must be proved and the degree of certainty that is required. In a criminal trial, the burden is upon the prosecution to prove the guilt of the defendant beyond reasonable doubt. Juries in Crown Court trials are directed that, unless the evidence makes them satisfied so they are sure of guilt, their verdict must be one of not guilty. Magistrates also work to the same standard of proof.

Sentencing

Magistrates' Courts and the Crown Court have different **sentencing** powers. More serious cases are sentenced in the Crown Court and less serious offences are sentenced in the Magistrates' Court. When the defendant is convicted following a trial or a guilty plea, the court has a range of sentencing options available. These depend on the type, the seriousness and the circumstances of the crime, and on the maximum penalty available by law. When deciding upon the appropriate sentence, courts have guidelines to assist them. The judge or magistrate giving the sentence must consider the aims of: punishing the defendant, reducing crime, rehabilitating the defendant, protecting the public, and the defendant making reparation. The sentence will be a combination of these aims.

How cases and statutes are used in answers to AQA Unit 2

The question paper for Unit 2 is divided into three sections. The first section, Section A, is compulsory and is the introduction to criminal law. The question starts with a short scenario that sets the scene and is the basis of your discussions for some of the questions. A scenario taken from the sample paper is:

> Jenny had an argument with her boyfriend, David. This resulted in David hitting Jenny with a cricket bat. Jenny suffered a very badly broken leg that needed surgery. David, who has several previous convictions for violence, denies that he was involved.

The questions are of two general types:

Theory questions

These require an explanation of terms used and no reference to the facts given in the scenario. A typical question (taken from the sample paper) is:

1 Criminal offences usually require *actus reus* and *mens rea*, although some crimes are crimes of strict liability.

   i   Explain, using examples, the meaning of the term *actus reus*.

   ii Explain, using examples, the meaning of the term *mens rea*.

   iii Explain, using examples, the meaning of the term 'strict liability'.

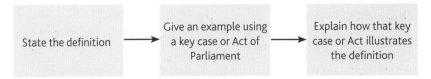

Fig. 9.3 *Content of theory answer*

Application questions

These usually require you to select the appropriate law or principles of sentencing and apply the law to the facts given in the scenario. You should assume that the facts as stated in the scenario can be proved. A typical question (taken from the sample paper) is:

Taking into account the explanations given in your answer to 1(a), discuss the criminal liability of David for the injuries suffered by Jenny.

Fig. 9.4 *Content of application answer*

Conclusion

Criminal law requires an understanding of the different aspects of the law that come into play in the criminal process. This Unit concentrates on the underlying concepts in criminal law and a little of the process. Your understanding of this will develop as you continue through the topics and chapters.

Activities

1 List two types of wrongdoing not mentioned in this topic that you believe should be a crime, and two crimes that you think should not be a crime. Compare your list with someone else and think about why you came up with those ideas.

2 Look at the criminal cases reported in your local newspaper and identify the stage in the process each has reached, or outline the process that will have been followed where a person has been found guilty.

You should now be able to:

▪ understand the underlying principles to the study of criminal liability

▪ understand how to use cases and statutes to justify your answers.

■ **Key terms**

Actus reus: the guilty act.

AQA Examiner's tip

The examination will have a number of theory-only questions that need to be answered accurately, using decided cases as examples.

■ Link

For more information on the Offences Against the Person Act 1861 see Topic 8 of this chapter, p182.

■ **Key cases**

Hill v Baxter (1958): an involuntary action does not form the actus reus of a crime.

Pittwood (1902): here a contractual duty created criminal liability for an omission when the defendant failed to act as required.

💡 2 Actus reus

A voluntary deliberate act

As you have seen in Topic 1, a criminal offence usually requires both a guilty act (*actus reus*) and a guilty mind (*mens rea*). The **actus reus** of a crime is the voluntary, deliberate act of the defendant. One of the offences that you will be studying is found in the Offences Against the Person Act 1861 s20, which states:

Whosoever shall unlawfully and maliciously wound or inflict any grievous bodily harm upon any other person, either with or without any weapon or instrument …

The *actus reus* is any act of the defendant that: (i) is unlawful; and (ii) has the consequence of causing an injury to the victim that (iii) the law classifies as a wound or grievous bodily harm. You can see that the act might be a punch or a shot from a gun or hitting with an iron bar. All these appear to be voluntary deliberate acts of the defendant, and so would form the actus reus of s20.

There are, however, different considerations when:

1 the act appears to be involuntary; or
2 there has been no positive act, merely a failure to act: an omission.

Involuntary acts

When describing the term *actus reus*, you need to look at involuntary acts and omissions too, but not causation, unless the question specifically asks for causation.

Everybody performs involuntary acts, such as closing their eyes whilst sneezing. This can be seen in **Hill v Baxter (1958)**. In this case the court gave examples of situations where a driver of a car would not be driving voluntarily. These included being stung by a swarm of bees and being hit on the head by a stone. Such actions would not form the *actus reus* of a crime and so a defendant could not be guilty.

It is clear that, if a strong person holds a knife in the hand of a weaker person and uses the knife to stab another person, then the weaker person could not be guilty of stabbing the victim. That would be because the act was not a voluntary deliberate act of the weaker person.

Omissions

An omission, being a failure to act, is not an act. The law only makes a person liable for his failure to act where he has a duty to act. That duty can arise in a number of ways.

Where a person's contract requires him to act

A case involving a contract is **Pittwood (1902)**. In that case, Pittwood was employed as a gatekeeper at a railway crossing. One day he went for lunch, leaving the gate open. This meant that road traffic could cross the railway line. A cart crossing the line was hit by a train. One man on the cart was killed. Pittwood was convicted of manslaughter, based on his failure (omission) to carry out his duty to close the gate when a train approached. The duty to close the gate was part of his contract of employment.

Where a person's public position requires him to act

A case involving a person's public position is **Dytham (1979)**. In that case a uniformed police officer saw a man who ended up being kicked to death. He took no steps to stop the attack and drove away when it was over. He was convicted of the offence of misconduct in a public office, as he had neglected to act to protect the victim.

Where an Act of Parliament requires a person to act

There are many examples of this, ranging from the requirement to wear a seatbelt whilst driving a car, to neglect (failure to look after) of a child under the Children and Young Persons Act 1933.

Where a person fails to minimise the harmful consequences of his act

In **Miller (1983)**, Miller had been squatting in a house and fell asleep on a mattress whilst smoking a cigarette. He was awoken by the flames, but instead of putting the fire out, he simply got up and went into another room, where he found another mattress and went back to sleep. As a result, the house was damaged by fire. He was convicted of criminal damage. Once he awoke and realised what had happened, he had a duty to minimise the harmful effects of the fire.

Where a person voluntarily takes on a duty

In **Stone and Dobinson (1977)**, the defendants lived together, but were of low intelligence and had many personal difficulties. Despite this, Stone's sister came to live with them. The sister was anorexic, and although ill she refused to leave her room to seek medical attention. Stone and Dobinson made some effort to care for the sick woman, but did not call the medical services. Eventually she died. Stone and Dobinson were convicted of manslaughter, as they had taken on a duty of care, by allowing her to live in their home and making no other arrangements for her, whilst knowing that she relied on them.

Conclusion

The *actus reus* of a crime is an essential ingredient of a crime. It is usually a voluntary deliberate act, but can, in some circumstances, be an omission. The next topic examines whether the act caused the consequence required for the crime.

When you are asked to explain the meaning of the term *actus reus*, you will need to describe:

1   the idea of a guilty act
2   the idea of a voluntary act
3   the fact that there is no liability if there is no act
4   the exceptions where there is liability for an omission.

Key cases

Dytham (1979): here a person's public position created liability for an omission.

Miller (1983): the defendant's failure to minimise harm, caused by a dangerous situation he had created, created liability for an omission.

Stone and Dobinson (1977): a person can take on responsibility for another and create liability for an omission if they fail to fulfil the duty.

Activities

1 Consider the following situation. John stopped his car at a pedestrian crossing to let a family cross the road. As the family crossed, a car drove into the back of John's car. Despite John having the brakes on, his car was pushed onto the crossing and knocked down a member of the family who were on the crossing. Is John's act of knocking the person down voluntary or involuntary?

2 Consider the following situation. You have been left to look after a friend's three-year-old daughter. Think of situations in which you would be liable and situations in which you would not be liable if the child were injured. Would it make any difference if you were a paid babysitter?

3 Take each of the cases mentioned in this chapter and make a table as in the example set out below. Note you do not need to remember the dates of the cases.

Case	Key facts	Legal principle
Pittwood	Left crossing gates open and man was killed.	His omission to close the gates whilst not an act was the *actus reus* of the crime.

You should now be able to:

■ understand the meaning of the term *actus reus*

■ explain, using cases as examples, aspects of the term *actus reus*.

In this topic you will learn how to:

■ state the meaning of the term 'causation'

■ distinguish between factual and legal causation

■ describe and give examples of the meaning of factual causation

■ describe and give examples of the meaning of legal causation.

Key terms

Causation: the link between the defendant's act and the criminal consequence.

💡 **3** Causation

The problem of causation

The *actus reus* of a crime is the defendant's guilty act. For many crimes, that act must have caused a particular consequence. The rules of **causation** are applied to decide whether the defendant's guilty act caused the required consequence in the definition of a particular crime. Thus in homicide, the defendant's act must have caused the death of the victim. In offences against the person, the defendant's act must have caused the injury that is relevant for the particular offence. If it does not, or the act is not unlawful, there is no criminal liability.

Crimes can be categorised as 'conduct' or 'action' crimes, where the act is the *actus reus* and the consequences are immaterial, or 'result crimes', where the *actus reus* must produce a particular consequence such as death or a particular type of harm.

In many cases causation is not in issue. If I hit another person very hard over the head with an iron bar and their skull is then fractured, there is no question that I caused the broken skull. Where it is less clear, the prosecution must prove both factual and legal causation. These two terms will now be explored in more detail. Most of the cases involve homicide, but the principles apply equally to all cases where the prosecution has to prove that the defendant's act caused a particular consequence.

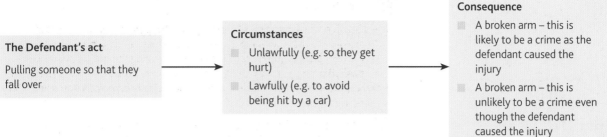

The Defendant's act

Pulling someone so that they fall over

Circumstances

- Unlawfully (e.g. so they get hurt)
- Lawfully (e.g. to avoid being hit by a car)

Consequence

- A broken arm – this is likely to be a crime as the defendant caused the injury
- A broken arm – this is unlikely to be a crime even though the defendant caused the injury

Fig. 9.5 *Link from act to consequence*

Factual causation

The defendant can only be guilty if the consequence would not have happened 'but for' his act. This can be seen in the case of **White (1910)**. In that case, White put the poison cyanide in his mother's drink, intending to kill her. She died shortly thereafter as a result of a heart attack. The poison had not taken effect at that time. Whilst he had intended to kill her and she had died, he had not caused her death and therefore could not be guilty of murder.

A different way of stating the test is to ask whether the prohibited result would have occurred if the defendant had not acted. If the prohibited result would still have occurred, even without the defendant's actions, then something other than the defendant's actions caused it and the **factual causation** is not present.

This principle can also be seen in an unusual way. In the case of **Pagett (1983)**, the defendant used his girlfriend, Gail, as a human shield while he shot at armed police. The police fired back and killed Gail. Pagett was convicted of Gail's manslaughter, as she would not have died 'but for' his use of her as a human shield.

Legal causation

Once it is established that there is factual causation, the prosecution must also prove **legal causation**. This is so that there is little chance of the conviction of a truly innocent person. The link between the act and the consequence is known as the chain of causation, which must remain unbroken if there is to be criminal liability.

Suppose you invite a friend to visit you at your house. On the way to visit you, your friend is stabbed and seriously injured. It could be said that, but for your invitation, your friend would not have been stabbed. Clearly, you are not guilty of causing the injuries, as your invitation was not the 'operating and substantial' cause of them. The 'operating and substantial' cause is the key test for legal causation and has several different aspects to consider.

The original injury must be the operating and substantial cause. This can be illustrated by two cases involving medical intervention. It should be noted that, in medical intervention cases, there is a degree of sympathy for the doctors, who will be considered to have caused the injury or death only if the treatment is seriously incorrect. The general sequence of events is as set out below.

Key cases

White (1910): there was no factual cause of death because the actual cause was natural and not affected by the defendant's act.

Pagett (1983): this is an unusual result of the 'but for' test, but is quite logical.

Key terms

Factual causation: this is the 'but for' test: but for the defendant's act, would the consequence have occurred?

Legal causation: this is the 'operating and substantial cause' test to find the link between the defendant's act and the criminal consequence.

AQA Examiner's tip

Some candidates confuse factual and legal causation. Make sure you are clear about the distinction and that both factual and legal causation is needed for there to be criminal liability.

Fig. 9.6 *Sequence of events in causation cases involving bad medical treatment*

The first case is **Jordan (1956)**. In that case the defendant had stabbed the victim, who was taken to hospital. A week later, when the wound was almost healed, doctors gave him an incorrect injection and he died. As the medical treatment was 'palpably wrong', there was no legal causation and the defendant was acquitted. The original injury was not the operating and substantial cause of death, but the defendant would still be guilty of wounding.

The second case is **Smith (1959)**. In that case two soldiers were involved in a fight. The victim received a stab wound that pierced his lung. The victim was taken to the medical station, where he died about one hour later. On being charged with murder, the defendant argued that the chain of causation between the stabbing and the death had been broken by the way in which the victim had been treated, in particular the fact that: (a) the victim had been dropped twice whilst being carried to the medical station; (b) the medical officer, who was dealing with a series of emergencies, did not realise the serious extent of the wounds; and (c) the treatment he gave him was 'thoroughly bad and might well have affected his chances of recovery'. The defendant was convicted of murder and appealed unsuccessfully. The court held that the defendant's stabbing was the 'operating and substantial cause' of the victim's death. In this case the victim clearly died from loss of blood caused by the stab wounds inflicted by the defendant.

It can also be seen that rare medical complications can break the chain of causation, but only where the original injury is no longer having any real effect. This can be seen in the case of **Cheshire (1991)**, where the victim was shot in the thigh and stomach. The victim died as a result of rare complications from a tracheotomy that had not been spotted by the doctors. Even though the original wounds were no longer life-threatening, the tracheotomy given to help breathing problems and the rare complication were not seen as independent of the gunshot wounds, so the chain of causation was not broken.

Intervening acts or events

Sometimes the sole cause of the death or injury seems to be a completely independent act. This is known as a ***novus actus interveniens***, or new act intervening. This can be seen in the case of **Malcherek (1981)**. Here, the defendant attacked a woman causing injuries that were so severe that the victim had to be placed on a life support machine. Doctors decided to switch off the machine after determining that the victim was 'brain dead' and that there was no prospect of recovery. Half an hour later, the victim was pronounced dead. The defendant was convicted of murder and appealed on the ground that the doctors had broken the chain of causation between the defendant's attack and the death of the victim by deliberately switching off the life support machine. However, the operating and substantial cause of death had been the original wounds inflicted by the defendant. The effect of the life support machine was merely to hold the effect of the injuries in suspension; as soon as the machine was switched off the original wounds continued to cause the death of the victim, even if death followed within seconds of the machine's disconnection. There was therefore no break in the chain of causation.

Take your victim as you find him

The general principle is that you take your victim as you find him: in other words, the law does not take into account any particular characteristics of the victim. In *Watson* (1989), it did not matter that the victim was an old man: if he was therefore more likely to suffer a heart attack, then that was a risk the defendant must take. This is clearly illustrated by the case of **Blaue (1975)**. The defendant had stabbed the victim, who was a Jehovah's Witness. The victim was rushed to hospital where doctors told her that she would die if she did not have a blood transfusion. The victim refused on religious grounds and died from her wounds shortly after. The defendant argued that the victim's refusal of treatment was unreasonable and so broke the chain of causation. However, the defendant had to take his victim as he found her, meaning not just her physical condition, but also her religious beliefs. The question for the court was what caused the death. The answer was the stab wound, so the defendant caused the victim's death.

The victim's own act

If the defendant causes the victim to act in a foreseeable way, then the victim's own act will not break the chain of causation. This depends on whether the victim's conduct is reasonable or unreasonable. Contrast the cases of **Roberts (1971)** and **Williams (1992)**. In *Roberts* (1971) a girl who was a passenger in the defendant's car injured herself by jumping out of the car while it was moving. Her explanation was that the defendant had made sexual advances to her and was trying to pull her coat off. The defendant was convicted, as it was held that the correct test for causation in law was to ask whether the result was the reasonably foreseeable consequence of what the defendant was saying or doing. However, the chain of causation would be broken by the victim doing something 'daft' or so unexpected that no reasonable man could be expected to foresee it. In *Williams* (1992) the defendants gave a lift to a hitch-hiker and allegedly tried to rob him. The victim jumped from the moving car and died from head injuries caused by falling into the road. Here, his own voluntary act was one which could be a *novus actus interveniens* and consequently break the chain of causation. It should of course be borne in mind that a victim may, in the agony of the moment, do the wrong thing.

Conclusion

Once it has been established that the defendant performed an act, the *actus reus*, the prosecution then must prove that his act caused the criminal consequence. Causation has two parts to it, factual and legal causation. These are the elements you will need to explain if the exam requires you to deal with causation.

> **Key cases**
>
> **Blaue (1975):** here the victim's religious beliefs led to refusal of possible life-saving treatment. This is an example of the principle of take your victim as you find him.
>
> **Roberts (1971):** the victim's own act was reasonable so there was causation.
>
> **Williams (1992):** the victim's own act might be unreasonable and so break the chain of causation. The victim thus caused their own injuries.

> **AQA Examiner's tip**
>
> There are many aspects to causation. You will need to deal with all aspects in a theory question, even though the scenario only points to some aspects of causation.

Activities

1. It is not always easy to find out whether the defendant's act is the cause of the criminal consequence. In the case of *Watson* (1989), the question before the court was 'did the defendant cause the victim's death?'

    Watson and another man burgled an old man's house at night. They knew he was very frail. When they saw him, they shouted abuse but took nothing. Shortly after, the police arrived, as did council workmen, who repaired a window broken by the burglars. Ninety minutes after the burglary the old man had a heart attack and died. The court had to decide whether there was sufficient evidence that the burglars caused the heart attack as anyone seeing him would have known he was frail.

    Discuss whether you think Watson caused the death of the old man.

2. Explain the causation issues in the past examination scenario set out below:

    Jamal, a man of middle-eastern appearance, was walking to work when Sam ran up behind him. As he ran up, Sam shouted racial abuse and made suggestions that Jamal was a terrorist. Jamal was afraid that Sam was going to attack him, so he ran across the street without looking. Unfortunately, he ran in front of a moving car and suffered a badly broken leg.

3. Explain the causation issues in the past examination scenario set out below:

    Anna was walking alongside Tara, when she tripped Tara up with her foot. Tara fell over and grazed her knee. She ignored the graze until three days later, when her knee became swollen by an infection. She went to her doctor, who prescribed her a drug to deal with the infection. Tara's doctor did not check her medical records. Tara is in fact allergic to this drug and has become paralysed as a result of her reaction to taking the drug.

4. Using the general layout in Fig. 9.6 on p170, add the facts of the cases in this topic area and show whether the chain of causation has been broken.

You should now be able to:

- understand the meaning of the term 'causation'
- explain, using cases as examples, the meaning of factual and legal causation.

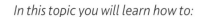

4 Mens rea

The general principle of *mens rea*

Many crimes need *actus reus* and also **mens rea**. The *mens rea* is the guilty mind and is often the distinguishing factor between different crimes. For example, the main difference between s18 and s20 of the Offences Against the Person Act 1861 is the *mens rea* required. *Mens rea* must be distinguished from motive. Whilst the motive behind a criminal act may give an indication of the defendant's *mens rea*, it is generally irrelevant. Motive can be relevant in some crimes such as a racially motivated assault and can also be a factor that the court will take into account in passing sentence. In this specification the only types of *mens rea* are intention and subjective recklessness.

Intention

Intention can be either direct intention or oblique (indirect) intention. The idea that a person will be guilty of a crime if he intends to perform a criminal act is perfectly reasonable. One definition of direct intent can be seen in the case of **Mohan (1976)**, where it was said that direct intention is a decision to bring about, so far as it lies in the defendant's powers, the criminal consequence, no matter whether the defendant desired that consequence of his act or not.

The offence under s18 of the Offences Against the Person Act 1861 sets out the *mens rea* as '… intent to do some grievous bodily harm to any person, or with intent to resist or prevent the lawful apprehension or detainer of any person …'. Thus, if I am angry and want to seriously injure someone, I might deliberately hit them on the head many times with an iron bar. This would be direct intent to cause grievous bodily harm. It is seen as **direct intent**, as the resulting injury is my aim or purpose.

Difficulties arise when the defendant's aim is something different to the actual consequence. This is known as oblique intent: the defendant intended the act but not the consequences.

Key terms

Mens rea: the guilty mind of the defendant.

Direct intent: this occurs where the consequence is the defendant's aim or purpose.

Key cases

Mohan (1976): this case is an example of, and gives a definition of, direct intent.

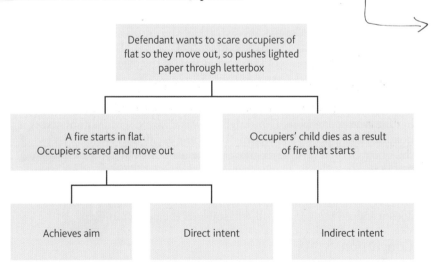

Fig. 9.7 *Distinction between direct and oblique intent*

F.C ⎱ "Forseeing the
V.C ⎰ consequences
⎱ of having a
predictable outcome"
↑
seen in
"R v Woolin"

Woollin (1998): sets out the 'virtual certainty' test for oblique intention.

Matthews and Alleyne (2003): confirms that the virtual certainty test in Woollin allows the jury to infer intention.

Cunningham (1957): sets out the essential definition of subjective recklessness which is used in the *mens rea* of many crimes.

■ Key terms

Recklessness: the level of *mens rea* lower than intention, wherein the defendant knows there a risk but goes ahead and takes it anyway.

The jury in a criminal trial must have a clear direction from the judge as to how they should decide whether the defendant had the necessary intention. The leading case on this is **Woollin (1998)**. In that case the defendant was feeding his three-month-old son. The baby choked on his food and the defendant lost his temper and threw the baby towards his pram. The baby hit the wall and suffered head injuries from which he died. Clearly, the defendant did not have direct intention to kill his son. The court stated a two-part test to decide whether the defendant had oblique intent. The test allows the court or jury to infer intention if:

a the consequence is a virtually certain result of the act; and

b the defendant knows that it is a virtually certain consequence.

Thus in *Woollin* (1998), a murder case where the required consequence is death or serious bodily harm, the jury would be able to infer (this is the precise word used in the case and means 'draw as a conclusion') intention, if:

a death or really serious harm to the baby was a virtually certain result of the baby being thrown and hitting the wall; and

b Woollin knew that it was a virtually certain consequence of the baby hitting the wall that the baby would die or suffer really serious harm.

This was considered again in **Matthews and Alleyne (2003)**. In that case the Court of Appeal stressed that the defendant's appreciation of death or serious bodily harm as a virtual certainty does not constitute the necessary intention for murder, but is something from which that intention can be inferred. The facts of that case were that Matthews and Alleyne pushed their victim from a bridge into a river, knowing he could not swim. They watched him head towards the bank, but did not stay to see if he succeeded in getting out. In fact, he drowned.

Be quite clear about the difference between direct and oblique intention: candidates sometimes confuse the two.

Recklessness

Some crimes require the lower level of *mens rea* of **recklessness**. The type of recklessness that is used is subjective recklessness. This occurs where the defendant knows there a risk of the criminal consequence, is willing to take it and takes it deliberately. This is also difficult to establish as it requires looking at what was in the defendant's mind. The leading case on this is **Cunningham (1957)**. In this case the defendant had broken a pre-pay gas meter to steal the money in it, with the result that gas escaped into the next-door house. The victim became ill and her life was endangered. Cunningham was charged with administering a noxious substance to the victim. The court decided that the *mens rea* of the offence could be intention or recklessness and defined recklessness as 'being recklessness as to whether such harm should occur or not (that is the accused has foreseen that the particular kind of harm might be done, and yet has gone on to take the risk of it). It is neither limited to, nor does it indeed require, any ill-will towards the person injured.'

Conclusion

The *mens rea* of an offence is often quite difficult to prove. There have been many cases where the courts have struggled to find suitable words to direct the jury. The present rules on this are reasonably clear and can be applied in examination questions.

Activities

1 Consider which type of *mens rea* is shown in the following example:

A young girl was struck twice whilst playing in the forecourt of a block of flats by two airgun pellets, which had been fired from a window by the appellant. He admitted to the police that he had fired a few shots out of the window, not in order to hit anyone, but to see how far the pellets would go. (Based on *Spratt* (1990).

2 Consider which type of *mens rea* is shown in the following example:

Unknown to the science tutor in charge, a student went out of the lesson and took with him a boiling tube of concentrated acid. He went into one of the toilets. He then heard footsteps in the corridor outside the toilet, panicked and poured the acid into the hot air dryer, the nozzle of which was pointing upwards. He intended to return later to deal with the acid in the dryer. However, some time later another student went to the toilet to wash his hands. He turned on the dryer. The acid was ejected onto his forehead and trickled down the right side of his nose. It caused a permanent scar. (Based on *DPP v K* (1990).

You should now be able to:

- understand the meaning of the term *mens rea*

- explain the meaning of intention as a form of *mens rea* using cases to illustrate the term

- explain the meaning of recklessness as a form of *mens rea* using cases to illustrate the term.

Examiner's tip

Make sure you can distinguish between oblique intent and recklessness. A common fault is confusing these two.

5 Coincidence of *actus reus* and *mens rea* and transferred malice

Coincidence of *actus reus* and *mens rea*

The general principle is that the *actus reus* and *mens rea* of a crime must occur at the same time. This is also called the contemporaneity rule. The idea is that a person cannot be guilty of a crime if he performs an act that causes a previously desired result. Thus, if I go out on Saturday with the intention of finding and injuring X, but fail do so, it does not make my activity on Tuesday a crime when I accidentally injure X in a car crash, not knowing that X was in the other car.

The courts have modified this rule so that a series of linked acts or omissions can be treated as a single continuing event. This establishes the coincidence of *actus reus* and *mens rea*. A simple example of this is the case of **Fagan v Metropolitan Police Commissioner (MPC) (1969)**.

In that case the defendant accidentally stopped his car on a policeman's foot. When the policeman asked him to remove the car from his foot, he replied 'F*** off, you can wait.'

The court found Fagan guilty of causing the injury to the policeman as leaving the car on the foot was seen as a continuing act. Even though he did not have the *mens rea* for the crime when he stopped the car on the foot (it was purely accidental), he did form the *mens rea* when he refused to move it and the act of placing the car on the foot remained.

In this topic you will learn how to:

- identify the circumstances where there is coincidence of *actus reus* and *mens rea*

- describe the cases involving continuing acts

- describe the concept of transferred malice.

Key cases

Fagan v MPC (1969): here there was a continuing act, so there was coincidence of *actus reus* and *mens rea* when the *mens rea* was later formed.

Fig. 9.8 *Fagan v MPC*

Sometimes the continuing act is a series of connected acts. This can be seen in a similar manner to the chain of causation considered in Topic 3 of this chapter; each act or omission is part of the continuing act and the *mens rea* can be said to continue throughout. This can be seen in the case of **Thabo Meli (1954)**, where the defendant hit the victim over the head, intending to kill him. Believing the victim was dead and trying to make it look like an accident, the defendant threw the victim over a cliff, where the victim later died of exposure.

mens rea

| Beating | Thrown off cliff | Dies of exposure |

Fig. 9.9 *In Thabo Meli, the courts viewed the three separate incidents as one long continuing act*

In *Thabo Meli* (1954) the *mens rea* continued throughout, as the defendant had set out to kill the victim. In **Church (1966)**, the defendant panicked, believing his victim was dead. This was not his desired consequence. What actually happened was the defendant had gone to his van with a woman for sexual purposes. She mocked his impotence and he had attacked her, knocking her out. The defendant panicked and, wrongly thinking he had killed her, threw her unconscious body into a river, where she drowned. He argued that all he had done wrong was to dispose of or conceal a dead body and that the *mens rea* for the attack on the woman ended when he thought her unconscious body was in fact dead. The court decided that the *mens rea* continued even after he thought she was dead, so as to include her death from drowning.

Transferred malice

Transferred malice occurs when the defendant's *mens rea* is transferred from the intended victim to the actual victim. This can occur either by, for example, hitting one person and knocking them into another whom you have no intention of hitting, or by shooting at one person, missing, and injuring another. Thus in the case of **Mitchell (1983)** the defendant, having become involved in an argument whilst queuing in a post office, pushed an elderly man, causing him to fall accidentally on an elderly woman, who subsequently died in hospital from her injuries. The defendant unsuccessfully appealed on the ground that his unlawful act had not been directed at the victim. The court said that although there was no direct contact between the defendant and the victim, she was injured as a direct result of his act and that the *mens rea* was transferred to the victim. There was, of course, also a crime committed against the person originally pushed over.

Conclusion

The general principle of coincidence between *actus reus* and *mens rea* is sometimes interpreted quite widely to ensure that there can be a conviction where someone is truly guilty. These interpretations include continuing acts and transferred malice.

Activities

Consider the elements of coincidence of *actus reus* and *mens rea* in the following situation:

Lyn had broken up with her boyfriend, Carl, and was very angry that he continued to climb onto the branches of a tree in the park next to her garden and shout at her when she was out in her garden. She went out one night and partly sawed through some of the branches on the tree, hoping that they would break and that Carl would fall and be injured next time he pestered her. Unfortunately, the next day, Jan, aged 6, climbed the tree. She fell and was seriously injured when one of the branches broke.

You should now be able to:

■ understand the meaning of the term 'coincidence of *actus reus* and *mens rea*'

■ understand the meaning of the term 'transferred malice'

■ explain those terms with the help of decided cases.

6 Strict liability → actus reus but no mens rea

The general principle of strict liability

Crimes of **strict liability** are crimes where the definition of the crime includes an *actus reus* and no *mens rea*. Merely performing the act is sufficient to make a person guilty. There are many crimes of strict liability, many of which are purely regulatory and are not always seen by some sections of society as 'real' crimes. Many motoring offences are included in these crimes, and in many cases the decision to prosecute or not is seen, in part, as an indication of whether there is a truly wrongful act.

Strict liability offences were originally created to make it easier to prove guilt for business-related offences. In the 19th century, with the industrial revolution, there were many abuses of factory workers that were the subject of criminal law, but there were very few successful prosecutions, as showing *mens rea* on the part of the factory owner was very difficult. In addition, there was a view that, as the magistrates were often factory owners as well, there was a temptation to find factory owners not guilty, and lack of *mens rea* was often the reason given. When *mens rea* did not have to be proved, conviction rates increased and so did factory safety.

AQA Examiner's tip

You can recognise the need to discuss this topic in applying the law to a given scenario where there is a time gap between different parts of the story.

AQA Examiner's tip

Make sure you state and apply the relevant law when tackling a problem question.

In this topic you will learn how to:

■ explain the meaning of strict liability, giving reasons for its use

■ state and explain examples of strict liability using decided cases and Acts of Parliament.

Key terms

Strict liability: these are crimes defined as requiring an *actus reus* only; *mens rea* has no relevance.

Key cases

Sweet v Parsley (1970): this case is not one of strict liability as the House of Lords decided that the statute did not specifically exclude *mens rea*.

Gammon (Hong Kong) Ltd v Attorney-General for Hong Kong (1985): this case sets out the general criteria for a crime to be a crime of strict liability.

Strict liability today

The vast majority of strict liability crimes are statutory offences. However, statutes do not always state explicitly that a particular offence is one of strict liability. Where a statute uses terms such as 'knowingly' or 'recklessly' then the offence being created is one that requires *mens rea*. Sometimes, particularly in more recent statutes, it may be made clear that an offence of strict liability is being created. In many cases it will be a matter for the courts to interpret the statute and decide whether *mens rea* is required or not. The famous case of **Sweet v Parsley (1970)** was decided in The House of Lords, and established that the offence of being involved in the management of premises which were used for the smoking of cannabis was not an offence of strict liability under the Dangerous Drugs Act 1965. The facts were that Miss Sweet, a teacher, let out her cottage to students and only visited rarely to collect post and see that things were in order. She kept a separate room locked for her use when she visited the cottage. She knew nothing of the drug-taking and was acquitted when it was decided that an element of *mens rea* was needed for there to be a conviction for this crime.

In **Gammon (Hong Kong) Ltd v Attorney-General for Hong Kong (1985)**, the court considered the scope and role of strict liability offences in the modern criminal law. The court started with the principle that in criminal law there is a presumption of *mens rea*. This means that it is presumed that all criminal offences require some form of *mens rea* unless the definition of the offence states the opposite. Unfortunately, as is seen in Unit 1, not all statutes are clear, so Lord Scarman laid down the criteria upon which a court should decide whether or not it is appropriate to impose strict liability. These criteria were as follows.

- There is a presumption of law that *mens rea* is required before a person can be held guilty of a criminal offence.
- The presumption is particularly strong where the offence is 'truly criminal' in character.
- The presumption applies to statutory offences, and can be displaced only if this is clearly or by necessary implication the effect of the statute.
- The only situation in which the presumption can be displaced is where the statute is concerned with an issue of social concern, and public safety is such an issue.
- Even where a statute is concerned with such an issue, the presumption of *mens rea* stands, unless it can be shown that the creation of strict liability will be effective to promote the objects of the statute by encouraging greater vigilance to prevent the commission of the prohibited act.

These can be summarised as follows:

- presumption of *mens rea*
- truly criminal
- statute must clearly exclude *mens rea*
- only for public safety or social concern
- encouraging greater vigilance.

Examples of strict liability

Many cases of strict liability result in a very minor penalty, which makes one wonder why there was a prosecution in the first place. A typical case is **Alphacell v Woodward (1972)**, where the defendants were

Key cases

Alphacell v Woodward (1972): here the defendant company was guilty even though event could not be predicted. This encourages greater vigilance in business.

papermakers. There was an overflow from settling tanks which allowed polluted water to be discharged into a river. The overflow had happened because pumping equipment had become blocked. The company had alarm systems and a regular maintenance and inspection programme, but could not predict if and when there would be a blockage. Despite this the company were found guilty and fined £20.

From the company's point of view, the main problem with a prosecution is often the hidden costs: engaging lawyers; non-productive time investigating the alleged offence and going to meetings about it; and bad publicity if there is a conviction (would you go to a fast food outlet that had just been prosecuted for selling unfit food?) Bad publicity affects future business, and fines affect profits. The result is that the real people punished are the shareholders who may be far removed from the business. Consider **Smedleys v Breed (1974)**, where one tin of peas, out of millions of tins produced by the defendants, contained a caterpillar. The defendants were convicted under the Food and Drugs Act 1955, even though they had taken all reasonable care.

Sometimes the conviction and publicity will have little lasting effect on the defendant but serves as a reminder to others of their legal obligations. In **London Borough of Harrow v Shah (2000)**, the court held that the offence of selling a national lottery ticket to a person under 16 was a strict liability offence because the offence was not truly criminal but dealt with a matter of social concern (gambling by young people).

In **Blake (1997)**, investigation officers heard an unlicensed radio station broadcast and traced it to a flat, where the defendant was discovered alone standing in front of the record decks, still playing music and wearing a set of headphones. Though the defendant admitted that he knew he was using the equipment, he claimed that he believed he was making demonstration tapes and did not know he was transmitting. The court was told that pirate radio broadcasts might interfere with public service transmissions and so create a risk to public safety. The defendant was convicted as it was a crime of strict liability.

Conclusion

Strict liability offences require no *mens rea*. Even though these offences may seem unfair, the reasons behind strict liability usually make prosecution a just outcome. These reasons include:

- easier to prove
- takes less time in court
- encourages compliance with the law
- prevents defences being raised as an excuse
- makes regulation straightforward
- protects the public.

 Benefits.

You should now be able to:

- understand the reasons for the use of strict liability
- describe the use of strict liability by reference to authority.

Key cases

Smedleys v Breed (1974): the defendant company was guilty, even though all reasonable care had been taken.

London Borough of Harrow v Shah (2000): this is another example of the characteristics of a strict liability offence: it is not truly criminal, but is of social concern.

Blake (1997): the characteristic of strict liability in this case is that of public safety.

Activities

1. Look in your local paper and find examples of prosecutions for crimes of strict liability.

2. Find out as many offences as you can that are crimes of strict liability with respect to driving a car.

AQA Examiner's tip

If you use *Sweet v Parsley* (1970) as an example, do make it clear that the House of Lords decided the offence was NOT one of strict liability.

7 The offences of assault and battery

The nature of the offences

Assault and battery are two different offences that together are called common assault. The word 'common' is used because the definitions of the offences come from the common law: in other words, all the sources of this law are decided cases. The Criminal Justice Act 1988, s39, does not define these offences; it merely states the maximum sentence (six months' imprisonment) and establishes that the offences are summary offences, that is, triable only in the Magistrates' Court. They are the least serious of the non-fatal offences against the person.

The essential distinction between the two offences is that assault is all about fear of suffering harm, whereas battery is the actual harm. It therefore follows that a person who is asleep cannot suffer an assault but can suffer a battery. Both these crimes require *actus reus* and *mens rea* and it is essential to be able to explain these accurately.

Assault

The *actus reus* of **assault** is any act which causes the victim to apprehend an immediate infliction of unlawful violence. This might be waving a fist at someone in an aggressive manner or aiming a gun or a catapult at that person. The House of Lords in *Savage* (1991) stated that the *mens rea* is 'an intention to cause the victim to apprehend unlawful and immediate violence or recklessness whether such an apprehension be caused.'

The *actus reus* has the following elements:

1 causing the victim to apprehend violence
2 immediate violence
3 unlawful violence.

In the first element, causing the victim to apprehend violence, there is no need for any physical contact between the defendant and the victim. The emphasis is on what the victim thought was about to happen. So even if the defendant meant his threat as a joke, an assault is nevertheless committed if the victim is sufficiently frightened. This can be seen in the case of **Logdon (1976)**, where the defendant, as a joke, pointed a gun at the victim, who was terrified until she was told that it was in fact a replica. The court held that the victim had apprehended immediate physical violence, and the defendant had been at least reckless as to whether this would occur.

Logdon (1976) involved more than just words as a replica gun was shown. In **Smith v Chief Superintendent of Woking Police Station (1983)** there were no words, merely actions. In that case, the victim was at home in her ground-floor flat dressed in her nightdress. She was terrified when she suddenly saw the defendant standing in her garden, staring at her through the window. The court held him liable for assault, on the grounds that the victim feared immediate violence, even though he could not physically attack her as she was locked in.

Words alone or even silence can be assault. This is consistent with the law that was developed to deal with stalkers prior to the Protection from Harassment Act 1997. In **Ireland (1997)**, the making of silent telephone calls that caused psychiatric injury to the victim was capable of amounting to an assault in law where the calls caused the victim to apprehend an immediate application of force.

In this topic you will learn how to:

■ distinguish between common law offences and statutory offences

■ distinguish between assault and battery

■ describe, using authority, the *actus reus* of assault

■ describe, using authority, the *mens rea* of assault

■ describe, using authority, the *actus reus* of battery

■ describe, using authority, the *mens rea* of battery

■ apply the above to a given situation.

■ **Key terms**

Assault: intentionally or recklessly causing the victim to fear immediate, unlawful harm.

■ **Key cases**

Logdon (1976): the court decided that an assault could be by words and actions.

Smith v Chief Superintendent of Woking Police Station (1983): in this case there was an assault by actions alone.

Ireland (1997): it was decided that silence or words alone can be an assault.

The second element is that the violence threatened must be immediate. Immediate means as a part of the current activity. This can be seen in *Smith* v *Chief Superintendent of Woking Police Station (1983)* where the immediacy arose as the victim was behind glass, even though the defendant did not have immediate access to her. The immediacy in the telephone calls in *Ireland (1997)* is that the verbal contact made by the defendant with the victim caused the fear.

The third element is that the threatened violence must be unlawful. Thus it is not a criminal offence for a policeman to threaten to handcuff someone or restrain them if they do not cooperate during an arrest.

The *mens rea* of assault stated in *Savage (1991)* was an intention to cause the victim to apprehend unlawful and immediate violence or recklessness whether such an apprehension is caused. This means:

- direct or oblique intention as to causing immediate, unlawful fear in the victim that he might suffer some harm;
- subjective (*Cunningham*) recklessness as to causing immediate, unlawful fear in the victim that he might suffer some harm.

Battery

The *actus reus* of **battery** is the unlawful application of force to another. The force involved can be very slight: indeed, it is suggested that touching a person's clothes may be sufficient. Typical examples are hitting someone or throwing a drink at someone. In **Thomas (1985)** a school caretaker was charged with indecent assault after taking hold of the hem of a 12-year-old girl's skirt. Whilst the act was not indecent because there was no evidence of circumstances making it so, the court said that there can be no dispute that if you touch a person's clothes while he or she is wearing them, that is equivalent to touching him or her.

Consent can make the touching lawful. There is an implied consent in normal social situations, such as tapping someone on the shoulder to bring attention to something, or consent to touching in normal sporting activities. There is no consent when the touching goes beyond the rules of the sport, although in such cases the consequences are usually more severe than a battery.

The force can be applied only by an act not an omission which is why *Fagan* v *MPC (1969)* was considered a continuing act. It is also possible to cause a battery by indirect force, as in the case of **Haystead (2000)**, where the defendant punched his girlfriend, causing her to drop her baby onto the floor. He was convicted of battery on the baby.

The *mens rea* of battery was stated by the court in **Venna (1976)** as 'proof that the defendant intentionally or recklessly applied force to the person of another.' This is very similar to the *mens rea* of assault except as to the intended or reckless consequence. In *Venna (1976)*, the defendant was arrested along with some friends for a public order offence. He struggled violently with the arresting officer and he was judged to be reckless as to whether he caused some harm to the officer.

Battery only requires the slightest touching. Other offences may be more appropriate if the consequences to the victim are more severe.

AQA Examiner's tip

Look for events such as shouting at someone or waving a weapon at someone, to consider whether assault should be discussed as an offence.

Key terms

Battery: the unlawful application of force to another.

Key cases

Thomas (1985): here it was decided that touching a person's clothes can be a battery.

Haystead (2000): in this case it was decided that indirect force is sufficient for there to be battery.

Venna (1976): this case defines the *mens rea* of battery.

AQA Examiner's tip

Always select the most appropriate offence(s) to discuss, rather than setting out the *actus reus* and *mens rea* of every offence in the Unit specification.

Activity

For each of the cases listed in this section, set out the *actus reus* and *mens rea* of the offences disclosed by the facts.

Conclusion

Assault and battery are two crimes that have distinct *actus reus* and *mens rea*. Assault is all about the fear that the victim will suffer a battery, the physical touching of the other person.

You should now be able to:

■ describe, using authority, the offences of assault and battery

■ apply the law on assault and battery to given situations.

In this topic you will learn how to:

■ describe, using authority, the *actus reus* of s47, s20 and s18 of the Offences Against the Person Act 1861

■ describe, using authority, the *mens rea* of s47, s20 and s18 of the Offences Against the Person Act 1861

■ apply the above to a given situation.

💡 8 The three offences under the Offences Against the Person Act 1861

The nature of the offences

The three offences that we are concerned with in the specification are the more serious personal injuries offences. They are listed in terms of seriousness as can be seen in Fig. 9.10.

Section 47 is the least serious offence. It is also the offence that, of the three, gives rise to the most convictions. The other two offences, being more serious offences, also include the possibility of a charge and conviction for the lesser offence. In some of the cases you may read about, you might wonder why a more serious charge was not brought against the defendant. The practical reason is that conviction and appropriate sentence is more important than a conviction for the more serious offence. It should also be noted that the maximum sentence under both s47 and s20 is five years imprisonment; that gives the court plenty of scope to choose a suitable level of punishment.

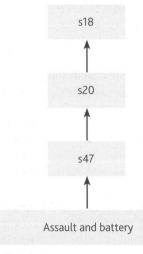

Fig. 9.10 *The hierarchy of harm*

The next step is to understand the distinction between the different offences, as it essential that these are understood and can be applied.

AQA Examiner's tip

Make sure you can explain the *actus reus* and *mens rea* of each offence accurately. Many candidates fail to do this.

Section 47 of the Offences Against the Person Act 1861

Section 47 of the Offences Against the Person Act 1861 states that:

> Whosoever shall be convicted on indictment of any **assault occasioning actual bodily harm** shall be liable to be imprisoned for any term not exceeding five years.

This offence is triable either way, that is, in either the magistrates' court or the Crown Court. The correct name for this offence is assault occasioning actual bodily harm, often referred to as ABH.

The *actus reus* has three elements:

- assault
- occasioning
- actual bodily harm.

The first element, assault, includes both assault and battery. The first essential part of the *actus reus* is to prove that there was an assault or battery as set out in the previous topic. This is usually not a problem, but can become one if the limitations on assault and battery are not taken into account.

The second element, occasioning, means bringing about the consequence. This is causation that has been looked at in Topic 3 of this chapter. One of the distinctions between s47 and the other offences under the Offences Against the Person Act 1861 is the degree of harm caused. This aspect is vital, but sometimes is very straightforward and requires no discussion. Thus, if I hit someone with a stick and the victim is bruised where the stick hit them, there is no issue of causation and it would not need to be discussed further.

The third element is the key distinction. In **Chan-Fook (1994)** the court said that 'harm' means 'injury', and that 'actual' indicates that the injury should not be so trivial as to be 'wholly insignificant'. The court also said that 'bodily harm' is not limited to harm to the skin, flesh and bones of the victim. It includes the organs, nervous system and brain. It can include psychiatric injury, but it does not include emotions or states of mind that are not in themselves evidence of an identifiable medical condition. Where there is expert evidence of psychiatric injury, the injury is capable of being actual bodily harm.

The scope of the offence has been extended to include a person's hair in the case of **Smith (2006)**. In that case, the defendant cut off his former partner's pony-tail with a pair of scissors. The court said actual bodily harm is not limited to injury and extends to hurt and damage so long as it is not trivial. It is not limited to the skin, flesh and bones but applies to all parts of the body including the hair. It also seems that if paint or similar material were put on the hair, that could also be actual bodily harm.

The *mens rea* of the offence is intention or recklessness as to assault or battery. This was made clear in the case of **Roberts (1971)**, where a girl who was a passenger in the defendant's car injured herself by jumping out of the car while it was moving. This was dealt with in more detail in Topic 3 of this chapter. In that case, the defendant had the *mens rea* to cause a battery; the subsequent injuries were merely a consequence of his unlawful act, and so there was sufficient *actus reus* and *mens rea* for a conviction under s47. There need not be a separate *mens rea* for the actual bodily harm, so the requirements are exactly the same as those set out in Topic 7 of this chapter. This can be seen in **Savage (1991)**, the facts of which are set out in detail below. In that case, the intentional

Key terms

Assault occasioning actual bodily harm: the offence requiring the consequence of more than minimal harm to the victim.

Key cases

Chan-Fook (1994): in this case it was decided that 'harm' in s47 of the Offences Against the Person Act 1861 includes physical or psychiatric injury.

Smith (2006): in this case it was decided that actual bodily harm can include all parts of the body including the hair.

Roberts (1971): this case is authority for the proposition that *mens rea* for s47 Offences Against the Person Act 1861 is intention or recklessness as to assault or battery.

Savage (1991): this case confirmed the *mens rea* for s47 Offences Against the Person Act 1861 is as set out in *Roberts* (1971), that is, where a crime states the *mens rea* as 'maliciously', this requires either intention or recklessness.

Key terms

Grievous bodily harm: this is serious harm and can cover a wide range of injuries.

Wounding: this is where the victim's skin is cut and therefore usually results in some blood loss.

Key cases

JCC v Eisenhower (1984): this case explained that a wound requires breaking of both layers of the skin.

Brown and Stratton (1998): in this case a collection of relatively minor injuries amounted to grievous bodily harm.

throwing of the beer was sufficient for the offence of battery, and as the result was something more serious, factually and legally caused by that act of the defendant, there is sufficient *mens rea* for the more serious offence under s47 (or indeed s20).

Section 20 of the Offences Against the Person Act 1861

Section 20 of the Offences Against the Person Act 1861 states that:

> Whosoever shall unlawfully and maliciously wound or inflict any **grievous bodily harm** upon any person, either with or without any weapon or instrument, shall be guilty of an offence …

This offence is triable either way, that is, in either the Magistrates' Court or the Crown Court. The correct name for this offence can be either malicious wounding or inflicting grievous bodily harm, often referred to as GBH, depending on the nature of the injuries to the victim.

The *actus reus* has three elements that need explanation:

■ unlawful

■ wound

■ grievous bodily harm.

The first element is that the act must be unlawful. In the context of s20, this usually means that there must have been no consent to the act. Thus, subject to age restrictions set out by statute, it is not an unlawful act to have a tattoo or a piercing. The issue is whether the consent is genuine: this is clearly of importance for those providing a tattoo or piercing service.

The second element is the definition of a wound. **Wounding** requires there to have been a break in the surface of the skin; this is both layers of the skin and is therefore seen to be an open wound, usually with blood loss. This can be seen in the case of **JCC v Eisenhower (1984)**, where the victim was hit by an airgun pellet in the eye. He suffered bruising and internal bleeding in the eye. The court decided there was no wounding, since there was no wound breaking the skin.

The third, separate, element is that of grievous bodily harm. This has been defined in various ways such as 'really serious' harm. This means that it is a phrase that should be given its ordinary and natural meaning in the circumstances of the case. Thus, in the case of **Brown and Stratton (1998)**, where the victim was a transsexual, the victim went to the market stall where her father worked. The father felt humiliated to see his son as a woman and, along with his cousin, attacked the victim with a chair, causing a broken nose, three lost teeth and concussion. Together, these injuries were considered to be grievous bodily harm.

The *mens rea* required is set out in the definition above as 'maliciously'. Many older Acts of Parliament set out the *mens rea* of an offence as 'maliciously'. This was discussed in *Cunningham (1957)* and has been considered again in *Savage (1991)*. The court transcript sets out the facts of *Savage (1991)* as:

> On 3 October 1989 in the Crown Court at Durham the appellant, Mrs Savage, was indicted and convicted on a single count of unlawful wounding contrary to s20 of the Offences Against the Person Act 1861, the particulars of the offence being that on 31 March 1989 she unlawfully and maliciously wounded Miss Beal. She was ordered to undertake 120 hours of community service.

The victim, Miss Beal, was a former girlfriend of Mrs Savage's husband. There had been some bad feeling between these two young women, although they had never previously met. On the evening of 31 March 1989 they were both in the same public house, but not together. Mrs Savage pushed her way through to the table where Miss Beal was sitting with some friends. She had in her hand a pint glass which was nearly full of beer. Having said 'Nice to meet you darling', she then threw the contents of the glass over Miss Beal. Unfortunately, not only was Miss Beal soaked by the beer, but, contrary to Mrs Savage's evidence, she must have let go of the glass, since it broke and a piece of it cut Miss Beal's wrist. The Jury, by their verdict, concluded either that the appellant had deliberately thrown not only the beer but also the glass at Miss Beal or, alternatively, that while deliberately throwing the beer over Miss Beal, the glass had accidentally slipped from her grasp and it, or a piece of it, had struck Miss Beal's wrist, but with no intention that the glass should hit or cut Miss Beal.

It is clear that Mrs Savage did not intend to cause serious injuries to Miss Beal, but she had been reckless. The court confirmed that 'maliciously' meant intentionally or recklessly and she had been reckless.

Therefore, in order to prove that the defendant acted maliciously, it is sufficient to prove that he intended his act to result in some unlawful bodily harm to some other person, albeit of a minor nature, or was subjectively reckless as to the risk that his act might result in such harm. There is no requirement that the intent or recklessness must be as to anything more than that some harm might occur.

Section 18 of the Offences Against the Person Act 1861

Section 18 of the Offences Against the Person Act 1861 provides:

> Whosoever shall unlawfully and maliciously by any means whatsoever wound or cause any grievous bodily harm to any person, with intent to do some grievous bodily harm to any person, or with intent to resist or prevent the lawful apprehension or detainer of any person …

This offence is triable only on indictment, so will be tried at Crown Court only. The *actus reus* of the offence is either wounding or grievous bodily harm as set out in s20. The *mens rea* is that the defendant must be 'malicious' (see above, under s20) but in addition he must be proved to have had a further specific intent, in that it must have been the defendant's intention either to do some grievous bodily harm to the victim or to resist or prevent a lawful arrest or detention. This can be seen in the case of **Belfon (1976)**. In this case, the defendant had slashed the victim with a razor, causing severe wounds to his face and chest. The court said that, in order to establish the offence under s18, it was essential to prove the specific intent. References to the defendant foreseeing that such harm was likely to result or that he had been reckless as to whether such harm would result, would be insufficient.

AQA Examiner's tip

Remember there are two aspects of this offence, grievous bodily harm and wounding. You should be able to distinguish between the two.

Key cases

Belfon (1976): it was decided in this case that for there to a conviction under s18 of OAPA 1861, the defendant must have had the specific intent to do grievous bodily harm or resist arrest.

Summary of offences

The table below summarises the three offences under the Offences Against the Person Act 1861.

Table 9.2 *The three offences under the Offences Against the Person Act 1861*

Offence	*Actus reus*	*Mens rea*
s47	Assault occasioning actual bodily harm	Intention or recklessness as to either putting the victim in fear of unlawful force or applying unlawful force
s20	Wounding or inflicting grievous bodily harm	Intention or recklessness as to some harm
s18	Wounding or inflicting grievous bodily harm	Specific intent to wound or cause grievous bodily harm or resist arrest

AQA Examiner's tip

Only use the charging standards in your conclusion. The exam is a law exam and so you need to explain the law. The charging standards are guidelines for practice only.

Conclusion

The three offences under the Offences Against the Person Act 1861 have a number of overlapping essentials and a number of subtle differences. It is important to understand these, but also to recognise that the offences provide a framework for defining different levels of seriousness of harm that can occur.

Activities

1 Analyse the cases set out below and decide what offence or offences are disclosed by each set of facts, explaining and applying the relevant *actus reus* and *mens rea*:

   a These are the facts of *Mowatt* (1968): the defendant attacked his victim by sitting astride him, raining a series of blows on his face, and lifting his head up and throwing it down again. The Court of Appeal upheld the defendant's conviction for inflicting grievous bodily harm, saying the offence required the defendant to have foreseen the risk of some physical harm, which was clearly the case.

   b These are the facts of *Grimshaw* (1984): following an offensive remark in a pub, the woman defendant struck a man, her victim, who suffered serious eye injuries from the glass he had been holding.

2 Read the article opposite taken from the *Yorkshire Evening Post,* 12 May 2007, and discuss the offence(s) that might have been committed. Look for similar articles in your local newspaper.

Summary of general points relating to your answer to application of the law to the problem scenario:

■ An exam question starting 'Discuss the criminal liability of …' requires you to select the relevant offence or offences, state the law for the *actus reus* and *mens rea* of the offence selected (you can refer back to other answers in your paper if you have explained the offence there) and then apply the law to the facts in the scenario, coming to a conclusion as to which offence or offences have been committed.

Knife thug locked up for street attack

Mark Lavery

A teenage thug who repeatedly stabbed a Good Samaritan has been locked up indefinitely. Gary Hawley, 50, asked a group of drunken teenagers to stop abusing three women in the street in Yeadon, Leeds. Markus Lavelle, 17, and Reece Lupton, 16, began repeatedly punching him as he was getting into his car after collecting a meal from a Chinese takeaway on Yeadon High Street at 11.30pm on August 24 last year. A third teenager, Jason Pears, 17, then joined the attack armed with a knife. He stabbed Mr Hawley seven times in the chest and back and slashed him across the chest. The court was told Pears then ran off, buried his bloodied top and knife, stole a shirt from a washing line and returned to the crime scene to wipe his fingerprints on Mr Hawley's car.

Pears, of Gipton Gate, Gipton, was yesterday ordered to be detained for the public protection and must serve a minimum of two years before he is eligible for parole. Lupton, of Bradford, who was 15 at the time, was given an 18-month sentence and Lavelle of Henshaw Oval, Yeadon who was 16 at the time got 12 months. After the hearing Mr Hawley, of Yeadon, said: 'It's a result – they deserve everything they have got. Hopefully now there's some form of closure for me and I can get back to normality.'

Bleeding

The court heard that after the attack the three thugs ran off and left their victim bleeding and falling out of his car. He was unable to speak by the time he got to hospital and had developed fluid on both lungs and spent three days being treated. He has since suffered episodes of vertigo and his mental health has been impaired.

Judge Kerry Macgill told the three youths: 'It's a disgusting lawless assault on an innocent man. Mr Hawley having seen foul and abusive language coming from a group of youths does the gentlemanly thing and asks that to stop. Lupton and Lavelle, you started about him punching him to the face and head.' Lavelle who pleaded guilty has two previous convictions for racially aggravated assaults. Lupton who pleaded guilty to the attack and theft of Mr Hawley's mobile phone, has previous convictions for robbery and assault.

Pears who pleaded guilty to the attack, has previous convictions for burglary and assault.

PC Lee Fletcher of Pudsey Weetwood Police, said: 'Gary Hawley was subjected to a vicious attack for no other reason than asking a group of youths to stop shouting at people in the street.'

www.leedstoday.net

■ You should always refer to these offences by their correct names at least once in your answer. You can then use abbreviations to save time. This is best described in a manner similar to, 'The most appropriate offence in this case is assault occasioning actual bodily harm (ABH) under s47 of the Offences Against the Person Act 1861 (s47 OAPA).' If you then want to mention the expression 'assault occasioning actual bodily harm' again you can say ABH and if you want to refer to another section of the Offences Against the Person Act 1861 you can refer to OAPA.

- You only need to discuss causation in an answer where there is an issue relating to causation disclosed in the scenario.
- In the examinations you are expected to discuss and apply the law and not the charging standards. The only relevance of the charging standards in an answer is to use them as part of a conclusion.

You should now be able to:

- describe, using authority, the offences in ss47, 20 and 18 of the Offences Against the Person Act 1861

- apply the law in the above sections of the Offences Against the Person Act 1861 to given situations.

10 The criminal courts: procedure and sentencing

Link

The basic structure for appeals is as set out in Figs 6.1 and 6.2 on p94.

Key terms

Summary offence: a criminal offence that can only be tried by a Magistrates' Court.

Either-way offence: an offence for which the accused may be tried by the Magistrates' Court or in the Crown Court, where the defendant will be tried by jury.

Indictable offence: a criminal offence that can only be tried by the Crown Court.

Arrest warrant: an order of the court for a person to be arrested in connection with a criminal offence.

Search warrant: an order of the court that permits the police to search premises to look for evidence in connection with a crime.

Bail: release of a defendant from custody until his next appearance in court.

1 Outline of criminal courts and appeal system

The criminal courts

Criminal offences are summary, indictable or either-way offences. **Summary offences** are relatively minor offences triable only in the Magistrates' Court. Most offences are summary and include common assault, threatening behaviour and nearly all motoring offences. The maximum sentence is less than six months.

Either-way offences can, as the name suggests, be tried in either the Magistrates' Court or the Crown Court. The Crown Court tries the more serious offences although most pre-trial matters are dealt with in the Magistrates' Court.

Indictable offences are the most serious offences, such as murder, rape or robbery and are tried on indictment only. That means they must be tried in the Crown Court before a judge, who rules on the law and passes sentence, and a jury of twelve members of the public, chosen at random, who decide on the facts if the defendant is guilty or not guilty.

There are different possible appeals from decisions in either the Magistrates' Court or the Crown Court.

The jurisdiction of the Magistrates' Court in criminal matters

The Magistrates' Court has the following criminal jurisdiction:

- issuing **arrest** and **search warrants**: these will be applied for by the police. These are quite rare, as the police have such wide powers;
- deciding on **bail** applications: when the defendant appears at court, it is the court's obligation to decide bail and not the police;
- conducting sending-for-trial hearings: indictable only offences such as murder are sent directly to the Crown Court for trial without the Magistrates' Court taking any action, apart from the decision on bail, public funding of the defendant, and the use of statements and exhibits. Where the case involves an either-way offence, the more usual form of committal for trial is committal without consideration of the evidence, known as a short committal. This means the defendant's case will be sent to Crown Court for trial without the magistrates making a detailed review of the evidence;
- trying summary offences such as assault;
- trying either-way offences that are to be tried summarily such as theft.

The jurisdiction of the Crown Court

The Crown Court has the following jurisdiction:

- trying indictable offences such as murder
- trying either-way offences that are to be tried on indictment, such as theft
- sentencing, where the case has been sent by the Magistrates' Court to the Crown Court for sentence
- hearing appeals from the Magistrates' Court against conviction or sentence.

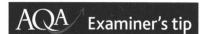
Table 10.1 *Summary of offences and the courts that hear them*

Offence	Type	Court
Assault	Summary	Magistrates
Battery	Summary	Magistrates
Section 47, Offences Against the Person Act 1861	Either way	Magistrates/Crown
Section 20, Offences Against the Person Act 1861	Either way	Magistrates/Crown
Section 18, Offences Against the Person Act 1861	Indictable	Crown

Classification of offences

Criminal offences are of three types: summary offences; either-way offences; and indictable offences. Summary offences are the most minor offences that can only be tried in the Magistrates' Court. The word 'summary' refers to the way in which the defendant is ordered to attend court, which is by a written order usually delivered by post.

Either-way offences, such as an offence under s47 of the Offences Against the Person Act 1861, can be tried in either the Magistrates' Court or the Crown Court. This is usually at the defendant's option but can be ordered by the magistrates. Indictable offences, such as under s18 of the Offences Against the Person Act 1861, are the most serious offences and can only be tried in the Crown Court.

The burden of proof in criminal offences

As has been seen, the general basis for imposing liability in criminal law is that the defendant must be proved by the prosecution to have committed the guilty act whilst having had the guilty state of mind for the crime with which the defendant is charged. It is the responsibility of the prosecution to prove both of these elements of the offence to the satisfaction of the magistrates or jury. This is known as the **burden of proof**. The **standard of proof** is beyond reasonable doubt. If this cannot be proved the defendant will be acquitted. Active case management of criminal cases is designed to make cases proceed more quickly and lead to fewer cases collapsing. This means that the criminal justice system should become more cost effective.

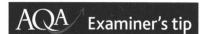
■ Key terms

Burden of proof: the obligation to prove the defendant committed the crime.

Standard of proof: the level to which the evidence must be proved to gain a conviction.

■ Activities

1 Review cases mentioned in the local paper and try to find out whether each is summary, either-way or indictable.

2 Choose one of the cases you have looked at in Activity 1 and outline the process that will have been followed and note the courts where those processes took place.

You should now be able to:

- understand the framework for the criminal process
- apply the criminal process in a given situation.

A Magistrates' Court summons looks like this:

Summons on Complaint (MCA 1980, ss 51, 52; MCR 1981, r98)

Magistrates' Court (Code   )

Date:

To the defendant:

Address:

You are hereby summoned to appear on
at   am/pm before the Magistrates' Court at
to answer the following complaint

Matter of complaint:

The Complainant is:

Address:

Date of complaint:

**Justice of the Peace
[Justices' Clerk]**

Fig. 10.1 *Magistrates' Court summons*

2 Outline procedure to trial

The principles behind the procedure

The main purpose behind the procedure is to ensure justice is done. The Criminal Procedure Rules 2005 sets out a number of aspects of achieving justice. These include:

1 acquitting the innocent and convicting the guilty (a straightforward objective)

2 dealing with the prosecution and the defence fairly (so that a fair trial ensues)

3 recognising the rights of a defendant, particularly those under Article 6 of the European Convention on Human Rights (to meet international standards)

4 respecting the interests of witnesses, victims and jurors, and keeping them informed of the progress of the case (to maintain confidence in the system)

5 dealing with the case efficiently and expeditiously (to save money for the Government and taxpayer)

6 ensuring that appropriate information is available to the court when bail and sentence are considered (to ensure individual justice occurs);

7 dealing with the case in ways that take into account

   a the seriousness of the offence alleged (the consequences of an incorrect verdict or sentence could be disastrous)

   b the complexity of what is in issue (this helps arguments in favour of abolishing the jury in complicated trials)

   c the severity of the consequences for the defendant and others affected (this takes into account the victims, victims' families, witnesses and jurors, as well as the defendant)

   d the needs of other cases (this takes into account the whole picture of the court system and the need to reduce cost and delays).

Much of this relates to topics studied in Unit 1.

Outline procedure for the different types of offences

The procedure to trial follows the diagram set out below:

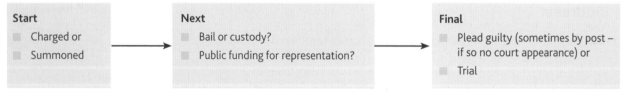

Fig. 10.2 *Outline for summary offence*

The process for a summary offence starts with the summons, as a result of inquiries having been made and a decision to prosecute having been taken. The Crown Prosecution Service normally makes the decision as to whether to prosecute or not. The Police only have the right to charge a person for certain minor offences.

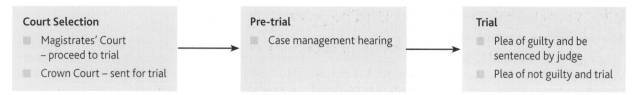

Fig. 10.3 *Outline procedure for either-way offences*

The first main hearing of an either-way offence is for a decision to be made as to whether the case should be heard in the Magistrates' Court or the Crown Court. This is called a 'mode of trial' hearing. At this hearing, both the prosecution and defence lawyers make representations as to which mode of trial should be adopted. The magistrates' clerk and his lawyers will explain to the defendant:

- that he may state whether he wishes to plead guilty or not guilty
- that, if he pleads guilty, the court will proceed to hear the case as a guilty plea and proceed to sentence
- that, if he pleads guilty, he may still be committed for sentence to the Crown Court if the magistrates consider that their powers of punishment are likely to be insufficient. (Magistrates have a maximum sentencing power of six months' imprisonment, or 12 months if there is more than one offence.)

If the defendant indicates a not guilty plea to an either-way charge, then the Magistrates' Court first considers whether its powers of sentence are sufficient to deal with the case in principle. If the magistrates decide that their powers are not likely to be sufficient, they send the case to the Crown Court. If the magistrates decide that they can hear the case, the defendant still has the right to elect trial by jury in the Crown Court. In other words, the defendant can choose whether to be tried by the magistrates in the Magistrates' Court or be sent for trial by jury in the Crown Court.

The defendant's choice is not straightforward. There are advantages and disadvantages to each court. Rates of acquittal on not guilty pleas are significantly higher in jury trials, and many defendants feel they receive a fairer hearing before a jury than before magistrates, who may have become case-hardened. There are some who believe that magistrates may still hear evidence that may be inadmissible, and that police evidence is never less than totally accurate. Jury trial, however, involves significant delays and greater defence costs. Many defendants prefer to get the matter over with and move on in their lives. The defendant is also opting for a court with greater sentencing powers in the event of conviction, even though the magistrates can send the case to the Crown Court if they decide their powers are insufficient. The choice is not always straightforward, and it is best to obtain legal advice before making it. The defendant is entitled to a summary of the prosecution evidence, or copies of their witness statements, before deciding. This is known as Advance Information.

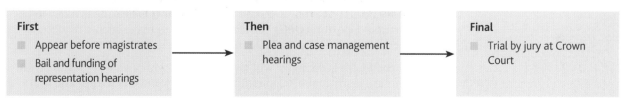

Fig. 10.4 *Outline procedure for indictable offence*

Indictable offences pass through the Magistrates' Court quickly for transfer to the Crown Court, even though the Crown Court trial may well take place some time in the future. The sending for trial procedure is quite straightforward and leaves the magistrates to decide on preliminary issues such as bail only. The outcome is an order based on the extract from Adult Court Bench Book, set out below.

Sending for trial

The offence[s] with which you are charged can only be tried at the Crown Court. We are therefore sending you to the Crown Court sitting at […] for trial.

(If applicable:) We are also sending you to the Crown Court for the connected offence[s] of [give details]. A [preliminary hearing/plea and case management hearing] will be held on […]. (If applicable:) A legal representation order is granted to cover the Crown Court proceedings. In the meantime you are [released on bail/remanded in custody].

[Proceed to give relevant pronouncement for the remand.]

www.jsboard.co.uk

The first hearing at the Crown Court is the plea and case management hearing (PCMH). A PCMH is designed to ensure that all necessary steps have been taken in preparation for trial and that sufficient information has been provided for a trial date to be arranged. The judge is required to exercise a managerial role in the case. At this hearing the defendant will enter a plea. If the defendant pleads guilty, sentencing can take place immediately. If the defendant pleads not guilty, then the prosecution and defence are expected to inform the court of things such as:

■ the issues in the case, such as conflicting witness statements
■ the number of witnesses and the order in which prosecution witnesses will be called: this will help assess the length of the trial
■ any formal admissions, for example, of guilt
■ exhibits that will need to be produced, such as a weapon
■ the documents to be used by the prosecution at trial, and how they will appear
■ any point of law, such as the definition of the *mens rea* of the offence
■ questions as to the admissibility of evidence: it might be that a statement was not obtained following the correct procedure
■ the estimated length of the trial and the availability of witnesses and counsel, so that a suitable date or dates can be found.

These matters are dealt with in a questionnaire, which must be completed by counsel for each party.

The defendant may use the PCMH to request an advance indication of sentence from the judge. This can help decisions to be made about the trial and whether the defendant's plea should change from not guilty to guilty with the hope of a further reduction in sentence for having pleaded guilty before the trial. It should be noted that this hearing is likely to be the first opportunity that the defendant has to make such a request, as the procedure is not available in the Magistrates' Court.

At the PCMH, the judge will give directions with a view to dealing with the case justly and bringing it to trial quickly and efficiently. The trial date will usually be fixed. The Crown Court will normally send a notice of fixture, which confirms that date and other agreed matters.

Her Majesty's Court Service
Bail Act 1976

Accused: .... Date of Birth: ....

Offences:...

DECISION OF THE COURT

☐ The accused is remanded to appear before the (..)

(above named) Youth/Magistrates' Court at............................ am/pm on ....

☐ The accused is committed/sent/transferred to the Crown Court at Cambridge/Peterborough/Northampton/

Norwich at.......................... am/pm on ....or such day, time and place as may be directed to the accused by the appropriate officer of the Crown Court

☐ The accused is granted unconditional bail

☐ The accused is granted bail/remanded to local authority accommodation subject to the following conditions:

Conditions to be complied with before release on bail		Conditions to be complied with after release on bail
☐ To provide Suret(y)(ies)	☐	To live and sleep each night at...
in the sum of £ ....(each)	☐	To be indoors at the above address between .... and ....
Continuous until ( )	☐	To report to .... Police Station between .... and ....
☐ To surrender Passport to		(daily) (on ....)
☐ To provide a security in the sum of	☐	Not to contact directly or indirectly ....
£	☐	....
Reasons to secure	☐	....
☐ Surrender to custody	☐	....
☐ That no offence is committed	☐	....
☐ No interference with witnesses/ obstructing justice	☐	Not to go to .... (except to attend court or see solicitor by prior arrangement)
☐ Accused makes him/herself available For the purpose of making report	☐	To keep any appointments with ....to enable enquiries or a report to be made

☐ The accused is refused bail and committed to custody/remanded to local authority accommodation

Exceptions to right on unconditional bail	**Reasons for applying exceptions**
All offences	☐ Serious nature of alleged offence (probable method of dealing with it)
☐ Arrested for absconding/breaching bail conditions	☐ Accused's character/antecedents/lack of community ties
☐ Custody for his/her protection/welfare	☐ Previous bail record
☐ Serving custodial sentence	☐ Strength of evidence
Imprisonable offences only	☐ Recent arrest and details not yet verified
☐ Believed would fail to surrender	☐ Behaviour towards/proximity to prosecution witness
☐ Believed would commit an offence	☐ No likelihood of co-operation for purposes of obtaining report
☐ Believed would interfere with witnesses or obstruct justice	☐ Already serving a custodial sentence imposed on ....
☐ Impracticable to complete inquiries or make report	
☐ Impracticable to obtain sufficient information since arrest	
☐ Either way/indictable offence committed on bail	
Non-imprisonable offences only	
☐ Previously failed to surrender and unlikely to surrender	

S.23(5) CYPA 1969 The Court is of the opinion that only remand to remand centre/prison is adequate to protect public from serious harm because ....

☐ I hereby certify that at the hearing today the Court heard full argument on an application for bail by or on behalf of the accused, before refusing the application and remanding the accused in custody under Section (5)(10)(18)(30) Magistrates' Courts Act 1980.

FAILURE TO SURRENDER TO BAIL OR COMPLY WITH YOUR BAIL CONDITIONS CAN RESULT IN YOUR ARREST
FAILURE TO SURRENDER TO BAIL IS AN OFFENCE PUNISHABLE BY IMPRISONMENT AND/OR FINE

Date: ....

(Clerk of the Court present during the proceedings)

1. White Copy - Register   2. Yellow Copy - Defendant   3. Blue Copy - CPS   4. Pink Copy - Court File

Fig. 10.5 *Bail notice*

💡 Bail

Under the Bail Act 1976 there is a general right to bail. Bail can be granted by the courts or the police. Police bail can be given at a police station or under the Criminal Justice Act 2003, where police officers can grant bail following arrest at locations other than at a police station, a process known as 'street bail'. Court bail is dealt with through the Magistrates' Court.

Where bail is granted, the person is released from custody until the next date when they must attend court or the police station, as stated on the bail notice. If bail is refused, this will be because the police or the court believes that the defendant, if released on bail, will: abscond (not turn up to court); commit an offence; interfere with witnesses; or otherwise interfere with the criminal justice process. There are two types of bail: conditional bail and unconditional bail.

Conditional bail

The police and courts can impose any requirements that are necessary to make sure that defendants attend court and do not commit offences or interfere with witnesses whilst on bail. Recommended bail conditions, and the reasons for such conditions, should be specific and justifiable. The conditions must be likely to be effective and capable of being enforced.

Bail conditions can be imposed before release on bail. These will be either surety, where the defendant or another person may be required to pay a sum of money up to that amount if the defendant does not attend the police station or court as required, or security, which is the same but secured on an asset such as a house. The security may be forfeited if bail is broken. Additionally, the defendant may have to surrender his passport.

Post-release conditions may also be imposed, so that the defendant is likely to attend and also is less likely to re-offend or interfere with witnesses. These conditions can include:

- reporting to the police at given times
- living at a stated address, for example the defendant's home, the home of a relative away from the scene of the offence, or a bail hostel
- staying away from certain people or places
- a curfew, for which the court (but not the police) can order an electronic tag to be used.

If a defendant is reported, or believed, to have breached a bail condition, he can be arrested and brought before the Magistrates' Court and may lose the right to bail and be placed on remand. Failing to appear at court as required is a criminal offence and can lead to prosecution for this offence.

Unconditional bail

If the police or court think that the defendant is unlikely to commit further offences, will attend court when required, and will not interfere with the justice process, the defendant will usually be released on unconditional bail.

AQA *Examiner's tip*

Bail may require some application to the scenario: read the question carefully and look for factors that might reduce the chance of being given bail in the scenario.

AQA *Examiner's tip*

When looking at bail questions, consider the three options of:

- unconditional bail, giving reasons for that decision;
- conditional bail, again giving reasons for that decision;
- refusal of bail, which means a remand in custody, again giving reasons for that decision.

Activities

1 Make a list of bail conditions that have been reported in the newspapers or that you have seen imposed on defendants in court and decide why the bail was conditional or unconditional in each case, and, where conditional, why the conditions were imposed.

2 Jack was arrested after a person was attacked by a group of people outside a nightclub. The victim suffered severe injuries and is still critically ill. Jack was one of 15 people who were interviewed about the attack, but only Jack and two others were arrested and charged with an offence. The others are likely to be witnesses who will help confirm the images captured on CCTV. Jack is not known by the police to be a man of violence, but one of those arrested and charged has a history of violent attacks. Jack had been in the pub in the company of the other two charged and knows many of the witnesses. Consider the criminal process that will be followed in Jack's case and the factors that will be taken into account in deciding whether Jack will be granted bail or not, and, if granted, what conditions might be imposed.

You should now be able to:

▪ understand the framework for the criminal process

▪ apply the criminal process in a given situation.

💡 3 Sentencing

The aims of sentencing

In this topic you will learn how to:

▪ describe the aims of sentencing

▪ state and describe the different sentences available to a court in sentencing an adult offender

▪ explain what is meant by aggravating and mitigating factors

▪ apply the above to a given situation.

Once the defendant has been found guilty either by the magistrates or the jury, the court must decide on sentence. There is an underlying concept that justice requires consistency in sentencing. This principle means that similar crimes committed in similar circumstances by offenders whose circumstances are similar should be given similar sentences. This is important not only to the offender, but also to those directly affected by the crime and to the public if there is to be public confidence in the criminal justice system.

When an offender is convicted following a trial or guilty plea, the court has a range of sentencing options available. The range of sentences available will be looked at later. These depend on the type, the seriousness and the circumstances of the crime, and the maximum penalty available by law. The judge or magistrates have a number of guidelines that are designed to help them make a decision. These guidelines, and the potential sentences available, can be seen in the light of the various traditional theories of punishment that there are as to the purpose of a sentence. These are:

▪ retribution
▪ deterrence
▪ prevention
▪ rehabilitation.

potential sentences available.

The Criminal Justice Act 2003, s142, requires judges and magistrates dealing with an offender in respect of his offence to have regard to the following purposes of sentencing:

- the punishment of offenders
- the reduction of crime (including its reduction by deterrence)
- the reform and rehabilitation of offenders
- the protection of the public
- the making of reparation by offenders to persons affected by their offences.

These follow the traditional principles, which will now be examined in turn.

Retribution – "Revenge"

Retribution is based on the idea of revenge. The demand for this is seen in the tabloid press demanding extreme sentences for notorious offenders that have come to the public eye, for example, a suspected child molester. In some ways all punishment has this effect, as many individuals and, often, society as a whole, feel better that someone has gone to prison for a long time. Retribution is one aspect of the view that a person who commits a serious crime such as murder should be executed. However 'To take a life when a life has been lost is revenge, it is not justice': this quotation is attributed to Archbishop Desmond Tutu. Sometimes retribution may be part of the idea behind punishment, but it is not always the major principle behind the sentence.

The Criminal Justice Act 2003 starts with the principle of punishment and adds in the idea of reparation, which includes the compensation of victims through, for example, paying for damage caused in a case involving vandalism.

Deterrence "Putting off"

Deterrence can be an individual deterrent where the sentence is designed to make the offender not wish to re-offend for fear of suffering the same or worse fate. An experiment with young offenders took place in the 1990s. A number of young offenders, who were likely to go to prison if they re-offended, were given a tour of an adult prison by serving prisoners. The result was a much better than normal reconviction rate, and for many it was seen as a turning point in their lives. There can also be a general deterrence, whereby the prospect of the potential punishment dissuades most people from offending. Thus, if the Government wanted to stop people parking illegally, it could make the offence a strict liability offence punishable by a minimum of 10 years in prison. It is also thought that the likelihood of being caught is also a major deterrent, so that better policing will help to reduce crime.

Prevention of crime

Prevention of crime works to protect the public by, for example, putting offenders in prison so they cannot re-offend whilst in prison. It could be said that all sentences aim to prevent crime by demonstrating the bad effect of conviction, but it could be argued that a criminal conviction tends to lead to other convictions as employers are less willing to employ an ex-offender.

Rehabilitation

Rehabilitation involves offering the offender help to overcome problems that he faces, thereby attempting to make it easier to avoid future offending. It can also be seen as 'curing' the offender. Much of rehabilitation is concerned with providing the offender with the skills to cope with life, and can be reflected in ways such as attending an anger management course or driver retraining. This follows from having an individual sentence rather than a fixed tariff.

Whilst most offences have a maximum set by law such as five years' imprisonment for assault occasioning actual bodily harm, some, such as using a mobile phone whilst driving, have a fixed penalty, and there are also minimum sentences in some circumstances, such as a minimum three-year prison sentence for third-time domestic burglary. The maximum penalty for burglary is 14 years' imprisonment.

Types of sentence available

Sentences can be classified as:

- custodial (a sentence of imprisonment)
- community (for example, a community rehabilitation order)
- financial (a fine)
- discharge (the offender is found guilty but no further action is taken)
- other (for example, a driving ban).

Custodial sentences

A **custodial sentence** is the most serious sentence and is reserved for the most serious crimes. A custodial sentence can be imposed if the offence is so serious that neither a fine alone nor a community sentence can be justified for the offence. The sentence imposed by the court represents the maximum amount of time that the offender will remain in prison. Despite these criteria, the prison population continues to rise, and the prison population in England and Wales is one of the highest in Europe. A prison sentence can be suspended which means that the prison sentence will not take effect unless there is a subsequent offence within a given period.

Community sentences

Minor crimes are often dealt with by giving the offender a community sentence. While these sentences offer a suitable punishment, they concentrate on making sure that the person does not commit more offences.

www.direct.gov.uk

This Government statement shows the purposes behind these sentences which the court can tailor-make for the individual. The idea is to combine punishment with changing offenders' behaviour and making amends. The range of options includes:

- compulsory (unpaid) work, so that something is put back into the community; here the offender works for up to 300 hours on local community projects such as cleaning up graffiti under a local payback scheme; programmes aimed at changing offending behaviour, such as anger management
- curfew, so that the offender must be at home between certain times such as 21.00–06.00. The offender must stay indoors, usually at their home, for the curfew period. A tag, worn on the ankle or wrist, notifies monitoring services if the offender is absent during the curfew hours
- exclusion from certain areas for a period of up to two years; there may be electronic monitoring of this, too, via a tag
- residence requirement, where the offender must reside at a place specified, for example, an approved hostel or private address
- drug treatment and testing

AQA Examiner's tip

The aims of sentencing are often used by the examiner to enhance the mark given to your answer, but you should concentrate on answering the precise question, which may not look particularly for the aims of sentencing.

Key terms

Custodial sentence: this is a sentence of imprisonment, which might be immediate or suspended (able to be implemented later if necessary).

Community sentence: these are alternatives to prison and are non-custodial options available to a court.

- alcohol treatment for offenders who are alcohol-dependent and who might benefit from reducing or eliminating their dependency
- supervision; this is where the offender is required to attend appointments with an Offender Manager from the Probation Service. The subject of the supervision and the frequency of contact will be specified in a sentence plan
- attendance; the court can direct the offender to spend a total of between 12 and 36 hours at an attendance centre, on a number of occasions over a set period of time. Here the offender addresses their offending behaviour with others in a group. This also restricts the defendant's leisure time at the weekend. This can be used to prevent football hooligans attending matches.

Financial sentences

Criminal fines are a simple financial penalty imposed on the defendant. A fine can be a fixed penalty, as with a fixed penalty speeding fine, or it can be given subject to a statutory maximum for the offence. A fine is the courts' most frequently imposed penalty. Magistrates can impose a maximum fine of £5,000, assuming that that sum is less than the statutory maximum for that offence.

Compensation orders are sometimes made. Some would argue that a compensation order is a financial penalty although that is payable to the victim of the crime rather than the State and is designed to repay, for example, damage caused to the victim's property.

Discharge

There are two types of **discharge** that can form the court's sentence. The first is an absolute discharge, which is where the court takes no further action against an offender, but the offender's discharge will appear on his or her criminal record. The second type is a conditional discharge, which is where a defendant is convicted without sentence on condition that he does not re-offend within a specified period of time. This period can be between six months and two years. If another offence is committed during this time, the court can look at the old offence as well as the new one in deciding on the sentence to impose.

Other sentences

There are other sentences, such as a driving ban, that can be imposed. None of these are within the scope of the AQA Law 2 specification.

How the court goes about selecting a sentence

Once a defendant has been found guilty, the court's function is to impose the appropriate sentence. It is at this stage that the defendant's previous convictions will be made available and it is likely that a pre-sentence report will be required for more serious offences. This report is prepared by the probation service. The probation service will be told how serious they consider the offence to be and the purpose of the sentence. This might be related to any of the purposes of sentencing.

To compile the report, an officer from the probation service will interview the defendant. Usually this will be at the probation office on a different day from the court hearing. The court will tell the probation service when they wish to receive the report. The defendant will be either remanded in custody or be bailed.

AQA Examiner's tip

Make sure your description of different sentences gives full explanations with examples and limits (for example, maximum hours for unpaid work). There are usually some high-profile cases where these sentences have been imposed, but make sure they are not from outside England and Wales.

Key terms

Discharge: this is a sentence where the offender is found guilty of the offence, and the conviction appears on his criminal record. It may be absolute or conditional.

Stating the reasons for sentence

1. We are dealing with an offence of:

   ....

2. We have considered the impact on the victim which was ....

   ....

3. We have taken into account these features which make the offence more serious:

   ....

   ....

4. We have taken into account these features which make the offence less serious:

   ....

   ....

5. (*where relevant*) We have taken into account the offence was:

   racially and/or religiously aggravated

   committed on bail

6. We have taken into account your previous record, specifically the offences of ....

   .... and your failure to respond to the sentences imposed.

7. We have taken into account what we have heard in your favour about the offence and about you:

   ....

   ....

8. We have taken into account the fact that you pleaded guilty [at an early stage] [but not until ....] and we have reduced the sentence by [state how much].

9. And, as a result, we have decided that the appropriate sentence for you is:

   ....

10. (*where relevant*) We have decided not to award compensation in this case because:

    ....

Update December 2006: Refer to the sentencing form and guidance notes at pages 1-48a to 1-48d of the adult court bench book.

© The Magistrates' Association   **103**   *Published October 2003 and revised December 2006*

Fig. 10.6 *Guidance for giving reasons for the sentence*

A pre-sentence report will look at the reasons why the person committed the offence, their attitude to the offence and to any victims and any other factors that affect their blameworthiness. These are aggravating and mitigating factors. The pre-sentence report will also include an assessment of the offender's risk of harm and risk of reconviction.

Aggravating factors are those that make the offence worse and therefore deserving of a harsher sentence. Examples of aggravating factors include previous convictions, use of a weapon in the crime, the seriousness of the consequences of the crime and racially motivated crime.

Mitigating factors make the crime less bad and therefore the court is more likely to give a lenient sentence. Examples of mitigating factors include the defendant having no previous convictions, pleading guilty at the first opportunity and therefore not wasting the court's time, evidence of remorse and provocation (even though words can never justify a blow).

For all offences, pleading guilty at the first opportunity is a mitigating factor, as is cooperation with the police and others involved with the court case. The courts use the Adult Bench book, which has some guidance on aggravating or mitigating factors. An extract from this is shown in Fig. 6.3 on p100.

The court will give reasons for the sentence, and the magistrates are helped by the questions set out in Fig. 10.6 on p201.

AQA Examiner's tip

There are usually some pointers in the scenario to the mitigating and aggravating factors you can apply in your answer.

AQA Examiner's tip

When applying the principles of sentencing, make sure you use the evidence given in the scenario.

Activities

1. Using the scenario in Topic 2, Activity 2, and assuming that the injuries turned out to be less severe, Jack is convicted of assault occasioning actual bodily harm. Using the guidance in Fig. 10.6 of this chapter and Fig. 6.3 on p100, consider what sentence might be imposed on Jack.

2. Look at each of the potential sentences available and consider which sentencing aim or aims is reflected.

You should now be able to:

- understand the way in which a court sentences an offender
- apply the principles of sentencing to a given situation.

Chapters 9 and 10

1   Alan was reversing his lorry into a narrow entrance to park against a wall. He suddenly heard people standing on the pavement shout, "Stop!" Alan stopped immediately and looked to see what the fuss was about. He found that he had trapped Denis against the wall. When he saw that it was Denis, he shouted, "I hate you, you can stay there!" He kept Denis trapped against the wall for several minutes and then drove off. As a result, Denis suffered a fractured spine. Denis was rushed to hospital, but an inexperienced surgeon operating on Denis back made a mistake and, as a result, Denis was permanently paralysed.

   (a) Criminal offences usually require both *actus reus* and *mens rea*.

     (i)   Explain, using cases and/or examples, the meaning of the term *actus reus*.   *(7 marks)*

     (ii) Explain, using cases and/or examples, the meaning of the term *mens rea*.   *(7 marks)*

     (iii) Explain, using cases and/or examples, the principle that *actus reus* and *mens rea* must coincide (the contemporaneity rule).   *(7 marks)*

   (b) Taking into account the explanations in your answer to part (a), and ignoring any possible driving offences,

     (i)   Discuss the criminal liability of Alan for Denis's fractured spine.   *(7 marks)*

     (ii) Discuss whether Alan would have been found to have caused the paralysis.   *(7 marks)*

   (c) (i)   Outline the procedure that would be used following Alan's arrest and charge up to the start of his trial.   *(5 marks)*

     (ii) Assuming Alan was convicted of an offence, discuss the range of factors that the court may take into account before he is sentenced.   *(5 marks)*

2A Review and examination techniques

■ Answering questions on criminal law in AQA Law 2

There are a number of different aspects of learning that need to take place to answer the questions fully:

■ being able to understand and explain the basic principles

■ being able to illustrate the principles by reference to decided cases or Acts of Parliament

■ being able to select appropriate material for a given question

■ being able to apply the legal principles to a given scenario and come to an appropriate conclusion.

The aspects listed above will enable all types of question to be tackled. These questions come in a number of formats. The first format is the short answer defining and explaining a term in theory only. A typical question would be:

> Explain, using examples, the meaning of the term *actus reus (5 marks).*

In answering such a question you should:

1 define *actus reus*

2 explain that it needs to be a voluntary act, and refer to a case such as *Hill* v *Baxter* (1958)

3 explain that there should be an act, but that sometimes an omission is enough; give examples of cases illustrating omissions and show how the cases illustrate the point by explaining the idea behind the case (see Topic 2 in Chapter 9).

Similar questions are based on the material in Topics 3–6, where typical questions might be:

> Criminal liability depends on proof that the defendant caused the criminal consequence. Outline the rules of causation. *(5 marks)*: Topic 3.

> Explain, using examples, the meaning of the term *mens re*a.
> *(5 marks)*: Topic 4.

> Explain, using examples, the rule that *actus reus* and *mens rea* must coincide (the contemporaneity rule). *(5 marks)*: Topic 5.

> Explain, using examples, the meaning of the term 'crime of strict liability'. *(5 marks)*: Topic 6.

The second format combines the first format with applying the law that has been explained to a scenario and coming to a conclusion.

A typical examination question scenario is:

> Richard was riding his mountain bike along an unmade road. He saw Sally, his former girlfriend, walking in the road with her new boyfriend, Tom. Richard was still upset that Sally had left him for Tom. He went past Sally and Tom as fast as he could, deliberately shouting 'Boo!' as he went past them. Sally was startled by the shout and jumped to the edge of the road where she slipped and fell into a ditch, suffering bruising.

The question that follows the scenario is:

Discuss Richard's criminal liability for the incident involving Sally.

(10 marks)

When answering such a question you should:

1 Define the appropriate offence(s) in terms of their *actus reus* and *mens rea*. This is the same format as in the first type, except that the requirement is to choose the offence(s) first and then explain the *actus reus* and *mens rea* by reference to decided cases.

2 Apply the law you have stated to the facts disclosed in the scenario. This requires it to be made clear that the facts fit the requirements of the scenario.

3 Come to a conclusion as to the liability of Richard.

The AQA mark scheme for this question was:

> **Potential content**
>
> (A) Appropriate explanation of assault and of battery and/or ABH.
>
> (Note that an explanation of ABH (s47) requires an explanation of the assault or battery.)
>
> (B) Application to the facts of the problem and conclusion.

The answer therefore needs:

■ Explanation of *actus reus* and *mens rea* of assault, using decided cases to give authority for the statements: see Topic 7. This is theory only, and is required for potential content (A).

■ Explanation of *actus reus* and *mens rea* of battery, using decided cases to give authority for the statements: see Topic 7. This is theory only and is required for potential content (A).

■ Application of the *actus reus* and *mens rea* of both offences to the facts in the scenario. This is application only, and is required for potential content (B). Discussion might include that shouting 'Boo!' was the *actus reus* of assault, and that the *mens rea* was recklessness, as Richard knew there was a risk she would fear some harm (being knocked into by a bike, perhaps) and went ahead anyway. Similarly, the *actus reus* of the battery is the bruising (there are no causation issues, so do not go into causation at all except to state there are no causation issues) and the *mens rea* is recklessness as to causing some harm.

An alternative offence is given in the mark scheme, as an argument can be made on similar lines for the offence of assault occasioning actual bodily harm. Either or both of the offences of battery and assault occasioning actual bodily harm were acceptable along with the initial assault.

It should be noted that, on occasions, the examination question comes broken into parts, where the first part requires you to explain the principle and the second part to apply the principle to the given scenario. In such questions there is no need to repeat the detail in the theory part in the second (application only) part. Repeating the material may lead to a shortage of time.

A similar approach is needed when dealing with the questions based on the material in this chapter. Both procedure and sentencing will have questions that are of the different types set out above, and the same techniques need to be used.

■ The examination

Law 2 makes the topics in Chapters 9 and 10 compulsory. The criminal liability section will be Section A of the paper, and there is no choice but to attempt the question (Question 1). There is no choice in the parts of the question – all must be attempted. The question is worth 45 marks (half the marks for the paper, apart from quality of written communication) and half the time for the full paper should be used on this section. A choice has to be made between Section B (tort) and Section C (contract) for the other half of the paper. This effectively means that there is a maximum of 45 minutes to answer the criminal liability questions: this is one minute per mark.

Activities

1. Using the questions set out in the text of this topic, practise writing answers to each of them in the time allowed. Once you are confident that you know the material, set a timer for five minutes and write the answer to one of the five-mark questions without notes within that time. Then compare your answer to one completed using notes. This will help you identify what parts of the topic you find difficult. Do the same for the 10 mark question.

2. Now attempt the questions from the paper set out below, using the techniques set out in Activity 1 but taking 25 minutes.

   Jo, her boyfriend Peter, and Karen shared a flat. Jo was angry and upset because she believed that Peter and Karen had slept together. Jo heard the door to the flat being opened, and assumed that Karen or Peter had come in. In fact it was the landlord, Richard, who was delivering a new fridge. Without looking, Jo threw a pan full of boiling water in the direction of the door to the flat, and Richard was badly scalded.

   a At a criminal trial, the prosecution is required to prove *mens rea* unless the crime is one of strict liability. Explain, with the help of decided cases, what each of these two terms means. *(15 marks)*

   b Discuss Jo's criminal liability for Richard's injuries. *(10 marks)*

   AQA, 2006

3. Now attempt Section A of the sample paper in 45 minutes. Your teacher will be able to provide you with a copy of this.

You should now be able to:

- apply the principles in AS examination questions involving the legal system.

Introduction

Unit 2A, together with Unit 2B or Unit 2C, constitutes Unit 2 of the AS specification. Unit 2 A is about criminal liability and is compulsory. Unit 2B is about tort, and Unit 2C is about the law of contract. Candidates must answer the questions on either Unit 2B or C, but not both, as well as the questions on Unit 2A. Candidates choose to study either Unit 2B or 2C in addition to 2A.

All three sections are examined together on one examination paper, which constitutes 50 per cent of the overall marks for the AS qualification and 25 per cent of the overall marks for the A2 qualification. The Unit 2 examination is of 1.5 hours' duration. Candidates must answer all the questions from Section A and all the questions from Section B or Section C. There is no choice of question in any of the sections.

The questions in each section are worth 45 marks each. Each question is divided into several parts, each part normally being worth 5, 7 or 10 marks. Candidates must answer all parts of the question. All parts of the tort question relate to the tort and there can be no overlap between sections of the AQA Law AS specification.

The tort section is covered by Chapters 11 and 12 of this book. Some parts of the question test the candidates' knowledge and understanding and some test application of the law to the scenario that introduces the question. Question 2 is the tort question and is broken into three main parts with sub-parts. Part (a) usually tests knowledge and understanding only, whilst parts (b) and (c) test a mixture of knowledge, understanding and application of the law to the scenario.

Questions require answers to be written in continuous prose rather than note form. There are no short answer or multiple choice questions. Attainment of high grades is dependent on correct identification of the issues raised by the question and sound explanation of each of the points using authority. Authority is usually reference to a decided case or to an Act of Parliament, but may be examples taken from other sources. Further exam tips are provided throughout each topic and at the end of the chapter.

Unit 2B comprises two chapters:

11 **Liability in negligence:** concerned with the underlying principles of duty, breach and damage in the law of negligence. This provides the foundation for considering the civil liability in negligence of the character or characters in the scenario in the question.

12 **The courts: procedure and damages for negligence cases:** looks at the procedure that takes place in the civil courts from the start of legal proceedings up to, but not including, the trial. Alternative methods of resolving the claim are also considered. The chapter finishes with the way in which a court awards damages to a successful claimant.

Liability in negligence

In this topic you will learn how to:

- distinguish between criminal and civil law

- distinguish between evidence and procedure

- define negligence.

Key terms

Civil law: the law concerned with the relationship between individuals.

1 Introduction to liability in negligence

Negligence is an area of the law of tort. A tort, from the French word 'tort', which means wrong, is a civil wrong other than a breach of contract or a breach of trust. The purpose of the law of tort is to provide remedies when one person has been affected by another's acts or omissions and the law considers that a remedy should be available. The most usual remedy is damages (financial compensation), and that is the remedy being considered in this section. Negligence requires three elements: (i) a duty of care being owed to the claimant by the defendant; (ii) that duty of care being broken, as the required standard of care has not been reached by the defendant; and (iii) that broken duty must have caused the loss complained of, and the loss must not be too remote a consequence. These three elements are known as duty, breach and damage.

Civil law

Civil law is concerned with settling disputes between individuals: 'individuals' including businesses and, sometimes, Government. The key difference between civil and criminal law is that civil law is primarily designed to settle disputes, not punish wrongdoing. There are many areas of civil law including the law of tort. Negligence is the one area of the law of tort that is to be studied in the AQA AS Law specification.

A civil case is started by the person who has suffered loss (the claimant) as the result of a wrong which only directly affects him. A typical negligence case is a claim for losses and injuries resulting from a car crash. The claim requires proof that the defendant was negligent. The claimant's usual remedy is financial compensation, known as damages. Thus a successful claim in negligence against a driver who caused a car crash will result in damages paid to the claimant to cover his financial losses and to compensate for his injuries. There are other remedies available in the law of tort but these are not relevant to the material in these chapters on the law of tort.

The civil process

The civil process is the procedure by which a claim makes its way through the court system, so that the court can decide whether the claim will succeed and, if so, what amount of damages should be awarded. The court processes and eventual award of damages can be a long and complicated business for both the claimant and the defendant, but the process is designed to keep delay to the minimum through case management. Once a person is advised that they are likely to have a good claim in negligence, the major consideration is to obtain sufficient evidence of the losses suffered. This is straightforward for a damaged car: it is the cost of repairs to, or the market value of the vehicle if it is written off. Incidental costs such as renting an alternative vehicle whilst the car is being repaired also have to be proved, but, again these are straightforward. Personal injuries are much more difficult to calculate, as is loss of future earnings.

Eventually, the claimant may have to go to court for some or all of the issues to be tried and, if the claim is successful, to calculate their award of damages. The length and complexity of the process depends on the nature of the injuries, whether the evidence is clear, and whether and how the defendant makes his defence and tries to establish that he has not been negligent. There are rules of procedure that prescribe the court in which the case will be heard and the framework for deciding the case. For many reasons, such as the length of time without compensation, the stress of a court case and the question of cost (especially as many claims are the subject of insurance, and the insurance companies have to take into account their overall financial status), most negligence cases are settled out of court.

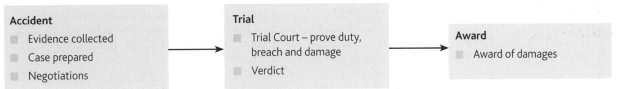

Accident
- Evidence collected
- Case prepared
- Negotiations

Trial
- Trial Court – prove duty, breach and damage
- Verdict

Award
- Award of damages

Fig. 11.1 *The civil process*

There are rules of **civil evidence** that set out how the facts must be proved and the degree of certainty that is required.

The burden of proof is the obligation on a party to establish the facts in issue in a case to the required degree of certainty (the standard of proof) in order to prove their case. In a civil trial the burden is upon the claimant to prove the liability of the defendant. The standard of proof is on a **balance of probabilities**. This is a lower standard of proof than in criminal cases, which is beyond reasonable doubt. The balance of probabilities has been defined as 'more likely than not' or '51 per cent'. Effectively, this is just a matter of convincing the judge that the claimant is right in his version of events. This is most likely to be relevant in assessing future losses or establishing that a particular loss was the result of the negligent act. Juries are not used in negligence trials, which take place in the County Court or High Court Queen's Bench Division.

Negligence

If a person is to succeed in a negligence case, there must be proof that the act of the defendant falls within the relevant definitions of what must be proved for a successful claim in negligence. There are three parts to any claim in negligence that must be proved:

- that a duty of care was owed by the defendant to the claimant
- that the defendant broke that duty of care; this means his act was not performed to the standard the law requires which is that of the reasonable man
- that the broken duty caused the loss complained of, and that the law recognises that the loss is not too remote from the act.

So far as the material in this book is concerned, all the authorities for the law come from decided cases. This means that the law is judge made and has developed over the years. It is important that the latest interpretations of the law are used, although the historical background can sometimes be useful in explaining why today's law is as it is. There are areas of negligence that have their basis in an Act of Parliament, but those areas are not part of the specification at AS.

How case law is used in answers to typical questions in AQA Unit 2

The question paper for Unit 2 is divided into three sections. As we have seen, the first section, Section A, is compulsory, and is the introduction to criminal liability. Section B is the law of tort and, like the other sections, has no choice within it. All questions must be answered. The tort question starts with a short scenario that sets the scene and is the basis of your discussions for some of the questions. A scenario, taken from the sample paper, is:

> Having bought herself a cheap sail board, Olga decided to teach herself to windsurf on a lake near her home. After several hours' practice, she began to tire and decided to have one last attempt at crossing the lake. She failed to notice Petra, who was fishing from a boat on the lake. Unfortunately, Olga crashed into the boat, which capsized, and Petra lost her fishing equipment, worth £3,000, in the lake.

The questions are of two general types:

Theory questions

These require an explanation of terms used but they require no reference to the facts given in the scenario. A typical question (taken from the sample paper) is:

> 1) Negligence requires proof of duty, breach and damage.
>
> a) i) Explain, using examples, the meaning of the term duty of care. *(7 marks)*
>
> ii) Explain, using examples, the meaning of the term breach of duty. *(7 marks)*
>
> iii) Explain, using examples, the meaning of the term damage. *(6 marks)*

Application questions

These usually require you to select the appropriate law or principles of damages and apply the law to the facts given in the scenario. You should assume that the facts as stated in the scenario can be proved. A typical question (taken from the sample paper) is:

> Using the explanations given in your answers to question 1(a) above, discuss whether Olga has been negligent towards Petra. *(10 marks)*

Negligence requires proof of three elements: duty, breach, and damage. Once this has been proved, damages can be assessed. The requirements for these elements need to be explored in more detail.

Links

■ For a diagram of how to structure a content of theory answer, see Fig 9.3 on page 165.

■ For a diagram of how to structure a content of application answer, see Fig. 9.4 on page 165. These methods of tackling a question will be dealt with in more detail in the Section Review in at the end of Chapter 12.

Activities

1 Think about your family and friends and remember accidents that have befallen them. Consider whether it is likely that someone had been negligent in the accident. Do you think one person was to blame?

2 Think about things you do every day, such as driving a car, riding a bike or playing football. What do you do to avoid being negligent?

You should now be able to:

■ understand the role of the civil law

■ understand the concept of negligence

■ understand how to use authority in answering questions on negligence.

🔍 ② The duty of care

The history of the test for a duty of care

The law of negligence has been developing for many years. The famous definition of negligence is 'Negligence is the omission to do something which a reasonable man, guided upon those considerations which ordinarily regulate the conduct of human affairs, would do, or doing something which a prudent and reasonable man would not do.' This is the definition given by Baron Alderson in **Blyth v Birmingham Waterworks Co. (1856)**.

This definition is still relevant today as it puts the idea of **the reasonable man** in the centre of negligence. What the reasonable man would do is to try to fulfil his duties to other people. This would include a duty of care owed to others. A duty of care is simply a duty to take care of others or look out for them. The legal definition is a little more complex, as will be seen later. The law has struggled to define what a duty of care is or at least how to decide the circumstances in which a duty of care is owed by one person to another. The famous case of **Donoghue v Stevenson (1932)** was an attempt to do this.

The facts of *Donoghue* v *Stevenson (1932)* were that Mrs Donoghue and her friend went to the Wellmeadow Café, Paisley, where her friend purchased ice cream, and ginger beer which, as was the fashion at the time, was to be poured over the ice cream as an iced drink. The ginger beer was contained in an opaque bottle, which meant that the contents could not be seen clearly. Mrs Donoghue drank some of the ginger beer. When the remaining ginger beer was poured into her glass the decomposed remains of a snail came out of the bottle. This appalled Mrs Donoghue and she became ill as a result of the sight and the ginger beer she had already drunk.

Mrs Donoghue had no direct claim against the manufacturer or the shopkeeper based on contract because she did not buy the ginger beer. Mrs Donoghue's friend could claim against the café in contract, but had not suffered any loss apart from the fact that she had bought defective goods; she could get her money back, but nothing for Mrs Donoghue's illness. Therefore, Mrs Donoghue claimed damages against the manufacturer, Stevenson. Her claim was for the resulting shock and stomach upset, which she claimed was caused through drinking the ginger beer.

The court had to decide whether her claim against the manufacturer of the ginger beer could succeed. This led to Lord Atkin's famous statement:

> The rule that you are to love your neighbour becomes in law, you must not injure your neighbour; and the lawyer's question, 'Who is my neighbour?' receives a restricted reply. You must take reasonable care to avoid acts or omissions which you can reasonably foresee would be likely to injure your neighbour. Who, then, in law is my neighbour? The answer seems to be: persons who are so closely and directly affected by my act that I ought reasonably to have them in contemplation as being so affected when I am directing my mind to the acts or omissions which are called in question.

The neighbour principle was based on the command in the Bible to 'love thy neighbour', and Lord Atkin used that as his starting point for his attempt to set out a general principle that he could then apply to Mrs Donoghue's case. This made it clear that there could be liability without

---

In this topic you will learn how to:

- define a duty of care in terms of the neighbour principle

- state the three-part Caparo test for the existence of a duty of care

- explain each part of the Caparo test by reference to decided cases

- apply the Caparo test to a given situation.

■ Key cases

Blyth v Birmingham Waterworks Co. (1856): this case defined the meaning of the term 'negligence' in the famous statement by Baron Alderson.

Donoghue v Stevenson (1932): this famous case set out the neighbour principle in the law of negligence. This principle is the foundation of the modern law.

■ Key terms

The reasonable man: the expression used to describe the basis of the law of negligence: the typical ordinary person.

a contract and gave the opportunity for the law to develop the rules of negligence. The law has developed these rules to the extent that there are a number of different areas of negligence that have developed in different ways. These are looked at in detail in A2 law. The AS specification looks at the general concept only in relation to liability for physical damage and personal injury.

Donoghue v *Stevenson* (1932) was the first successful attempt to set out a general principle with respect to the concept of the duty of care. The principle set out was satisfactory, but as the world became increasingly complex and increasingly willing to take legal action, the test was seen to be too simple. This led to many other attempts to make a general test for the existence of a duty of care after *Donoghue* v *Stevenson* (1932), but these, too, were unsatisfactory in various ways. The latest test comes from the case of **Caparo v Dickman (1990)**.

The three-part test in Caparo v Dickman

The case of *Caparo* v *Dickman* (1990) involved a claim by an investor who had lost money in a company. The investor claimed against the auditors of the company, as the auditors had produced inaccurate accounts. The court decided that the law should develop new categories of negligence incrementally and by analogy with established categories of negligence. This means that the court would first look at existing precedents and if none could be found or adapted to fit the case in question, then, and only then, would a general test be applied to see whether a duty of care should exist.

The general test set in *Caparo* v *Dickman* (1990) requires three elements to be demonstrated:

- it was reasonably foreseeable that a person in the claimant's position would be injured
- there was sufficient proximity between the parties
- it is fair, just and reasonable to impose liability on the defendant.

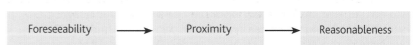

Fig. 11.2 *Summary of three-part test from Caparo v Dickman*

All parts of the test must be satisfied if there is to be a duty of care owed by the defendant to the claimant.

Each part of the test must be looked at in turn.

The first part – foreseeability

This is an objective test: would a reasonable person in the defendant's position have foreseen that someone in the claimant's position might be injured? In *Donoghue* v *Stevenson* (1932) it can be seen that failing to stop a snail getting into a bottle will affect the consumer (Mrs Donoghue) of the contents. This is a consequence of producing food that has foreign bodies in it, and a reasonable person in the defendant's position (a soft drink manufacturer) would foresee that the claimant (a consumer) might be injured.

It would equally apply, by analogy, to the caterpillar in the tin of peas in *Smedleys* v *Breed* (1974), noted in Chapter 9 (p179). So, if the consumer of the peas had not seen the caterpillar and had eaten it and become ill as

Key cases

Caparo v Dickman (1990): this case sets out the modern three-part test to decide whether a duty of care exists in situations where there is no precedent for a duty of care.

appeal?

[Kent v
  Griffiths
        (2000)

Bourhill v Young
no proximity
BUT was in
McLoughlin v O'Brien

a result, that person would have had a similar claim to Mrs Donoghue. In fact, as we have seen, criminal action was taken against the manufacturer and, presumably, the consumer was unaffected by the caterpillar and got a refund from Smedleys.

A good example of the first part of the test can be seen in the case of **Kent v Griffiths (2000)**. In that case it was decided that the ambulance service owed a duty of care to a member of the public on whose behalf a 999 call had been made. This was because it was reasonably foreseeable that a person in the claimant's position (an injured or sick person waiting for an ambulance to take them to hospital) would be further injured if the ambulance failed to arrive or took too long to arrive.

The second part – proximity

Proximity is related to the concept of foreseeability. Proximity just means closeness. There can be proximity by space, time or relationship. If I crash my car into yours, I am proximate in time and space, but not necessarily in relationship. If I crash into my son's car, whilst there is relationship, it is not relevant to my liability which is based on time and space. Relationship only becomes relevant when it makes the loss foreseeable to a person in the defendant's position. A good example of this can be seen in the case of **Bourhill v Young (1943)**.

In that case the claimant was getting off a tram in the centre of Edinburgh when she heard a motorcycle go past and almost immediately heard a collision. She did not see the accident and was in a safe place away from it when it happened. She decided to go and see what had happened and saw the dead motorcyclist and all the rest of the aftermath of the accident. She suffered shock from what she had seen and she claimed that the shock caused her to miscarry her baby. The defendant was found not to owe a duty of care to the claimant as she was in a safe place and had not seen the accident but went to see the aftermath voluntarily. In proximity terms, there was no proximity in space as she was away from the accident even though she was nearby at the time.

The result might have been different if she had been related to the victim as in the case of **McLoughlin v O'Brien (1983)**. Mrs McLoughlin was told of a serious accident involving her husband and children. She was nowhere near the accident when it occurred, but was told of it a short time afterwards. She, quite naturally, rushed to the hospital where the family had been taken. Here she discovered that one of her children had died, the other was seriously ill and her husband, whilst alive, had not yet been cleaned up or sedated and was very distressed and in great pain. She suffered shock and the court decided that the person that caused the accident owed a duty of care to her even though there was no proximity of time or space. The proximity of relationship was the deciding factor in establishing the duty of care in this case.

In most cases there is little issue of proximity as the accident victim is part of the event. However, where a person learns about an accident later or sees it from a safe distance and where the injury is psychiatric, (so-called 'nervous shock'), then relationship is the key factor. This is explored in greater depth in A2 in Unit 4.

The third part – reasonableness

The third part of the test, whether it is fair, just and reasonable to impose a duty of care, is really a matter of public policy. Traditionally, the courts were always concerned that any extension to the types of claim that could be brought before them would open the 'floodgates of litigation'. In other

AQA Examiner's tip

Make sure you can explain each part of the Caparo test fully and use a different negligence case to illustrate it.

Key cases

Kent v Griffiths (2000): this case is an example of foreseeability in that it is foreseeable that an injured person waiting for an ambulance may have more severe injuries if there is delay.

Bourhill v Young (1943): here there was no physical proximity, as the claimant was in a safe place away from the accident, and whilst she could hear it she could not see it. She later went to see the aftermath and then suffered her miscarriage.

McLoughlin v O'Brien (1983): the claimant was told of events and rushed to see her injured family. She then suffered shock. Even though there was no proximity of space and time, the relationship overrode this to make the defendant liable.

words, the concern was that there would be a huge number of claims and that the courts might be deceived into allowing a claim that had no validity. This was always a concern with nervous shock cases and has been a consideration in other areas of negligence too. The fear was that – and is possibly justified by the impression that – the nation is much more claims-conscious today and some individuals are always looking to make some claim in the hope of getting money for nothing, or at least very little.

Today, the courts are looking at what is best for society as a whole. Thus, defendants who are in the public sector are more likely to find that claims against them will fail, as it is not fair and reasonable to impose liability on them. The police need to be able to act without undue worry about legal action in negligence against them. Thus in the case of *Hill v Chief Constable of West Yorkshire (1988)*, the House of Lords refused to impose a duty of care on the police to the mother of the Yorkshire Ripper's last victim. The police had already interviewed and released the victim's killer before he killed again, but the court found no duty of care to potential victims of crime. This was partly on proximity grounds to an unknown member of the public and more on the policy consideration of allowing the police to work as efficiently as possible. This can be compared to *Kent v Griffiths* (2000). In that case the emergency service owed a duty of care to a known member of the public because it had taken on the responsibility to that person when the telephone call was taken.

Hill v *Chief Constable of West Yorkshire (1988)*: The police were found not to owe a duty of care to potential victims of crime and their families on policy grounds. This is an example of the reasonableness part of the Caparo three-part test.

However, the police do owe a duty of care in some circumstances. For example, they usually owe a duty of care to people taken into custody as can be seen from the following cases. In **MPC v Reeves (2001)** the police took a man into custody who was a prisoner known to be at risk of committing suicide. Whilst in police custody he hanged himself in his cell. The court found that the police owed him a duty of care.

There are limits to this duty of care, or at least as to whether the duty has been broken, as can be seen where the prisoner is not known to be a suicide risk as in the case of **Orange v Chief Constable of West Yorkshire (2001)**. In that case the increased risk of suicide among prisoners as compared with those in the community gives rise to an obligation, within the general duty of care owed by the police to a person in their custody for that person's health and safety, to take reasonable steps to identify whether or not a prisoner presented a suicide risk. The obligation to take care to prevent a prisoner from taking his own life deliberately only arose where the custodian knew or ought to have known that the individual prisoner presented a suicide risk. In this case, because of the lack of any evidence to suggest that the police officers knew or ought to have known that a person in Orange's condition (he had been arrested for being drunk and disorderly) presented a significantly increased suicide risk, the judge concluded that the police had not been negligent in permitting Orange to retain his belt with which he committed suicide.

Similarly, the police do not owe a duty of care to a prisoner who is injured whilst making an escape attempt, as can be seen in the case of *Vellino v Chief Constable of Greater Manchester* (2001). This is partly because of policy (the injured person is committing a criminal offence and should

■ Key cases

MPC v Reeves (2001): the police owe a duty of care to prisoners taken into custody.

Orange v Chief Constable of West Yorkshire (2001): the police's duty of care only extends to known risks to a particular prisoner.

Handwritten margin notes:
Police can only do what they can
Can't arrest on suspicion
Public Policy
Fair, Just, Reasonable

not profit from their wrongdoing) and partly as an escaping prisoner is no longer under the control of the police.

The fire service has a similar, limited, protection against claims in negligence, but the legal profession no longer has that immunity following the case of *Hall* v *Simons* (2000).

When applying the Caparo test, say why each part is or is not present in the scenario. You must give a reason for your decision, not just assert, for example, that it is fair, just and reasonable.

Conclusion

Proof of the existence of a duty of care, where there is not an existing duty, requires all three parts of the test in *Caparo* v *Dickman* (1990) to be established by the claimant. Proof of the existence of a duty of care is not, however, proof of negligence. Breach of that duty and resulting damage must also be proved.

Activities

1. Look at the facts of *Donoghue* v *Stevenson* (1932). Imagine that case was coming before the court for the first time today. Apply the Caparo three-part test to the facts and decide whether a duty of care would be found to exist.

2. Consider the scenario below, taken from a past examination paper, and consider whether a duty of care exists in that case.

   Yannick and Zoe, university students, were at a music festival organised by XS Ltd. They were sitting on the ground in the main tent, listening to a band, when one of the tent supports became detached and the tent collapsed. Yannick suffered severe head and neck injuries.

You should now be able to:

- understand the legal requirements for the existence of a duty of care
- describe and apply the *Caparo* test in examination-style questions.

AQA Examiner's tip

When answering problem questions on the existence of a duty of care, you need to assume there is no existing duty of care and apply the three-part test in *Caparo* v *Dickman* to the facts in the scenario. You will often have described the theory in a previous part question, so you will not need to repeat the theory, merely apply each part of the test to the facts saying why each part is or is not demonstrated in the scenario.

🔲 3 Breach of duty

The nature of breach – the reasonable man

Once it has been established that a duty of care exists, the claimant must satisfy the court that the defendant broke that duty of care by failing to reach the standard of care required. The standard of care is that of the 'reasonable man', which comes from the definition from Baron Alderson in *Blyth* v *Birmingham Waterworks Co.* (1856), set out at the start of Topic 2.

The reasonable man is the ordinary person performing the particular task: he is expected to perform it reasonably competently. Thus, when I am riding my bicycle, I am expected to be a reasonably competent cyclist; when I am building a wall, a reasonably competent wall builder and so on. This is an objective standard: the peculiarities of the person performing the task are irrelevant.

In this topic you will learn how to:

- describe the 'reasonable man' test
- list the factors that affect the standard of care of the reasonable man
- state and explain relevant examples for each of the above factors
- apply the test to a given situation.

■ **Key cases**

Wells v Cooper (1954): the standard of care required is of the reasonably competent person doing the job in question. Here a man doing DIY was expected to reach the standard of a reasonably competent professional doing the job.

Nettleship v Weston (1971): the standard of care expected of a learner driver is the same as that of any driver. This is logical from the point of view of those injured and because there is compulsory insurance.

Factors affecting the standard of care of the reasonable man

When the court looks at whether a duty of care has been breached, it bases the standard on the reasonable man performing the task in the circumstances. There are, therefore, a number of factors that can be considered to raise or lower the standard. This is logical because a reasonable person will rightly take greater risks in an emergency, and take more care when the risk of harm is greater. For example, I may well damage a person's clothing or cause minor injuries when pulling a person from a burning car; equally, I will be more careful when carrying a young baby than when carrying a sack of potatoes. These differences can be put into various categories for ease of explanation and illustration. Commonly used questions to define the categories include:

- Are there any special characteristics of the defendant?
- Are there any special characteristics of the claimant?
- What is the size of the risk?
- Have all practical precautions been taken?
- What are the benefits of taking the risk?

These will be looked at in more detail.

Are there any special characteristics of the defendant?

The defendant is expected to be a reasonably competent person performing the task. This is straightforward when dealing with everyday people doing everyday tasks. In **Wells v Cooper (1954)**, a man fitted a new door handle to the outside of the back door of his house. The door was at the top of some steps. The door was difficult to close on the day the accident happened as there was a high wind blowing against the door. The claimant was leaving the house and pulled hard on the door to shut it. The handle came away in his hand and he fell down the steps and was injured. The court decided that a reasonably competent carpenter would have done the work to a similar standard as the man doing DIY on his house, so he had reached the standard of a reasonably competent person attaching a door handle.

This can have some surprising, but logical results. In **Nettleship v Weston (1971)**, the claimant was a non-professional driving instructor and the defendant was a learner driver. The learner driver was on her third lesson in her car that did not have dual controls. She failed to straighten up the car after turning a corner at a road junction and hit a lamp post, injuring the passenger/instructor. The court decided that the learner driver's standard of driving should be that of the reasonably competent driver, not the standard of a learner driver.

The decision is perfectly logical. First, the defendant must be insured by law and, if not insured, personal injuries might be covered by the Motor Insurers' Bureau. Secondly, any claimant would find it unjust if he were told, 'Sorry, I am not liable to pay you compensation as I am only on my first lesson and you cannot expect me to be as good a driver as someone who has passed their driving test.' Thirdly, whilst you take more care whilst helping a person to learn to drive, there are some aspects you cannot be expected to control; those outside the vehicle have no need to look out for learners even though other drivers are a little more cautious in their vicinity.

The position is much the same when dealing with a professional. When you go to hospital for an operation, you expect the same standard from your surgeon whether it his first operation ever or not. This is no

Fig. 11.3 *Nettleship v Weston*

different to the learner driver. The test here is whether he is operating to the standard expected under a known and accepted procedure. This can be seen from the case of **Bolam v Friern Barnet Hospital Management Committee (1957)**.

Bolam was suffering from mental illness and was advised by a consultant attached to the defendants' hospital to undergo electro-convulsive therapy. This is a form of electric shock treatment. He signed a form of consent to the treatment but was not warned of the risk of breaking a bone whilst strapped down and being given electric shocks. On the second occasion when the treatment was given to him he suffered a broken bone. The hospital did not use relaxant drugs that would have prevented the risk of breaking a bone. Among the medical experts, however, there were two bodies of opinion, one of which favoured the use of relaxant drugs as a general practice, and the other of which confined the use of relaxant drugs to cases where there were particular reasons for their use. These reasons were not present in Bolam's case. The hospital had reached the standard expected and so had not broken their duty of care. The principle for professionals is established by asking two questions:

1 Does the conduct of the defendant fall below the standard of the ordinary competent professional?

2 Is there a substantial body of opinion within the profession that would support the course taken by the defendant? It should be noted that in **Bolitho v City and Hackney Health Authority (1997)** it is open to the court to find the practice of the entire profession wrong. In such circumstances, the duty of care would be broken even if the normal practice was being followed.

If the answer to the first question is 'no' and to the second question is 'yes', then the correct standard has been reached and the defendant has not broken his duty of care.

Finally, it should be noted that where a reasonable man cannot know that a standard procedure is in fact dangerous, he will not break the duty

> ### Key cases
>
> **Bolam v Friern Barnet Hospital Management Committee (1957):** the standard of a professional is judged by the standard of the profession. In this case, following either of two accepted medical methods was said to be acceptable in reaching the standard of care expected.
>
> **Bolitho v City and Hackney Health Authority (1997):** when judging the standard of care required by professionals, the court can decide that the normal standard of acceptable conduct set by the profession is not high enough and the defendant has therefore broken his duty of care.

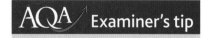

Examiner's tip

Make sure you do not confuse claimant and defendant.

of care. This is because the reasonable man is not expected to know and protect against risks of harm that are not yet known scientifically. Once the risk is known, there can be a breach of duty. This is illustrated by the case of **Roe v Minister of Health (1954)**. In that case, the claimant was injected with an anaesthetic contained in glass ampoules which were, prior to use, immersed in an antiseptic solution. The object of this was to keep the risk of infection to a minimum. Unfortunately, the claimant suffered permanent paralysis from the waist downwards, as the anaesthetic had been contaminated by antiseptic which had seeped through invisible cracks in the ampoules. At the time the risk of this happening was not appreciated by competent anaesthetists in general, and such contamination had not happened before. Therefore the duty of care owed by the hospital to the patient had not been broken.

Are there any special characteristics of the claimant?

The reasonable man takes more care where the situation demands it. This factor relates to risks known to the defendant as a result of peculiarities of the claimant. This is illustrated by the case of **Paris v Stepney Borough Council (1951)**. Here the claimant was employed as a fitter in a garage. His employer, the local council, knew he had the use of only one eye. While he was using a hammer to remove a bolt on a vehicle, a chip of metal flew off and entered his good eye. This resulted in his becoming totally blind. The council did not provide goggles for him to wear as, in 1950, it was not common practice for employers to supply goggles to men employed in garages on the maintenance and repair of vehicles. So had Mr Paris been fully sighted, the council might not have broken their duty of care. Because the council knew he was blind in one eye when they employed him, the court decided that the council owed him a higher standard of care because of this known, increased, risk.

This principle applies equally to illness. In **Walker v Northumberland County Council (1995)** the claimant was a social services manager who had been forced, because of local authority funding shortages, to take on a far higher volume of work than he could cope with. He suffered several weeks of being unable to work because of a stress-related illness. This then became a special characteristic of Mr Walker known to the defendant. When he returned to work the local authority made little or no effort to improve his situation. The claimant then suffered another long period of illness. The court referred to the principle in *Paris* v *Stepney Borough Council* (1951) that the standard of care expected of an employer is raised if the employer knows that an employee is more likely to suffer injury. Thus the claimant was owed a higher standard of care that had been broken.

Another example of this is that a higher standard of care is expected by organizers and sports coaches to disabled athletes because of their special needs; this can be seen in the case of *Morrell* v *Owen* (1983). The facts of that case were that at a sports event for disabled athletes, archery and discus activities took place in the same hall, separated by a curtain. The archery section was past this curtain, which billowed out from time to time when struck by a discus. The claimant was an archer, and was close to the curtain when a discus struck her head (through the curtain) and caused brain damage.

What is the size of the risk?

The principle is that the greater the risk, the more care need be taken. To some extent this is an extension of the ideas behind the previous factors. The reasonable man takes more precautions where the risk is greater, but does not take precautions against highly unlikely events. The classic case on this factor is **Bolton v Stone (1951)**. During a cricket match a batsman struck a ball which hit a person who was standing outside her house on the road outside the ground. The ball was hit out of the ground over a protective fence five metres high. The distance from the striker to the fence was about 70 metres and that to the place where the person was hit nearly 100 metres. The ground had been used as a cricket ground for about 90 years, and only on six occasions in the previous 30 years had a ball been hit out of the ground in that direction and no one had previously been injured. The court decided that the risk of injury to a person from a ball being hit out of the ground was so small that the probability of it happening would not be anticipated by a reasonable man. Therefore the cricket club had not broken its duty of care as it had reached the appropriate standard of care. The club had clearly thought about the risk and provided a reasonable solution.

A combination of this factor and a person with a disability can be seen in the case of **Haley v London Electricity Board (1964)**. A blind man was walking along the pavement on his way to work. He was using his white stick to go along a route he knew very well. The electricity board had opened a trench and warned of it in the then conventional manner of laying a tool on the ground to force people to walk round it. The blind man did not notice the tool with his stick and fell over it into the trench. The court decided that it was reasonably foreseeable that a blind person might be in the area as about one in 500 people is blind or partially sighted. Thus the reasonable man would take precautions to prevent such an accident happening as it was a reasonable risk to protect against and not a fantastic possibility. Of course, today's procedure for warning of such an obstacle protects against this risk.

Have all practical precautions been taken?

It follows from the previous factor that a defendant will have acted reasonably if he has taken reasonable precautions. Thus the nets around the cricket ground in *Bolton* v *Stone* (1951) were a reasonable precaution, but the tool left on the ground was not in *Haley* v *London Electricity Board* (1964). The idea behind this factor is that the reasonable man will do all he reasonably can to prevent harm coming to others. In situations that are unexpected, this may not always prevent an accident, but the key is the reasonableness of the action taken. In **Latimer v AEC (1952)** the defendant's factory was flooded after an exceptionally heavy rainstorm. The water, mixed with some oil, made the floor very slippery. The defendant put up warning signs, passed the message round the workforce and used all their supply of sand and sawdust to try to dry the floor. Despite this, the claimant slipped and was injured. The defendant owed a duty of care to the employees, but had not broken the duty as the precautions taken to prevent an accident were sufficient in the circumstances as all reasonable practical precautions had been taken.

What are the benefits of taking the risk?

This factor is sometimes called public utility. The idea is that there is a lower standard of care when reacting to an emergency. This is consistent with the idea of fair, just and reasonable in the third part of the test to establish a duty of care. The most famous example of this is **Watt v Hertfordshire County Council (1954)**. This case concerns firefighters, who were injured by lifting gear when travelling in a vehicle not specifically fitted for carrying that gear. The vehicle that the firefighters should have used was adapted to carry the gear. However, that vehicle was already in use attending an emergency when the call came to go to another emergency where a woman was trapped under a heavy vehicle.

Key cases

Bolton v Stone (1951): the reasonable man takes precautions against reasonable risks, not fantastic possibilities. The likelihood of a cricket ball clearing the protective fence at the ground and injuring a passer-by was not a risk the reasonable man would protect against.

Haley v London Electricity Board (1964): a reasonable risk to protect against is one that is statistically likely to occur. In this case, a blind pedestrian was not adequately warned of a trench across the pavement.

Latimer v AEC (1952): one factor in deciding whether the defendant has acted as a reasonable man is taking all practical precautions. After a flood, this was doing the best to mop up and warning the employees in the factory.

Watt v Hertfordshire County Council (1954): the benefits of saving a woman's life outweighed the risk of injury to a firefighter when using the best, but still unsuitable vehicle in an emergency.

Court must balance the risk against the measures

The court held that the firemen were ready to take the risk of using the vehicle to save life. The court must 'balance the risk against the measures' and the benefit of saving the woman was greater than the risk of injuring the firefighters by using a vehicle not suited to carrying the heavy gear which moved and crushed a firefighter. Thus the duty of care owed by the council to its employee firefighters had not been broken.

The approach of the courts is very realistic when an emergency arises as the courts want to encourage rescuers on the one hand, but also want to make sure employers are not put off encouraging employees to effect a rescue by the threat of being sued in negligence because they had not taken all reasonable precautions. In another recent case, **Day v High Performance Sports (2003)**, Ms Day, a reasonably experienced climber, fell while climbing on an indoor climbing wall belonging to the defendant. Unfortunately, she suffered serious brain injury. At a height of 30 feet she had discovered she was not tied to her top rope and had had to be rescued by the duty manager because she was 'frozen' in her position. The court recognised that this was an emergency situation and that the circumstances of the emergency had to be taken into account. In fact the centre was one where a concern for safety was prominent and workshops on safety were given to employees. The court concluded that the climbing centre had not broken its duty of care and had reached the standard of care of a reasonably competent climbing centre.

Conclusion

Breach of duty is concerned with the question of whether the defendant has reached the standard of care of a reasonable man. There are a number of factors that are relevant to this duty which raise or lower the standard expected.

■ Key cases

Day v High Performance Sports (2003): the standard of care can be lower when making a rescue, in this case on a climbing wall.

■ Activities

1. Think about things you do and decide what standard of care is required. Situations could include driving a car, babysitting, taking a person in a wheelchair shopping. In order to do so, you need to decide on the people to whom you would owe a duty of care and then decide the standard of care owed to each of those people.

2. Consider the following case and decide whether there is a duty owed and the standard of care required, concluding with a decision as to whether any duty of care owed has been broken.

   On 26 August 2000, the Saturday before the late summer Bank Holiday, Mary Abrew, a pensioner in her mid-60s living in Thornton Heath, was shopping in the Thornton Heath branch of Tesco, when, in aisle 23, she slipped on some dried spaghetti, which had apparently been spilt onto the floor near the shelves which she was approaching. She was helped to her feet by an employee of the defendants, and taken by that employee to the first aid room, where she was treated with the utmost courtesy, and the incident was entered in the incident book in her presence. (These are the facts of *Abrew* v *Tesco* (2003)).

memo

AQA / Examiner's tip

Make sure that you start from the reasonable man test.

Breach of duty does not need a repeat of the Caparo three-part test.

You should now be able to:

- understand the concept of breach of duty
- describe and apply the test for the standard of care in negligence.

4 Damage caused by the defendant's breach

General principles

At the start of this chapter it was seen that the third aspect that must be proved if there is to be liability in negligence is that the broken duty caused the loss complained of, and that the law recognises that the loss is not too remote from the act. This is often referred to as **damage** and must be distinguished from **damages** which is the amount of compensation awarded.

There are two parts to damage: causation and remoteness. Causation is the idea that the defendant must have caused the loss complained of. This is causation in fact. This is the same concept as in criminal law, but is illustrated by examples from the law of negligence. If no loss is caused then there is no claim in negligence. Remoteness is concerned whether the loss is reasonably foreseeable: causation in law. Both must be proved following a broken duty of care if there is to be liability for a claim in negligence.

This can be illustrated by the following diagram:

Situation	Causation in fact	Causation in law
▪ Defendant's act or omission ▪ Drives car into claimant's car	▪ Apply 'but for' test ▪ Minor damage to car and whiplash injury to claimant	▪ Take your victim as you find him/unusual form of forseeable injury ▪ Claimant already has a weak neck from previous accident and in fact breaks neck

Fig. 11.4 *Causation and remoteness*

Causation in fact

Causation in fact is the starting point. If there is no causation in fact, there is no point in considering whether there has been causation in law. Causation in fact is determined by the 'but for' test. The test is satisfied if it can be said that, but for the defendant's act or omission the claimant would not have suffered the loss or harm. A different way of stating the test is to ask whether the prohibited result would have occurred if the defendant had not acted. If the prohibited result would still have occurred, even without the defendant's actions, then something other than the defendant's actions caused it and factual causation is not present.

This is clearly illustrated in the case of **Barnett v Chelsea and Kensington Hospital Management Committee (1968)**.

The facts of the case are that the defendants managed a casualty department at a hospital. One night, three night-watchmen arrived at casualty, complaining to a nurse on duty that they had been vomiting for three hours after drinking tea. The nurse reported their complaints by telephone to the duty medical casualty officer, who instructed her to tell the men to go home to bed and call their own doctors if they still felt ill in the morning. The casualty officer did not speak to the men or offer to examine them which would have been normal practice. The men then left, and, about five hours later, one of them died from poisoning by arsenic. It seems that the arsenic had got into the tea, probably as a result of the mugs or teapot being used for mixing poison by someone else at the workplace. The medical opinion was that the claimant was likely to have died from the poisoning even if he had been admitted to the hospital wards and treated with all care for the five hours before his death.

In this topic you will learn how to:

▪ distinguish between causation in fact and remoteness of damage

▪ distinguish between damage and damages

▪ state and explain factual causation in negligence

▪ state and explain the test for remoteness of damage.

Key terms

Damage: the resulting loss to a claimant from a breach of a duty of care.

Damages: the amount of compensation payable to the claimant who has proved the defendant has been negligent.

Key cases

Barnett v Chelsea and Kensington Hospital Management Committee (1968): this is an example where there was no causation in fact as the hospital could not have done anything to save Barnett's life. The cause of death was the original poisoning, not the hospital's failure to examine him properly.

AQA Examiner's tip

Many candidates confuse damage and damages. Make sure you answer the question asked!

Key cases

Fairchild v Glenhaven Funeral Services Ltd (2002): the normal rule on causation in fact can be modified on policy grounds where there are 'special circumstances'. Here this was because it is impossible to prove when asbestos actually entered the system to cause illness.

Barker v Corus (2006): this case modifies the 'but for' test in asbestos cases only and should be seen as a special exception to ensure some remedy for the victim.

The judge stated in his decision, 'My conclusions are: that the plaintiff, Mrs Bessie Irene Barnett, has failed to establish, on the balance of probabilities, that the death of the deceased, William Patrick Barnett, resulted from the negligence of the defendants, the Chelsea and Kensington Hospital Management Committee, my view being that had all care been taken, still the deceased must have died. But my further conclusions are that the defendants' casualty officer was negligent (owed a duty of care and broke it) in failing to see and examine the deceased, and that, had he done so, his duty would have been to admit the deceased to the ward and to have treated him or caused him to be treated.'

In other words, the hospital owed the deceased a duty of care; the hospital broke the duty of care by not reaching the standard of the reasonably competent hospital; but the hospital had not caused the death of the deceased as their failure to examine him had not been proved to be the factual cause of his death. It should be noted that the judge stated the hospital had been negligent and only ruled out liability for the death. This means that the hospital could be liable for any other losses following from their failure to examine the deceased. Note also how the judge specifically referred to the standard of proof as being 'on the balance of probabilities'.

Multiple causes

It is not always straightforward to establish that the defendant's act or omission caused the loss complained of. Sometimes there is more than one possible cause. The courts have started to use a modified rule on the grounds of public policy where there are 'special circumstances'. This was set out in the case of **Fairchild v Glenhaven Funeral Services Ltd (2002)**.

This case decided that a worker who had contracted mesothelioma (a form of cancer caused by exposure to asbestos dust) could sue any of his previous employers following multiple exposures to asbestos caused by employers' negligence, even though the claimant could not prove which particular exposure had been the cause of the disease. It is understood that just one fibre from asbestos can cause the disease, but not every fibre inhaled will cause the disease. As a result of this uncertainty, the court decided all possible exposures to asbestos could have triggered the disease, and if any and all employers were not to be held to be the cause of the disease, the claimant would not succeed. It was, therefore, unjust on policy grounds to leave this type of claimant without a remedy in law.

This problem has been revisited by the courts in **Barker v Corus (2006)** which has similar facts. In this case liability was placed on all those responsible for the exposure to asbestos so that liability is shared. This seems to mean that, in the case of exposure to asbestos at any rate, the normal rule of causation in fact is modified. The difference between Fairchild and Barker is that the defendant in Fairchild had to take full responsibility for compensation and then try to find and claim against other possible sources of asbestos (which might be difficult where a potentially responsible defendant has gone out of business); in Barker, each defendant sued by the claimant was liable for a given percentage of the award in proportion to the likelihood of having been the source of the asbestos that caused the disease. This then led to a further variation in the Compensation Act 2006. This whole area is similar in concept to contributory negligence, which is dealt with in A2 law.

Intervening events

As with criminal law, an intervening act can break the chain of causation. As has been seen, the intervening act is known as a *novus actus interveniens* (new act intervening) and can be seen diagrammatically as:

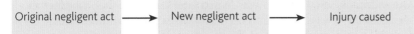

Fig. 11.5 *Diagram of* novus actus interveniens

AQA Examiner's tip

The law on multiple causes is very complex and no more than an awareness that there is a problem for the law is needed.

The defendant's act may be said to cause the claimant's damage, in that it satisfies the 'but for' test, but a second factual cause is the real cause of the damage. For example, suppose your head was injured at school by a tile falling off the roof (because the roof was badly maintained), and you were taken to casualty by a teacher. On the way to casualty, the teacher's car was hit by a bus that was being driven badly, causing you leg injuries. It could be said that 'but for' the tile falling off the roof you would not have suffered the leg injury. However, the real cause of the leg injury is the bus, not the tile. The bus is the *novus actus interveniens*. This means the injury to your head is caused by the tile, the injury to your leg by the bus.

Many of the cases we have looked at have an element of an intervening act in them and the argument is often used that if there is duty and breach, the intervening act prevents liability. These arguments were used in *MPC* v *Reeves* (2001) (the case where a prisoner was known to be at risk of committing suicide) and *Orange* v *Chief Constable of West Yorkshire* (2001) (the case where the prisoner was not known to be a suicide risk). In Orange it was a *novus actus interveniens* and in *Reeves* it was not.

The principle that is applied is whether the resulting damage was a foreseeable consequence of the original act. The cases often appear to be decided on the basis of producing a just result as each set of facts are very different.

In **Smith v Littlewoods (1987)** the defendants purchased a cinema with a view to demolishing it and replacing it with a supermarket. They closed the cinema and employed contractors to make site investigations and do some preliminary work on foundations, but then left the cinema empty and unattended but locked. Vandals started a fire in the cinema which seriously damaged two adjoining properties, one of which had to be demolished. The court decided that a reasonable person in the position of the defendants would not foresee that if he took no action to keep the premises fully secured rather than just locked in the short time before the premises were demolished they would be set on fire and that would result in damage to neighbouring properties. The defendants had not known of vandalism in the area or of previous attempts to start fires, so the events which occurred were not reasonably foreseeable by the defendants and therefore they owed no duty to the plaintiffs, the vandalism being a *novus actus interveniens*.

A more recent example is **Corr v IBC Vehicles (2006)**. In 1996 Mr Corr was employed by the defendant as a maintenance engineer when he suffered severe head injuries in an accident at work caused by malfunctioning machinery. Following lengthy reconstructive surgery, he began to suffer post-traumatic stress disorder causing him to lapse deeper and deeper into depression. This was in contrast to his mental health before the accident, which had no known depression. In February 2002 he was admitted to hospital after taking a drug overdose; by March he was diagnosed as being at significant risk of suicide; in May he was further diagnosed as suffering from severe anxiety and depression and three days later he committed suicide. The court decided that the question was not whether the particular outcome was foreseeable but whether the kind of harm was foreseeable (this is an example of 'take

Key cases

Smith v Littlewoods (1987): vandals breaking into an unoccupied, but secured, building and setting fire to it was a new act intervening when vandals were not common in the area.

Corr v IBC Vehicles (2006): depression following a serious accident and subsequent suicide is seen as a result of the original accident and not as a novus actus interveniens.

your victim as you find him', discussed later) and, if it was, whether the eventual harm was, on grounds of policy or fact, too remote. Suicide does not necessarily break the chain of causation, and, as the evidence clearly established that there was no other cause than the depression that drove Mr Corr to suicide, there was no break in the chain of causation, and the defendant had been negligent.

Key terms

Remoteness of damage: the defendant is liable for damage only if it is the foreseeable consequence of the breach of duty.

Remoteness of damage – the test of reasonable foreseeability

Where there is factual causation, the claimant may still fail to win his case, as the damage suffered may be too remote. The breach of duty may have significant results, but the defendant will not be liable for everything that can be traced back to the original act. Clearly there are some far-fetched results that are not foreseeable and therefore are not recoverable. For example, consider the negligent driving of someone who bumped into the back of my car. There are almost infinite consequences: the car suffers very minor damage (a broken tail light); I might miss the train; I might not get the job, the interview for which I was travelling to when the accident occurred; the reason I did not get the job was that I was late for the interview; I might then be unemployed for many months; I might have to sell my car to cover living expenses as I have little income (being unemployed); I might then buy an old cheap car that has not got modern safety features; I might crash that car and be injured, become depressed and commit suicide – all because of a minor traffic accident. The law has to draw the line and say that some events are too remote to be considered to have been caused by the negligent act.

The test is that the defendant is liable for damage only if it is the foreseeable consequence of the breach of duty.

The case that this principle stems from is **Overseas Tankship (UK) Ltd v Morts Dock and Engineering Co. Ltd (1961)** usually known by the name of the ship involved: **The Wagon Mound**. In that case, the defendant spilt a quantity of oil whilst refuelling another ship. The oil spread over the water to the claimant's wharf, which was some distance away. The claimant was carrying out repair work to a ship. This involved welding. Molten metal (part of the welding) from the claimant's wharf fell on floating cotton waste which smouldered and then ignited the oil on the water. The claimant's wharf was severely damaged by fire. The defendants did not know and could not reasonably have been expected to know that the oil could be set alight when spread on water. They had made enquiries about the possibility of fire as soon as the oil was noticed and suspended welding whilst the situation was checked. They were told that it was safe to continue and took precautions to stop flammable waste falling into the water. Despite this, the fire started. The court decided that the damage by the oil was foreseeable but the damage by the fire was too remote and was not foreseeable.

Key cases

The Wagon Mound No. 1 (1961): damage by the spilt oil was foreseeable; damage by fire was not foreseeable and was therefore too remote.

Bradford v Robinson Rentals (1967): as long as the type of damage is foreseeable, it does not matter that the form it takes is unusual. In this case, frostbite was an extreme form of injury from the cold.

Remoteness of damage – the kind of damage must be reasonably foreseeable

The principle here is that as long as the type of damage is foreseeable, it does not matter that the form it takes is unusual. A classic example of this is **Bradford v Robinson Rentals (1967)**. The claimant was required by his employer to take an old van from Exeter to Bedford and collect a new one. The weather was very cold and there was advice not to travel unless it was necessary. The vans had no heater (an optional extra in those days!), and the windscreen kept freezing over, so Bradford had to drive with the window open. The old van's radiator leaked and had to be topped up regularly. Bradford suffered frostbite. It was foreseeable that he would suffer some cold-related injury, so the defendants were liable for his frostbite even though that is very unusual. The reason for the claimant succeeding is that frostbite is merely an extreme form of injury from being cold.

Similarly, in **Hughes v Lord Advocate (1963)** the claimant succeeded. Two boys took a paraffin warning lamp down an unattended open manhole. On emerging from the hole, one of the boys knocked the lamp back into the hole, causing an explosion, and suffered severe burns. Since the risk of injury by burning was foreseeable, this extremely unlikely form of burning meant that there was factual and legal causation and the boys' claim succeeded. This is another example of case law helping develop safety standards, as this method of warning is no longer used.

However, in **Doughty v Turner Asbestos (1964)**, the claimant was burned when an asbestos lid was knocked into a vat of molten metal; the lid slid into the liquid with no noticeable effect for a few minutes. However, a chemical reaction then caused a violent eruption that scientific knowledge at the time did not expect to happen. It could be foreseen that knocking things into the liquid might cause a splash of molten metal, but this was an event of a wholly different type from that which could have been foreseen. Therefore, the claim failed as the result was not reasonably foreseeable.

Remoteness of damage – take your victim as you find him

This is similar to the concept in criminal law. A person's liability in negligence is not extinguished or lessened because the claimant had a pre-existing condition that made the injuries worse. We have already seen that in *Corr v IBC Vehicles* (2006). An earlier case that illustrates the principle is **Smith v Leech Brain (1962)**.

In that case, the claimant suffered a very minor splash by molten metal that caused a burn on his face. The burn triggered his pre-existing cancerous condition, and the claimant developed cancer. Some minor injury at least was foreseeable. His extreme reaction was a result of his condition and as the principle is that you take a person as you find them, the claim succeeded.

Remoteness of damage – a recent example of how a judge should apply the principle of reasonable foreseeability

In **Gabriel v Kirklees Metropolitan Council (2004)**, the claimant was six years old. He was walking past a building site owned by the local council in Huddersfield, when he was hit in the eye by mud thrown by children playing on the site. The site was not fenced at that time. It was decided that the correct way to decide whether the council were liable in negligence involved the following tests:

- whether it was reasonably foreseeable that children would go onto the construction site
- whether, whilst on the construction site, it was reasonably foreseeable that the children would play there
- whether it was reasonably foreseeable that, in playing on the site, they would throw whatever came to hand
- whether in playing with material on site it was reasonably foreseeable that they might cause injury to those passing by on the pavement.

Key cases

Hughes v Lord Advocate (1963): another example of a claimant succeeding for injury caused by an extreme type of harm (an explosion and fire being an extreme type of a burn).

Doughty v Turner Asbestos (1964): the claimant was injured when a lid was knocked into a vat of molten metal and the vat erupted. Scientific knowledge could not predict the eruption, so the event was unforeseeable. The claim failed.

Smith v Leech Brain (1962): the claimant had a pre-cancerous condition. He was splashed on the lip by some molten metal. The burn turned into a cancer as a result of his condition. His claim succeeded.

Gabriel v Kirklees Metropolitan Council (2004): this example of how a judge should apply the reasonable foreseeability test involved children playing on an unfenced building site.

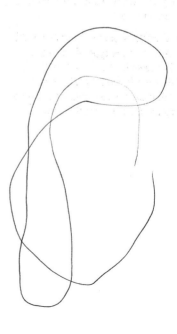

The original judge had not followed these tests and so a retrial was ordered. Thus it can be seen that the idea of reasonable foreseeability is still the backbone of the modern test.

Conclusion

Damage caused by the defendant's breach has two principles that equate to factual and legal causation. Factual causation is the 'but for' test. Legal causation is the idea of remoteness of damage, which has a test of reasonable foreseeability.

Activities

1. The text in Topic 4, pp222–3 on *novus actus interveniens* states, 'These arguments were used in *MPC* v *Reeves* (2001) and *Orange* v *Chief Constable of West Yorkshire* (2001). In *Orange* it was a *novus actus interveniens* and in *Reeves* it was not.' Consider why that was the case.

2. Consider the scenario below, taken from a past examination paper, and consider whether there is duty, breach and damage in that case.

   Seema was an amateur mountain-bike racer who was preparing for the Student Championships in Austria. She bought some expensive new wheels from Spokes Ltd that had been made to their new design. Whilst she was training abroad, a design fault in her new front wheel caused the tyre to burst and she crashed, breaking several bones. She can no longer ride competitively.

AQA Examiner's tip

Always use negligence cases for causation in this part of the specification rather than those learned for criminal law.

You should now be able to:

- understand the concept of damage
- describe and apply the test for damage
- decide, giving reasons, whether a person has been negligent or not in a given situation.

The courts: procedure and damages for negligence cases

In this topic you will learn how to:

- draw a diagram of the civil court structure showing appeal routes

- state the jurisdiction of each court

- distinguish between different classifications of cases in negligence

- describe the burden of proof and standard of proof in a civil case

- apply the above to a given situation.

Key terms

Court of first instance: the court which first tries a case.

Small claims track: a straightforward claim for damages of less than £5,000 or, if personal injuries, less than £1,000.

Fast track: a claim of between £5,000 and £15,000, with limited oral evidence, that is likely to be completed in less than one day.

Multi-track: a claim that does not fall within small claims or fast track; it is likely to be complex and/or high value.

1 Outline of civil courts and appeal system for a negligence case

The civil courts

The majority of negligence cases are heard in the 218 County Courts. The manner in which each case is dealt with depends on the nature and size of the claim. The largest claims are heard in the High Court, Queen's Bench Division. Usually, appeals go to the Court of Appeal (Civil Division). For most legal cases in England and Wales, the House of Lords is the final point of appeal.

The basic structure is set out in the diagram below:

Initial hearing	First appeal	Final appeal
County Court	Court of Appeal (Civil Division)	House of Lords
High Court		

Fig. 12.1 *Court structure for a negligence case*

The courts of first instance

A **court of first instance** is the court where a case is first tried. The court of first instance will be either the County Court or the High Court. The County Court and the High Court have different jurisdictions so will hear different cases. The courts hope most cases will be settled out of court or by alternative dispute resolution, with only a minority actually being tried. In the 2005–2006 County Court Annual Report, Lord Justice Thomas, Senior Presiding Judge for England and Wales, wrote:

> **The division between the County Court and the High Court**
>
> The figures in this report reflect solely the work of the county court. However in reality outside the Royal Courts of Justice, there is very little distinction in practice between the way in which High Court and county court work is done. We have in practice a 'single civil court', but unfortunately the figures in this report do not reflect this. A distinction is still perpetuated between the High Court and the county court, even for reports such as this.

He went on to quote from the report for South Wales: 'there is no rational reason why a case is issued one or the other. Practitioners frequently issue and pursue personal injury cases worth a seven-figure sum in the county court.'

The reality is that the cases are heard dependent on the track into which they fit. The courts are responsible for case management, with all cases allocated to one of three 'tracks' (**small claims, fast track, multi-track**) according to their value and complexity. If a negligence case is to be heard in the High Court, it is heard in the Queen's Bench Division.

Appeals

Either side of a civil case can appeal against the judge's decision based on supposed errors of law or fact. If the appeal is from the decision of a District Judge, the first appeal will normally be to a Circuit Judge. Such appeals are usually on procedural matters or smaller claims in the County Court. Thereafter, appeals go to the Court of Appeal with a further appeal to the House of Lords. The leapfrog procedure, which bypasses the Court of Appeal, is only used where the case is of great legal importance, and will take the appeal directly to the House of Lords. The appeals do not take the form of a complete rehearing, but a consideration of the documentary evidence in the case and the judge's notes of witness evidence. Appeal judges rarely change the trial judge's finding of fact, as the trial judge will have seen the way the witnesses behaved whilst on oath in the witness box.

The appeal court has three options: it may affirm the original judge's decision, which means that the result is totally unchanged; it may vary the decision, usually by changing the amount of damages awarded; or it may reverse the judgment in the first hearing by finding in favour of the other party (usually the party making the appeal).

Claims involving small sums and appeals to the House of Lords require leave of the court, either from the court where the appeal is coming from or the court it is going to. Leave to appeal just means permission to appeal.

The burden and standard of proof

As we have seen in Chapter 11, in civil law cases the burden of proof is on the claimant to prove his claim on a balance of probabilities. There is a lower standard than that in criminal cases. This means that the party bearing the burden of proof, the claimant, must demonstrate that it is 'more likely than not' that the defendant has been negligent. The burden of proof is the obligation on a party to establish the facts in issue in a case to the required degree of certainty (the standard of proof) in order to prove their case. In a civil trial the burden is upon the claimant to prove the liability of the defendant. The standard of proof is on a balance of probabilities.

There are, however, two exceptions to the rule that the claimant must prove his case. The first is that, if the defendant has been convicted of a crime based on the same event, the claimant's case in negligence will be satisfied as a court has already been satisfied that the defendant caused the wrongful act beyond reasonable doubt which is a higher standard. This comes from the Civil Evidence Act 1968. Thus a claim for personal injuries arising from a car crash where the driver has been convicted of dangerous driving will not require proof of the driver's negligence. The driver would then have to prove he was not negligent – an impossible task one would assume, given the conviction! The only issue before the court is the amount of damages to be awarded.

A more important exception is **res ipsa loquitur.** *Res ipsa loquitur* literally means 'the thing speaks for itself'. The idea is that the accident causing the damage complained of would not have happened unless someone had been negligent and the thing that caused the accident was wholly under the control of the defendant. This can be seen as a three-part test:

■ Key terms

Res ipsa loquitur: this literally means 'the thing speaks for itself'. It is a rule whereby negligence can be inferred from the fact that the accident happened.

1   The thing that caused the harm was wholly under the control of the defendant.

2   The accident that caused the damage complained of would not have happened unless someone had been negligent.

3   There is no other explanation of the injury caused to the claimant.

The classic example is **Scott v London and St Katherine's Docks (1865)**.

The claimant was walking along the dock when he was hit on the head by a sack of sugar which had fallen from an overhead crane. The claimant did not have to prove that the dock company were negligent as the required elements for *res ipsa loquitur* were present:

▪ The thing that caused the harm was under the control of the defendant; the sack of sugar fell from a crane controlled by the dock company.

▪ Sacks of sugar do not fall from cranes unless someone has been negligent.

▪ There is no other explanation of the injury caused to the claimant.

Since these conditions were fulfilled, the claimant does not have to prove his case. The burden of proof shifts to the defendant who has the opportunity to prove that he was not in fact negligent, in other words, that there was some other explanation for the accident.

The modern explanation of *res ipsa loquitur* was summarised in *Bergin v David Wickes Television Ltd* (1994) as simply a convenient label for a group of situations in which an unexplained accident is, as a matter of common sense, the basis for an inference of negligence. *Res ipsa loquitur* has been successfully used in cases involving a car knocking over someone on the pavement and an aircraft crashing on take off. A particularly clear case is **Mahon v Osborne (1938)**.

In that case the claimant went into hospital for an abdominal operation, and after the operation he remained in pain and died when he should have made a recovery. In fact, a swab had been left inside his body. *Res ipsa loquitur* applied, as a swab is not left inside a body unless someone has been negligent, the swab is wholly under the control of the hospital and there is no other explanation for the incident. It should be noted that this rule is particularly helpful to the claimant who was not even conscious when the event happened.

There are occasions where the defendant can show that he was not negligent and so the claimant does not succeed despite using *res ipsa loquitur*. In **Pearson v North Western Gas Board (1968)** the gas main outside the claimant's house exploded, killing her husband and destroying the house. The gas board were able to show they had not been negligent as they had taken all reasonable precautions to deal with gas leaks. There had been particularly cold weather and this had caused the ground to freeze and then buckle during the thaw. This had caused the pipe to fracture. Having regular inspections and 24-hour emergency call-out teams was a sufficient standard of care so the board had not been negligent.

Conclusion

Most negligence cases are heard in the County Court. The actual timing and venue will depend on the track to which the case is allocated. Whichever track the case is allocated to, the claimant has to prove his case on a balance of probabilities. This may be easier where he can establish *res ipsa loquitur* which shifts the burden of proof to the defendant.

▪ **Key cases**

Scott v London and St Katherine's Docks (1865): the claimant was walking along the dock when he was hit on the head by a sack of sugar. *Res ipsa loquitur* applied to the situation.

Mahon v Osborne (1938): this is an example of *res ipsa loquitur*, where a surgeon left a swab inside the patient's body during an operation.

Pearson v North Western Gas Board (1968): in this case the defendant was able to show there was no negligence despite a claim using *res ipsa loquitur*.

AQA **Examiner's tip**

Remember that the fact that *res ipsa loquitur* applies does not automatically mean the defendant has been negligent. You should still apply the Caparo three-part test and then explain that *res ipsa loquitur* applies (showing why it applies).

Read this extract below from the case of *Carroll* v *Fearon* (1998) and decide whether you think *res ipsa loquitur* could be applied.

At about 11.00am on 9 July 1988 Alan Carroll was driving his Austin Princess along the M4 westbound to Wales. He and his wife, Susan, together with their children, Catherine and Stephen, were off on their summer holiday. Mr Carroll was driving a well-maintained car carefully and safely in excellent driving conditions.

Among the traffic travelling in the opposite direction in the eastbound carriageway there was a Ford Cortina owned by Alexander Bent. He was travelling as a passenger in his own car which was being driven by his friend Lundy Fearon. Mr Bent's partner, Astrid Barclay, was sitting in the back seat, immediately above the rear nearside tyre. It is relevant to the issues in this appeal to note that she was a heavily built lady. In addition his son Delroy, aged fifteen years, and her daughter Lolita, aged twelve years, were also travelling on the back seat.

This Ford Cortina was first registered in 1982. It had travelled nearly 82,000 miles. Mr Bent acquired it in May 1987. By 9th July 1988 he had driven it about 4,000 miles. He ensured that his car passed its MOT tests as and when required. It had not passed its MOT test on 22 May 1988 until the two front tyres had been replaced, as it happened by second-hand tyres, not retreads. In addition to the condemned two front tyres the tests revealed problems with the trailing arm bushes and the nearside wishbone bushes, the offside front shock absorber was broken and there was slight play on the front hubs. These faults were corrected. Nevertheless the evidence demonstrated 'a car which was plainly not being maintained unless and until parts were condemned.' For present purposes the most significant feature of this car was the condition of the rear nearside tyre. The tread, although within legal limits, was worn down to some 25 per cent–30 per cent of its life. There were signs on its outer wall of crazing and cracking consistent with degradation, but this tyre passed its MOT test in May 1988 and had covered a further 1,052 miles before the accident.

The car had travelled some 33 miles from Bristol and the party was going to a wedding in Swindon. They were not far from their destination when disaster, in the form of a sudden and virtually complete tread strip of the rear nearside tyre occurred. Mr Fearon lost control of the car. As it happened there was a twenty seven metre gap in the crash barrier between the two carriageways on the motorway, and near to the Swindon exit marker post 146, the Cortina spun through 360 degrees and careered through the emergency crossing gap in the central reservation into the westbound carriageway and crashed virtually head on with Mr Carroll's car. There was nothing he could do to avoid a collision at a converging speed of 140 miles per hour or more.

Everyone in Mr Carroll's car was injured. His wife's injuries were of the utmost gravity and she has suffered and will suffer from the most severe long term consequences. The state of the group in Mr Bent's car if anything was worse. Lolita Barclay was killed. The driver and other passengers were injured.

Arising out of this collision three actions were brought. Mr Carroll and his wife and their children brought proceedings against Mr Fearon, Mr Bent and Dunlop Ltd, the manufacturers of the tyre. Astrid Barclay and Delroy Bent brought proceedings against Mr Bent, Mr Fearon and Dunlop Ltd and Mr Fearon himself took proceedings against Dunlop Ltd who joined Mr Bent as a third party. In the meantime, to protect their own position, the insurers for Mr Fearon and Mr Bent involved themselves in the litigation.

www.bailii.org

You should now be able to:

- understand the framework for the civil process
- apply the civil process in a given situation.

💡 2 An outline of the procedure of a negligence case up to trial

Starting a negligence case

Once it has been established that court proceedings need to be started (most claims are settled by negotiation without the need to go to court), the formal procedure must be started. Claims where there are personal injuries and the claimant does not expect to be awarded more than £50,000 must be started in the county court. All other claims may be started in either the County Court or the High Court. Most claims are started in the County Court and we will now concentrate on claims starting in the County Court. The first step is to complete a claim form. Information about this is available online to download or can be collected from one of over 200 court offices in the country.

This form is simple to complete, requiring names and addresses for claimant and defendant, brief details of the claim (such as 'Damages for personal injuries caused when the defendant knocked down the claimant on a pedestrian crossing'), and the value of the claim. The purpose of this is to establish the fee payable and to help establish the choice of court and track. If the claim is expected to be worth less than £5,000 in total with some element being personal injuries and there being some losses that have a fixed value (for example, replacement of ruined clothes, loss of earnings for a week whilst recovering), the claimant would put 'My claim includes a claim for personal injuries and the amount I expect to recover as damages for pain, suffering and loss of amenity is not more than £1,000.'

The particulars of claim on side two of the form will give details of the claim being made. This may be sent separately within 14 days, but most simple claims have it included. The particulars of claim give a simple statement of the facts on which the claimant bases the claim. This might include the time, date and place of the accident, and an outline of why the claimant considers the defendant has been negligent.

The fee payable depends on the size of the claim. In the example in the preceding paragraphs, the fee would be £150 (as at June 2007).

There is also the possibility of having the fee lessened or pay no fee at all in certain cases for claimants with low income and few assets.

In this topic you will learn how to:

- describe the procedure from the start of court action to trial
- apply the above to a given situation.

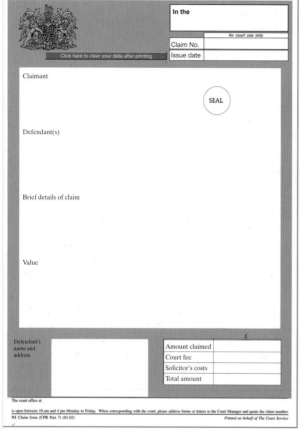

Fig. 12.2 *County Court claim form*

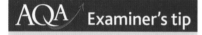
This claim form is then served on the defendant, usually by post. In addition to the claim form, the defendant is sent forms for use in dealing with the claim made. At this stage the claimant chooses which County Court he wishes to start the claim in, although the claim may get transferred to a different court later in the process.

The defendant receives the claim form

Assuming the defendant's details and address are correct, the claim form and defendant response pack will not be returned to the court by the Post Office and will be deemed to have been received by the defendant. The defendant's response pack includes an admission form so that the defendant can admit the claim, a defence form to be completed if the claim is not admitted, and an acknowledgement of service form, which confirms receipt of the claim. This means that the defendant can do nothing and not reply to the claim at all, admit all or part of the claim, or dispute all or part of the claim. The defendant must do this within 14 days of receiving the claim. If the defendant does not file a defence within 14 days or any extension the court may give, the claimant can file for a default judgment and effectively win the case. The court will then only be concerned with awarding the appropriate amount of damages and costs. This can be done either by allocating the case to the small claims track or to a disposal hearing in those cases where the claim is more complicated.

In many cases the defendant may attempt to settle the claim by making an offer of payment. The great majority of claims are settled without the need for a court hearing. However, the defendant may dispute the claim in which case the defendant may well just complete an acknowledgement of service, as this will give additional time to complete the defence: from 14 to 28 days. In these circumstances the claimant may well discover that the defendant has instructed a solicitor. The defendant will then complete his defence and send it to the court.

The claimant receives the defence

When the claimant receives the defence, the court will also send an allocation questionnaire to all parties to the case. The purpose of this is to establish the location, track and timing of a trial. There is usually (apart from money claims of less than £1,500) an allocation fee payable of £100. This is another incentive to negotiate a settlement of the case as the expense of taking the case forward mounts up. There will also be a trial fee which for a multi-track case is £500. The court will keep records of when the allocation questionnaires are due to be returned and if they have in fact been returned. This is part of case monitoring. **Case monitoring** is where judges receive support from court staff in carrying out their case management role. The court uses a computerised diary monitoring system to record court orders and requests, the deadline for the return of documents such as the allocation questionnaire and whether the deadline has been met.

Once the allocation questionnaires have been completed, a procedural judge (normally a District Judge) will allocate the case to the appropriate track. If a party to a case does not comply with a court order or time limit, that party may be struck out of the action. The effect of this is that the party would be unable to take further part in the case and would lose any right to claim or defend the court action. This is part of judicial **case management**, which aims to keep the process moving along at a reasonable speed and help reduce the average time taken to deal with a claim. One reason for case management being introduced is to avoid the former problem of even quite trivial cases dragging on for years. The judge now has the power to summon the parties to court to find out what is going on in the event of inactivity.

> **Key terms**
>
> **Case monitoring:** the system by which the court monitors progress of a case to help achieve a quick conclusion.
>
> **Case management:** the active role taken by a judge in the life of a case to help reach a speedy and just resolution of the issue.

The three tracks

The court rules and practice direction explain the limits of the tracks. There are three tracks: small claims, fast track and multi-track. Which court and judge will hear the case depends on the scope and size of the case.

Small claims	Fast track	Multi track
▪ Up to £5,000	▪ £5,000–£15,000	▪ Over £15,000
▪ Personal injury up to £1,000	▪ Trial up to one day	▪ Complex cases
▪ Simple cases	▪ Moderately complex cases	

Fig. 12.3 *The three tracks*

The small-claims track is the normal track for claims of a monetary value of less than £5,000. It is also the track for cases in which the financial value of any claim for damages for personal injuries is less than £1,000. Personal injuries include claims for pain, suffering and loss of amenity. There will be no complex issues involved. This type of case is usually heard by a District Judge.

An example of a small-claims track case is where a horse jumped over a broken fence in the field in which he was grazing and ran into a parked car. The car suffered £2,000 of damage. The car owner claims the owner of the horse had been negligent by not keeping the horse securely fenced in. This would be small-claims track, as the value of the claim is less than £5,000

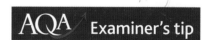

AQA Examiner's tip

Make sure you know the differences between the tracks, as you are quite likely to have to identify the relevant track for the exam scenario.

and there are no complex issues of law or evidence and no personal injury claim (if there were one it would have to be less than £1,000).

The fast track is the normal track for a claim that does not fall within the small-claims track and has a claim value of less than £15,000. In addition, the trial must not be expected to last more than one day and there is limited oral expert evidence. There may be some complex issues involved. This type of case is also usually heard by a District Judge.

A fast-track case might be a claim following a road accident where a pedestrian had been knocked down whilst crossing the road. The injuries were straightforward – some bruising and a broken leg – and the medical evidence is all done by written reports. The issues for trial might be amount of special and general damages, and whether the accident was caused by the injured person. This would be supported by witness statements rather than oral evidence. The documentary evidence is likely to be receipts for expenses and damage items such as spectacles and loss of earnings. This is likely to be a fast-track case as the issues are straightforward, the value is likely to be between £5,000 and £15,000 and the expert evidence is written.

Any claim that is not within the scope of small-claims track or fast track is a multi-track case. A multi-track case would be more complex and also (usually) involving a larger sum of money. Multi-track cases are almost always heard by a Circuit Judge.

This might be following a road accident where the claimant is a 17-year-old person who has suffered multiple injuries and is unlikely to make a full recovery from the injuries. Questions the court might have to decide might include: whether the injuries were caused by the hirer of the car involved in the accident not maintaining the car properly (was the seat belt defective) rather than the driver; whether the injured person knew the driver had taken drugs and would therefore be unfit to drive; and what the effect of the accident is on the claimant's future earnings. This would be fast track because of the value of the claim, the complex nature of the evidence – some expert evidence might not be written – and the likely length of a trial.

Between allocation and trial

After the case has been allocated the court sets a date for the trial. This date will be at least 21 days later and the actual date will depend on what other directions need to be made. These other directions include providing copies of documents to the other party or parties to the case and copies of experts' statements. The stage is now set for the trial.

Conclusion

The procedure from issue of a claim up to trial is designed to bring the claim to a conclusion fairly and speedily. The aim of the civil justice system is to reduce the average time a claim takes to be resolved and thus reduce the criticism that the law is very slow. The aim is to reduce the time from over a year at the end of the 1990s to about 30 weeks on average for a fast-track case. The procedure is relatively straightforward and is backed up with much help and guidance through leaflets, the court offices and online.

AQA Examiner's tip

You may be asked to describe the process in the exam. This may well require reference to the scenario.

Court proceedings

All court cases vary slightly but this is a general overview

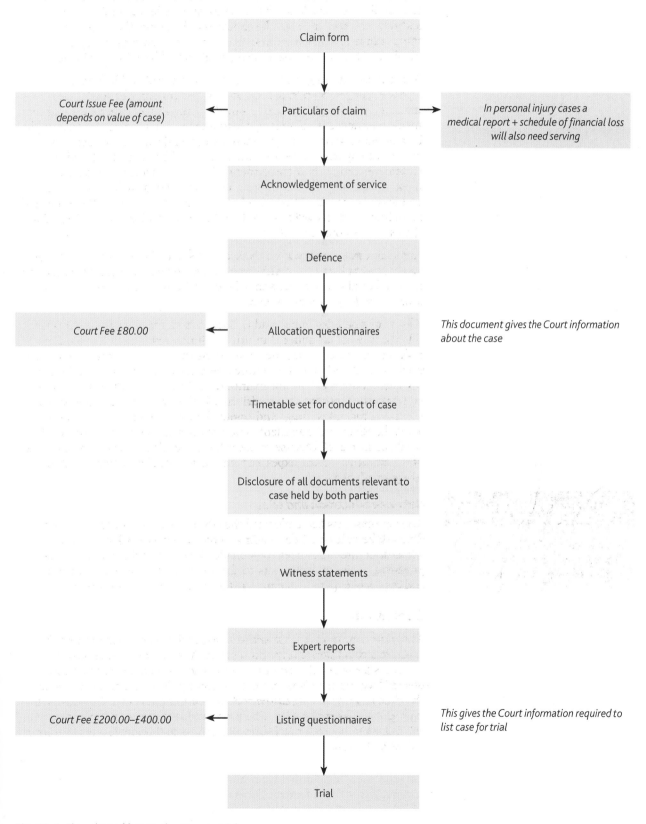

Fig. 12.4 *Flow chart of fast-track case up to trial*

Activities

1 Set out below is a slightly expanded past examination question. Using the information in the scenario, complete a claim form as far as possible and explain to the claimant how the case would proceed up to any trial.

Having bought herself a cheap windsurfer, Ursula Langer decided to teach herself to windsurf on a lake near her home. After several hours' practice, she began to tire and decided to have one last attempt at crossing the lake. She failed to notice Vera Unsworth, who was fishing from a boat on the lake. Unfortunately, Ursula crashed into the boat, which capsized, and Vera lost her expensive fishing equipment in the lake. The equipment cost £2,000 and the boat needed £400 worth of repairs. Vera suffered some injuries including being cut by a fish hook which imbedded itself in her cheek. She now has a permanent scar and has been advised that she is likely to be awarded £1,500 in damages for her injuries.

2 A friend of yours has just been involved in a minor car accident which appears to have been the fault of the other driver. Write a short guide to him as to how he might take legal action to recover the cost of repairs to his car.

3 If the case in Activity 1 above were heard today, explain which track would be used.

You should now be able to:

- understand the procedure from up to trial in a case of negligence
- apply the procedure in a given situation.

In this topic you will learn how to:

- state the meaning of the term 'compensatory damages'
- distinguish between general and special damages
- distinguish between pecuniary and non-pecuniary damages
- distinguish between lump sum and structured settlements
- apply the above to a given situation.

💡 **3** Damages

The purpose of damages

Damages in a negligence case are compensatory. The purpose is to put the claimant in the position he would have been in had the negligent event not occurred. This means that the claimant will have his actual losses repaid and will also get a further sum of money to compensate for future losses. It is relatively easy to compensate the victim of a car crash for a damaged car, but much harder to compensate for personal injuries and the effect of the accident on life in the future. The purpose of damages is to do this as fairly as possible. The law is not concerned with punishing the defendant, only with compensating the victim of the defendant's negligent event.

As the claimant is not expected to profit from the award of damages (they are compensatory although it can be argued that some claimants do gain financially), the claimant must follow the general principle of mitigation of loss. This means minimising the loss by taking reasonable action to do so. An example of this might be replacing a car that has been written off as soon as possible rather than hiring a car for many weeks as part of the claim against the defendant. This is often reflected in guidelines given by employers to their staff following losses that might result in an insurance claim as insurance companies operate the principle of mitigation of loss.

An example of this is set out below:

> In the event of flood damage on premises for which you are responsible, you should take sensible actions to mitigate the loss such as:

1. Clean or mop up the affected areas as best you can.

2. If necessary, turn off gas, mains water stop cock, but do not switch off electricity supply unless clearly advised by a qualified electrician that circuits are unsafe. If you have to switch off the electricity, arrange for emergency supply of refrigeration and freezing appliances if there are perishable goods.

3. Identify items lost and prepare lists for costing. You should expect these lists to be closely scrutinised. No action should be taken to replace or repair damaged items until agreed by the Insurance Section.

4. Try to protect key/critical equipment from further deterioration; retrieve important documents/items. No items should be disposed of until Loss Adjusters have given approval.

5. If possible, copy any computer files to portable storage to prevent further damage.

6. Ensure safety checks are made of power and light circuits before turning the power back on and arrange for safety checks of all equipment. Retain all evidence of safety testing, dated and signed. Keep a list of the time and date and actions taken by you.

In practice, the claimant does not have to be too careful about ensuring mitigation of loss; the key criterion is that the action taken by the claimant is reasonable. Thus, in a case involving an unwanted pregnancy resulting from a negligently performed sterilisation, it was not reasonable to expect the claimant to undergo an abortion.

Since damages are compensatory, the claimant can only receive damages once even if there are several people who contributed to the accident as in the case of *Barker* v *Corus* (2006), an asbestos case, studied in Chapter 11. Similarly, the amount actually received can be reduced where the court considers the claimant is partly responsible for his losses. This is known as contributory negligence and the reduction is in proportion to the claimant's own proportion of blame. Contributory negligence is not part of the AQA AS specification so will not be explored further.

Where the event has resulted in personal injuries, it is usual to get a preliminary idea of the amount (technically called 'quantum') of damages likely to be awarded. This helps negotiation and often avoids the need to start proceedings. Whilst this is time consuming, it can often result in an earlier settlement of the claim or at least an interim payment to help the claimant with immediate expenses. Typically this would occur like this:

When calculating the quantum of damages, there are two types of damages: special and general. The distinction between them arises as the idea is that special damages reflect losses that are particular to the claimant in the event that has occurred, and general damages are those that are presumed to follow from the negligence. A distinction is also made between pecuniary and non-pecuniary losses. **Pecuniary losses** are those involving financial loss such as loss of earnings (any claim for lost wages is for net wages – again, so the claimant does not make a profit) or damage to goods. **Non-pecuniary losses** are compensation for those things that do not have a ready financial value such as pain and suffering after an injury.

AQA Examiner's tip

Remember damages are compensatory. As you will have few precise details of losses in the exam, only be precise where the scenario gives the information (for example, the car worth £1,500 was destroyed ...) and explain how other losses (for example, he cannot work again as a hairdresser ...) would be calculated in theory.

Key terms

Pecuniary losses: the claimant's losses that are financial losses, such as loss of earnings.

Non-pecuniary losses: the claimant's non-financial losses, such as pain and suffering.

■ Key terms

Special damages: this is compensation for the financial costs incurred up to the date of the trial, such as repair of a damaged car.

Special damages

Special damages are compensation for the financial losses incurred up to the date of the trial. These losses must follow from the negligent event and the losses that are particular to the claimant rather than those that can be foreseen to affect any claimant. The things included can all be given an exact figure.

This includes medical expenses such as prescription fees and hospital charges. For example, the driver of a vehicle involved in a road accident may be charged for any emergency medical treatment provided by a doctor and any hospital involved. The 2007 tariff is set out in Table 12.1 below. The driver's insurance company will usually pay this charge without affecting their no-claims bonus.

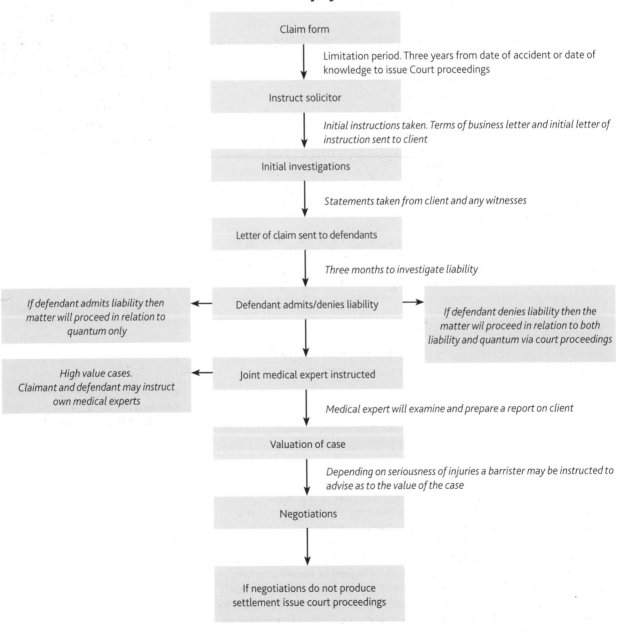

Personal injury case

Claim form

↓ Limitation period. Three years from date of accident or date of knowledge to issue Court proceedings

Instruct solicitor

↓ Initial instructions taken. Terms of business letter and initial letter of instruction sent to client

Initial investigations

↓ Statements taken from client and any witnesses

Letter of claim sent to defendants

↓ Three months to investigate liability

If defendant admits liability then matter will proceed in relation to quantum only ← Defendant admits/denies liability → *If defendant denies liability then the matter wil proceed in relation to both liability and quantum via court proceedings*

High value cases. Claimant and defendant may instruct own medical experts ← Joint medical expert instructed

↓ Medical expert will examine and prepare a report on client

Valuation of case

↓ Depending on seriousness of injuries a barrister may be instructed to advise as to the value of the case

Negotiations

↓

If negotiations do not produce settlement issue court proceedings

Fig. 12.5 *Flow chart of activities before issue of proceedings in a personal injuries claim*

Table 12.1 *Tariff for NHS motor vehicle accident medical charges: an example of special damage*

Accident/ incident Date (on or after)	Out-patient (not admitted)	In-patient (admitted) Per day/part day	Maximum amount (Cap)	Maximum days in-patient
Pre-02.07.1997	£295	£435	£3,000	6.9
02.07.1997	£354	£435	£10,000	23.0
01.01.2003	£440	£541	£30,000	55.5
01.04.2003	£452	£556	£33,000	59.4
01.04.2004	£473	£582	£34,800	59.8
01.04.2005	£483	£593	£35,500	59.9
01.04.2006	£505	£620	£37,100	59.8
01.04.2007	£505	£620	£37,100	59.8

www.dwp.gov.uk

In addition there will be an ambulance charge, currently £159 per journey.

Also included is loss of earnings up to the date of trial. This is straightforward where the claimant is salaried and has sick pay arrangements that do not cover fully pay for the actual duration of time off work. Deductions are made for benefits actually received; if that were not the case, the claimant would make a profit as a result of the negligence. Where the claimant has had irregular overtime or works for varying hours each week, the calculation is less clear and would have to take into account the history of earnings and the likelihood of missed overtime and work. The usual calculation is to take the average earnings from the previous 26 weeks' earnings. Loss of future earnings is part of general damages and will be considered there.

Damage to goods such as repairing a car or replacing ruined clothes are easy to calculate as special damages, as there is evidence of the cost from receipts. A car that is written off would attract damages of the market value before the accident. This principle is applied to all such losses that occur as a result of the negligent act.

General damages: the principle

General damages are designed to cover anything that does not have a readily quantifiable figure that can be put on it. There are three major areas that need to be explored:

- ▪ pain, suffering and loss of amenity
- ▪ future medical care and personal assistance
- ▪ loss of future earnings.

Pain, suffering and loss of amenity

Pain, suffering and loss of amenity are very difficult to calculate. The damages awarded under this heading include the physical and mental suffering of the claimant, the injury itself and the reduction in the quality of life of the claimant, known as loss of amenity. The Judicial Studies Board lays down guidelines with respect to the size of the award for different injuries. This enables there to be a general consistency in approach, but provides some range to allow for different levels of severity. Having the range of figures available also helps claimants and defendants to settle the claim without the need to go to court. There are many calculators available on the internet.

AQA Examiner's tip

Make sure you can distinguish between special and general damages: many candidates get them confused.

▪ Key terms

General damages: these cover any loss that does not have a quantifiable sum attached to it.

Some examples of typical awards of damages for physical injuries are:

■ infertility in a woman who already has children: £10,000–£20,000
■ moderate knee injury: £8,000–£14,750
■ total loss of sight in one eye: £27,000–£30,000.

The court takes into account many factors when making the overall calculation, as every claimant's injuries are different, even if there are similar outward appearances such as loss of a limb. The factors taken into account include:

■ time spent in hospital and the number and type of treatments
■ whether the injury is temporary or permanent, and if temporary, the length of time it will affect (or has affected) the claimant
■ loss of expectation of life: how much shorter the claimant's life is likely to be
■ loss of quality of life: how much worse his life is as a result of the accident
■ inability to have children and loss of marriage prospects
■ cosmetic injury and the effect that has on the claimant
■ psychological and emotional damage, such as depression
■ whether there is continuing pain and discomfort and a greater likelihood of serious disease later: in this case there can be an award of provisional damages, with further damages later with the onset of the disease.

Loss of amenity is the effect of the injury on everyday life activities and on the claimant's enjoyment of life. This, therefore, covers things such as not being able to do the housework and being unable to perform personal care activities such as shaving, as well as being unable to follow a sport or recreation, such as cycling or driving.

Future medical care and personal assistance

Personal assistance follows on from the concept of loss of amenity and the inability to look after oneself fully. The problem for the courts is when a member of the victim's family become the carer and has to lose earnings as a result. In many such cases there is a claim for compensation in respect of the care provided to the claimant by family members or friends free of charge. This type of care happens naturally and so the claimant can be awarded damages for the care and domestic assistance. This money is then used for the carer.

Even with relatively minor cases, an award of damages can be made for care, particularly where the victim is a child. This can be seen from the case of *Giambrone* v *JMC Holidays* (2002), where 652 people staying at a hotel in Majorca on a holiday provided by the defendant tour operator suffered food poisoning, giving rise to the claims. Many of the victims of the food poisoning were children, and their parents were successful in claiming damages for the extra care they had to carry out.

Loss of future earnings

Loss of future earnings is very difficult to predict and depends on the evidence that can be provided and the arguments that can be made to reduce the claim. There are many firms offering forensic and investigative services who become expert witnesses in such cases. The problem is illustrated by a simple example. Suppose an 18-year-old A Level student was involved in a car crash which resulted in his paralysis and reduced mental abilities. Earnings at the time of the accident are likely to be very low, perhaps from a part-time job at a supermarket checkout. The argument made on his behalf would be that he had a very bright future, would get good results (this could be based on AS results, progress tests and Units taken at A2), and has received an offer of a place at university, and so on. After the accident, he has limited capacity for employment, and is currently still a part-time supermarket checkout operator. How would you calculate his future lost earnings?

The answer is not clear and relies on likely outcomes based on the evidence and not fanciful outcomes: after all not every teenage guitar player will become an enduring rock musician earning millions! This is one reason why most claims are settled by negotiation without going to court.

In many cases a formula is used to help make the calculation.

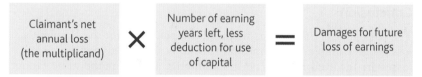

Fig. 12.6 *Loss of earnings calculator*

This formula works on the principle that the income from the capital sum of damages invested will produce the lost earnings and that the capital will also be used up during the expected working life used in the calculation. This is on the basis that the damages awarded are compensation and that the claimant will not make a profit. However, these calculations are not accurate and some claimants benefit and others do not. Clearly, a claimant who then dies before the end of the anticipated period would benefit, but similarly, a claimant who far exceeded his life expectancy would lose out. The courts do take into account loss of life expectancy and, under the Damages Act 1996, the expected rate of return from investments.

Suppose a 30-year-old man suffered an accident following which he could no longer work. His income was £20,000 and it was decided that he was unlikely to work for the next 30 years. In theory, he would be awarded £20,000 × 30 = £600,000. In practice, because of the effect of using capital and other factors, the multiplier is rarely more than 18, so the maximum award is likely to be £20,000 × 18 = £360,000.

Method of payment of damages

Traditionally all damages were paid as a lump sum. This meant that the claimant received his payment and did with it as he wished. A lump sum could then be invested and the interest earned would give the defendant much more than he would have earned had he not been injured. This is the reason for the reduction in the multiplier for calculating an award for loss of future earnings and all other payments that are to represent money for the claimant's future needs.

Lump sum payments are, however, entirely appropriate for loss of or damage to goods, but periodical payments, such as monthly payments, are more appropriate where the claimant is going to need a regular income during his life. Damages for personal injuries paid in this way are known as a structured settlement and are dealt with in the Damages Act 1996.

A structured settlement is usually paid by the defendant's insurer. Once a lump sum figure has been agreed, some of that sum takes the form of periodic payments 'structured' to meet the claimant's individual needs. The lump sum, or part of it, is effectively spent on getting these payments made through an annuity provided by a financial institution. Thus the payments can be guaranteed to increase with inflation and to continue for the rest of the claimant's life. There can be tax advantages to this as damages are tax-free. The main advantages of a structured settlement are greater certainty and security compared to the traditional lump sum and the fact that the claimant does not have to manage his lump sum or pay someone to do that. The structured settlement is therefore an excellent solution where the victim is a child or is so severely injured that management of a large sum of money would be an unnecessary burden. Structured settlements, based on an annuity, also solve the problem of a claimant living for a very short or a very long time and being over- or under-compensated by the lump sum system.

Conclusion

The basic idea of damages as financial compensation for the claimant's loss is quite simple. It becomes more complicated where non-financial losses are involved, such as personal injuries, and where the value cannot easily be calculated such as care costs and future earnings. The payment of damages is usually by way of a lump sum, but large claims are increasingly paid though a structured settlement.

 Activity

Using the scenarios in Topics 1 and 2 of this chapter (pp230–1 and 236):

1 Identify the types of damages that can be claimed in each case.

2 Explain how the court would go about calculating the amount of damages in each case.

You should now be able to:

■ understand the principles behind an award of damages

■ apply the principles in examination questions.

AQA Examination-style questions

✔

Chapters 11 and 12

1   William was sorting out some files that were on a high shelf next to the open window in his office. As William could not reach the files easily, he used a pole to push them to the end of the shelf, and then tried to catch them as they fell.

William tried to catch a heavy file, but he failed to do so and it fell out of the window onto Lyn, who was sitting outside in her car. The car's sunroof shattered, and Lyn suffered a broken collarbone.

Because of the injury, Lyn was unable to work as a freelance hairdresser for three months, and had to cancel a planned skiing holiday.

(a) Negligence requires proof of **duty**, **breach** and **damage**.

  (i)   Explain, using examples, the meaning of the term **duty of care**.   *(7 marks)*
  (ii) Explain, using examples, the meaning of the term **breach of duty**.   *(7 marks)*
  (iii) Explain, using examples, the meaning of the term **damage**.   *(7 marks)*

AQA specimen question

(b) (i)   Using the explanations given in your answers to (a) (i), discuss whether
          William owes Lyn a duty of care.   *(7 marks)*

   (ii) Using the explanations given in your answers to (a) (ii), and assuming that
          William was found to owe Lyn a duty of care, discuss whether William has
          broken that duty of care.   *(7 marks)*

(c) Assuming William was found to be liable in negligence,

  (i)   Identify which court would hear Lyn's claim and outline the procedure that
        would be followed **before** any trial.   *(5 marks)*

  (ii) Outline how the court would calculate an award of damages, if appropriate,
        to Lyn in the situation given.   *(5 marks)*

▮ Answering questions on tort in AQA Law 2

There are a number of different aspects of learning that need to take place to answer the questions fully, namely being able to:

- understand and explain the basic principles
- illustrate the principles by reference to decided cases
- select appropriate material for a given question
- apply the legal principles to a given scenario and come to an appropriate conclusion.

The aspects listed above will enable all types of question to be tackled. These questions come in a number of formats:

- theory-only questions on the lines of 'Explain what is meant by the term duty of care'
- theory and application questions, such as 'Explain what is meant by the term duty of care and explain whether X owes Y a duty of care in the scenario above'
- application-only questions, such as 'Using the terms you have explained in question n, explain whether X owes Y a duty of care in the scenario above.'

In the first type of question, theory only, no reference needs to be made to the scenario. All you are expected to do is explain the term asked for, using relevant decided cases as examples. In the second type, theory and application, it is easiest to explain the theory as if it had been a separate question, and then apply the rules you have described to the facts set out in the scenario. The final type does not require repetition of the theory, merely a clear application of the principles to the facts. It should be noted that application is different from assertion. An assertion would be where the answer gives no reason for the statement made. Application goes on to give reasons for the assertion. In negligence questions this will be by use of the relevant cases to show how the legal principle applies to the facts.

Answering a theory only question

A theory-only question taken from the sample paper is:

> (a) Negligence requires proof of duty, breach and damage.
>
> Explain, using examples, the meaning of the term duty of care.
> *(7 marks)*

The potential content in the mark scheme is:

> (A) Explanation of the meaning of the term duty of care, e.g. neighbour test and/or Caparo three part test;
>
> (B) Relevant examples/cases.

What a good answer would include is:

- a statement that a duty of care is a legal concept that sets the situation in which a person can be liable to another in negligence;

- a statement that the test started off from the case of *Donoghue* v *Stevenson* (1932) and the neighbour test;
- a statement that the modern test as to the existence of a duty of care is set out in the case of *Caparo* v *Dickman* (1990);
- an explanation of each of the three parts of the *Caparo* test, with each part having a different case used as an example to illustrate each part.

Answering a theory and application question

A question from a past paper that has both theory and application in it is set out below:

> Pearl is a singer with a rock band. At the end of the band's concert at a big festival, Pearl decided to leap into the crowd, who were prepared to catch her. Unfortunately, Pearl misjudged the distance and landed on top of Tom, a security guard. Tom was facing the crowd at the time, as required by his job, and had no idea of what was about to happen. Tom suffered a severe neck injury.
>
> a) (i) Explain what is meant by a duty of care in negligence, and (ii) discuss whether Pearl owes a duty of care to Tom.
> *(10 marks)*
>
> b) Assuming Pearl owes a duty of care to Tom,
> (i) explain the legal principles relating to breach of duty.
> (ii) Discuss whether or not she is in breach of that duty.
> *(15 marks)*

When you answer part (a) of this question, you should set out the theory of duty of care as set out above in the theory only question. You should then apply the theory clearly to the facts set out in the problem. This requires each part of the Caparo test to be applied in turn.

A good answer to the application part would be:

- The first part of the test is whether it was reasonably foreseeable that a person in the claimant's position would be injured. It clearly is foreseeable that if a person jumps off a stage in the direction of a person who is not looking at them, then if there is a collision with that person, that person will suffer some injuries.

- The second part of the test is whether there was sufficient proximity between the parties. There is sufficient proximity, as they are both present in time and space. Relationship is not relevant here.

- The third part of the test is that it must be fair, just and reasonable to impose liability on the defendant. It is, as there is no policy reason why performers should be protected if they undertake activities such as jumping off the stage.

- Therefore, all three parts of the test have been satisfied and Pearl owes a duty of care to Tom.

Activities

1 Write up, using continuous prose, your answer to part (a) of this question.

2 Plan and then write up the answer to part (b) of this question.

Answering an application only question

When answering such a question, you only need to write the application part, as you will be able to refer back to the theory part that you almost certainly will have answered. The answer will be much as set out in the previous section. Now try the following activity based on a past paper question.

Activities

1   Look at the question set out below, and answer each of the parts in turn using the techniques set out above.

Pamela suffers from severe learning difficulties and is unable to read. She enrolled at West Coast College on a course for special needs students. On her first day, she became separated from the rest of her group and wandered into a laboratory which a member of staff had forgotten to lock. She saw a bottle containing a clear liquid, which she believed to be water, and drank some. In fact it was acid, as the label indicated, and Pamela was severely injured.

a Explain what is meant by the term duty of care.   *(7 marks)*

b Explain how the law decides whether there has been a breach of duty.
   (8 marks)

c Using your explanation above, discuss whether West Coast College owes a duty of care to Pamela.   *(5 marks)*

d Assuming West Coast College owes a duty of care to Pamela, and using the explanation you have made in part (2) above, discuss whether or not the college is in breach of that duty.   *(5 marks)*

2   Now attempt Section B of the sample paper in 45 minutes. Your teacher should be able to provide you with a copy of this.

You should now be able to:

■   apply the principles in AS examination questions involving negligence.

2C The law of contract

Introduction

Chapters in this section:

Unit 2A, together with Unit 2B or Unit 2C, constitutes Unit 2 of the AS specification. Unit 2A is about criminal law and is compulsory. Unit 2B is about tort and Unit 2C is about the law of contract. Candidates must answer the questions on either Unit 2B or C, but not both, as well as the questions on Unit 2A. Candidates choose to study either Unit 2B or Unit 2C in addition to Section A.

All three sections are examined together on one examination paper, which constitutes 50 per cent of the overall marks for the AS qualification and 25 per cent of the overall marks for the A2 qualification. The Unit 2 examination is of 1.5 hours' duration. Candidates must answer all the questions from Section A and all the questions from Section B or Section C. There is no choice of question in any of the sections.

The questions on each section are worth 45 marks each. Each question is divided into several parts, each part normally being worth 5, 7 or 10 marks. Candidates must answer all parts of the question. All parts of the law of contract question relate to the law of contract and there can be no overlap between sections of the AQA Law AS specification.

The law of contract section is covered by Chapters 13 and 14 of this book. Some parts of the question test the candidates, knowledge and understanding and some test application of the law to the scenario that introduces the question. Question 3 is the law of contract question and is broken into three main parts with sub-parts. Part (a) usually tests knowledge and understanding only, whilst parts (b) and (c) test a mixture of knowledge, understanding and application of the law to the problem scenario.

Questions require answers to be written in continuous prose rather than note form. There are no short answer or multiple choice questions. Attainment of high grades is dependent on correct identification of the issues raised by the question and sound explanation of each of the points using authority. Authority is usually reference to a decided case or reference to an Act of Parliament, but may be examples taken from other sources. Further exam tips are provided throughout each topic and at the end of the chapter.

Unit 2C comprises two chapters:

13 Formation of contract: concerned with the underlying principles of formation of contract; these elements can be seen as the agreement, having legal intention and the bargain made.

14 Breach of contract and the courts: procedures and damages: the courts – procedure and damages for breach of contract: investigates what happens when a contract is broken. This is followed by considering the procedure that takes place in the civil courts from the start of legal proceedings, up to but not including the trial. Alternative methods of resolving the claim are also considered. The chapter finishes with the way in which a court awards damages to a successful claimant.

13 Formation of contract

In this topic you will learn how to:

- distinguish between criminal and civil law
- distinguish between evidence and procedure
- define a contract.

Key terms

Civil law: the law concerned with the relationship between individuals.

1 Introduction to formation of contract

Contract is an area of **civil law**. A contract is an agreement that the law will recognise. The purpose of the law of contract is to decide whether there is a valid contract or not and to provide remedies when one person has been affected by another's failure to perform their part of the contract. The most usual remedy is damages (financial compensation) and that is the remedy being considered in this section. A valid contract starts with the acceptance of an offer made to the person accepting the offer.

Civil law

As discussed above, civil law is concerned with settling disputes between individuals: 'individuals' including businesses and, sometimes, Government. The key difference between civil and criminal law is that civil law is primarily designed to settle disputes, not deal with punishing wrongdoing. There are many areas of civil law including the law of contract. Contract is one area of civil law that is to be studied in the AQA AS Law specification.

A civil case is started by the person who has suffered loss (the claimant) as the result of a wrong which only directly affects him. A typical contract case is a claim for losses for failure to deliver goods, such as bread to a restaurant. The claim requires proof that the defendant had a contract with the claimant and that he did not carry out his part of the bargain. The claimant's usual remedy is financial compensation, known as damages. Thus a successful claim for failure to deliver bread under a contract with a restaurant will result in damages paid to the restaurant claimant to cover the financial losses which might be the cost of getting bread elsewhere or, in some circumstances, possible loss of trade. There are other remedies available in the law of contract but these are not relevant to the material in these chapters on the law of contract.

The civil process

The civil process is the procedure by which a claim makes its way through the court system so that the court can decide whether the claim will succeed and, if so, what amount of damages should be awarded. The court processes and eventual award of damages can be a long and complicated business for both the claimant and the defendant, but the process is designed to keep delay to the minimum through case management. Once a person is advised that they are likely to have a good claim in contract, the major consideration is to obtain sufficient evidence of the losses suffered. This is straightforward for non-delivery of a car; it is the difference between the contract price and the market value of the vehicle at the time of breach of contract. Any incidental costs would have to be proved, but, again these are straightforward. Contracts involving services are much more difficult to calculate, as is loss of future business.

Eventually, the claimant may have to go to court for some or all of the issues to be tried and, if the claim is successful, to calculate their award of damages. The length and complexity of the process depends on the nature of the claim, whether the evidence is clear, whether and if so how the defendant makes his defence and whether or not he tries to establish that he had not broken the contract. There are rules of procedure that set out the court in which the case will be heard and the framework for deciding the case. For many reasons, such as the effect of publicity on the businesses involved, the stress of a court case and the question of cost, many contract cases are settled out of court. A successful claimant needs to prove that a contract existed and that it has been breached.

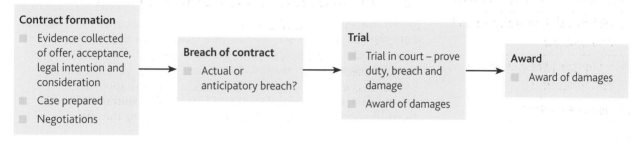

Fig. 13.1 *The civil process for a contract case*

There are rules of **civil evidence** that set out how the facts must be proved and the degree of certainty that is required. In civil law cases the burden of proof is on the claimant to prove his claim on a balance of probabilities. There is a lower standard than that in criminal cases. This means that the party bearing the burden of proof, the claimant, must demonstrate that it is 'more likely than not' that the defendant has been negligent. The burden of proof is the obligation on a party to establish the facts in issue in a case to the required degree of certainty (the standard of proof) in order to prove their case. In a civil trial the burden is upon the claimant to prove the liability of the defendant. The standard of proof is on a **balance of probabilities**. Effectively this is just a matter of convincing the judge that the claimant is right in his version of events. This is most likely to be relevant in assessing future losses or establishing that a particular loss was the result of the breach of contract. Juries are not used in contract cases, which take place in the County Court or High Court Queen's Bench Division or the Commercial Court.

Contract

A **contract** is an agreement between two parties that the law will enforce. The central part of the concept is that of agreement made voluntarily between the parties to the contract. If a person is to succeed in a contract claim, there must be proof that there is a valid contract and that the contract has been broken. There are four elements that need to be considered in the formation of a valid contract:

- that there has been a valid offer made by one party to the contract
- that there has been a valid acceptance of the offer: together offer and acceptance constitute an agreement
- that there is an intention to create legal relations: in other words, an intention to have a legally enforceable contract
- that there has been consideration: the idea that each party has given up something or contributed something to the agreement. If one party contributes and the other does not then there is a gift rather than a contract.

You also have to study breach of contract: if a contract has been performed satisfactorily, there will be no dispute and so no possibility of the courts being involved. Two aspects of breach of contract are studied: actual breach, where the defendant fails to perform his side of the

Key terms

Civil evidence: the rules that set out how the facts of a civil case must be proved.

Balance of probabilities: the standard of proof in a civil case. It means that the claimant must prove his case is more likely than not to be as presented by him.

Contract: a contract is an agreement between two parties that the law will enforce.

contract; and anticipatory breach, where the defendant states he will not perform his part of the contract when the time comes for him to do so.

So far as the material in this book is concerned, most of the authorities for the law come from decided cases. This means that the law is judge-made and has developed over the years, and that the rules of precedent studied in Unit 1 are used. It is important that the latest interpretations of the law are used, although the historical background can sometimes be useful in explaining why today's law is as it is. There are a few areas that have their basis in an Act of Parliament and those areas require the Act of Parliament to be interpreted in accordance with the rules of statutory interpretation that are studied in Unit 1.

How case law is used in answers to typical questions in AQA Unit 2

The question paper for Unit 2 is divided into three sections. As we have seen, the first section, Section A, is compulsory and is the introduction to criminal law. The choice of area of study of civil law is between tort and contract. Section C is the law of contract and, like the other sections, has no choice within it. All questions must be answered. The contract question starts with a short scenario that sets the scene and is the basis of your discussions for some of the questions. A scenario, taken from the sample paper, is:

Umar wanted to buy a large quantity of mobile phones for his shop. He phoned Mobiles plc, who agreed to supply him with a quantity of phones for £60,000. Mobiles plc immediately realised they had been using an old price list and tried to contact Umar on the phone, but failed to do so. Mobiles plc therefore posted a new one to Umar, which he received on the next day. Mobiles plc refused to supply the phones at £60,000 and Umar refused to pay the revised price of £70,000. Mobiles plc's new prices were the same as other suppliers of the phones.

The questions are of two general types:

Theory questions

These require an explanation of terms used but they require no reference to the facts given in the scenario. A typical question (taken from the sample paper) is:

(1) (a) A valid contract requires an offer to be accepted.

(i) Explain, using examples, the meaning of the term 'offer'.

(8 marks)

(ii) Explain, using examples, the meaning of the term 'acceptance'. *(7 marks)*

Application questions

These usually require you to select the appropriate law or principles of damages and apply the law to the facts given in the scenario. You should assume that the facts as stated in the scenario can be proved. A typical question (taken from the sample paper) is:

(b) Using the explanations given in your answer to 3(a), discuss whether Umar has made a valid contract with Mobiles plc.

(10 marks)

Link

These methods of tackling a question will be dealt with in more detail in the Unit 2C Review at the end of Chapter 14.

Conclusion

Contracts have a number of elements that have to be considered to decide whether the contract is valid. Once this has been proved, the court can assess whether the contract has been broken and then damages can be assessed. The requirements for these elements need to be explored in more detail.

Activities

1. Think about what you have bought today. Each time you bought something you made a contract. How did this contract take place? What do you think the situation might be if you put a coin in a vending machine or clicked to buy something from a website?

2. Think about contracts that have gone wrong, such as buying a DVD that would not play. Was there a breach of contract and what was done about it?

You should now be able to:

- understand the role of the civil law

- understand the concept of contract

- understand how to use authority in answering questions on contract.

2 The offer

What is an offer?

An **offer** is the starting point for a contract. It is essential to understand what amounts to an offer and when the offer comes into existence. The difficulty is in deciding whether a statement amounts to an offer or whether it is just a statement preparatory to an offer (known as an **invitation to treat**).

Much of the law is found in precedents set in the 19th century, so the facts may seem rather dated. Most of the law is based on sensible ideas and is easy to apply providing a logical approach is taken.

The next essential aspect of an understanding of the operation of the law is to look for communication of the offer. Unless a person knows about an offer, it cannot be acted upon. Once it is known to exist, the essential point is to establish the duration of an offer, as it can only be accepted whilst the offer remains open. Once the offer has ended it cannot be accepted and so it cannot be the basis of a contract. A new offer would then have to be made to start the process of forming a contract. The contract is formed when an offer has been accepted.

In this topic you will learn how to:

- define an offer

- distinguish between an offer and an invitation to treat

- describe the rules that decide when an offer comes to an end

- apply the rules to a given scenario.

Key terms

Offer: an offer is a statement of the terms upon which the person making the offer is willing to enter a contract: it can be verbal or written.

Invitation to treat: an invitation to treat is merely an indication of a willingness to start negotiations and is not an offer.

Fig. 13.2 *Duration of an offer*

An offer or an invitation to treat?

An invitation to treat is merely an indication of a willingness to enter negotiations. This is not always understood by the general public and leads to the situation that arose in 1999 set out in the article below.

> Catalogue retailer Argos was swamped with online orders after a software blunder led to TV sets being mistakenly priced at £3 each.
>
> The 21-inch television sets should have been priced at £299.99 – but were offered at the bargain price after that figure was rounded up to £300 and the decimal point put in.
>
> By the time Argos discovered the mistake there were reported to have been hundreds of orders worth more than £1m.
>
> Argos decided to refuse to honour any of the orders placed for the £3 TV sets – a decision which could lead to a legal test case on Internet trading.
>
> Argos said it had consulted its lawyers and the Advertising Standards Authority before making its decision.
>
> They added that because it had not confirmed that any of the orders had been accepted, no contract existed to sell the TV sets at the £3 price.
>
> © bbc.co.uk/news

Argos was correct that the advertisement on the internet was just an invitation to treat: they were following precedents that have been set for many years. Therefore, there was no offer that could be accepted and therefore no contract between the customers and Argos. This is a logical decision for many reasons, for example, there are usually a finite number of articles for sale. If you advertised your car for sale, you only have one to sell and you would be in legal difficulties if the advert were an offer as each person telephoning to accept would create a contract, only one of which you could fulfil.

Generally, an advertisement in a newspaper or magazine is not an offer but an invitation to treat. There are a number of examples of cases setting the precedent that such advertisements are an invitation to treat and not an offer. One such case is **Partridge v Crittenden (1968)**.

This was a criminal case where an advertiser in a newspaper advertised 'bramble finch cocks and hens 25/– [£1.25]' It was an offence under the Protection of Birds Act 1954 to offer wild birds for sale. The defendant was found not guilty as he did not offer the birds for sale; there was merely an invitation to treat.

The same conclusion is reached with respect to goods in a shop window. This can be seen in **Fisher v Bell (1961)**, another case involving a criminal prosecution.

A shopkeeper in Bristol was prosecuted because he had a flick knife in his shop window with a price label on it. It was a criminal offence under the Restriction of Offensive Weapons Act 1959 to offer such knives for sale. The shopkeeper was found not guilty as he was not offering the knife for sale; it was merely an invitation to treat. Again it is a logical decision as the shopkeeper may wish to choose the person to whom to sell the goods.

The idea of choosing to whom a shopkeeper wants to sell goods is even more important in a self-service shop such as a supermarket. There are many restrictions on those who can buy certain types of goods, ranging from alcohol, potential weapons such as chef's knives, solvents and other dangerous items to lottery tickets. In all such cases the seller has the right to refuse to sell the item to the potential customer, as the advertisement of the lottery or the display of bottles and cans of alcoholic drink are not an offer, just an invitation to treat. The customer makes the offer and the shopkeeper decides whether to sell or not, often after establishing that the buyer is of the appropriate age.

Thus in the case of **Pharmaceutical Society of Great Britain v Boots Cash Chemists (Southern) Ltd (1952)**, the well-known high street shop was prosecuted for offering medicines for sale when a pharmacist was not present. This was an offence under the Pharmacy and Poisons Act 1933. Boots were found not guilty as the court decided that the offer was made by the customer at the point of sale, that is, the counter or checkout till. This is reflected in the practice of assistants in pharmacies of seeking approval from the pharmacist before selling some medicines.

Where a shop assistant does not make the necessary checks on age, there can be a prosecution as can be seen in the case of **Harrow London Borough Council v Shah (1999)**. The Shahs owned a shop and explained to all of their employees about the regulations with respect to the selling of lottery tickets. There were signs around the shop telling customers of the minimum age for buying a lottery ticket. One of the employees sold a lottery ticket to a boy under 16, so the shop owners were prosecuted.

There are some variations on this principle, again being based on common sense. Where a person buys something from a vending machine, it can be said that the offer is made by the owner of the machine and that it is the buyer from the machine who accepts the offer and makes the contract come into existence. This has some implications for cigarette machines and access to them by those who are under the legal age for buying cigarettes.

However it would be impractical to use any other principles on vending machines and this can be seen in the case of **Thornton v Shoe Lane Parking (1971)**. In that case the court decided that a contract was formed by a customer entering a car park via an automatic barrier. On the facts, Mr Thornton put money in a machine to open the barrier and was given a ticket. It would be the same if he had just taken a ticket and paid on exit as is more common today. Lord Denning said, 'The offer is made when the proprietor of the machine holds it out as being ready to receive the money. The acceptance takes place when the customer puts the money in the slot.'

An even more unusual example of an offer can be seen in the case of **Chapelton v Barry UDC (1940)**, where the act of taking a deckchair from a pile of deckchairs and sitting on it formed the contract where a local council hired deckchairs to people on its beach. The offer was the placing of the pile of deckchairs that could be taken. There would not be an offer if the deckchairs were secured and an attendant had to release one

Key cases

Pharmaceutical Society of Great Britain v Boots Cash Chemists (Southern) Ltd (1952): goods in a self-service store are an invitation to treat, not an offer.

Harrow London Borough Council v Shah (1999): a shop assistant sold a lottery ticket to an underage person. This is an offence which could have been avoided by the shop assistant refusing to accept the customer's offer to buy a ticket.

Thornton v Shoe Lane Parking (1971): a ticket from an automatic machine in a car park involved the car park owner making the offer and the customer accepting the offer by putting money in the machine.

Chapelton v Barry UDC (1940): a pile of deckchairs for hire on a beach was an offer that the customer could accept.

to a customer who requested it. In the last case it would be the customer making the offer and the attendant accepting it on behalf of the council.

It should also be noted that just giving information does not amount to an offer – it is just a common courtesy to reply to an enquiry should the person owning the item decide to sell. There are a number of cases that involve this point and each one is decided on the key aspects of the evidence. The most famous of these cases is **Harvey v Facey (1893)**. In this case the claimants were interested in buying some land and sent a message, 'Will you sell us Bumper Hall Pen [the land]? Send lowest cash price.' The defendants replied, 'Lowest cash price for Bumper Hall Pen £900.' The claimants then replied, 'We agree to buy Bumper Hall Pen for £900.' The court decided that there was not a contract as the original message was merely a request for information.

Finally, a statement is not an offer if it is not definite in the terms it uses. In **Gibson v Manchester City Council (1979)** the council's response when asked by Mr Gibson whether he could buy his council house was, 'the corporation may be prepared to sell the house to you at the purchase price of £2,725 less 20 per cent.' The court decided that this reply was not an offer, but an invitation to treat. The word 'may' indicated a lack of certainty so there was not an offer. The uncertainty showed that negotiations were still continuing, not that there was a readiness to make a contract.

■ Key cases

Harvey v Facey (1893): a response to a request for information is just an invitation to treat not an offer.

Gibson v Manchester City Council (1979): a statement is not an offer if the words you use show uncertainty as to whether there is a willingness to make a contract.

AQA Examiner's tip

There are many cases on the law on offer and acceptance. Make sure you know the legal point each case is authority for. The examiner will expect accurate authorities.

Table 13.1 *Cases distinguishing offers and invitations to treat*

Invitation to treat	Offer	Case
Advertisement in newspaper		Partridge v Crittenden
Goods in a shop window		Fisher v Bell
Goods on a supermarket shelf		Pharmaceutical Society of Great Britain v Boots Cash Chemists (Southern) Ltd
	Dealing with an automatic machine	Thornton v Shoe Lane Parking
	Taking chair and awaiting attendant to collect money	Chapelton v Barry UDC
Response to a request for information		Harvey v Facey
Uncertain words ('the corporation may …')		Gibson v Manchester City Council

Communication of the offer

An offer cannot be accepted unless the person who is seeking to accept it knows of its existence. Thus if I offer a reward for finding my missing cat, a person who returns the cat but is unaware of the offer cannot claim the reward. Similar problems arise with answerphones which do not play back messages and fax machines which fail to print out. This has implications for potential purchasers who are responding to an invitation to treat who do not realise that they have failed to communicate with the person making the invitation. However, they will have no legal claim as there is no contract.

There is one famous case that illustrates a number of points, but is unusual because the offer was made to anyone and everyone rather than to a specific person. This is the case of **Carlill v Carbolic Smoke Ball Co. (1892)**.

■ Key cases

Carlill v Carbolic Smoke Ball Co. (1892): an advertisement could contain an offer if it was clearly meant to be taken seriously.

In that case Mrs Carlill claimed the reward offered by the Carbolic Smoke Ball Co. for anyone who used its smoke ball (a sort of medicinal vaporiser or inhaler) but caught influenza. The company refused to pay stating that the so-called offer of £100 was a mere marketing 'puff' and not intended to have any basis for a contract. Mrs Carlill argued that it was an offer which she had accepted by buying and using the smoke ball in accordance with the instructions. Mrs Carlill won the case, as the court decided that it was an offer that could be taken seriously and was not just an advertising gimmick. The court also said that an offer could be made to the whole world, and that anyone hearing the offer could accept: it just had to have been communicated to the individual claiming to have accepted it. Mrs Carlill apparently lived to the age of 96. She died in 1942 of … influenza.

Ending an offer

As an offer can only be accepted whilst it is open, it is important to know when an offer comes to an end. It can come to an end in the following ways:

- lapse of time
- revocation
- rejection
- counter-offer
- death.

Lapse of time

Some offers are made for a fixed period of time, such as seven days or one month. At the end of that period, the offer lapses and comes to an end. Most offers do not have any fixed time limit and so will come to an end after a reasonable time. What is reasonable will depend on all the circumstances. It is clear that a short period would be appropriate for something perishable such as a cake and a long period for something large and complex such as a ship. In the case of **Ramsgate Victoria Hotel v Montefiore (1866)**, the defendant offered to buy shares in the Ramsgate Victoria Hotel on 8 June. On 23 November, the company tried to accept the offer but the defendant no longer wanted to buy the shares. The court decided that the five-month gap after the offer was too long and so the offer had lapsed and so could not be accepted.

Revocation

A person who makes an offer can revoke (withdraw) his offer at any time before it has been accepted. For this to happen, the person to whom the offer was made must receive notification of the withdrawal, at which point he can no longer accept the offer. A withdrawal of an offer can even occur during any period when the offer is said to be open, and an example of this is **Routledge v Grant (1828)**. In that case Grant made an offer o buy Routledge's house, the offer to remain open for six weeks. Grant decided not to buy the house three weeks later and told Routledge he was withdrawing his offer. Two weeks later, Routledge tried to accept the offer. The court decided that the offer had been withdrawn, so it could not be accepted.

Revocation can be implied by other actions. Once an offer for an object is accepted, it cannot be accepted again. However, where the offer has been made to more than one person, there are potential difficulties, as there could be two contracts with respect to one object. Suppose I offer my car for sale to Y and Z at a price of £1,000 even though the market price for my car is £1,500. If I agree to sell to Y, I will need to tell Z that the car I offered to sell him was in fact sold or I risk being sued for breach

Fig. 13.3 *The advertisement in Carlill v Carbolic Smoke Ball Co.*

AQA **Examiner's tip**

Remember the important part of the case is the *ratio decidendi* rather than the facts. Some candidates spend a great deal of time describing the facts of cases and forget to mention the legal principle that the case proves.

Key cases

Ramsgate Victoria Hotel v Montefiore (1866): an offer made to buy shares in a company had lapsed when the company responded five months later. The person making the offer was entitled to assume that the company did not want him to invest.

Routledge v Grant (1828): an offer can be revoked at any time even if it is said to be open for a fixed period that has not yet ended.

Key cases

Dickinson v Dodds (1876): where a reliable person informs the person to whom an offer has been that the offer has ended, it is as if the revocation of the offer had been made by the person who had made the offer.

Stevenson v McLean (1880): an enquiry about whether credit was available did not reject the offer which could still be accepted.

of contract. If Z found out I had sold the car from a reliable source, he would also know that the offer had ended. This can be seen from the case of **Dickinson v Dodds (1876)**, where Dodds offered to sell his house to Dickinson. The offer was open until Friday. On Thursday afternoon, Dickinson heard from someone else, whom he knew to be reliable, that Dodds had sold the property to someone else. On the Friday morning, Dickinson delivered a formal acceptance to Dodds but the court decided that the offer made to Dickinson had been revoked on the Thursday when he heard of the sale of the house. There was no longer an offer in existence to accept and so no contract could be formed. Hearing about the sale from a reliable source is the implied revocation of the offer.

The situation where one person wants an offer to remain open for a period of time is quite common as the time period is to be used for getting financial and other plans drawn up. So as to make sure that the offer will remain open, a separate contract has to be made. This is usually a contract to keep the offer open for an agreed fixed period in exchange for an agreed sum of money. This is known as 'buying an option'.

Rejection

Once an offer is rejected, it cannot be accepted and the offer comes to an end. The person to whom the offer is made does not have a second chance to accept the offer. If he attempts to accept the offer, he is in fact making a fresh offer that the person who originally made the offer can accept or reject. The rejection must be a clear rejection and not just a request for more information as in the case of *Harvey v Facey* (1893). In **Stevenson v McLean (1880)** there was an enquiry from a person to whom goods had been offered for sale as to whether he could have two months' credit. There was no reply, so assuming that there would be no credit, he accepted the offer being prepared to pay cash. The court decided that this enquiry about credit was not a rejection of the offer or a counter-offer and the offer remained open and had been accepted.

Counter-offer

A counter-offer both rejects the original offer and creates a new offer that can then be accepted or rejected. This commonly takes place during negotiations. If I were selling my car, the sequence might be like this:

- Advertisement to sell car for £2,000: this is an invitation to treat (*Partridge v Crittenden*)
- X offers to pay £1,800 for the car: an offer
- I refuse, saying I could go to £1,950: rejection of X's offer of £1,800; new offer made by me at £1,950.

This process then continues until agreement is reached or there is no sale. Note I cannot go back to X and 'accept' his offer of £1,800 as that offer ended when I originally rejected the offer and made an offer to sell at £1,950.

A case that illustrates counter-offer is **Hyde v Wrench (1840)**. The facts of that case were:

- 6 June: Wrench offered to sell his farm to Hyde for £1,000. Hyde offered £950
- 9 June: Wrench rejected Hyde's offer
- 21 June: Hyde tried to accept the offer to sell at £1,000. Wrench refused to sell at £1,000, as his original offer had ended with Hyde's counter-offer of £950.

Key cases

Hyde v Wrench (1840): a counter-offer ends the original offer. In this case this occurred in negotiations over the price to be paid for a farm.

Death

In English law contracts can be enforced against a dead person's estate, if necessary by suing the deceased's executors or administrators. However, an offer made by a person who dies before the offer ends cannot be accepted if the person to whom the offer is made knows of his death. If he does not know of the death, then the offer can still be accepted. This is logical as it could otherwise provide hardship for the family of a business owner who died, as contracts in the course of negotiation would have to be restarted. Obviously if the contract involves a service to be provided by the deceased, the contract will not be valid as performance of it would be impossible.

Conclusion

An offer is a statement of the terms on which the person making the offer is willing to be bound, whereas an invitation to treat is only preliminary to that. Once an offer is open it can be accepted by the person to whom it has been made until the point where the offer ends. There are a number of different ways in which an offer can end although it is most usually by lapse or acceptance.

Activities

1. Consider how internet sellers make sure their customers are of an appropriate age so they can decide whether to accept an offer made by an unknown person online.

2. Make a chart of the ways in which an offer can come to an end and give your own example of how each would occur.

You should now be able to:

- understand the nature and duration of an offer

- decide whether there is a valid offer in a given situation.

 ## 3 Acceptance

Acceptance

Once an offer is accepted there is a contract between the person making the offer and the person accepting it, provided the other essentials of formation of consideration and legal intention are present. The **acceptance** has to be positive and unqualified. In other words it is responding to the offer by saying 'Yes' and not 'Yes, but' or 'Yes, if'. The words can be said or written. Acceptance can be by conduct, in other words by doing something, but it cannot usually be by doing nothing. Acceptance must usually be communicated to the person making the offer. This is the most crucial aspect of acceptance as that communication establishes if and when the contract comes into existence.

Methods of communication of acceptance

The usual methods of acceptance do not present any problems. A verbal statement that is clearly heard and understood fulfils the requirements. There are potential difficulties where acceptance is by conduct, by post or by electronic methods.

AQA Examiner's tip

When explaining the theory of the ending of an offer, deal with all the ways it can be ended. When discussing an offer and acceptance problem, select the appropriate method for the facts in the scenario.

AQA Examiner's tip

There are no past papers on this topic. It is likely that the short answer questions on theory rather than application will be separated into questions on distinguishing an offer from an invitation to treat and those on termination of an offer. Answering both comprehensively would take too long. So a question such as 'Explain what is meant by an offer' requires you to deal with distinguishing an offer from an invitation to treat and not termination of an offer.

In this topic, you will learn how to:

- define acceptance

- describe when acceptance takes place

- apply the rules of acceptance to a given situation.

Key terms

Acceptance: the final expression of assent to the terms of an offer.

Conduct

In general, silence or inaction cannot be an acceptance as some positive act is needed. An example of this is seen in the case of **Felthouse v Bindley (1862)**, where the sale of a horse was being negotiated by letter and message.

Eventually Felthouse wrote saying that if he heard nothing further, he would consider the horse sold to him for a stated price. The court decided that this was just another offer that the seller could accept or reject and was not an acceptance, as acceptance required positive conduct. Today this is reflected in legislation such as the Unsolicited Goods and Services Act 1971 and the Consumer Protection (Distance Selling) Regulations 2000. This legislation means that someone who receives goods they did not request does not have to pay for them and may be able to keep them if the sender of the goods does not collect them or provide a mechanism for the cost-free return of the goods. In other words, just retaining the goods does not amount to an acceptance of any offer to sell the goods.

Positive conduct can be acceptance where that is a method of communication set out in the offer. This can be implied in the offer – for example starting to use goods sent on approval. It can also be seen in the case of *Carlill v Carbolic Smoke Ball Co.* (1892), where Mrs Carlill's use of the smoke ball was sufficient to accept the offer of the reward as the company clearly did not expect individual users to contact the company.

Communication of acceptance by post: the postal rules

The postal rules developed during the 19th century as the postal service became reliable and the main means of communication between businesses that were at a distance from each other. There is a risk that a letter may go missing so the court had to decide where the loss should fall. The following rules were set out:

- The postal rules only apply to letters of acceptance, not to offers, revocation of offers or counter-offers.
- The postal rules only apply if the post is the usual method of communication between the parties involved in the contract or is specifically stated as the only or an accepted method of communication of acceptance.
- Acceptance takes place when a correctly stamped and addressed letter is posted (the principle is based on the fact that once a letter is posted it cannot be got back).
- The claimant must be able to prove the letter was posted. This is reflected in a certificate of posting from a post office or a signed statement by the person putting the letter in the letter box.

These rules were first clarified in the case of **Adams v Lindsell (1818)**. The facts are best seen in date order:

- 2 September: Lindsell wrote to Adams offering to sell some wool asking for a reply 'in the course of post'.
- 5 September: Adams received the letter and sent a letter of acceptance.
- 8 September: Lindsell sold the wool to someone else.
- 9 September: Lindsell received Adams' acceptance letter.

The court set out the postal rules and decided that the offer for the sale of the wool had been accepted by Lindsell on 5 September when Lindsell posted his letter of acceptance and there was a contract.

This principle has been confirmed as the law in several cases since then and in the 1980s was used as the basis of a corporate promotion video made by an insurance company. The scenario was posting a letter accepting life insurance on the way to run a marathon and dying on the marathon. The deceased's widow was paid in full by the life insurance company even though he had died before the acceptance of the offer had reached the insurance company.

Electronic and instantaneous forms of communication

The advent of technology meant that the postal rules had to be reconsidered in the light of electronic communication. It is accepted that telephone is instant verbal communication, just as though the parties were in each other's presence. If the call was not heard because of a fault it appears there would be no communication of acceptance. This will be a question of evidence, but does not usually present a problem as most businesses keep written notes of important telephone calls and it is business practice to send confirmation of an order.

The first case on this was **Entores v Miles Far East Corporation (1955)**. In this case the question was when a telex machine communication was made. The court decided that the acceptance by telex took place when it was received. A similar decision was arrived at in *Brinkibon* v *Stahag Stahl* (1983).

Whilst this still seems to be the law for telex and fax communications, all other electronic communications are now covered by The Electronic Commerce (EC Directive) Regulations 2002. Regulation 11 states that an order and the acknowledgement of receipt of it (these can be taken to be the offer and acceptance) are deemed to be received when the person to whom they are addressed are able to access them. This covers all contracts made with internet companies.

How to approach an offer and acceptance problem

All offer and acceptance problems require the same logical approach:

- Identify the sequence of events and list them in chronological order.
- Identify each event as an invitation to treat, offer, counter-offer, revocation of offer, acceptance, etc., as appropriate.
- State the reasons why you identified the event as you did using decided cases to back up your argument.
- Identify when the offer opens and when it ends.
- Identify whether there is an acceptance within that period (if so, there is a contract).
- Come to a conclusion.

Note that problems involving consideration and legal intention have other issues that may need to be identified and dealt with too.

Here is a sample question, together with an outline answer following the template above:

The scenario:

> On 29 April, Richard placed an advertisement in the local paper offering his car for sale for £17,000. Jennifer telephoned Richard on 1 May and offered to buy the car for £15,000. Richard said he was not prepared to accept such a low price, but kept Jennifer's details. On 8 May Richard had still not sold his car and wrote to Jennifer offering to sell it to her for £16,000. Jennifer received the letter on 9 May. On 10 May, Jennifer wrote back stating that she would not pay

AQA Examiner's tip

Look out in the scenario for the characters writing a letter. If there is a letter, at least consider whether the postal rules apply.

Key cases

Entores v Miles Far East Corporation (1955): communication by telex machine takes place when the message is received rather than when sent. It is not the same as using the post.

more than £15,500 for the car. On 11 May Jennifer wrote another letter to Richard saying that she accepted his offer and would pay £16,000 for the car. Richard received both of Jennifer's letters on 12 May but refused to give the car to Jennifer as he had found another buyer who would pay him £16,500.

The approach:

29 April – advertisement (£17,000) – invitation to treat – *Partridge* v *Crittenden*.

1 May – offer (£15,000) – Jennifer to Richard – Richard can accept or reject it; he rejects it instantly on the telephone ending Jennifer's offer.

8 May – offer (£16,000) Richard to Jennifer – offer open when Jennifer receives the letter (9 May).

10 May – rejection of offer in the letter from Jennifer to Richard by counter-offer (*Hyde* v *Wrench*) – rejection takes place when this letter is received by Richard (12 May).

11 May – acceptance of offer in the letter from Jennifer to Richard – acceptance takes place when put in the post box as the postal rules apply (post is usual mode of communication, evidence of posting and correct address, etc. as letter arrived the next day (12 May)) – *Adams* v *Lindsell*. Contract therefore made as acceptance takes place whilst the offer is still open (it is open till 12 May). If Richard does not sell the car to Jennifer he will be in breach of contract.

Conclusion

Acceptance is agreeing to the terms of the offer, and requires understanding of when the acceptance takes place as the consequences are a legally binding contract. One consequence might be the need to insure the item bought from that moment as it then belongs to the buyer.

Activities

1 Here are the facts of *Byrne* v *Van Tienhoven* (1880). Van Tienhoven, a Cardiff businessman, offered goods to Byrne, a New York trader, at a fixed price in a letter of 1 October. Byrne accepted as soon as he received the offer. On 8 October Van Tienhoven had sent a letter revoking the offer. The letter of 1 October arrived on 11 October. On 12 October, Byrne sent a telegram accepting the offer and a confirmatory letter of acceptance on 14 October. The letter of 8 October arrived on 20 October and the letter of 14 October arrived on 30 October.

Apply the methodology for solving offer and acceptance problems to those facts.

2 Considering the facts of *Byrne* v *Van Tienhoven* (1880), discuss how a business would avoid such a dispute today.

You should now be able to:

■ understand when acceptance takes place

■ apply the rules on offer and acceptance to a given situation.

🔦 4 Intention to create legal relations

Background

So far we have looked at the formation of the agreement that forms the contract. Any agreement includes an offer and an acceptance, but the law will not enforce such an agreement if there is no **intention to create legal relations**. Whilst some may try to avoid the use of the courts to settle disputes, it is an essential principle that there is an intention that legal rights and duties will follow from a commercial contract. Everyone expects to have some legal rights should goods bought turn out to be defective or services ordered not provided. The law presumes that there is an intention that such contracts will be legally binding.

However, it is equally clear that we do not expect our domestic arrangements to be legally binding, with the prospect of a court case in the event of failure. I do not expect my children to sue me if I am late in paying their pocket money; if a friend fails to turn up and give me a lift to a venue for an evening out in their car, I, again, will consider that I have no legal right to claim damages. The law will take the same view, and presume that there is no intention to create legal relations in domestic or social arrangements.

There are some situations where these two presumptions will be rebutted; in other words, the law will find a legally binding contract in what appears to be a domestic arrangement or the law will find no intention to create legal relations in a business arrangement.

Commercial agreements

The general principle is that an intention to create legal relations is presumed in commercial agreements. This can be rebutted by the words used in the agreement. There are some older cases where the agreements had specific terms referring to 'honour clauses', but these are rarely seen in today's commercial world and are likely to be interpreted very strictly by the courts. The agreement must be quite clear as to the nature and effect of this restriction. A clear, express statement excluding legal intention can be seen to have been effective in the following examples:

A football pool coupon

In **Jones v Vernons Pools (1938)** and in **Appleson v Littlewoods Pools (1939)** claims were made by claimants who believed they had a winning coupon. In both cases the courts refused to deal with the claim as the coupon clearly stated 'binding in honour only' and the claimants had signed the coupon.

A sale of a house 'subject to contract'

It is quite usual to see a house sale board with the addition 'sold, subject to contract' added to it. This is reflecting the situation that an agreement has been reached between the owner of the house and the prospective purchaser, but that a written contract has not yet been completed. The delay may occur while the purchaser checks financial and other details. A contract to sell land, and therefore a house, has to be evidenced in writing to be legally valid under the Law of Property Act 1925. The idea of 'sold, subject to contract' is common practice in such transactions but can still lead to unpleasant disputes where a house seller ignores the agreement and then sells to another person for more money. The seller is legally, but, arguably, not morally correct in taking this action. It should be noted that some commercial agreements are also made 'subject to contract'

In this topic you will learn how to:

- explain the term 'intention to create legal relations'
- distinguish between the rules for commercial and domestic agreements
- state relevant cases and examples.

Key terms

Intention to create legal relations: the parties to a contract must intend the agreement to be legally binding. This is implied in commercial agreements, but presumed not to exist in social and domestic agreements.

AQA Examiner's tip

In most contracts legal intention is not an issue. The examiner will make it clear in the scenario if this area of law is to be applied. If the scenario does not hint that the area is to be discussed in the application questions, there may still be a theory only question on this topic.

Key cases

Jones v Vernons Pools (1938) and Appleson v Littlewoods Pools (1939): in both cases a claim that money had been won on a football pool coupon could not be enforced in the courts as the football pool coupon clearly stated it was 'binding in honour only'.

where the agreement is a basic intent to proceed with the need to draw up precise terms. In these cases, it is a matter of interpretation as to whether there is a contract or not.

Social and domestic arrangements

Social and domestic arrangements are not usually legally binding. The exceptions to the rule are those where there is a more formal situation. Two matrimonial cases illustrate this.

In **Balfour v Balfour (1919)**, Mr Balfour worked in Ceylon, and came to England with his wife on holiday. He later returned to Ceylon alone but his wife stayed in England for health reasons. He promised to pay her £30 per month as maintenance whilst she stayed in England, but he stopped paying her when the marriage broke down. The court decided she could not take legal action for the promised maintenance payments as, amongst other reasons, the agreement was a purely domestic arrangement that they did intend to be legally binding. It would then be a question in divorce proceedings for the court to decide what payments he should make to her.

In **Merritt v Merritt (1970)**, the situation was different because the husband and wife were already living apart when the agreement was made. Mr Merritt left his wife. Shortly after he left, they met to make arrangements for the future. He agreed to pay £40 per month maintenance, out of which she would pay the mortgage. When the mortgage was paid off he would transfer the house from joint names to the wife's name. He wrote this down and signed the paper, but later refused to transfer the house. The court decided that they must have intended the agreement to be binding, as they would base their future actions on it and had put it in writing. Therefore there was a legally binding agreement rather than a purely domestic arrangement.

This principle has been applied to many other domestic arrangements including support for students by parents at university. For such an agreement to be a contract there needs to be something much more formal, such as a deed (a formal written and witnessed document).

Finally there can be social arrangements that are legally binding such as an agreement to share winnings in a lottery syndicate. These arrangements are usually set out in writing and signed, which again helps the evidence that the agreement is meant to be legally binding. This can be seen in the case of **Simpkins v Pays (1955)**. Mrs Pays, her granddaughter, and Mr Simpkins, a lodger, shared a house. They all contributed one-third of the stake in entering a weekly competition in the *Sunday Empire News*. On 27 June 1954, the competition was to place, in order of merit, eight women's fashions. They took it in turns to pay the entry fee and fill in the form and send it off. On that week a prize of £750 was won for correctly placing the fashion items in order but as Mrs Pays had entered the form that week, she refused to share the prize. The court decided that the arrangement was a joint enterprise to which cash was contributed in the expectation of sharing any prize. Thus each was entitled to a one-third share of the winnings.

A similar case arose in Scotland in 2002 with the same outcome. This was the case of *Robertson* v *Anderson*, where two women set off together on 21 November 1997 to play bingo at the Mecca Bingo Hall in Drumchapel. The defendant won a big prize; and, when she declined to share it with the claimant, proceedings were brought for payment of half the winnings, alleging that there had been an agreement to 'go halfers'.

Conclusion

Generally there is presumed to be an intention to create legal intention in commercial agreements and no intention in social or domestic arrangements. There are exceptions, but they are quite clear and seem to have been sensible decisions.

Activities

1 Consider the agreements you have made today and decide whether each is legally binding or not.

2 Decide how you make sure you had sufficient evidence to show you were entitled to any winnings on a competition entered jointly by you and your friend.

You should now be able to:

▪ understand the meaning of intention to create legal relations

▪ apply the rules to a given situation.

AQA Examiner's tip

When an exam question is set involving two closely related people making an agreement, look for the issue of intention to create legal relations.

💡 5 Consideration

Consideration means that each party to a contract must give something of some value. This is because the law is concerned with bargains and not gifts. This has been defined by Sir Frederick Pollock as follows: 'An act or forbearance of one party, or the promise thereof, is the price for which the promise of the other is bought, and the promise thus given for value is enforceable.' The idea in the definition is that each party to the contract does something of some value for the other – either a positive act, such as giving something or doing some work, or forbearance, that is, not doing something. Consideration must be present for any valid contract unless the agreement is made by a deed (a form of legal document). There are a number of aspects of consideration that need to be understood. There are two types of valid consideration: executed consideration and executory consideration.

Types of valid consideration

Executed consideration is the term used to describe the status of a person's promise in a contract where that part of the bargain has been performed. For example, if A agrees with B to pay B £10 to wash A's car, and B washes the car, B's consideration is executed, that is, complete, because he has then performed his side of the bargain. He can then hold A to his promise to pay the £10.

Executory consideration is the term used to describe the status of a person's promise in a contract where that part of the bargain has not yet been performed. Thus in the previous example, it would be the payment of the £10 that had not yet happened.

Consideration must have some value

As the law is concerned with bargains and not gifts, the consideration must have some value but does not have to be of equal value. The whole point of business is to get more for your goods than you paid for them: clearly this is not equal value. Thus contract law recognises the rule that consideration must be sufficient but need not be adequate.

In this topic you will learn how to:

▪ define consideration

▪ explain the term 'past consideration'

▪ state relevant cases and examples.

Key terms

Consideration: 'an act or forbearance of one party, or the promise thereof, is the price for which the promise of the other is bought, and the promise thus given for value is enforceable': Sir Frederick Pollock. In other words, each party to a contract gives something of value to the other.

Executed consideration: consideration in a contract which has been completed.

Executory consideration: consideration in a contract which has not yet been completed.

The idea of adequacy is that there must be some economic value, but not necessarily equal value. This can be seen in the case of **Chappell v Nestlé (1959)**, where chocolate bar wrappers were taken as part payment for a record as part of a promotion. It was acknowledged that used chocolate bar wrappers have little value, but there was some value, all that is needed. This is reflected today in the use of vouchers that are often described as having a value of 0.0001 pence.

Past consideration is not valid consideration

Past consideration is not a valid form of consideration. It is defined as something already done at the time the agreement is made. Where the consideration is past, there will not be a valid contract. An example of this can be seen in the case of **Re McArdle (1951)**. In this case a person died and in his will left his assets in equal shares to his five children. The wife of one of the children paid out of her own money for alterations to one of the houses that were included in his assets. The children wrote to the wife, 'In consideration of your carrying out certain alterations … we hereby agree to repay you [£488] from the estate.'

The court held that the promise of payment did not create a contract as the alterations were over and done with by the time the promise of payment was made, so in relation to that promise her 'consideration' was past. In other words, she had given no consideration for the promise of payment, there was no contract and she could not claim the £488.

This is different where A requests some performance from B before the contract comes into existence but on the common understanding that there will be a contract and that there will be a payment. An example is asking a plumber to fix a leak in an emergency. A case that illustrates this is the very old case of **Lampleigh v Braithwaite (1615)**. In that case, Braithwaite killed someone and then asked Lampleigh to get him a pardon from the king. Lampleigh got the pardon and gave it to Braithwaite, who promised to pay Lampleigh £100 for his trouble. The court decided that although Lampleigh's consideration was past (he had got the pardon) Braithwaite's promise to pay could be linked to Braithwaite's earlier request and treated as one agreement. Therefore, it could be implied at the time of the request that Lampleigh would be paid and so was valid consideration.

Consideration must move from the promisee

This means that the person making the promise must provide the consideration. It does not matter that the contract was made for the benefit of another person. Thus if A agrees to wash B's car if B pays £10 to C, there is no promise that is enforceable by C, as he has given no consideration for the £10. This basic rule has been altered by the Contracts (Rights of Third Parties) Act 1999 so that a person who is not a party to a contract can enforce the contract if he is named in the contract or he gains a benefit from it. There are a number of possible examples of how this applies, such as where a person has ordered goods on the internet to be delivered to someone else, where someone makes a group booking for an event or travel, and where someone has bought the bride and groom a wedding present from a wedding list in a shop.

Conclusion

All contracts require consideration. It is important to know what amounts to consideration and what does not. The main basis of the principle is that the law is concerned with bargains and not gifts.

Activities

1 Identify whether the consideration in the example below is executed or executory.

Umar agreed with Mobiles plc that they should supply him with 1,000 mobile phones for £60,000. Mobiles plc has now delivered the phones, but Umar has not yet paid for them.

2 State your own examples of executed consideration, executory consideration and past consideration.

You should now be able to:

- understand the concept of consideration
- apply the rules to a given situation.

Breach of contract and the courts: procedure and damages

In this topic you will learn how to:

- explain the meaning of the term 'breach of contract'

- distinguish between actual breach and anticipatory breach

- use cases and examples to help provide a solution to breach of contract problems.

AQA Examiner's tip

The exam question may ask for an explanation of the legal principles on breach, but is also likely to require you to apply the law to the facts in the scenario.

Key terms

Condition: a condition is a term of the contract that, if not performed, will go to the heart of the contract. Breach of a condition gives the innocent party the right to end the contract, if he chooses, in addition to the right to claim damages for any losses.

Warranty: a warranty is a minor term of the contract that, if not performed, will cause loss but does not go to the heart of the contract. Breach of warranty will not end the contract but will give rise to a claim for damages.

Innominate term: a term in a contract that can be treated as either a condition or a warranty, depending on the nature of the breach of that term.

1 Breach of contract

Introduction

A breach of contract occurs when one party to the contract fails or states that he will fail to perform part or all of his side of the bargain.

If the breach has serious consequences for the innocent party he will have the choice of ending or continuing with the contract, as well as claiming damages; if the breach is only trivial, the innocent party must continue with the contract, although he can claim damages for any losses. Consider the difference between an electrician who has made a contract to renew all the electrical circuits, lights and sockets in a landlord's two houses, who fails to renew: (i) one socket in one house; and (ii) the electrical circuits in the upstairs of one house. These are both breaches of contract, as they both result in loss to one party to the contract. The first is a minor loss in having to get a socket renewed: a relatively small cost, even if it is essential work. But the second is much more serious and expensive to rectify and would probably end the contract. The house owner may well agree a small reduction in the price he is paying for the minor failure and expect other work to continue. However, he may lose confidence in the electrician after the major failure and not wish him to continue to work on the second house. The first essential therefore is to decide which breaches are sufficiently serious that the innocent party can choose to end the contract.

Types of term

The law decides whether a breach of contract is serious enough by deciding which type of term in the contract has been broken. A term in a contract is known as either a **condition** or a warranty. A **warranty** is not the same as the promise made by manufacturers of goods in relation to repair or replacement if it should fail within a fixed period of time, often 12 months.

A term which can be either a condition or a warranty depending on the nature of the failure is known as an **innominate term**.

A condition is a term of the contract that goes to the heart of the contract. If I rent a car, one term of the contract that will be a condition is that the car will actually go and stop. If it does not, then clearly I would want to end the contract and either rent a different car or go elsewhere. The failure to provide a car that goes and stops would be a breach of condition of a contract and I would be entitled to treat the contract as ended. If the problem was easily fixed, I might delay renting the car and continue the contract, but seek damages as compensation for the delay. In law it is my choice if a condition has been broken.

A warranty, on the other hand, is a minor term of the contract. If it is broken, loss will result, but the main purpose of the contract will still be achieved. If I rent a car and the rental company offers me one which has a CD changer, if the CD changer does not work I will still have a useable car, but would expect to pay less and to be compensated for any CD of mine that I loaded that could not be recovered from the broken changer. This would be a warranty and I would have to continue with the contract, but would expect compensation for my lost CD and perhaps very minor compensation for the car not having a CD changer.

Two cases that illustrate the distinction between a condition and a warranty are **Poussard v Spiers and Pond (1876)** and **Bettini v Gye (1876)**. In *Poussard* v *Spiers and Pond*, an opera singer made a contract to sing in an opera. She failed to attend the first six performances and was replaced for the entire run of the opera. She could only be replaced if her failure to attend was a breach of condition. The court decided that this was a breach of condition as her role was central to the performance and a replacement singer would not want to perform only for a few days. The promoters could therefore replace the singer without paying compensation as she had broken a condition of her contract.

In *Bettini* v *Gye* an opera singer made a contract to perform from March to July and was also required to attend six days before performances were due to start, for rehearsals. He failed to attend the first two days of rehearsals. This was a breach of warranty and not a breach of condition, as his failure to attend only caused some inconvenience; other parts of rehearsal could continue without him and the promoters would not lose much, if any, money. They could not treat the contract as ended and replace the singer. Damages were the only remedy available. If the promoters had refused to use the singer in the performances, they would have broken their side of the contract and the singer could then have taken legal action against them for damages.

Actual breach and anticipatory breach

Breach of contract can occur in two ways: actual breach and anticipatory breach. Actual breach occurs either through poor performance of the contract, where there is performance of the contract but the work is done badly or the goods are substandard, or by non-performance where the work is not done or the goods are not provided at all.

Anticipatory breach occurs where one party to the contract states or otherwise indicates that there will not be performance of the contract. This is usually that goods or services will not be provided. As soon as this has happened, the person affected can start legal action under the contract. This would occur in the situation where a person told a mobile phone provider that he did not wish to continue with the contract after two months of a 12-month contract. An example of this can be seen in the case of **Hochster v De La Tour (1853)**, where a tour guide was told that his services would not be required despite the contract for him to work in two months' time. Here the guide has a choice: he could wait and see if the guide work was in fact wanted after all on the due dates, or treat the contract as ended and take immediate legal action to recover damages for his losses.

The consequences of breach of contract

Whatever type of breach has occurred, the party to the contract affected by the breach automatically has a right to damages. That party can also treat the contract as repudiated and take no further action under the contract where the breach is a breach of a condition or an innominate term that has been broken in a serious way so that it is in effect a breach of condition.

Conclusion

Breach of contract can either end the contract because the breach is serious, or be a minor breach where damages are payable. Breach can be actual breach – the breach has happened – or anticipatory breach, a statement of intention not to perform the contract in the future.

AQA Examiner's tip

When applying the law on breach to a scenario, make sure you explain why you have decided that the breach is a breach of condition or a breach of warranty. This requires reference back to the legal authorities you are likely to have explained in your answer.

Key cases

Poussard v Spiers and Pond (1876): Poussard's inability to sing the lead role in an opera for the first six days of performances was a breach of condition. The opera promoter was therefore able to end the contract and replace the singer.

Bettini v Gye (1876): Bettini was unable to attend the first two days' rehearsal for an opera. This was considered to be a warranty as it was only for part of the rehearsal, not the performances, so the singer could not be replaced without the opera company breaking their contract.

Hochster v De La Tour (1853): anticipatory breach occurs where one party states he will not perform his side of the contract: in this case, to be a tour guide in future months.

AQA Examiner's tip

Look out in the scenario for evidence of when the breach took place. That will establish whether the breach is anticipatory breach.

267

You should now be able to:

- understand the concept of breach of contract
- apply the rules to problem situations.

In this topic you will learn how to:

- draw a diagram of the civil court structure showing appeal routes
- state the jurisdiction of each court
- distinguish between different classifications of cases in contract
- describe the burden of proof and the standard of proof in a civil case
- apply the above to a given situation.

2 Outline of civil courts and appeal system

Initial hearing	First appeal	Final appeal
County Court	Court of Appeal	House of Lords
High Court	(Civil Division)	

Fig. 14.1 *Court structure*

The civil courts

The majority of contract cases are heard in the 218 County Courts. Simple money claims can all be dealt with online using the Money Claim Online scheme. The manner in which each case is dealt with depends on the nature and size of the claim. The largest claims are heard in the High Court, Queen's Bench Division. Part of the Queen's Bench Division is the Commercial Court. Usually, appeals go to the Court of Appeal (Civil Division). For most legal cases in England and Wales, the House of Lords is the final point of appeal.

The courts of first instance

A court of first instance is the court where a case is first tried. The court of first instance will be either the County Court or the High Court. The County Court and the High Court have different jurisdictions, so will hear different cases. The courts hope most cases will be settled out of court or by alternative dispute resolution, with only a minority actually being tried. In the 2005–2006 County Court Annual Report, Lord Justice Thomas, Senior Presiding Judge for England and Wales wrote:

> **The division between the County Court and the High Court**
>
> The figures in this report reflect solely the work of the county court. However in reality outside the Royal Courts of Justice, there is very little distinction in practice between the way in which High Court and county court work is done. We have in practice a 'single civil court', but unfortunately the figures in this report do not reflect this. A distinction is still perpetuated between the High Court and the county court, even for reports such as this.

Money Claim Online is part of the County Court and was set up in 2001 to support Government policy in making justice affordable and accessible to all. This online service allows county court claims to be issued for fixed sums up to £100,000 by individuals and organisations over the internet, anywhere, anytime. Its use is growing enormously each year.

Apart from Money Claim Online, the reality is that the cases are heard dependent on the track into which they fit. The courts are responsible for case management, with all cases allocated to one of three 'tracks' (namely, small claims, fast track and multi-track) according to their value and complexity. If a contract case is to be heard in the High Court, it is heard in the Queen's Bench Division. The Commercial Court is part of the Queen's Bench Division. It deals with complex cases arising out of business disputes, both national and international. In the Commercial Court there is particular emphasis on international trade, banking, commodity and arbitration disputes. All Commercial Court cases are treated as multi-track cases; these are explained later. Whilst there are few cases in the Commercial Court (fewer than 100 went to trial in 2005), they are often quite lengthy. The procedure is successful because the number of full trials is about 10 per cent of the number of cases started. For example, the case *Man Nutzfahrzeuge Aktiengesellschaft* v *Freightliner Ltd* began on 11 January 2005 and continued for 18 weeks. It involved a dispute about the acquisition of a company. The existence of the Commercial Court is important because many international contracts contain a term that any dispute will be settled in accordance with English law in the English courts. This is good for the business of UK law firms and barristers.

The three tracks

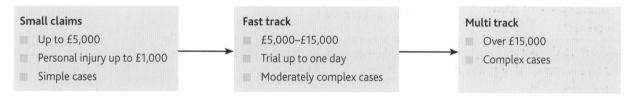

Small claims	Fast track	Multi track
▨ Up to £5,000	▨ £5,000–£15,000	▨ Over £15,000
▨ Personal injury up to £1,000	▨ Trial up to one day	▨ Complex cases
▨ Simple cases	▨ Moderately complex cases	

Fig. 14.2 *The three tracks*

As outlined in Chapter 12, cases are heard in the court appropriate to the track into which they fit. The courts are responsible for case management, with all cases allocated to one of three 'tracks' (small claims, fast track or multi-track) according to their value and complexity. If a contract case is to be heard in the High Court, it is heard in the Queen's Bench Division, some large cases being allocated to the Commercial Court.

Which court and judge will hear the case depends on the scope and size of the case. Multi-track cases are almost always heard by a Circuit Judge, the others more often by a District Judge. A number of factors are taken into account in deciding the track apart from the normal financial limits set out above. These include the complexity of the case and the amount of oral evidence that will be given.

An example of a small-claims track case is a dispute about the performance of a custom-built computer system that cost £4,000. This would be small-claims track as the value of the claim is less than £5,000 and there are no complex issues of law or evidence. It might be fast-track if specialist IT evidence were required to decide the case.

Links

▨ The three tracks are discussed in more detail on pp233–40

▨ For information on Appeals, see Chapter 12 (The courts: procedure and damages for negligence cases), p227.

AQA Examiner's tip

Make sure you know the differences between the tracks, as you are quite likely to have to identify the relevant track for the exam scenario.

A multi-track case would be more complex and also (usually) involving a larger sum of money. This might involve a dispute about the construction of a new office block that appears to have been built with substandard foundations.

The burden and standard of proof

As we have seen in Chapter 13, in civil law cases the burden of proof is on the claimant to prove his claim on a balance of probabilities. There is a lower standard than that in criminal cases. This means that the party bearing the burden of proof, namely the claimant, must demonstrate that it is 'more likely than not' that the defendant has been negligent. The **burden of proof** is the obligation on a party to establish the facts in issue in a case to the required degree of certainty (the standard of proof) in order to prove their case. In a civil trial the burden is upon the claimant to prove the liability of the defendant. The **standard of proof** is on a balance of probabilities.

As most cases are for non-payment of a debt, there is often little need for complex evidence unless the defence is that the debt was not paid as the goods were faulty. These simple cases sare usually dealt with following the Money Claim Online procedure and are rarely defended, so the claimant quickly obtains a default judgment which he can then try to enforce against the defendant.

Conclusion

Most contract cases are heard in the County Court. The vast majority start as a Money Claim Online. The actual timing and venue will depend on the track to which the case is allocated. Whichever track the case is allocated to, the claimant has to prove his case on a balance of probabilities.

Key terms

Burden of proof: the obligation to prove the defendant committed the crime.

Standard of proof: the level to which the evidence must be proved to gain a conviction.

Activity

Read the extract from the blog below and consider whether the procedure that is said to have taken place is accurate. How well do you think the law served the individual involved?

Money Claim Online

Firstly - is response to Tony's question, and to fill any of you who haven't been through the process in:

When you submit a claim to Money Claim on line, the case is initally handled by Northampton County Court - in the event that the defendant chooses to defend themselves (as persimmon did in this case), the case is referred to the claimants local court (in this case Barrow-in-Furness). At this point an allocation questionnaire is sent to both parties. This is used to decide which track the case should be allocated to (Small Claims Track, Fast Track or a third option that i can't remember). Both the defendant and the claimant fill this in and return it with supporting evidence and any other details relevent to the case. This is seen by the Judge, and the Judge then makes a decision as to which track it should be allocated, and how long the session will be.

Righto - on with the blog!

I got bored this week, and rang the local court to chase them up, found out they are running three weeks behind (shocker) but my case was allocated late last week, for a two hour hearing, and the paperwork would be in the post. THis is promising, as Persimmon's representation had only one defence: That the case had no merit. And they made a motion to have hte case dismissed on the grounds that i'd signed the inspection form. The fact that the Judge hasn't dismissed the case as requested fills me with hope that i may be able to win this one. I can't say for certain whether the allocation is good or bad at this point, but i'm optimistic.

www.newhomeblogs.co.uk

You should now be able to:

■ understand the framework for the civil process

■ apply the civil process in a given situation.

3 An outline of the procedure of a contract case up to trial

Starting a contract case

Once it has been established that court proceedings need to be started (most claims are settled by negotiation without the need to go to court), the formal procedure must be started. Claims where there are personal injuries and the claimant does not expect to be awarded more than £50,000 must be started in the County Court. All other claims may be started in either the County Court or the High Court. Most claims are started in the County Court and many use the Money Claim Online procedure such as is mentioned in the blog in the activity in the previous topic. We will now concentrate on claims starting in the County Court. The first step is to complete a claim form. Information about this is available online to download or can be collected from one of over 200 court offices in the country.

This form is simple to complete, requiring names and addresses for claimant and defendant, brief details of the claim (such as 'Damages for breach of contract resulting from the failure of the defendant to complete building works at the agreed time'), and the value of the claim. The purpose of this is to establish the fee payable and to help establish the choice of court and track. The claimant needs to assess the value of his claim. This is easy for an unpaid debt, but for other claims it is more difficult. If the claim is not for a fixed amount of money (an 'unspecified amount') under 'Value' the claimant would write 'I expect to recover' followed by whichever of the following applies to the claim:

▮ 'not more than £5,000', or

▮ 'more than £5,000 but not more than £15,000' or

▮ 'more than £15,000', or

▮ 'I cannot say how much I expect to recover'.

This is done to select the track that will be relevant.

The particulars of claim on side two of the form will give details of the claim being made. This may be sent separately within 14 days, but most

In this topic you will learn how to:

■ describe the procedure from the start of court action to trial

■ apply the above to a given situation.

Link

A County Court claim form can be seen illustrated in Chapter 12 (The courts: procedure and damages for negligence cases), Fig. 12.2, p232.

AQA Examiner's tip

You will not be asked to complete a claim form in the exam, but you need to have an appreciation of the detail in it and consider why that detail is needed.

simple claims have it included. The particulars of claim give a simple statement of the facts on which the claimant bases the claim. This will include the date and terms of the contract and an outline of why the claimant considers the defendant has broken his contract and the loss that resulted.

The fee payable depends on the size of the claim.

There is also the possibility of having the fee lessened or paying no fee at all in certain cases for claimants with low income and few assets.

This claim form is then served on the defendant, usually by post. In addition to the claim form, the defendant is sent forms for use in dealing with the claim made. At this stage the claimant chooses which County Court he wishes to start the claim in, although the claim may get transferred to a different court later in the process.

The defendant receives the claim form

Assuming the defendant's details and address are correct, the claim form and defendant response pack will not be returned to the court by the Post Office and will be deemed to have been received by the defendant. The defendant's response pack includes an admission form so that the defendant can admit the claim, a defence form to be completed if the claim is not admitted and an acknowledgement of service form, which confirms receipt of the claim. This means that the defendant can do nothing and not reply to the claim at all, admit all or part of the claim, or dispute all or part of the claim. The defendant must do this within 14 days of receiving the claim. If the defendant does not file a defence within 14 days or any extension the court may give, the claimant can file for a default judgment and effectively win the case. The court will then only be concerned with awarding the appropriate amount of damages and costs. This can be done either by allocating the case to the small claims track or to a disposal hearing in those cases where the claim is more complicated.

In many cases the defendant may attempt to settle the claim by making an offer of payment. The great majority of claims are settled without the need for a court hearing. However, the defendant may dispute the claim, in which case the defendant may well just complete an acknowledgement of service, as this will give additional time to complete the defence (from 14 to 28 days). In these circumstances the claimant may well discover that the defendant has instructed a solicitor. The defendant will then complete his defence and send it to the court.

The claimant receives the defence

When the claimant receives the defence, the court will also send an allocation questionnaire to all parties to the case. The purpose of this is to establish the location, track and timing of a trial. There is usually (apart from money claims of less than £1,500) an allocation fee payable of £100. This is another incentive to negotiate a settlement of the case as the expense of taking the case forward mounts up. There will also be a trial fee, which for a multi-track case is £500. The court will keep records of when the allocation questionnaires are due to be returned and if they have in fact been returned. This is part of case monitoring. **Case monitoring** is where judges receive support from court staff in carrying out their case management role. The court uses a computerised diary monitoring system to record court orders and requests, the deadline for the return of documents such as the allocation questionnaire and whether the deadline has been met. **Case management** has been introduced to avoid the former problem of even quite trivial cases dragging on for years. The judge now

Key terms

Case monitoring: the system by which the court monitors progress of a case to help achieve a quick conclusion.

Case management: the active role taken by a judge in the life of a case to help reach a speedy and just resolution of the issue.

has the power to summon the parties to court to find out what is going on in the event of inactivity, and then make an appropriate order to speed up the process. Failure to comply can result in the party at fault being prevented from continuing the case.

Once the allocation questionnaires have been completed, a procedural judge (normally a District Judge) will allocate the case to the appropriate track. If a party to a case does not comply with a court order or time limit, that party may be struck out of the action. The effect of this is that the party would be unable to take further part in the case and would lose any right to claim or defend the court action. This is part of judicial case management which aims to keep the process moving along at a reasonable speed and help reduce the average time taken to deal with a claim.

Between allocation and trial

After the case has been allocated the court sets a date for the trial. This date will be at least 21 days later, and the actual date will depend on what other directions need to be made. These other directions include providing copies of documents to the other party or parties to the case and copies of experts' statements. The stage is now set for the trial.

Conclusion

The procedure from issue of a claim up to trial is designed to bring the claim to a conclusion fairly and speedily. The aim of the civil justice system is to reduce the average time a claim takes to be resolved and thus reduce the criticism that the law is very slow. The aim is to reduce the time from over a year at the end of the 1990s to about 30 weeks on average for a fast-track case. The procedure is relatively straightforward and is backed up with much help and guidance through leaflets, the court offices and online.

 Activity

Set out below is a sample examination question. Using the information in the scenario, complete a claim form as far as possible and explain to the claimant how the case would proceed up to any trial.

Umar wanted to buy a large quantity of mobile phones for his shop. He phoned Mobiles plc, who agreed to supply him with a quantity of phones for £60,000. Mobiles plc immediately realised they had been using an old price list and tried to contact Umar on the phone, but failed to do so. Mobiles plc therefore posted a new one to Umar, which he received on the next day. Mobiles plc refused to supply the phones at £60,000 and Umar refused to pay the revised price of £70,000. Mobiles plc's new prices were the same as other suppliers of the phones.

You should now be able to:

- understand the procedure up to trial in a contract dispute
- apply the procedure in a given situation.

 Examiner's tip

You may be asked to describe the process in the exam. This may well require reference to the scenario.

Link

A flowchart of a fast track case up to trial can be found in Chapter 12 (The courts: procedure and damages for negligence cases), Fig. 12.4, p235.

 Examiner's tip

Make sure that you present the order of events in a clear logical manner using the correct legal terminology. You will gain your marks more easily if you do so. It is usually a good idea to plan your answer and then write it out. The planning exercise will help you get the procedure in the correct order.

AQA Examiner's tip

Make sure you read the examination paper carefully. Some candidates answer questions on damage with material on damages and some do the opposite. The examiner is specific as to which he wants. Answer damage with material on damage and damages with material on damages.

💡 4 Damages

The purpose of damages

Damages in contract are compensatory. The purpose is to put the claimant in the position he would have been in had the contract been properly performed. This means that the claimant is entitled to the benefit of his bargain. It is easy to calculate the loss where a bill has not been paid, but much harder to calculate where services have not been performed or goods not delivered, as there are losses that could be said to be a consequence of the failure to perform or deliver. Consider, for example, what losses there might be if the copy of this book that you are reading were delivered late, or the losses that would follow from a cancelled restaurant reservation. The purpose of damages is to do this as fairly as possible. The law is not concerned with punishing the defendant, only with compensating the victim of the defendant's breach of contract.

Calculation of damages

The court has to take into account a number of factors when awarding damages. The first thing is the easiest: the amount payable for what is known as the 'loss of the bargain'. The idea is to put the claimant in the same situation as if the contract had been performed. For example, in a contract to buy for £400 a television normally costing £500 and where the television is either defective or is not delivered, the claimant will be entitled to damages reflecting the difference between the price paid under the contract and the actual value of the non-delivered or defective television. This will usually involve the return of any money paid and the difference between the contract price and the general selling price of the television at the date the contract was broken: in other words, £100.

There are also consequential losses that are more difficult to calculate. The extent of the losses that can be claimed depends on whether the consequence is too remote to be recovered or not. The principles behind this will be discussed later in this topic. The basic principle is that the loss is foreseeable. Thus if a television is defective and catches fire, it is foreseeable that other goods may be damaged by the fire. This damage would also be recoverable. The damages would reflect the value of the other goods that were damaged.

Additionally there will be costs incurred by the claimant as a result of sorting out the consequences. A simple example of this is the additional costs incurred in getting another television to replace the one that was defective – in that case it could be the cost of an additional trip to the shop or a delivery charge for a replacement television bought over the internet.

Where a business is claiming a loss of profit, it will have to show how the broken contract affected its earnings. This is usually done by calculating the loss of profits on the basis of previous profits, contracts made and the consequences of those contracts being broken. The detail of a claim can be seen from the case of *Wiseman* v *Virgin Atlantic Airways* (2006), where the claimant was wrongly not let on board an aircraft in Port Harcourt, Nigeria, flying to Stansted airport in England. It was another 12 days before he could return to England. The successful claim resulted in damages of around £2,300 which was based on:

1 hotel bill for the additional stay

2 restaurant bills for the additional stay

3 taxi fares in and out of town for the purpose of trying to rearrange his flight to England

4 postage and telephone calls.

However, nothing was awarded for:

1 expenses incurred by his fiancée who had arranged to meet him at Stansted

2 the breakdown of their relationship which is not a recoverable type of damage, even if that was caused by the breach of contract

3 the additional expenses of his Nigerian friends who had come to see him off

4 his hurt feelings and the alleged damage to his reputation

5 a robbery suffered during the time he was delayed in Nigeria; this was a supervening event not caused by the delay.

In exceptional cases there can also be damages for emotional distress following a breach of contract. This relates to consumer contracts and particularly holidays. Lord Denning said in the case of **Jarvis v Swan Tours (1973)**, 'It has often been said that on a breach of contract damages cannot be given for mental distress … I think those limitations are out of date. In a proper case damages for mental distress can be recovered in contract … One such case is a contract for a holiday, or any other contract to provide entertainment and enjoyment.' *Jarvis* v *Swan Tours* was a case where a winter sports holiday had failed to live up to expectations with respect to the activities on offer. The original trial judge awarded damages of approximately half the cost of the holiday, but on appeal, twice the cost of the holiday was awarded even though that sum could not possibly reflect the actual financial loss. This seems to be contrary to the basic principles of an award of damages, but is the just result which is reflected in the quotation from Lord Denning.

Mitigation of loss

The claimant must do his best to keep the losses he has suffered to a minimum. Thus in *Wiseman* v *Virgin Atlantic Airways* (2006), the claimant could not do nothing or be extravagant. Chartering an aircraft to fly out from England to Nigeria and collect him would have been irrecoverable, as it would not have been keeping his losses to a minimum. In practice, the claimant does not have to be too careful about ensuring mitigation of loss; the key criterion is that the action taken by the claimant is reasonable. Thus Wiseman did not have to buy the cheapest meal available or walk into town rather than take a taxi.

Causation and remoteness

The general principle is that the loss complained of must have been caused by the breach and not be too remote. The rule with respect to **causation** is that the breach of contract must be the main cause of the claimant's loss: in other words, but for the defendant's breach of contract, the claimant would not have made the loss. For example, if I have made a contract to have my new car delivered on Friday and it is not delivered on Friday, I would then have to hire a car until delivery took place. The cause of my loss is the defendant's breach of contract in not delivering on the stated day. If, however, the car was delivered late because I was not able to pay for it on Friday, as my bank had failed to deliver the funds to pay for it on time, the cause of my loss is the bank's failure, not the seller of the car.

AQA Examiner's tip

In the exam you would not be expected to guess at these figures. Only quote a figure in your answer if you have been given figures in the question.

AQA Examiner's tip

If there is a clear and simple calculation of damages, then you will be expected to state it. A breach by failure to deliver, where the cost of the goods has risen from £10 to £15, should be explained as the difference between the contract price and the market price at breach: in this case, £5. You will not be penalised for poor maths!

Key cases

Jarvis v Swan Tours (1973): damages could be awarded for mental distress following a breach of contract. This is particularly relevant to holidays.

Key terms

Causation: the link between the defendant's breach of contract and the loss being claimed.

■ Key cases

Hadley v Baxendale (1854): damages for breach of contract will cover naturally occurring consequences of the breach and those that are in the contemplation of the parties to the contract.

Victoria Laundry v Newman Industries (1949): the claimant could recover damages for their normal lost profit, but not for an especially valuable contract the defendant did not know about.

The Heron II (1969): the claimant could recover damages for late delivery of a cargo of sugar as the defendant knew the cargo and that there was a market for it. This was an ordinary, known risk.

AQA Examiner's tip

When answering a question on damages, you will often have to describe the theory (the law) as to how damages are calculated and/or what damages are recoverable. The next part of the answer will often be applying the law to the facts in the scenario. This requires an explanation of how the law is used in connection with the facts so that you produce a reasoned conclusion.

With remoteness of damage, it would clearly be impossible to make the defendant liable for all the consequences of his breach as they could be, arguably, never ending. The decision the law has to make is where to draw the line. Remoteness is the test used by the courts to decide whether losses resulting from a breach of contract are recoverable. The first case to really establish the law was **Hadley v Baxendale (1854)**. In that case, the claimants needed to have the main shaft that powered their mill repaired, as it had broken. Until it was repaired, the mill could do no work, and so they were losing money. It could be repaired only in London; they hired the defendant to take it from Gloucester by the next day. For some unexplained reason, the shaft took several days to arrive. The delay caused continuing losses. The question before the court was whether the defendant was liable for the money that the Hadleys had lost while the mill was without its shaft. The court decided that since the defendant did not necessarily know that the mill would be idle until the shaft could be returned (they might have had a spare shaft), the defendant was not liable for the loss. The decision was based on the 'foreseeability' test for contract breaches: you cannot be held liable for losses that you could not reasonably have anticipated. This test has been restated in various ways on many occasions. Two categories of loss are recognised:

■ Direct or normal loss: loss of a type that would usually arise from a breach of contract. This is assumed to have been in the 'reasonable contemplation' of the parties at the time they made the contract.

■ Indirect or abnormal loss: loss of a type that is out of the ordinary. This is recoverable if, at the time of making the contract, the defendant knew it could happen in the event of breach. The defendant must also have accepted responsibility for that risk. Acceptance of risk is often implied from knowledge that the defendant has in relation to the situation.

There are a number of cases that have looked at these abnormal losses. The first to be considered is **Victoria Laundry v Newman Industries (1949)**. In that case the defendants contracted to sell a new, larger, boiler to the claimants, which the defendants knew was required for immediate use. Delivery was made five months late. The claimants lost not only the £16 a week profit that they could have made from normal customers, but also a £262 a week dyeing contract with a Government department. The court decided that the £16 per week was recoverable as it was a normal loss, but the £262 was not recoverable, as the defendants did not know about the Government contract.

The case of **The Heron II (Czarnikow v Koufos) (1969)** shows that business people know of, and are therefore responsible for, losses occurring in normal business situations. In that case the defendants were ship owners who made a contract to carry a cargo of sugar to Basra for the claimant. They knew a great deal about the claimant client and the world of business: they were sugar merchants; there was a sugar market in Basra. What they did not know was whether the claimant intended to sell the sugar as soon as the ship arrived. The ship arrived in Basra nine days late as a result of the defendants' fault. In the course of those nine days the price of sugar fell significantly in the market and the sugar was sold for much less than it would have done had the cargo arrived on time. The claim was for the loss of profit on the sugar. The court decided that the claimant was entitled to their lost profit. Even though the ship owner did not know of the intention to sell the sugar immediately, 'if he had thought about the matter he must have realised at least that it was not unlikely that the sugar would be sold in the market at market price on arrival.' The defendant is liable for such loss as a reasonable man, knowing what the defendant knew or ought to have known, would consider 'not unlikely' to result.

A typical modern example is *Hotel Services Ltd* v *Hilton International Hotels* (2000), where the court decided that the claimant was allowed to recover both the costs of the removal of defective mini-bars and the consequent loss of profit from their non-availability. These were both direct losses.

You should now be able to:

- understand the principles behind an award of damages

- apply the principles in examination questions.

Activity

Using the scenario on p273 in the previous topic, outline how the court would calculate an award of damages to Umar in the situation given.

Chapters 13 and 14

1   Richard wanted to buy another car. He saw an advertisement in the local paper which stated '2007 Golf GTi – £16,000. Ring Janice on XXXX'. Richard telephoned Janice and was given details of the car. Richard said he would only pay £15,000 for the car. Janice said that was too low and rang off.

Richard spent the rest of the day looking at similar cars and discovered that £16,000 was a good price for the car as similar cars were not less than £18,000. He therefore rang Janice again and left an answerphone message, "I now accept your offer to sell the Golf GTi for £16,000. I will come and collect it tomorrow."

When Richard went to collect the car, he discovered that it was not a Golf GTi, but a Golf GT, a different and less expensive model. As this was not the model of car he wanted and was not what Janice had described, he refused to buy the car.

(a) A valid contract requires an offer and acceptance, an intention to create legal relations and consideration. If one party to the contract does not do what has been agreed, this is likely to amount to a breach of contract.

   (i)   Explain, using cases and/or examples, the meaning of the term 'offer'.   *(7 marks)*
   (ii) Explain, using cases and examples, the meaning of the term 'acceptance'.   *(7 marks)*
   (iii) Explain, using cases and examples, the meaning of the term 'breach of contract'.   *(7 marks)*

(b) (i)   Using the explanations given in your answer to 3(a), discuss whether Janice and Richard had made a valid contract.   *(7 marks)*

   (ii) Explain what is meant by consideration. Assuming there was a valid contract between Richard and Janice, identify the consideration in that contract.   *(7 marks)*

(c) Assuming that Janice breached her contract with Richard,

   (i)   Identify which court would hear the case and outline the procedure that would be followed before a trial.   *(5 marks)*

   (ii) Outline how the court would calculate an award of damages to Richard in the situation given.   *(5 marks)*

2C Review and examination techniques

Answering questions on contract in AQA Law 2

There are a number of different aspects of learning that need to take place to answer the questions fully:

- being able to understand and explain the basic principles
- being able to illustrate the principles by reference to decided cases
- being able to select appropriate material for a given question
- being able to apply the legal principles to a given scenario and come to an appropriate conclusion.

The aspects listed above will enable all types of question to be tackled. These questions come in a number of formats:

- Theory only questions, on the lines of 'Explain, using cases and/or examples, what is meant by the term "intention to create legal relations".'

- Theory and application questions, such as 'Explain what is meant by the term "valid consideration" and identify the consideration in the scenario above.'

- Application only questions, such as 'Using the terms you have explained in question ..., explain whether there is a valid contract between X and Y.'

In the first type of question (theory only), no reference needs to be made to the scenario. All you are expected to do is explain the term asked for using relevant decided cases as examples. In the second type (theory and application), it is easiest to explain the theory as if it had been a separate question, and then apply the rules you have described to the facts set out in the scenario. The final type (application only) does not require repetition of the theory – merely a clear application of the principles to the facts. It should be noted that application is different to assertion. An assertion would be where the answer gives no reason for the statement made. Application goes on to give reasons for the assertion. In contract questions this will be by use of the relevant cases to show how the legal principle applies to the facts.

Answering a theory-only question

A theory-only question might be:

> A valid contract requires an offer and acceptance, an intention to create legal relations and consideration. If one party to the contract does not do what has been agreed, this is likely to amount to a breach of contract.
>
> Explain, using cases and examples, the meaning of the term 'acceptance'. *(7 marks)*

The potential content in the mark scheme would be:

(A) Explanation of acceptance, e.g. definition; communication of acceptance; postal rules;

(B) Cases and/or examples relevant to offer and acceptance.

A good answer would include:

■ a definition of acceptance, such as the final expression of assent to the terms of an offer; that definition is then explained and exemplified

■ an explanation of the idea of communication of acceptance

■ an explanation of acceptance by conduct: possible reference to *Carlill* v *Carbolic Smoke Ball Co.* (1892)

■ an explanation of the postal rules, exemplified by a case such as *Adams* v *Lindsell* (1818)

■ an explanation of other means of communication, using examples such as *Entores* v *Miles Far East Corporation* (1955).

Answering a theory and application question

A question from the sample paper that has both theory and application in it is set out below:

> Umar wanted to buy a large quantity of mobile phones for his shop. He phoned Mobiles plc, who agreed to supply him with a quantity of phones for £60,000. Mobiles plc immediately realised they had been using an old price list and tried to contact Umar on the phone, but failed to do so. Mobiles plc therefore posted a new one to Umar, which he received on the next day. Mobiles refused to supply the phones at £60,000 and Umar refused to pay the revised price of £70,000. Mobiles plc's new prices were the same as other suppliers of the phones.
>
> (c) Assuming there is a valid contract between Umar and Mobiles plc, Mobiles plc may be in breach of that contract. Briefly explain the meaning of breach of contract and discuss whether Mobiles plc is in breach of its contract with Umar. *(8 marks)*

When you answer the first part of this question, you should set out a theoretical explanation as set out above in the theory only question. You should then apply the theory clearly to the facts set out in the problem.

A good answer to the application part would be:

■ Refusal to supply the phones is an anticipatory breach of contract, because Mobiles plc has said it will not perform in the future (the due date for delivery).

■ When the contract date for delivery passes without the phones being supplied, that will be an actual breach of contract.

■ Explanation of effect of breach including when Umar can start legal action.

■ Activity

Write up, using continuous prose, your answer to the two-part questions set out above.

Answering an application only question

When answering such a question, you only need to write the application part, as you will be able to refer back to the theory part that you almost certainly will have answered. The answer will be much as set out in the previous section. Now try the following activity based on a past paper question.

 Activity

Now attempt Section C of the sample paper in 45 minutes. Your teacher should be able to provide you with a copy of this.

You should now be able to:

- apply the principles in AS examination questions involving contract.

Index

Acknowledgements

The authors and publisher are grateful to the following for permission to reproduce photographs and other copyright material in this book:

p7 Russell Boyce/Reuters/Corbis; p9 Handguns extract reprinted from the World Council of Churches; p11 Jim Young/Reuters/Corbis; p21 Nicholas Kane/Arcaid/Corbis; p25 Railways Act 2005 reprinted under Crown copyright PSI License C2008000256; p26 Dog Control Orders extract reprinted with permission from Eastbourne Borough Council; p27 Richard Klune/Corbis; p28 The Smoke-free Regulations Act 2006 reprinted under Crown copyright PSI License C2008000256; p34 Nuclear Consultation was flawed extract reprinted with permission from © NI Syndication, London (2007); p56 Paul Doyle/Alamy; p61 Purity ring is not intimately linked to religious beliefs extract reprinted with permission from © NI Syndication, London (2007); p96 Justices of Peace in England and Wales reprinted under Crown copyright PSI License C2008000256; p106 Bar council guidance for barristers extract reprinted with permission from the Bar Council; p108 Controversy flares over magistrate aged 19 extract reprinted with permission from the *Yorkshire Evening Post*; p116 Typical day of a barrister extract reprinted with permission from the Bar Council; p116 Bar statistics extract reprinted with permission from the Bar Council; p119 Number of Solicitors at 31st July 2006 extract reprinted with permission from the Law Society; p121 All take and no give? extract reprinted with permission from © NI Syndication, London (2007); p122 Hall v Simons appeal extract reprinted under Crown copyright PSI License C2008000256; p129 My plumber gets £90 an hour extract reprinted with permission from © NI Syndication, London (2007); p131 Availability extract reprinted under Crown copyright PSI License C2008000256; p139 Criminal trial chaos over lack of judges extract reprinted with permission from © NI Syndication, London (2007); p142 Extract from judicial post information pack reprinted under Crown copyright PSI License C2008000256; p145 Office for Judicial Complaints extract reprinted under Crown copyright PSI License C2008000256; p145 How well behaved are Britain's judges? extract reprinted with permission. © NI Syndication, London (2007); p146 Judge found guilty after drunken fracas extract reprinted with permission from Northern Echo © Newsquest Media Group 2003; p147 Judges' misdeeds will remain secret extract reprinted with permission from Guardian News & Media Ltd 2005 © copyright Guardian News & Media Ltd; p151 Judicial Statistics extract reprinted under Crown copyright PSI License C2008000256; p152 Women Judges in Post extract reprinted under Crown copyright PSI License C2008000256; p156 Definitely no regrets extract reprinted with permission © NI Syndication, London (2006); p187 Knife thug extract reprinted with permission from the *Yorkshire Evening Post*; p194 Sending for Trial extract reprinted under Crown copyright PSI License C2008000256; p230 *Carroll* v *Fearon* extract reprinted under Crown copyright PSI License C2008000256; p239 NHS Motor Vehicle Accident Charges extract reprinted under Crown copyright PSI License C2008000256.